Orientalism and the Figure of the Jew

Orientalism and the Figure of the Jew

Jeffrey S. Librett

FORDHAM UNIVERSITY PRESS

New York 2015

Copyright © 2015 Fordham University Press

All rights reserved. No part of this publication may be reproduced, stored in a retrieval system, or transmitted in any form or by any means—electronic, mechanical, photocopy, recording, or any other—except for brief quotations in printed reviews, without the prior permission of the publisher.

Fordham University Press has no responsibility for the persistence or accuracy of URLs for external or third-party Internet websites referred to in this publication and does not guarantee that any content on such websites is, or will remain, accurate or appropriate.

Fordham University Press also publishes its books in a variety of electronic formats. Some content that appears in print may not be available in electronic books.

Visit us online at www.fordhampress.com

Library of Congress Cataloging-in-Publication Data

Librett, Jeffrey S., author.
Orientalism and the figure of the Jew / Jeffrey S. Librett.
  pages cm
Includes bibliographical references and index.
ISBN 978-0-8232-6291-5 (hardback) —
ISBN 978-0-8232-6292-2 (paper)
1. Orientalism—Germany—History. 2. Orientalism.
3. Germany—Intellectual life. 4. Philosophy, German.
5. Jews—Public opinion. 6. Public opinion—Germany.
7. Jews in literature. 8. Orientalism in literature.
9. East and West. I. Title.
DS61.85.L53 2014
303.48′2430509034—dc23
                           2014014999

Printed in the United States of America
17 16 15 5 4 3 2 1
First edition

for Dawn and Malachi and Sasha

CONTENTS

List of Illustrations ix
Preface xi
Acknowledgments xiii

Introduction: Orientalism as Typology, or How to Disavow the Modern Abyss 1

Part I HISTORICIST ORIENTALISM: TRANSCENDENTAL HISTORIOGRAPHY FROM JOHANN GOTTFRIED HERDER TO ARTHUR SCHOPENHAUER

1. Ordering Chaos: The Orient in J. G. Herder's Teleological Historicism 29
2. Figuralizing the Oriental, Literalizing the Jew: From Letter to Spirit in Friedrich Schlegel's *On the Language and Wisdom of the Indians* 52
3. Goethe's Orientalizing Moment (I): "Notes and Treatises for the Better Understanding of the *West-East Divan*" 73
4. Goethe's Orientalizing Moment (II): The Poetry of the *West-East Divan* 90
5. Thresholds of History: India and the Limits of Europe in Hegel's *Lectures on the Philosophy of History* 129
6. Taking Up Groundlessness, Fulfilling Fulfillment: Schopenhauer's Orientalist Metaphysics between Indians and Jews 176

Part II HOW NOT TO APPROPRIATE ORIENTALIST TYPOLOGY: SOME MODERNIST RESPONSES TO HISTORICISM

7. Dialectical Development or Partial Construction? Martin Buber and Franz Kafka — 209
8. The Dreamwork of History: Orientalism and Originary Disfiguration in Freud's *Moses and Monotheism* — 235

Conclusion: For an Abstract Historiography of the Nonexistent Present — 265

Notes — 279
Index — 353

ILLUSTRATIONS

Baruch (Benedictus) Spinoza, painting	13
J. G. Herder, engraving by Faustino Anderloni	31
Friedrich Schlegel, charcoal drawing by Philipp Veit around 1810	54
J. W. Goethe, steel engraving based on pastel drawing by Ferdinand Jagemann, from 1817	106
Maria Anna von Willemer, pastel drawing	107
J. J. Willemer, pastel drawing	108
G. W. F. Hegel, in his office, lithograph after painting by Ludwig Sebbers, from 1804	137
Arthur Schopenhauer, sometime between 1855 and 1860	181
The circuit of negative fulfillment in Schopenhauer	185
Martin Buber, 1937, during unrest in Palestine, in white suit, boarding an armored bus	219
Martin Buber, 1937, in rearview mirror of a bus in Tel Aviv	219
Franz Kafka, in 1918	220
Franz Kafka in context: The Alchemistry (or Goldmaker) Alley, where Kafka lived when he most likely wrote "The Great Wall of China," photo from 1931	221
Sigmund Freud, with his two chow-chows on his apartment balcony, 1930	244

PREFACE

The ground of modern German Orientalism is the absence of the ground. This somewhat gnomically provocative formulation of my approach to German Orientalism can be spelled out, still in an extreme condensation, as follows. Around the late eighteenth century, Western modernity finds itself, as if suddenly, without its own absolute foundations, or bereft of grounding, and this not only in the theological dimension but also in the realms of politics, gender, family form, and philosophy generally, to name only the most prominent areas. This lack of foundations—which implies also a loss of all guidance and measure—creates uncertainty, hence anxiety, and at the limit panic, in those who become aware of it. One fairly pervasive defensive response to this state of affairs among intellectuals—during the period and for many subsequent decades—both in Germany and in Europe as a whole, is the disavowal of the lacking ground. This is how and why the cognitive and affective uncertainty is often kept in check. And in turn one major modality of this disavowal, I argue, is precisely modern Orientalism (both in its discursive and in its more real, commercial, and colonialist dimensions). Such Orientalism, especially in its historicist articulations, places a fetishized Oriental origin in the place of the lacking absolute foundations, thereby holding nihilism apparently at bay. But the alien origin thus posited must be appropriated in order to become the West's own. The fetish must become "mine."

How does one make one's own an origin one finds radically outside of oneself? In the case of modern Orientalism, the appropriation is accomplished—and this is a main theme of the book—through the application of medieval typology, or *figura*, to the East-West relation. Whereas the Jewish-Christian relation was traditionally conceived as that between the prefigural "dead letter" and its fulfillment in the "living spirit," now the Oriental-Occidental relation in general is conceived along exactly these lines. This is one of the (generally ignored or underappreciated) points I emphasize throughout: One cannot adequately understand the Orientalist problematic—especially but not exclusively in the German tradition—

without exploring in detail its constant entanglement with the problematic of Christian anti-Judaism. The Jew is not only always one particular type of Oriental, but the prefiguration, as it were, of the position of the Oriental in general as a prefiguration of the West. To examine the typological appropriation of the Oriental origin from this point of view enables us to understand the (otherwise baffling) combination of idealization and disparagement that characterizes the Orientalist discourse in general. And it further enables us to formalize the necessity in terms of which the Orient must at every turn be subjected to bifurcation into an appropriable aspect and an abject, inappropriable aspect that must always be made responsible for the otherness of the alien origin. The most prominent case of such a bifurcation in the German tradition (and more generally in Europe) is the opposition between the Semitic Orient—which must remain utterly foreign—and the Aryan Orient—which functions as the Orient that is essentially and radically "our" own. The sad logic that underlies the disastrous development of this opposition is one of the things that this book attempts to clarify. The book pursues this argument in close readings of major German-language thinkers and writers from Johann Gottfried Herder to Sigmund Freud. But in order to be able to focus in the individual chapters on close textual readings of these main figures, it is necessary to establish in greater detail my crucial conceptual and historical points of reference. Accordingly, in the introduction I develop elucubrations on the abyssal character of modernity and on Orientalism as a typological disavowal of this vertiginous situation, especially beginning with the panic about pantheism around the philosophy of Baruch, or Benedict, Spinoza.

ACKNOWLEDGMENTS

I have worked on this German Orientalism project off and on for so many years that I will certainly fail to do justice to the several institutions and many people who have supported both me and the project along the way, but here goes.

Parts of this book were written with the help of grants by the Zentrum für Literaturforschung in Berlin (Summer 2005) and the Oregon Humanities Center (Fall 2005). A Summer Humanities Grant at the University of Oregon (2010) also aided research and writing.

Different parts and aspects of the book have been presented as lectures at Cornell, Duke, the University of Washington, the University of Oregon, the Free University Berlin, Cardozo Law School, New York University, and the University of Central Florida, and at the annual conferences of the German Studies Association conference, the Midwest Modern Language Association, the Modern Language Association, and the Western Humanities Alliance, and I thank all of those who invited me or otherwise enabled me to present these talks, and those who listened and gave me useful critical responses.

Essentially the same text as chapter 2 appeared first as "Figuralizing the Oriental, Literalizing the Jew: On the Attempted Assimilation of Letter to Spirit in Friedrich Schlegel's *Über die Sprache und Weisheit der Indier*," in *The German Quarterly* 69, no. 3 (1996): 260–76, reprinted here by permission. To use a nineteenth-century metaphor where it is most appropriate: This essay was the germ from which the book grew. Chapter 7 contains much material that was originally published as "Orientalism and Panic in Franz Kafka's 'The Great Wall of China,'" in *(a): A Journal of Culture and the Unconscious* 3, no. 1 (2003): 1–12, reprinted here by permission of the editors, Dean MacCannell and Juliet MacCannell. Chapter 1 is almost identical to my article "Historicist Orientalism as a Public Absolute: On Herder's Typo-teleology," published in *Telos* 159 (Summer 2012): 19–34, and reprinted here by kind permission. Thanks are due to the Bildarchiv

Preussischer Kulturbesitz for their permission to reproduce the images used throughout the book.

To my friends and colleagues at Groupe interdisciplinaire freudien de recherches et d'interventions cliniques et culturelles (GIFRIC) and at the École freudienne du Québec, in Québec City, I am grateful for their ongoing support and in particular for the opportunities (a) to develop my thinking about Orientalism further in "Perversion and Freedom at Abu Ghraib," my contribution to the essay collection *Les enjeux de perversion aujourd'hui / The Stakes of Perversion Today* (Quebec: GIFRIC, 2005); (b) to present in the Clinical Seminar in 2006 a paper on Orientalism and fetishism in "The Mummy's Foot," by Théophile Gautier; and (c) to present the reading of *Moses and Monotheism* in the Clinical Seminar in 2009. I thank Tracy McNulty for encouraging me to write a chapter on *Moses and Monotheism*.

I am forever grateful for the strong support of this project (and of my work in general) shown by Peter U. Hohendahl, whose devotion to German Studies and Comparative Literature as emancipatory enterprises has always provided for me and so many others an admirable standard of integrity and intelligence in the profession of the humanities.

Among my former colleagues at Loyola University Chicago, I owe a continuing debt of gratitude to Wiley Feinstein and Andrew Cutrofello for our ongoing conversations about our work, including this project. Thanks to Paolo Giordano for inviting me to start drafting the chapter on Freud for the conference titled "The Hyphenate Writer and the Legacy of Exile," at the University of Central Florida in 2008. I still benefit from Andrew McKenna's rigorous writing and reading lessons and from Anne Callahan's inspiring and always insightful love of literature and life.

My colleagues at the University of Oregon have made working there both an ongoing pleasure and an uninterrupted intellectual adventure. In particular I thank Susan Anderson, Tres Pyle, and Michael Stern for reading and responding critically to parts of the manuscript, Kenneth Calhoon for conversations about methodology and Freud in particular, John McCole for our continuing conversation about German intellectual history, and David Luebke and Matthias Vogel, for their intellectual companionship in the melancholy task of teaching courses and reflecting in a sustained manner on the Shoah.

Other colleagues and friends whom I thank for conversation and inspiration concerning specific subject matter in this book include William Donahue, Martha Helfer, Sander Gilman, Winfried Menninghaus, Robert Stockhammer, Nikolai Hormeß, and—the person who has taught me

Acknowledgments

more about Judaism and modernist art than anyone else, and who has graciously allowed me to use a reproduction of one of her paintings as my jacket image—Colette Brunschwig.

My students—both long ago at Loyola University Chicago and in the past decade at the University of Oregon, graduate and undergraduate—have shown great patience and fortitude in working with me during the development of many of the readings contained in the following pages.

I am deeply grateful to David Martyn and the other outside reader at Fordham University Press for their rigorous reading of the manuscript and extremely useful comments. I feel particularly fortunate to have had as my editor for a second time Helen Tartar, whose support of this project was essential. Her untimely death still feels incomprehensible, and she is and will remain sorely missed. I am fortunate also to have had the opportunity to work with Tom Lay and the other fabulous people at Fordham University Press.

To my extended family of origin (and that of my spouse), a heterogeneous mélange of Americanness and Ostjudentum, I owe my continuing existence somewhere within the thematic nexus of this book.

I thank above all my wife and children: my wife, Dawn Marlan, for her judicious and intense intelligence, as applied in her critical responses to parts of this manuscript as well as everywhere else, for her emotional warmth and depth, and for her unfailing wisdom and insight. I am finitely indebted to her for her support of this particular project, but infinitely for her willingness to put up with me in general. I am more grateful to my children, Malachi and Sasha, than they can possibly know, for the endless riches they have brought to my life, and for the inspiring example they set—in the courage of their instinctual insistence on the pursuit of justice, in their sense of humor, in their aesthetic attunement, in their understanding of others and themselves, in their searching intelligence, and in their great capacity for joy and love.

Orientalism and the Figure of the Jew

Introduction: Orientalism as Typology, or How to Disavow the Modern Abyss

> Hearing the cry of anxiety, we feel the anxiety
> of the one who cries out.
>
> —JOHANN GUSTAV DROYSEN, *"Historik"*

> ruinstrewn land, little panic steps
>
> —SAMUEL BECKETT, *"Afar a Bird," in Fizzles*

My theme is German Orientalism in the context of modernity since the Enlightenment. The contours of this context are elusive, however, because the period involves a radical loss of certainty precisely about context (or coherence or cohesion). The German word, which will recur frequently, is *Zusammenhang*. In this general situation, individuals are increasingly uncertain about their metaphysical situation and foundations.

The Modern "Context"

The period I treat here extends from the late eighteenth century (the 1780s) through German idealism and historicism into German literary modernism. This stretch of time falls within modernity broadly conceived. Both early modernity and early modern Orientalism and colonialism have been going on for almost three centuries by the 1780s.[1] Thus, although it is not possible to do justice here to these developments, I sketch the context of this later modernity by situating the late eighteenth century in relation to the immediately preceding period, a period of relative European stability that begins in the mid-seventeenth century.

To do this, however, it is necessary to take one step further back and begin (moving very quickly) with Europe at the turn from the fifteenth century to the sixteenth. At that point, European history is marked by a particularly powerful, but also manifestly intimidated, Spanish Catholic combination of anti-Jewish and anti-Muslim policies in conjunction with imperialist undertakings to dominate the Indian Far East.[2] The complex subsequent processes of the sixteenth and the first half of the seventeenth centuries both extend the reach of European power and exacerbate European uncertainties.[3] Of these various interconnected processes, let us consider briefly the religiopolitical dimension, namely, the Reformation and its aftermath, in order to contextualize the later modernity when this book begins. As Reinhard Koselleck describes the effects of the Reformation:

> The traditional order had fallen apart in the sixteenth century. As a result of the division of the Church's unity, the entire social order was thrown out of joint. . . . The general anarchy led to duels, violence, and murder, and the pluralization of the Sancta Ecclesia was a ferment of depravity for everything that was otherwise still united: families, classes, nations, and peoples.[4]

One of the main forms of this anarchy was the Thirty Years' War, the "religious civil war" that devastated middle Europe from 1618 to 1648.[5] In terms of German history, the most striking shift in the mid-seventeenth century was the conclusion of the Thirty Years' War in the Treaty of Westphalia, which (with the principle of *cuius regio, eius religio* [whose realm, his religion]) subordinated church to state. This development attempted to adjust to the new political-religious necessities by "disarming" religion.[6] As Koselleck shows, the subordination of church to state was predicated on a radical split between morals (as private inwardness) and politics (exteriority under the ultimate rule of the sovereign in pursuit of *raison d'état*). By instituting this split, the age of absolute monarchy put an end to religious civil war across Europe.

This moment around 1648 has been seen as the achievement of a new stability that introduced a new phase of modernity.[7] Heinz Kittsteiner attributes the stabilization principally to three internal (i.e., more or less strictly European) matters and one external (or foreign-political) concern, all of which are religiopolitically significant: the end of the Thirty Years' War; the taming of the fear of witches and evil powers through the rise of the new cosmologies (here Kittsteiner draws in part on Jean Delumeau's research); the transformation of the dominant image of God from one of anger (*Zorn*) to one of merciful grace (*Gnade*) through new religious and philosophical discourses; and the defeat of the Ottoman Turks (295–318).[8]

According to Kittsteiner's historical reckoning, the post-1650 period of stability lasted until the final third of the eighteenth century.[9] It concluded politically with the French Revolution, economically with the industrial revolution, and culturally with the late Enlightenment (and more specifically with Lessing's text "The Education of the Human Race" and the Spinoza controversy, which is the point of departure for my own treatment of German Orientalism [297]). This phase of modernity that starts in the late eighteenth century involves what Kittsteiner calls the "acceleration of time," a matter of changing values that "continues unabated today" (296), and that Koselleck characterizes as a crisis called forth by Enlightenment critique, a renewal of the "religious civil war" in new forms. Enlightenment critique already "anticipates itself," however—as both of these historical thinkers, as well as earlier intellectual historians such as Paul Hazard, stress—in the late seventeenth century, in thinkers such as Spinoza, Toland, and Locke (Kittsteiner, 297).[10] The multidimensional (i.e., political, economic, and cultural) destabilization of the already fragile stability that had been fleetingly achieved in the post–Thirty Years' War European order of absolutist monarchies provides the context in which my readings of modern German Orientalism begin. But it is still important to know more precisely in what the instability or self-contradictoriness of absolutist monarchy consists in its political-religious sense as subordination of church to state and to determine how this instability produces value uncertainties that generate anxiety and virtual panic (or crisis) in new forms in the late eighteenth century and beyond.

Enlightenment as Response to Absolutist Monarchy, or The Dawn of Nihilism

The subordination of church to state does not just temporarily silence the individual's conscience by rendering it apolitical through the establishment of a radical rift between politics and morals, as Koselleck argues. It does both more and less than this. It does less, because it doesn't silence or depoliticize all faith equally. Rather, it silences the consciences only of those whose religious faith is not in accord with the state religion. The morals of those who are in accord with the absolute monarch's choice of religion are politically legitimated; in principle, they can express their faith without finding themselves in conflict with power.

However, the subordination of church to state also does more than separate morals from politics in Koselleck's sense. It not only generates (from Locke on) the Enlightenment discourse of "tolerance," that is, the demand that the conscience-claims of the religions excluded from the state be given some place within the state. In addition, it leads to the radical relativization as well as privatization of absolute values. For if each absolute monarch can freely choose his religion, then evidently—in the case of the monarch qua free subject—religion has become a matter of the subject's free choice. It is no longer objectively universal because it no longer exceeds the arbitrary (and soon tyrannical) authority of this particular monarch in this particular state. To speak the language of the Harry Potter novels, the wand no longer chooses the magician, but the magician the wand. Even if, in 1555 at Augsburg, there are only two recognized religions and in 1648 in Westphalia only three, and even if only absolute sovereigns are endowed with the right to choose their own faith, the doctrine of "cuius regio, eius religio" has introduced, as the legitimate ordering principle of European political theology, the rift between religion and the absolute (i.e., the rift between religion and itself). Religious faith is henceforth relative to the subject free to choose one among several religious directions. The change in the status of faith is more radical even than the fact that faith is now no longer justifiably political, as Koselleck notes (although he fails to note adequately that through this principle absolutism is already in contradiction with itself). Rather, and beyond this, the point is that faith is now no longer absolute and no longer objective. This implies—that is, it dictates—that all people should be free to choose their own religions, but at the same time that no one should or can be free to do so, not even the king, because religion—as objectified absolute—is now nowhere to be found.[11] Radical secularization follows in principle from the privatization of religion and the relativization of the absolute (and subjectification of the objective) that arise from the subordination of church to state. Enlightenment does not simply reverse an absolutism that it fails to understand; instead, *pace* Koselleck, it draws the consequences of an absolutism it understands better than that absolutism understood itself. These consequences will overturn or at least contest the Enlightenment itself, however, and in short order.

In Enlightenment discourse, the task of reason is to substitute for revealed or positive religion a universally shareable set of values and truths, a foundation for our lives on which we can all agree. And since, as a substitute for religion, this set functions like a religion, it makes sense that the Enlighteners, from Spinoza to Kant, speak in terms of a "religion of reason" (or in some cases of a rational God that is nature). But the attempt to impose a universally shared set of truths and values as foundations of a life must at such a juncture appear immediately suspect.[12] As the objective has turned out to be subjective (or the absolute to be relative), only—at best—the subjective (or relative) can now function as objective (or absolute). Ostensibly objective values immediately appear as merely particular, subjective values that someone is trying to impose on all the others for his own advantage. Conversely, only the radically subjective qualifies as (the remnant of) the objective, as real value, as the fundamental and essential truth. Especially but not exclusively in a (post-)Protestant world where "only faith" saves—and in this sense Luther anticipated the Counter-Enlightenment, or *Sturm und Drang*—irrationalism and subjectivism function as (anti)doctrinal foundations for new absolutes in an age that despairs and virtually panics over the loss of credible access to objective absolute foundations.

What Koselleck finds troublesome—that is, the politicization of Enlightenment reason—is thus less disruptively dangerous than the next step it calls forth. This next step is the absolutization of subjectivity and the politicization of irrationality in the Counter-Enlightenment, which lives on today in fundamentalisms of various shapes. The modernity that arises in the late eighteenth century is therefore the modernity of a particularly acute crisis of foundations, in which rationalism and irrationalism are locked like mirror images in a battle to the death, a nightmare from which in many respects we have still not awakened. The separation of subjective from objective value ramifies, across a series of homological and associated oppositions, as a separation of matter from spirit, of particular from general, of concrete from abstract. Debates about the relationships between, and relative values of, these oppositions (and other equivalents or concretizations of them) will structure the pervasive and sustained, institutional and philosophical crisis of values that is coterminous with the modernity inaugurated by the resistance to absolutist monarchy.

The loss of (absolute) foundations follows, then, from the subordination of church to state even though this subordination was a necessary and desirable solution to the Thirty Years' War. This loss comes provisionally to a (headless) head in the late Enlightenment period as the Counter-Enlighteners question (from the 1760s on) the reasonableness of reason itself. The loss can be organized in terms of six modes or manifestations of foundation that are found lacking in this moment.[13] The first three correspond to three main forms of institutional leadership: religious (or theological), political, and familial. The last three correspond to the main subdivisions of philosophical discourse: epistemology, ethics, and aesthetics. Just a word on each before proceeding to the question of how Orientalism responds to this lack of absolute foundations.

The theological uncertainty subtends and stands synecdochically for all of the others because it is a question of lost absolute values. But it is also its own specific theme. As revelation becomes questionable (in principle), the foundations of God begin to wobble, despite attempts to articulate rational and natural theology. Concerning the loss of the political ground, the Enlightenment erosion or destruction of absolutist monarchy asserts itself, for example, in the English tradition of Locke's *Two Treatises*, in the French *philosophes*, and above all in the French Revolution, as well as in Kant's cautious dance with Frederick the Great, and in early romantic German sympathies for the Revolution. Each of the thinkers treated in this book is responding to this loss of political authority in their Orientalist writings. In addition, the terms in which the relationship between religion and politics is mediated are likewise in question. And this is not just a matter of the unity of church and state, or the specific form of their disunity. Rather, and quite prominently (both in reality and in letters), the patriarchal family—as an institution through which the relationship between the objectivity of the state and the subjectivity of individual inwardness is to be established and maintained—is in suspension and transition. The volatilization of God and king entails the tendency toward the evaporation of patriarchy, or rather its redefinition, especially in terms of bourgeois sentimentality.[14] The bourgeois nuclear family is in the process of establishing itself, in this period of the rising bourgeoisie, as a place where radical interiority and exteriority, the private and the public, might achieve some sort of mediation. The chapters that follow address questions about figures of patriarchy, paternity, and maternity in every author.

On a theoretical level, the Enlightenment crisis of foundations makes itself felt in epistemology, ethics, and aesthetics, as it becomes increasingly necessary and impossible to decide in all of these philosophical subdisciplines between rationalist and empiricist methodological dogmas.[15] In epistemology, these dogmas posit the grounds of our knowledge in thought and things, respectively. In ethics, rationalism represents an ethics of principles, whereas empiricism represents one of customs. And in aesthetics, tensions between perfection (*Vollkommenheit*) and beauty, and between beauty and sublimity, instantiate the uncertainty about the relative priorities of empirical perception and rational thought.

Of course, the Kantian transcendental turn proposes solutions to all of these conceptual dilemmas. It incorporates both the sensuous givenness of empiricism and the categorial a prioris of rationalism into one epistemic system. Further, it gives reason its due in ethics through the categorical imperative, while granting empiricism its proper voice in that Kant acknowledges that we cannot know freedom empirically, or even speculatively. Finally, it attempts to unite perfection, sublimity, and beauty under the aegis of reflexive judgment. However, Kant is generally taken by the following generation to have solved the problems of knowledge, ethics, and aesthetics only at an excessive cost: the loss of the unity of the subject and the loss of immediacy qua *Ding an sich*. As is commonly acknowledged, German idealism—which culminates in Hegel's historicist Orientalism—comprises the attempt to resuture this lost unity of the subject and to reattach the *Ding* to the subject, thus restoring to the subject its lost substantial ground in a historical teleology.[16]

Orientalism as a Disavowal of Groundlessness: The Typological Extension of the "Jewish Question"

By the late eighteenth century, then, in the German (and more broadly European) cultural discourses at the center of this book, the intellectuals are anxiously seeking a new foundation for the West, and thus new modalities of guidance, leadership, and orientation.[17] Because the lack of foundation implies the lack of any absolute guidance, whether political, religious, familial, or philosophical, the subjects of this period are without reliable points of reference and thus exposed, according to the Freudian theory of groups, to the danger of panic, both individual and social. Why panic? In *Mass Psychology and the Analysis of the Ego*—which, despite its flaws, remains rich in implications for studies of group or mass formations and identity—Freud proposes that panic points us to the "essence of a mass" (90; 35).[18] It shows us the way in which libidinal ties—affectively laden posits of existence or cathexes (*Besetzungen*) that always tend toward excess—structurally constitute the mass. More specifically:

> A primary mass of this kind is a number of individuals who have put one and the same object in the place of their ego ideal and have consequently identified themselves with one another in their ego. (108; 61)

How does panic reveal the essence of a mass? Considering the case of military masses above all, Freud writes that panic arises "when such a mass disintegrates" (or dissolves, decomposes, disarticulates itself: *sich zersetzt*) (90; 35).[19] When panic occurs,

> none of the orders given by superiors are any longer listened to, and . . . each individual is only solicitous on his own account, and without any consideration for the rest. The mutual ties have ceased to exist, and a gigantic and senseless anxiety is unleashed. (90–91; 35–36)

Panic is the moment when the mass arrives at its limit or end.[20] This occurs, according to Freud, not because of any increase in danger, but owing to a loss of faith in the leader. And so panic reveals the essence of the mass by showing how the mass relates to the figure of the leader.

> The loss of the leader in some sense or other, the birth of misgivings about him [*das Irrewerden an ihm*], brings on the outbreak of panic, though the danger remains the same; the mutual ties between the members of the group disappear, as a rule, at the same time as the tie with their leader. (92; 38)[21]

The leader is the embodiment of the ego ideal whom all subjects in the mass share as their own ideal. When this ego ideal is disrupted, the mass dissolves.[22] Panic is a liminal group experience of the dissolution or dismemberment of the group (and of the members of that group) consequent upon some loss of its leader. In this experience, a sense of imminent annihilation—literal or figural, physical or spiritual, or both—and a desperate desire to be saved combine with a radical uncertainty about the direction in which to pursue such salvation. Hope and fear (or despair), aggression and flight, collude in panic when any group begins to experience the loss of its leadership. Finally, the leader-figure does not have to be a person or personification in order to function as the unifying principle of the group or mass. An idea, belief, or project will function just as well. Freud writes, for example, that when being in love takes on extreme idealizing proportions, such that "the object has put itself into the place of the ego-ideal" (106; 57), then the "'abandonment' of the ego to the object . . . can already no longer be distinguished from the sublimated abandonment to an abstract idea" (106; 57).[23]

But nobody likes to experience anxiety or panic, and one way of avoiding the anxious-making encounter with the void of absolute value is to disavow or deny whatever it is that questions our belief in a comforting figure of groundedness, wholeness, and protected safety. Indeed, I argue throughout the book that such a disavowal constitutes the fundamental reason for the positing of an Oriental origin as the transcendent yet historical foundation of Occidental culture in the narratives of historicist Orientalism. In arguing thus I am making reference to the complex discussion of disavowal that begins with Freud's essays "Fetishism" and "The Splitting of the Ego in the Process of Defense" and includes, for example, the crucial essay by Octave Mannoni, "I Know Very Well, But All the Same . . ." and the application of fetishism to colonial discourse in Homi Bhabha's essay "The Other Question: Stereotype, Discrimination, and the Discourse of Colonialism," as well as more recent applications of the notion to German-Jewish themes, for example in David Levin's *Richard Wagner, Fritz Lang, and the Nibelungen: The Dramaturgy of Disavowal* and in Jay Geller's *The Other Jewish Question: Identifying the Jew and Making Sense of Modernity*.[24]

To begin to trace the movement of this disavowal it is useful to recall that, as the Bible in its totality gradually ceases to function literally as a divine revelation (and as a reliable genealogy of the human), increasingly appearing as the merely human expression of Oriental peoples, the Orient—spreading in European awareness from the Near East to the Far—gains a quasi-sacral prestige as ostensible origin of the Occident.[25] The less a vertical revelation from on high seems convincing, the more the history of a horizontal development of human truth from East to West must carry the burden of the absolute grounding of the West. History supplements revelation. Oriental culture comes to supplement the Bible as source of absolute knowledge.

But as the invocation of the notion of development here already implies, disavowal is not just a one-step operation. It is not accomplished by the mere act of positing an Oriental origin. For as soon as one (in the Occident) posits the Orient as origin, one finds oneself confronted with the problem of the alienness of one's own origin, and with the pressing need to appropriate this origin as one's own, like a child making faces in the mirror, grimacing at the other who grimaces back or perhaps bursts out in terroristic laughter. The modern West confronts this situation, however, with a ready-made solution in hand. I argue that the West generally appropriates this Eastern "origin"—this fetish established by disavowal of the absence of any absolute ground—through the application of the tradition of "figural interpretation," or "typology," which previously structured the Jewish-Christian relation, to the East-West relation. The fetish, in short, becomes a figure.

This early Christian and medieval figural interpretation (which modern Orientalism redeploys in a displaced manner) is summarized importantly in Erich Auerbach's famous essay "Figura." "Figural interpretation," or "typology" was a hermeneutic model that involved an entire conceptual organization of the imagined progress from pagan idolatry to Jewish monotheism to Christian trinitarianism. This progress was structured therein as a passage from materiality to spirituality that was overdetermined by semiological and rhetorical notions. Rooted in Paul's theorization of the binary opposition between Jewish and Christian as that between the anticipatory dead letter of the law of works and the fulfilled living spirit of merciful faith, the system of figural interpretation ultimately involved, in its most complete formulation, three levels, sometimes traditionally referred to as *littera*, *figura*, and *veritas*, or what one can call the "pre-prefiguration," the "prefiguration," and the "fulfillment."[26] According to this triune version of the typological system, paganism was associated with radical materiality, with crude sensuality or referentiality (*littera*), and with lack of ideal signification or meaning; Judaism (the *figura*) was understood as a religion of the signifier (something that pointed to a meaning to which it could not itself attain), situated uncannily between matter and spirit, and as operating on the level of figural or indirect signification; Christianity, finally, construed itself here as the religion of the signified, or the spirit, and of meaning literally present to itself in its ideality (*veritas*).[27] In 1492 this typology was still being applied to the pagan–Jewish–Christian relationship in a medieval Catholic and purely sacred modality. But in post-Enlightenment modernity, in one of its transformations this entire code will be secularized and applied to the East-West relationship in general.[28] The modern Orientalist displacement of *figura*, which I detail in each thinker treated throughout this book (each thinker altering this pattern in a different way), goes in general as follows. (1) Pagan idolatry (the "literal" level) becomes in modern Orientalism the model of that which one cannot or will not appropriate from the East, that is, the model for the East as alien: the "bad" Orient. (Within the Aryan myth, for example, this will be the "Semitic" Orient.)[29] (2) The prefiguration of the triumph over idolatry, that is, the dead letter of the Jewish law, becomes in Orientalism the model for the part or aspect of the East that is destined to become Western and is in the process of becoming so. (This is the position of the ancient Aryan culture and race according to the modern Aryan myth, a myth that constructs the white West as the realization of the Aryan in the modern period.) As "prefiguration" of the West, this "good" (or "better") Orient will have to anticipate, but not quite realize, above all the "proper" forms of religion, political leadership, paternity (or maternity), truth, goodness, and beauty. The story of historicist Orientalism is centrally the story of this list of forms of "almost, but not quite." (3) The New Testamentary realization, the living spirit of Christian faith, becomes in Orientalism the model for the West as such. In the most widely diverse ways, the modern admirers and detractors of the Orient attempt to make the Orient (or rather their favorite part of it) into the prefigurative origin of the Occident. They thereby provide (or regain) for the Occident a quasi-transcendent but also historical basis without renouncing the possibility of the Western appropriation and fulfillment of this—always only promising—basis.[30]

But it is impossible to extend the typological tradition in such a manner, and this for both structural and philosophico-historical reasons. First, in terms of semiological structure, as Jacques Derrida insistently taught us, it is not possible for a signified—a literally spiritual term or meaning, without any dimension of what is called the "letter" (or figurative and material vehicle)—to avoid finding itself transformed into (or replaced by, or having always already been) a signifier, that is, a material and opaque "letter" that still needs to be read or interpreted anew. The "realization"—regardless of its content—always becomes another "prefiguration." It always repeats the structure of its anticipation. In turn, the prefiguration always becomes a mere prefiguration of itself, to the extent that a signifier can always be regarded as a referent, a mere thing. Indeed, the destabilizations of the Christian tradition in the Reformation and Enlightenment arose precisely out of this structure. (I analyzed this structure with respect to German Jews, Protestants, and Catholics in my earlier book, *The Rhetoric of Cultural Dialogue: Jews and Germans from Moses Mendelssohn to Richard Wagner and Beyond.*)[31]

Second, for a number of reasons, in the late Enlightenment and Counter-Enlightenment period I am considering, the typological program comes to be blocked by the daunting figure of Spinoza's philosophy. On a number of different levels, Spinoza and his pantheism represent a particularly threatening absence or alienation of the Western ground. It will be useful now to mention the most important of these deeply discomfiting aspects of Spinoza's text, before outlining the gesture through which, most generally, the period from the Enlightenment through idealism tries to acknowledge but also dispense with his menacing thought.

The Pantheism Panic and the Specter of an Oriental Modernity

First, Spinoza's ethnic-religious identity is unsettling for Christian thinkers of this period. An excommunicated Jew—descendant of Marranos and thus a distant side effect of 1492 and the expulsion of the Jews from Spain—who is seen in the late eighteenth century still as a pagan materialist, he represents to these modern German Christian readers the Oriental origin itself, because at this time Jews are still considered Orientals.[32] In terms of typology, he represents a protospiritual figure that has fallen back to the level of the literally material. But he also represents the modern thinker par excellence (as Friedrich Heinrich Jacobi argues in 1785 in *Über die Lehre des Spinoza in Briefen an den Herrn Moses Mendelssohn* [*On the Doctrine of Spinoza in Letters to Mr. Moses Mendelssohn*]): the very perfection of modern reason. Hence, he seems to represent the realization of the Judaeo-Oriental "letter" as rational modernity.[33] That is, he stands for the regressive fall of (Christian-Western) modernity back into an ancient Judaeo-Oriental self-anticipation and self-refusal of spiritual presence, which is in turn, in Spinoza's case, taken to be a regression to pagan literality. Modernity thus would be "realizing" the ancient preorigination precisely as a radically disoriented groundlessness; the signified become referent; God become a mere material thing.

Second, as these remarks already imply, not just Spinoza's ethnic-religious identity but his views on the religious tradition are still unsettling in the late eighteenth century in a number of respects, even if they are about to become *hoffähig*, or fashionable, in various displaced forms. His radical proposals for a historical biblical criticism reduce the scriptures to their historical ground, but it is a ground that ungrounds them in their truth. The Bible now consists of merely human utterances by authors whose prophetic credentials are based on their vivid imaginations, rather than on their superior insights or access to transcendent truths. The truth of the moral doctrines of the Bible is to be determined from without, that is, philosophically, by the natural light of reason, and only this determination can confirm the "divinity" of the text. Natural knowledge now rivals prophecy and even exceeds it, both in that it is repeatable rather than singular and in that it has shed the extraneous imaginary garb still worn by the biblical prophecies.

Further, Spinoza undermines the play of typology in terms of which the Christian narrative "realizes" the "figures" contained in the Judaic narrative in accord with the notion of an intention that "realizes" itself. He argues both in the *Theologico-Political Treatise* and in the *Ethics* that no divine intention, no intentionality at all, directs the course of nature or history.[34] History is without purpose (as Schopenhauer will repeat, when he "realizes" Spinoza's philosophy in his turn, as I discuss in chapter 6). How is it possible to read an earlier cultural form as the substantial anticipation of a later one—which would fulfill the intentions announced by its predecessor—if such intentions are no longer given?

Baruch (Benedictus) Spinoza (1632–1677). Anonymous painting. Seventeenth century. (Erich Lessing/Herzogliche Bibliothek, Wolfenbuettel, Germany/Art Resource, N.Y.)

Beyond the authorities within the Bible itself, Spinoza questions the leading authorities of the religious traditions more generally. He suggests, indeed, that the priests always merely manipulate the superstitious masses. At the outset of the *Theologico-Political Treatise*, Spinoza argues that the reason the masses are so easy to manipulate is that they operate on the basis of a combination of fear and hope. We should understand this combination, I believe, as a version of panic.

> [Because people] are often reduced to such straits that they can bring no plan into operation, and since they generally vacillate wretchedly between hope and fear, from an immoderate desire for the uncertain goods of fortune, for the most part their hearts are ready to believe anything at all. While they are in doubt, a slight impulse drives them this way or that; and this happens all the more easily when, torn by hope and fear, they are at a loss to know what to do; at other times they are too trusting, boastful, and overconfident. (6–7)[35]

So Spinoza diagnoses panic—an immoderate combination of hope and fear—as the foundation of positive religion qua superstition. In diagnosing the panic, moreover, he also evokes in many of his early readers a feeling of panic, which his own doctrines seem to render inescapable. For he undermines the foundations of positive religion, even as his own intention is evidently to provide new and more rational foundations for appropriate faith and action.

Spinoza's relation to the tradition leaves little ground on which to stand, further, in terms of his complex and subtle relationship to the question of the subordination of church to state. (He was sixteen when the Treaty of Westphalia was concluded, and in Holland he was embroiled in tensions between the Calvinist Orthodoxy in favor of a strong state church and the freethinkers, such as John de Witt, who favored a more tolerant regime.) Suffice it here to recall two traits of his analysis in the *Theologico-Political Treatise*. First, he acknowledges that the state must govern the outward observances of religion in order to ensure that these observances remain in accord with the public welfare (chapter 19). In the following chapter (20), however, he argues for freedom of thought and expression. The resultant tension—typical perhaps of the ambiguities of advanced thinking in the period of "Enlightened" Absolutism—leaves unclear where the jurisdiction of private conscience ends and that of public authority begins. Again, this is a problem of grounding.

But of course it is not only Spinoza's views on the tradition of revelation per se that make his philosophy scandalous still more than a century after its first publication. His philosophy itself is more generally scandalous, particularly in its pantheistic theology and its deterministic ethics. As for the pantheism: Spinoza's God—the one "substance"—presents himself as nature (*Deus sive Natura*), but at the same time therefore withdraws qua God, that is, God disappears into and from creation itself (which then appears to lack any grounding or source of presence in a creator). At least, this is what happens to God in Spinoza according to those who read him as an atheist despite the fact that he speaks of God throughout the *Ethics*, albeit in a radically anti-anthropomorphic and secularizing manner.

The other possible interpretation, offered by Moses Mendelssohn in his defense of a "purified Spinozism" against Jacobi's attack in the abovementioned letters, is the one that sees Spinoza as an "acosmic" thinker. On this interpretation, to the degree that all "modes"—or what one would normally consider appearances or accidents—become mere expressions of the one substance itself, Spinoza's substance is tantamount to a picture of the world prior to creation, when all still existed within God. This interpretation, which mitigates the scandal of Spinoza's thought by absolving him of the atheism charge, nonetheless leaves the reader with a potential problem of foundations. This time, the foundations are there, but they found nothing: There is nothing founded to be found. This confounding doctrine undoes the founding function of the foundation and thus leaves us once again without foundations worthy of the name.

The other main metaphysical scandal for which Spinoza is known, and to which all the authors I treat here respond directly or indirectly, is his "determinism." This determinism, which is entailed by Spinoza's approach to the notion of "substance," undoes the foundations of the subject by denying freedom of the will. And this undoing applies equally to humans and to God.[36] God operates according to his essence, the order of nature, not according to his whims, as Spinoza's critique of miracles also explains. But in part 5 of his *Ethics* Spinoza proposes guidelines for the self-emancipatory mitigation of excessive affect that seem tantalizingly close to a doctrine of the will. And yet, what Spinoza principally requires in ethical terms is that one distance oneself through understanding from the will to the will, that one desire freedom—in limited degree, within the range of the possible—from the desire for freedom itself. This paradoxical ethics upends both rational and irrationalist doctrines of the will. It also wreaks havoc with traditional notions of good and evil, insofar as Spinoza defines good and evil as the useful and the destructive or useless, thus producing what looks to hasty or simply traditionalist thinkers like an amoralism.

Finally, when Spinoza illuminates the world with the "natural light" of reason and, for example, shows "more clearly than the noon light that there is absolutely nothing in things on account of which they can be called contingent" (*Ethics*, I, prof. 33, scholia 1, 106), it is not possible for the mythological connotations of the Pan hour *not* to emerge.[37] Pantheism as Enlightenment occurs at the noon hour, when Pan appears and all of nature goes mad—here, with rationality. When the shadows disappear, the light—which as Spinoza repeatedly says, illuminates both itself and the darkness—becomes the equivalent of darkness because there is no darkness with which it could be contrasted. When the sun is overhead, we cannot in principle know which way it is moving: We lose our orientation. Pantheism, as the hour of Pan midway between Orient and Occident, where both meet, binds rising with setting. As a determinism, Spinoza's pantheism makes it impossible to distinguish likewise between the living and the ghosts—another traditional trait of the Pan hour—because the distinguishing characteristic of free will has disappeared. The hour of pantheism is the hour of panic.

Pursued by the specters or spectrality of pantheism, historicist Orientalism—which is consistently teleological throughout the nineteenth century—tends to respond by trying to position pantheism as the essential doctrine of (ancient) Oriental thought. It places Spinozistic pantheism at a distance but also makes pantheism the originary anticipation of the West's proper theism. In order to do so, however, historicist Orientalism must deny the very insights of pantheism that are also those of modern reason in Spinoza himself, centrally the absence of the teleological will in history. This denial emerges with striking simplicity, for example, in Herder's philosophy of history, where my reconstruction of the trajectory of historicist Orientalism begins, but it continues in different ways in Schlegel, Goethe, Hegel, and even (inverted and displaced) in Schopenhauer. Which brings us to our outline, or *Gliederung*, and to the question of historicism.

Gliederung: *The Sunrise and Sunset of Historicism*

This book focuses on German Orientalism in two separate subperiods within modernity since the age of reason. In Part I, I examine German idealism, which I understand here as a systematic historicism, or a transcendental cultural historiography. Taking Herder's philosophy of history as my point of departure, I consider further examples ranging from Friedrich Schlegel's later phase, to Goethe's postclassical period, to Hegel's maturity, to Schopenhauer's dissent from the historical System. Subsequently (in Part II), I examine posthistoricist modernism. The main instances I treat under this rubric are Martin Buber, Franz Kafka, and Sigmund Freud. Through the diverse illustrations of these two period-discourses, I show how the approach to the Orient tends to be different in each epoch, as follows.

Beginning already in the Counter-Enlightenment, the idealist gesture stands out most clearly when viewed against the background of the Enlightenment approach to the Orient, which in key figures such as Lessing and Kant is precisely not yet historicist. In the late Enlightenment, as I have argued elsewhere, a rationalist (or in Kant's case transcendentally idealist) and structurally interested ethicotheology governs the interest in the Orient.[38] Indeed, the late Enlightenment critically questions Christian supersessionism and in conjunction with this it relativizes or marginalizes in advance any construction of a linear historical-teleological narrative that would trace the development of an anticipatory Oriental origin toward its Occidental realization. For example, in Lessing, the parable of the ring in *Nathan the Wise* promotes the understanding of faith precisely as good works, a proposal that undermines Lutheran supersessionism. In Kant, the notion of rational faith (*Vernunftglauben*) as articulated in "What Does It Mean: To Orient Oneself in Thinking?" collapses into one term the reason and faith that openly stand for the "dead letter" of Judaism and the "living spirit" of Christianity respectively in the anti-Spinozistic writings of F. H. Jacobi against which Kant is polemicizing in that very essay. Thus, even if with reservations and limitations, the most advanced thinking of the German late Enlightenment pushes beyond Christian supersessionist rhetoric. The Counter-Enlightenment will resist this insight, insisting instead that the empty and "dead letter" of rational structures be filled with the spiritual-sensuous content of "living history."

In the idealist period broadly conceived, beginning with Herder's critique of the ahistoricism that characterizes the Enlightenment's systematic rationality, numerous writers construct different variants of the historicist Orientalist typology I have sketched.[39] I trace these developments from Herder to Schopenhauer, who represents an early and proleptic end of the historicist movement. Although my understanding of historicism is informed by, and largely accords with, the standard account as it appears, for example, in Georg Iggers's *The German Conception of History*, my notion of historicism is somewhat broader than the notion generally proposed.[40] Like others, Iggers rightly distinguishes between historicism proper, on the one hand, with its emphasis on the importance of individuality in history (a principle often associated with the asystematic legacy of Goethe), and, on the other hand. the German idealist tradition in its Hegelian form, which subordinates the individual givens of history more aggressively to conceptual patterns. But Iggers also indicates repeatedly that what binds these two traditions is the teleological view of history as tending toward the world hegemony of the European cultures (10–14, 24–25).[41] The common teleology is what I stress.[42] That is, this teleological conception—the construction of an overarching typological narrative running from the origins of civilization to the modernity of the West—is the central piece in the metaphysics of historicism as I use the term here.[43] And the Orient is always conceived within historicism as the origin of that narrative.

But the historicist tradition passes through a crisis in the late nineteenth century with the simultaneous, and in part mutually conflictual, rise of neo-Kantian epistemologies, ahistorical pessimisms, and (Nietzschean and other) vitalist irrationalisms. As a result, in the aesthetic, philosophical, and psychological modernisms of the twentieth century, historicism's main presuppositions are no longer as consistently embraced as in the early and mid-nineteenth century. This shift has important consequences for constructions of the Orient in German letters.[44] The realism of historicism—whose compatibility with its idealism is as evident as the transformability of Hegelian idealism into Marxist materialism—fades from the literary scene in the 1890s as decadence (or aestheticism) reduces both meaning and apparent reality to effects of artifice.

In twentieth-century modernism—whose proponents try to draw the consequences of these displacements—some crucial writers and thinkers (such as Franz Kafka and Sigmund Freud, my main instances) question both the Enlightenment's structural ethicotheologies and idealism's genetic narratives of human history. Others (such as Martin Buber) perpetuate historicist constructs in altered form. The former, more skeptical, modernists return in various ways to face the panicky anxiety about lacking foundations that was at the origin of Orientalism (as reason and as history) in the first place. What these advanced modernists envision and enact is not a sublation (*Aufhebung*) but a disarticulation of both options—both the structural (or rationalist) and the historicist option—thereby questioning in a significant way the Orientalist legacy. The arrival of modernism onto the scene is not, therefore, evidence of history as progress in the consciousness of freedom (i.e., the Hegelian philosophy of history I examine critically in chapter 5). Nonetheless, it is a moment in which some insight into the impossibility of such a linear narrative of progress in consciousness of freedom comes to the fore. Perhaps a little (panic) step in the right direction(lessness). At any rate, the deluded, typological positioning of an

Oriental culture (or any other primitivized one) at the origin of a development culminating in the West is rendered questionable by such modernist insights, as are also the structural models of a universal rationality, or a system of values that, as shared substance (even if purely formal), would render superfluous precisely the mediation and representation that enable society at the cost of full presence.[45]

Edward Said's Historicist Metaphysics

It remains for me to say a few words in this introduction about how this book relates to the work and tradition of Edward Said. Because he both relaunched the study of Orientalism in the late seventies in a new and important way and exercised a formative influence on cultural studies more broadly, he is still worthy of close attention. I address in notes along the way some of the many others who have made significant recent contributions to this field.[46] Since I include in my final chapter an excursus on Said's reading of Freud's *Moses and Monotheism*, which functions also as an illustration of Said's strengths and weaknesses in general, I will keep my remarks here relatively brief.[47]

I begin with my admiration for Said's remarkable achievement: He established in public view both the field of critical Orientalism in general—as the study of the cultural-political connections between Western research, writing, and thinking about the Orient, on the one hand, and the politics and economics of Western imperialism, on the other—and the plight of the Palestinians as victims of the brutally unjust and disastrous Israeli occupation, in particular. His book, *Orientalism*, provides an important overview of Orientalist scholarship, literature, and colonialist theory and practice.[48] Its single-minded political reading of Orientalism brings the violence of Eurocentrism usefully to light. Without Said's achievement, this book certainly would not exist.

My sense of the limitations of that achievement concern three interrelated areas: his choice of specific historical objects (i.e., specific national traditions); his methodological self-reflection; and the implications of both of these in terms of a certain distortion of the interpretation of Orientalism, along with the ideological effects of this distortion. The distortion is best summarized as Said's underemphasis, and insufficient appreciation, of the inextricable involvement of modern Orientalism both with a metaphysics of absolute foundations in crisis and with Christian anti-Judaism (and typology in particular). The limitations of Said's choice of historical objects are determined by his self-restriction to the English, French, and American traditions (for the most part). Although this self-restriction is understandable both in terms of Said's interest in the imperialist histories of the English, French, and U.S. Americans in the Near East, and also in terms of the natural limits on any scholar's knowledge, it nonetheless entails certain deficits in Said's perspective on, and understanding of, the "scope of Orientalism." But the second and third limitations are the more serious ones, and all three are most usefully approached by way of the methodological one.

In his methodological ideology, Said is a historicist, and his methodological limitations, specifically with regard to Orientalism, arise from the necessary partial blindness of any historicist to what is at stake in the entanglement of historicism with Orientalism (and vice versa) in its nineteenth-century mode, which is also exactly the mode that coincides with the height of its imperialist expansionism. It is precisely as the work of a historicist that Said's work became influential, in contributing to the shift in the mid- and late 1980s away from textual-theoretical studies based on structuralism toward the New Historicism and the subsequent Cultural Studies movement. The latter movement—although sometimes incorrectly conflated with "theory"—advanced its agenda precisely as an opposition to the excesses of "high theory" and in the name of concrete historical specificity. (Whereas many of the attacks on Said have suggested that his historiography is slipshod or too focused on literary and cultural texts, my critical reservations will concern his [idealist-realist] historicism [in the nineteenth-century sense], which may in turn explain why he is not a better historian than he is. The frequent attacks on Said as either too Foucauldian or wrong-mindedly deconstructionist are misdirected: He is ultimately neither the one nor the other, although he does at times misleadingly claim to adhere to Foucauldian postulates.) Further, to anyone knowledgeable about the turn from the late Enlightenment to the Counter-Enlightenment and historicism in German-language culture, this shift to New Historicism and Cultural Studies must feel uncannily familiar, and I believe the similarity is not a mere illusion. I focus these very condensed remarks about Said's historicism on the methodological section in *Orientalism* and on its ramifications for his understanding of Orientalism in that book.

Said's main methodological concern in *Orientalism*, expressed as his "two fears" (8), is the fear of "distortion and inaccuracy, or rather the kind of inaccuracy produced by too dogmatic a generality and too positivistic a localized focus" (8). This tension between the "general and particular"

(8), between "abstraction" and "individual instances" (8), is the tension I have already mentioned in various modern forms: as the ambivalence of historicism between (Goethean) individuality and (Hegelian) conceptual systematicity; as the tension between rationalist and empiricist methods in the late Enlightenment; as the rift implicit in absolute monarchy between a sovereign who appropriates universality and the apparent particularity of the religious formation he chooses for his state; as the tension between the particularly flawed human father and his universally validated authority in bourgeois patriarchy; as the incompatibility between a knowledge of the empirical particulars of the world and an ethics of a pure ought, or ethical principles that are indifferent to what is; as the tension between imagination and understanding in the sublime, and so forth. Although this tension between the universal and the particular, or the abstract and the concrete, can be deconstructively displaced and complicated, it cannot ultimately be resolved in a harmonious synthesis, nor can it simply be circumvented. How does Said propose to resolve or avoid this tension, that is, to restore the unity and coherence of the ground?

Said's ostensible resolution of the dilemma takes three steps. First, he emphasizes that there is no radical distinction between pure and political knowledge. All scholarship, he asserts, is historically embedded and nolens volens engaged. There are three problems with such a stance, which has both left-wing and right-wing credentials. First, it repeats one more time the upgrading of subjectivity as absolute or objective universality that was characteristic of the Counter-Enlightenment. Second, there is always also an aspect of disengagement in knowledge, which Said underestimates, although he does acknowledge it intermittently. This disengagement can appear as the alienation of the subject from group identifications, or the dissolution of group identity, and as the possibility of objectivity. By arguing that knowledge is necessarily politically engaged because it is embedded in its circumstances (10), that is, its context, or *Zusammenhang*, Said disavows these two aspects of all knowledge, which accompany its embeddedness or engagement. Third, all context is infinitely overdetermined; it is not necessarily absolutely grounded in the political per se or in power, as Said presupposes, invoking politics as the last instance (despite his emphasis also on the interplay between culture and politics).

But Said discusses "two more aspects of my contemporary reality" that "point the way out of the methodological or perspectival difficulties I have been discussing" (8–9). The next is what he calls, somewhat oddly, "The Methodological Question" (15). I address only two of the various and somewhat scattered points he makes under this heading. First, he acknowledges here that the omission of German Orientalism is regrettable (especially in terms of biblical studies). But then he partially justifies this omission in two ways: He notes the lack of any real German imperialism in the Near East, and he argues that the discussion of Europe's involvement with the Near East is to some degree separable from the discussion of its involvement with other places in South Asia and East Asia. But as has often been remarked, to ignore the German case obviously makes it easier to suggest the reducibility of Orientalism to imperialism and colonialism in their most literal senses. This also makes it easier to ignore the contextual belonging of the Near East within a larger Orient that, for much of Europe, even if with particularly glaring clarity for the German tradition, includes the South Asian and Persian—Aryan—racial designations and their opposition to the Jewish and Arab, Semitic one.[49] More important for the methodological question, although Said does cut down the field of Orientalism to a somewhat more manageable size by reducing it to English, French, and U.S. involvements with Arabs and Islam (which obviously reduces the quantity of particulars to be dealt with), this move in no way deals with the problem of particular and general as a hermeneutic or philosophical concern.

Second, Said proposes two "principal methodological devices for studying authority here": "*strategic location*, which is a way of describing the author's position in a text with regard to the Oriental material he writes about," and "*strategic formation*, which is a way of analyzing the relationship between texts and the way in which groups of texts, types of texts, even textual genres, acquire mass, density, and referential power among themselves and thereafter in the culture at large" (20). But the former "methodological device" amounts to nothing more than looking at how someone writes about the Orient, and the latter to nothing more than seeing how groups of texts cohere or fail to cohere in terms of their common traits, mutual references, connections with organizations and institutions, and so on, while calling coherence "power." None of this solves the insoluble problem of grounding the particular in the general, the concrete in the abstract, the material in the spiritual, or the political in the cultural, and vice versa. There is no "device" here to be found, and the relation between particular and general remains ultimately unregulated.

Finally, Said refers to the third escape route as "the personal dimension" (25). His personal experiences both motivate him to carry out such a study and provide him with the experiential knowledge necessary to do so. "In many ways my study of Orientalism has been an attempt to inventory the traces upon me, the Oriental subject, of the culture whose domination has been so powerful a factor in the life of all Orientals" (25). However, this argument—whose principle is in any case contested by significant historical literature that questions the historical validity of memoirs (in connection with Holocaust representation, for example)—essentially restates the (historicist) ontology that underlies the claim about engaged knowledge and the argument for the priority of the political/historical that we have seen.[50] According to this ontology, the concrete is ultimately to be favored over the abstract, as the real is more important than the ideal, the political more important than the cultural, the context determinant—in the last instance—of the text, and so on. It is not that, for Said, the abstract, the ideal, the cultural, and the text are not important (especially the text, since that can easily be aligned with the materially real, and New Critics thereby appeased or seduced), but that they best come into view when we read them out of their binary opposites. This historicist ontology is that of the concrete universal, or what is also known as the romantic symbol (the concretion that bears within itself an abstraction that is organically fused with it, freely shines through, but can never be separated from it as such).[51] As a methodological preference, it is arbitrary, its claim to priority dogmatic.

But how do these limitations of Said's methodological rigor or self-transparency adversely affect his understanding of Orientalism? First, as indicated above, Said does not seem to see the extremity and the importance for modern Orientalism of the crisis of foundations in Western modernity since the late eighteenth century (and as generated in stages since 1492, the Reformation, the installation of absolutist monarchy, and so on). Otherwise, he could not argue, as he always does, that the West is simply in a position of power with respect to the Orient, whereas I argue that it imposes its violence—in accordance with Hannah Arendt's notion of violence—on the Orient paradoxically out of a position of cultural weakness and need, though not a position of material or military weakness. Said would also not be able to say, as he does in the section of the introduction we have been considering: "The difference between representations of the Orient before the last third of the eighteenth century and those after it (that is, those belonging to what I call modern Orientalism) is that the range of representations expanded enormously in the later period" (22). Of course, this claim is not incorrect, yet the quantity or range of representations is not, on my view, the essential point, but rather the character of, and the reasons for, the investment. Moreover, if the range were to be taken into account, then studies of India would have to figure more prominently in Said's historiography of Orientalism. Said's insufficient attention to the problem of modern groundlessness entails, and is supported by, his historicist and materialist investments through which he claims to provide a grounded discourse, and also his relative indifference to the intellectual-historical overdeterminations of Orientalism, its "why," even though he is in principle interested in the cultural (12) role in coconstituting what he nonetheless understands as the Occident's ultimately political interest in the Orient.[52]

Further, Said fails to see how the Occident appropriates the fetishistically posited Oriental origin, namely through the application of typological arguments derived from the Jewish-Christian relationship according to the Christian traditions. Not only does Said not quite glimpse this, although he comes very close, and although it is the obvious answer (once one sees it) to the question as to why the West thinks the East cannot represent itself. Beyond this, he also falls prey to typological thinking in his own responses to the Orientalist discourse.

For the failure to see that typology is involved induces Said to oversimplify the Western accounts of the East and to return what he takes to be the Western accusation of the East in inverted form. That is, Said repeatedly inveighs against the tendency of Occidental discourses to accuse the Orient of being excessively concrete, material, and particularist. Overgeneralizing, he then falls into the opposite tendency, the desire to say that this is the fault of the Occident, because the Occidentals are too abstract.[53] This polemic implies that, if the West could learn to stop being so abstract, it could perhaps realize itself in and as the very concreteness of the Orient.[54] The Orient in this sense would be the realization of the Occident, and not the reverse. For the Orient represents here the value of concrete reality as such. But clearly there are also many cases where Orientalist texts accuse the Orient of being too abstract, too dreamy, too lofty, or too unrealistic, while the Occident claims to have its feet on the ground, to be in reality, and so on.

This oscillation follows the pattern of *figura*. According to this pattern, the Jewish "dead letter" is always too material, too concretely specific (ceremonial, etc.), but also too abstract (empty monotheism, rootlessness, etc.), whereas the Christian "spirit" is always just concrete enough (God embodied as human in Christ), yet abstract enough to be truly spiritual (merciful rather than caught up in legal trivialities, etc.). The Jewish principle lacks any mediation between particular and general, whereas the Christian principle establishes a mediation. Christian supersessionism sometimes accuses the Jewish tradition of just one or the other extreme, but the accusation as a whole is that of having failed to achieve a wholeness through the mediation of the extremes. This structure is demonstrably applied to the Orient by the Occident: Indeed, Said's book is full of examples, but he doesn't quite grasp the structure as a whole.

Thus despite the manifest truth of Said's claim that Western thinking about the East has often been grotesquely stereotypical, it is senseless to accuse the Occident of being abstract (as Said does) except if one wants to avenge oneself for accusations of being "too concrete," accusations with which one identifies, both because of the traumatizing repetition of these accusations throughout history and because in Western historicism, itself a Christian formation, the "concrete" is what one has become accustomed to praising qua dialectical mediation of universality and particularity. Said repeatedly falls prey to this senseless temptation, for instance, very strikingly in the section of his argument where he polemicizes against the "*textual* attitude" (92) of the Orientalists. The senselessness appears here in a few different ways. First, it suffices to consider Said's own attempt to write a useful book about real things, in light of his praise of Voltaire and Cervantes in the following terms: "What seems unexceptionable good sense to these writers is that it is a fallacy to assume that the swarming, unpredictable, and problematic mess in which human beings live can be understood on the basis of what books—texts—say" (93). Not only does Said hereby unwittingly place in question his own entire enterprise, but he also repeats here a gesture with which we are familiar from the empiricists, the Counter-Enlightenment, and the early to mid-nineteenth-century historicists, not to mention the late-nineteenth-century vitalists. Not that one could possibly disagree or want to disagree with the criticism of thinking in stereotypes about the Other, but the escape from textuality, here too, seems in principle hard to find. How does one get beyond language, thought, and tradition, in order to engage directly—that is, immediately—with reality itself, or with "the human ground (the foul rag-and-bone shop of the heart, Yeats called it)"? (110). Here, the second absurdity or contradiction emerges. For Said asks us to go beyond linguistically sedimented preconceptions precisely by means of this poetic, that is, textual evocation of the human "ground" by Yeats. (The gross mistakenness of those who think Said is a deconstructionist appears here most strikingly.) Third, Said explicitly, although accidentally, registers, for example, that the very literature on the Orient (in Nerval, for example) often enough writes down the ways in which the reality of the Orient diverges from stereotypical Western (textually or conventionally given) expectations (100). Clearly, like the problem of the particular and the general, the concrete and the abstract, the problem of representation is not simply one that we can leap beyond by investing in the metaphysics of presence itself, even if we determine presence as historical reality. Nor can it be either productive or remotely true to claim that one cultural group or historical period—here the modern Westerners (and the poststructuralists) caught in the evil "dead letter" of abstract representations—is more entangled or culpably entangled in representations than another. Indeed, this last point constitutes perhaps the most important emphasis of all that follows.

In the field of German Orientalism, much has been done, of course, since Said's *Orientalism*, especially since the 1990s, filling in the obvious lack of attention to the German tradition in his work, and responding to his methodological limitations.[55] Work by Dorothy Figueira,[56] Todd Kontje,[57] Nina Berman,[58] Andrea Polaschegg,[59] and Suzanne Marchand[60] is particularly noteworthy here. Other work has pursued the topic of Germany and colonialism, not necessarily with respect to the Orient.[61] In general, all of this scholarship willingly grants Said's political reading of Orientalism, but it often takes issue with what is seen as the one-sidedness and totalizing character of his reading, with regard to both European involvements with the Orient in general and especially German involvements.[62] Where these scholars criticize Said's work, they accuse him of oversimplifying the reality from the standpoint of a totalizing theory, that is, of being an imprecise, dogmatic historian. And they answer with the empiricist demand for more concrete specificity. Thus, if I am not mistaken, they never rigorously question his historicism. My own gesture, in contrast (but not exactly in contradiction), is to question the theoretical claim to master the problem of general and particular qua spiritual and material by investing in (symbolic) concretion as supposedly particular historical materiality. Instead, I read German Orientalism in connection with historicism's trajectory from a perspective that combines philosophical, psychoanalytic, and religiohistorical interests.

PART I

Historicist Orientalism: Transcendental Historiography from Johann Gottfried Herder to Arthur Schopenhauer

CHAPTER I

Ordering Chaos: The Orient in J. G. Herder's Teleological Historicism

Thus does fear make men insane.

—SPINOZA, *Theological-Political Treatise*

In the discourse of the late German Enlightenment, figures of the Orient from the Near East to China play a role in a wide range of discussions, from the anthropological to the theological to the political. In these discussions, however, notions about exemplary ethics tend to outweigh concerns with historical narrative. That is, the predominant aim in the late Enlightenment is to establish a universally valid ethical structure. It is to this project that notions about Oriental virtues and vices are subordinated. An Oriental culture can function, in the late German Enlightenment, as a potentially useful comparison or contrast with "our own" manners and values, but the historical-philosophical project of deriving Western from Eastern cultures in a continuous narrative is much less in evidence. Thus, for example, G. E. Lessing (1729–1781), in his later Orientalizing texts, *Nathan the Wise* and *Ernst and Falk: Dialogues for Freemasons*, ultimately uses the Oriental setting as an occasion to argue for an ahistorical ethics of the pure gift. Similarly, even in what looks like a sketch of progressive revelation, *The Education of the Human Race*, Lessing ends his narrative by returning it to its point of departure, and he defines this repetitive and anticipatory beginning point as the site of an eternal, infinite task: the ahistorical, ethical task of uniting the spiritual with the sensuous.[1] Similarly, Immanuel Kant (1724–1804) takes an essentially ahistorical, architectonic approach to reason. Indeed, when he intervenes in the pantheism controversy, he mobilizes the term "orientation," which Moses Mendelssohn (1729–1786) has introduced into the debate in *Jerusalem*, in order to argue that we must figure out where we are, and which way we are headed, not by any cultural-historical narrative, but by transcendental reflection on the faculties of knowledge that we bring to experience, and by striving infinitely to realize the categorical imperative. That is, the "Orient," as a place of the ostensible origin of the human culture that supposedly culminates in the West, plays in his thought no significant role whatsoever. Further, his critique of dogmatic teleology, which represents his moderate appropriation of Spinoza's antiteleological thought, articulates his distance from the historicist narrative mode that will predominate in nineteenth-century Orientalism.[2]

In contrast to these late Enlightenment figures, Lessing's and Kant's younger contemporary, Johann Gottfried Herder (1744–1803) broaches German historicism on the basis of the Counter-Enlightenment suspicion of abstract reason. His work may appear as a concretization, or fleshing out, of the kind of minimal abstract structure Lessing provides in the *Education* text. But Herder does not just flesh out Lessing's abstract schemas, he relinearizes the historical narrative that Lessing had delinearized, by reasserting the validity of typological thinking and the privilege of history over ethics. And he resituates the ethical will within the context of a (natural and divine) teleological will that he posits as the underlying subject of history itself.

Herder's *Ideas for a Philosophy of History of Humanity* (*Ideen zur Philosophie der Geschichte der Menschheit*), on which I concentrate the discussion of Herder here, appeared in four sprawling volumes from 1784 to 1791.[3] It is certainly one of the few most importantly influential inaugural works of the modern historicist tradition. I consider it here as an exemplary illustration of some of the main argumentative structures of that tradition (above all its dogmatically teleological and Orientalist dimensions), which will extend across the nineteenth century and beyond. As Raymond Schwab already showed very usefully in *The Oriental Renaissance* (1950), the second volume of Herder's *Ideas* (published in mid-1785) appeared just prior to a flurry of translations of Sanskrit texts to which Herder would be quite responsive.[4] Herder was struck by recent work on non-Western cultures as early as 1776 when he became aware of Abraham Hyacinthe Anquetil-Duperron's translation of the Zend Avesta. Sir Charles Wilkins's translation of the

Ordering Chaos: Herder

J. G. Herder (1744–1803). Engraving by Faustino Anderloni. (Bildarchiv Preussischer Kulturbesitz, Berlin/Art Resource, N.Y.)

Bhagavad Gita was published in 1784, the same year in which the Asiatic Society of Bengal was formed in Calcutta. And it was in the later 1780s and the 1790s that the first burst of translations from Sanskrit (and modern scholarly reports on ancient Indian culture) appeared in English, French, and German. Georg Forster sent his translation of *Shakuntula* to Herder in 1791, and Herder registered his enthusiasm in the preface he wrote for that work and in his further writings concerning India. As Schwab summarizes it:

> It is well known how Herder, in rekindling for a deciphered India the enthusiastic interest that had been felt for an imagined India [such as that contained in the *Ideas*], spread among the Romantics the idea of placing the cradle of the divine infancy of the human race in India and he himself later conceived the *Gedanken einiger Brahmanen* [*Thoughts of Some Brahmins*]. (*Oriental Renaissance*, 58)

I explore some of this larger, later context in detail in ensuing chapters. Here, I am particularly interested in the conceptual and affective determination of this slightly earlier, more imaginary Orient as it appears in Herder's *Ideas*.[5] Since Herder's philosophy of history is largely driven by the project of answering—that is, suppressing—the threat of Spinoza's arguments against both teleology and freedom of the will,[6] I begin with those arguments.[7]

God's Plan as Projection of Human Projects: The Spinozistic Reduction

Spinoza states his rejection of teleology, among other places, in the *Ethics*, appendix to part 1 ("Of God"). Here, he exposes the widespread "prejudices" by which "men commonly suppose that all natural things act, as men do, on account of an end; indeed, they maintain as certain that God himself directs all things to some certain end, for they say that God has made all things for man, and man that he might worship God."[8] Spinoza explains the origins of these beliefs, which he holds to be false, as follows. Since people most commonly do not know that their desires are the effects of external causes, while they necessarily and self-consciously strive to attain their own advantage, they (wrongly) think their striving is freely chosen. Thinking themselves free, they experience themselves as acting intentionally, toward some end. They then ask, with respect to *all* perceived events (which they regard as results of actions), to what end these actions were performed, because they project their own way of imagining themselves onto the world of events in general. In other words, they always ask "why?"—the question to which, according to Nietzsche's definition of nihilism, by the late nineteenth century there will be no answer.[9]

Beyond this, because people constantly encounter means to their "own" imaginary ends in the world, many of which means they have not provided or created for themselves, they tend to assume that someone else must have provided these means for them. That is, if things in the world are essentially or solely meaningful for me insofar as they are means to my ends, and if, further, in order for these means to exist, they have to be constructed for my ends (both because they don't just make themselves and because things aren't produced to *no* purpose, according to my assumptions), all those many means toward my ends that I find in the world, without having constructed them myself, must have been constructed by some other person or subject. Hence, the common assumption that some invisible entity, a free subject, has prepared things for my use.

Finally, Spinoza argues that when people reflect on why such a free subject—the God or gods they posit—has prepared things for my use, they project their own self-centered manner of functioning onto this subject. This is the functioning of those who give gifts with a view to exchange as return on investment. They assume that this subject has been providing for them so that they will, in turn, provide for it—by honoring and glorifying it.

> So it has happened that each of them has thought up from his own temperament different ways of worshipping God, so that God might love him above all the rest, and direct the whole of Nature according to the needs of their blind desire and insatiable greed. . . . This was why each of them strove with great diligence to understand and explain the final causes of all things. (111)

Here we see in Spinoza the inscription of the gift-exchange problematic that plays a key role in Lessing's writings mentioned above as well as (in a less ethical, more aesthetic register) in Goethe's *West-Östlicher Divan* (chapters 3 and 4). Providential teleology supports itself by pressuring its adherents to commit their faith to the absolute subject in order to guarantee their continuing good fortune.

The problem of teleology leads here, moreover, immediately to the problem of theodicy, as the reciprocal gift structure already implies. As Spinoza explains, when people begin to see the world as the intentional action of God toward some end and then have to acknowledge that bad things happen—wars, sickness, death—these bad things threaten the good reputation of God. And although it is easy enough to rehabilitate God's reputation (or concept) by blaming the victims when they have been impious, Spinoza points out that things get more difficult when the pious, as happens every day, are equally visited with suffering. Theodicy can then succeed only by claiming ignorance of the "judgments of the gods" (111). But Spinoza considers such a choice unfortunate, as it conduces to an acceptance of ignorance, that is, an abdication of intellect, whereas the rejection of the construction of divine intentionality would lead to a more coherent result.

To these false beliefs, Spinoza opposes his own necessaritarian doctrine, as it applies to both humans and God (qua nature). In contrast to the imaginary illusions of teleology, Spinoza views God (i.e., nature), or substance, as acting in accordance with the necessity of God's (or its) essence, rather than through prompting by anything external such as an intention or incitement, which would signify desire (97–99). "Will does not pertain to God's nature" (106). For as Spinoza repeats on a number of occasions and in various ways, to assume that God has a will and can act in terms of ends is to assume that God can lack something, since desiring toward an end implies lack. But to assume that God can lack something "takes away from God's perfection. For if God acts for the sake of an end, he necessarily wants something which he lacks" (112). The perfection of God (or nature) guarantees its ultimate lack of any intentionality. God is never unfulfilled—nor fulfilled, for that matter, in the sense of having had a previous lack filled in.

But Spinoza doesn't just discuss the causes of the teleological illusion and the reasons why it contradicts the true nature of God. He also considers the consequences of this illusion, the ways in which it generates in turn a complex network of further illusions. Spinoza argues here, namely, that when we assume—as we do in a (eudaemonistic) teleology—that things in the world have been put there for our sake, then we start judging all things in the world in terms of whether or not they are useful to us. From this results an entire series of value judgments—"good, evil, order, confusion, warm, cold, beauty, ugliness" (113)—that are imaginary: "Each one has judged things according to the disposition of his brain; or rather, has accepted affections of the imagination as things" (114).[10] To focus on the example of "order," since it will return in our consideration of Herder below:

> And because those who do not understand the nature of things, but only imagine them, affirm nothing concerning things, and take the imagination for the intellect, they firmly believe, in their ignorance of things and of their own nature, *that there is an order in things*. For when things are so disposed that, when they are presented to us through the senses, we can easily imagine them, and so can easily remember them, *we say that they are well-ordered*; but if the opposite is true, *we say that they are badly ordered, or confused*.
>
> And since those things we can easily imagine are especially pleasing to us, *men prefer order to confusion*, as if *order* were anything in Nature more than a relation to our imagination. They also say that God has created all things *in order*, and so, unknowingly attribute imagination to God—

unless, perhaps, they mean that God, to provide for human imagination, has disposed all things so that men can very easily imagine them. Nor will it, perhaps, give them pause that infinitely many things are found which far surpass our imagination, and a great many which confuse it on account of its weakness. But enough of this. (113–14)

Spinoza's derivation of values from the imagination rather than the intellect, as what we might call subjective values, projections, or narcissism—what Kant will call the pathological realm—certainly presents a grave challenge to the value orientation of the individual late-Enlightenment reader who aspires to rationality. As a result, Spinoza's Counter-Enlightenment readers such as Jacobi will consider his position nihilistic.[11]

In turn, however, Spinoza himself claims that nihilism, or rather what he calls skepticism, arises not from the critical approach to subjective values (the critique of the assumption that the world is meant for one's own happiness), but rather from indulging in such fond illusions. (And here he is closer to Kant's critique of dogmatism in reason as leading to irrationalism.) Arguments that result from the differences in judgments of these illusions lead, he says, to skepticism, which is merely one further illusion. Instead, "The perfection of things is to be judged solely from their nature and power; things are not more or less perfect because they please or offend men's senses, or because they are of use to, or are compatible with, human nature" (115). Thus, in a secularizing modern modality, Spinoza's early Enlightenment deterministic critique of teleology pushes for the establishment of a rational discourse that would relativize private differences in taste and values.

We now need to see how Herder's philosophy of history positions itself against the background of Spinoza's mechanistic view of nature, for we know that Herder was reading Spinoza during the time of the composition of the *Ideas*, reading that will culminate in his *God: Some Conversations* (1797), published in the same year as the third volume of the *Ideas*.

Philosophy of History as a Teleological Theodicy, or Historicism as a Disavowal of Doubt

The most overwhelmingly evident thing about the *Ideas* in this regard, from the preface on, is Herder's emphatic insistence on a teleological point of view, and specifically, on his capacity to read the intentions of history empirically, straight out of historical reality itself. This insistence will rightly be characterized by Kant as "dogmatic."[12] Herder's affirmation of teleology in the preface to the *Ideas*, however, merits attention not just for its philosophical limitations. It is also important—at once inaugural and illustrative—for the ways in which it manifests the affective correlative of these limitations (viz., a kind of panic) and for the rhetorical means it employs to elicit the reader's sympathetic identification with Herder's disavowal of this affect.[13]

In the preface, Herder spells out that the point or end of his project, his reason for undertaking it, has been to determine God's plan for humanity. (Hegel will repeat this claim, with increased bravado, in his *Lectures on the Philosophy of History*, as we'll see in chapter 5.) As the plan is the origin, that is, the original plan, to know the plan immediately one must evidently place oneself *at* the origin. Accordingly, Herder rhetorically places himself at the origin in a number of different ways, only two of which I'll mention here.

First, Herder emphasizes—at the end of an extended and cringingly demanding appeal to the reader—that he has lost his way, that is, he has lost track of his own intention, which was to tell "the story [or "history"—*Geschichte*, Herder's word here, can mean both "story" and "history"] of how I came to work on this material and . . . how I came back to it" (*die Geschichte . . . wie ich zur Bearbeitung dieser Materie gekommen und . . . auf sie zurückgekommen bin*) (14; 112). In losing his way, however, Herder performs the way itself, the path of the beginning or the beginning of the path. For what led him to the project of a philosophy of history turns out to have been the desire (or plan) to demonstrate that God has a plan for humans—that there is a path, an absolute path on which we are walking. But because the desire to prove that there is a path is predicated on some felt absence of the path—or some uncertainty about its presence (albeit one accompanied by a sense of there having been a path that was subsequently left behind), Herder's loss of his way performs the way itself. In so doing, it also implies the alignment of his own path with God's path itself.[14]

Second, when Herder now comes back to his "story" (*Geschichte*)—the story of his turn to history—this story reduces to the claim that his intention to write such a philosophy of history goes back to the very morning of his life, that is, the Orient of his existence.

> Already in rather early years, as the meadows of the sciences still lay in all of their morning jewelry [*Morgenschmuck*] before me, from which the mid-day sun of our lives [*die Mittagssonne unsres Lebens*] subtracts so much, there came to me often the thought: *should not, since everything in the world has its philosophy and science, also that which concerns us most intimately, the history of humanity as a whole have a philosophy and science?* (14; 112)

The beginning (intention) of Herder's return to the beginning (God's plan) was at the beginning (of his life), the Orient of his existence, prior to the disruption that arrived (à la Rousseau), with language, culture, and Enlightenment, as the Pan hour of the day. (I return to *Morgenschmuck* below, where its earliness will assume for Herder the opposite, negative connotations of decorative rhetorical excess.)

For all its wondrous oneness, wholeness, and earliness, however, this emphatic beginning is nonetheless already marked by a certain negativity or doubt, by multiplicity, fragmentariness, and belatedness. In explaining his original project and concern, Herder raises a rhetorical question. Should not God have a plan for humanity, given that his "wisdom, goodness, and power" (14; 112) are so strikingly evident in the natural world that when we dare to try to follow God's intentionality in the natural arena we "lose ourselves in an abyss of his thoughts"? (*wir uns in einem Abgrunde seiner Gedanken verlieren*) (15; 112). The negativity announces itself here already, in fact, through the mention of this abyss into which we lose ourselves concerning God's intentions with regard to nature. This negativity is severely exacerbated, however, by Herder's questioning—rhetorical as it may be—with regard to God's intentions for humanity. Herder's way of raising the question provides us with a glimpse of what is at stake for him in the possibility that such a divine intention for humanity could be lacking. Herder begins: "This God should renounce his wisdom and goodness, in the determination and establishment of our species as a whole [*in der Bestimmung und Einrichtung unsres Geschlechtes im Ganzen*], and here have no plan [*und hier keinen Plan haben*]?" (15; 112). To be sure, Herder piously acknowledges in passing that the plan might include our lacking clear knowledge of its contours, a move Spinoza disparaged. But he goes on to insist, against this consideration, that our lack of knowledge of the plan can potentially mislead us into denying its very existence, or to a combination of faith and doubt—"doubting believing and believing doubting" (*zweifelnd glauben und glaubend zweifeln*) (15; 113)—that has the structure of panic. For it involves following a hypothetical plan for salvation, then abandoning it, then following another, and so on, in quick alternations, like someone running in a panic this way and that. But why exactly would one panic? The problem—as Freud would later make clear in *Mass Psychology and the Analysis of the Ego* and related writings—is that of the leaderless group. "What is the human species as a whole," Herder asks, shepherding us, "but a herd without a shepherd?" (15; 112). However, if God is not leading, the leader will be a tyrant—"where the foot of the stronger one . . . stomps on thousands . . . where finally the two greatest tyrants of the earth—chance and time—lead the great crowd away" (15; 113). And Herder grants that much of history supports such a view. His expression of these doubts indeed now culminates in the form of a rather complex reflection on the impossibility of articulating space with time, or of spatializing time, creating a spatial order that is reconciled with the temporal order.

> What is it that, on the earth, is completed as a whole? What is whole on earth? Are not the times ordered, as the spaces are ordered? and both are, of course, the twins of One fate. The former are full of wisdom; the latter are full of apparent disorder; but still evidently man is created to seek order, that he should have an overview of a piece [*Fleck*] of the times, that the later generations should build upon the past: for this is why he has memory and a capacity to recall [*Erinnerung und Gedächtnis*]. And doesn't precisely this building of the times upon each other make the whole of our species into a formless monstrous building [*zum unförmlichen Riesengebäude*], where One carries away what the other started to build, where what never should have been built remains standing and in centuries finally everything becomes One Ruin [*Ein Schutt*], amongst which, the more broken and crumbling it is [*je brüchiger er ist*] the more confidently the hesitating people live? (15–16; 113)

Succession appears here as incompatible with simultaneity, diachrony with synchrony, genesis with structure, or history with philosophy—a grave difficulty for a philosophy of history.[15] In terms of the "building of the times upon each other," and getting an "overview of a piece of the times," Herder is trying to envision here—to put it in the language of critical theory after Jakobson—an articulation of metaphor (as spatial figure of the moment) with metonymy (as a temporal figure of displacement). But the success of this effort is undone continuously by the ceaseless and unending progression of temporal moments themselves, which provide only the most problematic foundations each for the others, which disrupt them in turn. The passage provides a powerful articulation of exactly the sort of sentiment that Herder is trying to disavow through his philosophy of history. The temporally induced disordering of space or the spatializing disruption of time leads to a sensed formlessness, groundlessness, and disorder—Spinoza would call it imaginary—that prompts Herder to put his teleological systematic narrative in its place. Here, in the preface, Herder interrupts himself abruptly by saying, "I do not want to extend the series of such doubts or follow further the contradictions of the human with himself, amongst themselves, and with the rest of creation. Enough, I sought a philosophy of the history of humanity" (16; 113).

What's the Plan?

The plan, of course, is humanity.[16] That is, God's plan, as nature's plan, is that the human, as crown of creation, should develop its capacities to the fullest. In ontological terms, this takes the form of Herder's principal law of history: "That which can be will come to be."[17] That is, the purpose is to pass from possibility to reality, from potential to actualization. This is a doctrine of plenitude, in which no unfulfilled possibility, no emptiness, is tolerated or acknowledged. In terms of the history of Christianity, however, this ontological formulation of purpose amounts to a displacement and repetition of the typological relation between Judaism and Christianity, as prefigural "dead letter" and realized "living spirit."

But in order for the plan to unfold, it has to begin. And in order for it to be empirically historical, it has to begin in history. Indeed, Herder disavows—as does historicist Orientalism generally—the absence of foundation and replaces it with a (fetishistic) beginning in time, a beginning constituted by the Orient, which now realizes itself in the Occident, as the Jews were taken (prior to secularizing modernity) to realize themselves in Christianity. Through this realization, the alien Eastern origin is appropriated by and as the modern Western subject. But since Herder is very much in the middle of this development of a bourgeois secular rationality as replacement for public religious foundations, he will articulate the Jewish-Christian opposition with the Oriental-Occidental one. Specifically, he will situate the Jews in the Orient as a preliminary realization of this Orient so that their limitations can be overcome by Christianity in its quasi-secularized form as Occidental culture.

Culture Is Born in Chaos but Recalls Its Birth as Order

In order to place the Jews in the Orient as the Oriental (i.e., preliminary) realization, Herder posits that the Israelite revelation is the Oriental self-revelation of the Orient—the self-illumination of sunrise—par excellence. Through his peculiar method, which combines religious faith with scientific observation—a method Kant will characterize as a version of dogmatic metaphysics—Herder claims to read divine intentions in the book of nature.[18] But to this end, he reads the divine Hebrew book of Genesis as a clue to the origination of both the natural world and humanity, as manifestations of divine intentionality.[19] The chiasmic structure of this unification of theism with naturalism—to read the book of nature in order to access revelation, he reads revelation in order to access nature—matches the chiasmic structure of the unification of Jewish and Oriental that I will be tracing here, as Jews are inscribed in the Orient while the Orient is inscribed in Judaism. Through the two chiasmic structures, Herder broaches simultaneously the secularization of providence and the transformation of Christian *figura* into Western Orientalism in its historicist mode.

Herder's first step is to posit that human culture begins in the Orient. Asia is the "mid-point of the most lively organic forces" (*Mittelpunkt der regsten organischen Kräfte*) (386; 200), where the "materials of the chaos most rich in fruits in the greatest fullness" (*die Materien des fruchtreichsten Chaos in größester Fülle*) (386; 200) had settled. The origin of humanity, then, occurs at and as the site of a fertile chaos. This chaos combines fullness with lack, in that the fruit with which it is rich still needs to be born into the world. Fulfillment anticipates itself in this chaotic fullness. Accordingly, while the other continents were still submerged in water, land-animal life and even human life had already begun in Asia, from which over time it streamed forth into the rest of the world: "Africa and Europe are more like offspring, leaning against the lap of mother Asia" (*daß Afrika und Europa nur wie Kinder sind, an den Schoß der Mutter, Asien, gelehnet*) (388; 201), and this applies even more so to the New World. The chaotic womb of mother Asia is in turn linked here associatively to the divine voice of creation (*die Stimme, die allenthalben Meer und Land mit eignen Bewohnern bepflanzte*) and to the maternal figure of nature herself—"die Natur," who brought us forth "as the fruits of her ripest diligence, or if you like as sons of her old age" (*als Früchte ihres reifsten Fleißes, oder wenn man will, als Söhne ihres hohen Alters*) in the perfect place, where she could care for us "with a motherly hand" (*mit mütterlicher Hand*) (389; 202).[20] As we will see, it is the chaos of this maternal, feminine figure—whose offspring constitute a late earliness or an early lateness—that is necessary to order just as origin is necessary to development. But the linearity of the step from one term to the next and the separation of the two terms are unstable because structurally speaking chaos and order, origin and development, all begin not just with themselves but also with their opposites, especially for a monist like Herder.

Herder also produces somewhat more concretely historical arguments for the birth of humanity in Asia. He suggests, for example, that the various peoples of Europe and their languages all come from Asia. In addition, written language, culture itself (including domestication of animals), the sciences and arts, government, and so on, all originated in Asia. Being the most ancient, the Asian cultures are, in one sense at least, closest to God: "The lofty poetry of several peoples of South Asia is known worldwide; and the more ancient it is, the more it gains in dignity and simplicity, which by itself deserves to be called divine" (*die Würde und Einfalt, die durch sich selbst den Namen der Göttlichen verdienet*) (394; 206). Yet these cultures, in their foreignness, remain marked by a certain negative aspect of chaos, which Herder will have to appropriate by reducing it to a more familiar form of order.

Given that for Herder human culture begins in the Orient, when he attempts to situate that origin more precisely, he looks for clues in Oriental myths about the creation of both earth and humanity. Herder thus uses the myths of the Orient, the oldest myths—India, Tibet, ancient Chaldea, and "even the low-lying Egypt"—to trace the origin of humanity.[21] In particular, he figures the "voice" of Oriental myth as that of childhood memories of birth.[22] In this Rousseauistic manner, Herder tries to catch inarticulate origination at its earliest articulate internalization, chaos in its earliest ordering, materiality in its initial spatialization. Herder suggests we follow the voice back through tradition (as the only "means to education") to its "original source" (*Urquell*, 397; 208), at which point he inserts the image of childhood.

> As little as a child, although it was present at its birth, can recount that birth, so little may we hope that the human race can give us a historically strict report of its creation and first doctrine/learning [*Lehre*], of the invention of language and its first dwelling place. However, a child does recall some traits from its later youth, and when several children who were raised together and later separated recount the Same or Similar things, why should one not listen to them? . . . especially when one could have no other documentation? (397; 208)[23]

The child with the best memory or best account of its memory, however, turns out to be the ancient Hebrew one, the Old Testament creation myth. How does Herder justify this?

The Old Testament account is preferable not just because Herder still takes it to be the "oldest book" (402; 212), but more crucially because this tradition, more than any other Asiatic one, he says, possesses "coherence, simplicity, and truth" (*Zusammenhang, Einfalt und Wahrheit*) (411; 218). In contrast, although the other Asian myths contain some seeds (411; 218) of physics and history, they do so in a

> savagely confused state, a confabulated chaos as at the beginning of the world's creation. This nature-philosopher [Moses] overcame chaos and

presents us with a building that, in its simplicity and connection, imitates order-rich nature herself. How did he come to this order and simplicity? If we only compare it with the fables of other peoples, we see the ground of his purer philosophy of the history of the earth and humanity. (218)

Wild durcheinander, ein fabelhaftes Chaos wie beim Anfange der Weltschöpfung. Dieser Naturweise hat das Chaos überwunden und stellt uns ein Gebäude dar, das in seiner Einfalt und Verbindung der Ordnungreichen Natur selbst nachahmet. Wie kam er zu dieser Ordnung und Einfalt? Wir dörfen ihn nur mit den Fabeln andrer Völker vergleichen, so sehen wir den Grund seiner reinern Philosophie der Erd- und Menschengeschichte. (411)

The Old Testament overcomes the chaos of the Asiatic womb, which is in turn associated in Herder's text with the "pregnant sea" (*schwangeren Meer*) (381; 197) from which life first arose.[24] The Old Testament thereby attains to an order that—paradoxically, contradictorily, or perhaps chaotically—places it closer to the origin than that origin—chaos itself. Since simplicity is divinity, the Old Testament narrative, as the simplest of the Asiatic creation myths, is the most divine. By overcoming chaos, it becomes the most perfect realization of chaos itself. This is the typological achievement of a passage from (the chaos of) matter to (the order of) spirit. Ancient Hebrew culture realizes the Oriental as Oriental.

Genetic Forces in Genesis: The Surprising Actuality of the Oriental Origin

This result is ambiguous, however, as with all typological realizations of the (pre)figural. On the one hand, it suggests that the ancient Oriental origin in its Hebrew form reaches all the way to modernity and already speaks our language. But on the other hand, it suggests that this origin remains stuck in its own Orientality, a sun frozen forever in its initial rise above the eastern horizon. Both of these points of view, equally necessary to the logic of figural interpretation, require the forcing of the Oriental object or text, once into a radical continuity with modern, Western conceptions (i.e., with "ourselves") and once into a radical incomprehensibility and regressiveness. Let me consider one striking example of the first gesture at this point in Herder's text, and then go on to discuss at greater length the presence of the second in Herder's characterization of Oriental peoples (I'll consider Egypt, China, India, and the Hebrews specifically) in books 11 and 12 of the *Ideas*.

In his reading of Genesis, Herder effects the transition between material nature and spirit by means of the translation of the Hebrew for "spirit"—*ruach*—with the German approximate equivalent, *eine lebendige brütende Kraft*, "a living brooding force," moving upon the waters. Or again by *Lebensschwangere Naturkräfte* (natural forces pregnant with life) (403; 212).[25] This simultaneous naturalization of the supernatural and supernaturalization of the natural—which goes by way of a tendentious translation that supports Herder's theory of underlying organic "forces"—is particularly striking, in that Herder accompanies it with the claim that the translation simply goes without saying.

> *As once the creation of our earth and our heaven began,* so goes the saga, *the earth was first a deserted, formless body, on which a dark sea flooded and a living brooding force moved upon the waters.* If, in accordance with all modern experiences, the oldest state of the earth should be indicated, such as the (re)searching understanding is capable of giving it, without the flight of unprovable hypotheses: we rediscover exactly this old description. (212)

> Als einst die Schöpfung unsrer Erde und unsres Himmels begann, *erzählt diese Sage*, war die Erde zuerst ein wüster, unförmlicher Körper, auf dem ein dunkles Meer flutete und eine lebendige brütende Kraft bewegte sich auf diesen Wassern.—*Sollte nach allen neuern Erfahrungen der älteste Zustand der Erde angegeben werden, wie ihn ohne den Flug unbeweisbarer Hypothesen der forschende Verstand zu geben vermag: so finden wir genau diese alte Beschreibung wieder.* (403)

Herder claims that he is indicating (*angegeben*) the oldest state of the earth immediately, that is, as the understanding gives it without "unprovable hypotheses" (403; 212). And what the understanding gives us here is "exactly this old description" (403; 212). In other words, Herder disavows the necessary distortion that accompanies all translation, and indeed all understanding and retelling. He disavows, that is, the hermeneutic uncertainty that results from the radical break between intention and articulation, or articulation and rearticulation. And above all, he disavows this uncertainty at exactly the moment when he proposes a translation of an ancient Hebrew ostensibly spiritual conception into the fundamental term of his eighteenth-century vitalist teleology![26] (Moreover, my point holds, of course, regardless of whether one can say that Herder's translation is a relatively good one in pragmatic terms.) The disavowal of the otherness of the other's speech, or simply the disavowal of the difficulty of understanding, here as elsewhere in Herder—and in stark contrast to Kant in the "Conjectural Beginning of Human History," for example—is of a piece with his dogmatic teleology. Concerning not just divine but also human intentionality, Herder oversimplifies the question of access with a naïvely overconfident and credulous violence that denies the abyss of uncertain meaning. (Note that Herder here uses the term *formless* [*unförmlich*]—which he had applied to the panic-inducing disaster of a history without telos, in the passage I discussed above—for the original matter over which the teleological instance of the spiritual-organic forces brood. The abyss would be the original formless materiality that results from a deficit of intentional meaning.) But because translating Old Testament *ruach* immediately into the language of the eighteenth century implies that the eighteenth century (in the person of Herder) masters Old Testamentary intentions, it is not so surprising (although apparently paradoxical) that Herder combines this gesture (as we are about to see in more detail) with the incompatible but complementary claim that the Old Testament and its "people" (and indeed the rest of the Orient) do not reach forward into modernity but remain behind in a state of eternal underdevelopment. In fact, the equation of ancient Oriental text with modern interpretation always possesses this duplicity. The ancient Eastern origin reduces to the Western reading because "we" in the West constitute the realization it is destined to, but cannot on its own, attain.

Or Maybe Not So Up to Date after All: Letter as Hieroglyph

Accordingly—and this is the second gesture I sketched above—when Herder analyzes particular Oriental traditions in books 11 and 12, including the Hebrew tradition, he tends to reduce them all to passivity, or *Trägheit*: to an unfree anticipation of the free activity of the West.[27] In this negative aspect, too, traditional Christian views of the Jews become the model for Herder's view of the Orient in general. It is important to retrace briefly here the somewhat circuitous logic of this development.

As I indicated in passing above, Herder adduces the origination of language in Asia as one of his main arguments in support of the claim that human culture more generally originates in Asia. In fact, Herder privileges the history of languages as a mode of access to the history of culture. Within language, in turn, he privileges the written form: "The most certain sign of the culture [*Kultur*] of a language is its writing" (392; 204). In

Asia he situates the origin of all alphabetical as well as hieroglyphic writing. As opposed to Europe, America, and Africa, "Asia . . . as it were exhausted writing in letters [*Buchstaben*] and artificial hieroglyphs [*Kunsthieroglyphen*] so that one can find amongst its written characters [*Schriftzügen*] nearly all genres [*Gattungen*] of how the speech of man can be contained [*gefesselt*]" (392; 204). (We will see this word, *fesseln*, below used with respect to the Jews, taken by Herder to "bind" the others in a negative sense.) Although the Asian languages include alphabetical ones, however, the essence of Asian language qua original language is for Herder its hieroglyphic character. Hieroglyphics means here not just to paint speech in pictures of the world but also to be incomprehensible, because in the 1780s Egyptian hieroglyphics had not yet been deciphered. Thus Herder can write of Asian languages in general that "the older they are," the more they "are hard for a European to learn: for he must give up the useless richness of his tongue and comes in them as to a finely-thought-out, lightly regulated hieroglyphics of the invisible language of thoughts" (391–92; 204). In sum, Asian culture is essentially hieroglyphic. But what is a hieroglyphic language, other than original language that forces us to give up our own language and become radically alienated in the (futile) attempt to make sense out of it?

As this last characterization already suggests, although he makes hieroglyphs the model for Oriental culture, Herder understands hieroglyphs in turn as "dead letters." He thereby connects the culture(s) of hieroglyphs with all of the material characteristics traditionally associated (by Christian discourse) with Judaism.[28] Through the mediation of the Egyptian hieroglyph, he thus extends the traits of the Jewish "prefiguration" across the cultural terrain of the East in general. This will put the West in a threatened but still dominant position vis-à-vis the East, in terms of typology.

The imaginary Christian reasoning here goes as follows. On the one hand, through its identification with Judaism, Christianity appropriates for itself the myth of enslavement in Egypt. But on the other hand, through its self-differentiation from Judaism, Christianity finds itself constantly threatened by regression into Judaism, that is, by a metaphorical enslavement in Judaism itself, an entrapment in the dead letter to which it is constitutively indebted: Judaism functions as the Egypt of Christianity. As a result, the suggestion that the West is exposed to the ongoing danger of an Egyptian/Jewish bondage in the unfree Eastern origin becomes plausible as soon as one posits that the East is a hieroglyphic culture in general. Now let me show some of the places where Herder establishes this network of suggestion in his text.

In the chapter on Egypt, Herder focuses extensively on the limitations of hieroglyphs, on their essential meaninglessness and lifelessness. For example: "To lively observation [the hieroglyphs] added not only a dark but rather also a dead image [*ein totes Bild*], that certainly did not advance the progress of the human understanding but rather inhibited it" (505; 268). The very attempt to decipher them is deadly:

> Inappropriate is the demand to learn to understand something through itself which can be interpreted in a thousand different ways and deadly is the effort [*tötend die Mühe*] that one expends upon arbitrary signs [*willkürliche Zeichen*], as if they were necessary, eternal things [*notwendige, ewige Sachen*]. Therefore Egypt always remained a child in knowledge, because it remained a child in the indication of knowledge, and for us these children's ideas are probably lost forever. (506; 268)

As incomprehensible images of "mummified forms" (*Mumiengestalten*) (502; 266), the Egyptian hieroglyphs—the model for all Asian or original language as such in its very origination—constitute a language of dead bodies.[29]

In his extension of this notion of hieroglyphic Orientality to the Oriental cultures in general, which is sometimes only implicit, the most explicit instance is his discussion of Chinese culture. Due to its ideographic language, China induces in Herder a hostility similar to the hostility he shows to Egypt, but even more so. For Chinese culture, unlike ancient Egyptian culture, is still alive, like the living dead, or like a large number of Jews who would possess a (very large) country of their own. Thus, for example, Herder says that the Chinese Empire "is an embalmed mummy [*eine balsamierte Mumie*] painted with hieroglyphs and wrapped in silks" (438; 235), and the people there live in a state of slavery (439; 235). The "entire learned mode of thought of the Chinese is painted in by artificial and State hieroglyphs" (*in künstliche und Staats-Hieroglyphen vermalet*) (440; 236). This type of writing "unnerves thoughts into image-traces and makes the entire mode of thought of the nation into arbitrary characters painted or written into the air" (440; 236). Again Herder emphasizes the arbitrariness of the signifier in these mimetic forms of writing with a vehemence matched and, as it were, driven by the manifest fallaciousness of the claim that alphabetical systems are less arbitrary, and a vehemence underwritten by the hostility toward the materiality of writing, or the body of language, that is carried by the pervasive phonocentrism of Christian, Western discourse. China is an Egyptian mummy that refuses to die.

If ancient Egypt still stood before us: we would see in many respects a
similarity, without dreaming of mutually deriving them, which in accordance with given traditions only the world-region modified differently....
Ancient China at the edge of the world is like a ruin of primeval times, in
its half-Mongolian institutions. (440; 236–37)[30]

At the same time, however, behind this hieroglyphic facade, China shares
a certain affinity with the Jews. For example: "The Chinese, in their corner
of the world, like the Jews, have kept free from mixing with other peoples
[as] is demonstrated by their vain pride" (436; 233). And less explicitly, the
artificiality and excessiveness of their written language (439; 236), their
subjection to "coercion and necessity" (436; 234), their lack of "human
heart and spirit" (437; 234), of any concern with "masculine strength and
honor" (437; 234), their nomadic or diasporal character (436; 233), which
Herder connects with their "Mongolian" essence—all link them to Christian stereotypes about Jews consistent with Pauline conceptions of the Jewish law as dead letter. The Egyptian-Jewish character of China, as of all the
Orient, will ultimately explain why it gets left behind by history, overcome
by a regrettable but inevitable modern European imperialism.

In contrast to the Egyptians and the Chinese—that is, the cultures associated with writing that is taken to imitate (material) images rather than
(spiritual) voice—the ancient Indians are ranked very high in Herder's
estimation. (And evaluative discourse is ubiquitous in the *Ideas* despite his
intermittent attempts and claims to cleave to descriptive objectivity.)[31]
Herder speaks, for example, of the ancient Indians' "artful and beautiful
language" (*künstliche und schöne Sprache*) (454; 242). And he goes so far as
to argue that the Garden of Eden must have been situated in Kashmir. In
the reception, indeed, he is known as one of the forerunners or founders
of German romantic Indomania. But at a certain point Herder nonetheless
takes his distance—as will Hegel, Goethe, and others—from the Indians'
fatalism, their caste system, and their associated belief in metempsychosis,
which he sees as forms of necessity and coercion.[32] This failure to escape
the sphere of necessity, to accede to freedom, is a trait that Herder links to
all Oriental peoples, and that is powerfully overdetermined by Christian
perceptions of the Judaic law as a deadly constraint. Further, to provide an
example of the explicit presence of such perceptions in Herder's text: As
he has said of the Jews and the Chinese, Herder writes in his chapter "In-
dostan" that the Indians, too, refuse to mix with any others (453; 241). In
this sense they remain caught within themselves. Consequently, they fail to

develop, like the chaotic materiality of the origin they represent, an origin whose development must always be situated outside itself, in the West.

But lest one think that Herder, the good-willed and evidently philo-Semitic author of *The Spirit of Hebrew Poesy*, could not be thought to purvey problematically stereotypical, Pauline, anti-Jewish ideas about ancient Hebrews (or modern Jews), it is necessary now to show briefly how he does, especially since I've been arguing for the importance of typology in his conception of the Orient as a whole.[33] We have seen that Herder marked the Hebrews as the order that masters the chaos of the more radical Oriental origin, functioning as the development of that origin or its realization. In "Hebrews," the third chapter of book 12, however, Herder reverses the polarities (without explicitly marking the reversal). In this context, he associates order with the undeveloped origin, and opposes it to the fruitful chaos—sometimes also called "freedom"—that now occupies the position of the development (or realization). With this reversal—always available to Herder because of the very instability of the binary oppositions with which he is working—the Hebrews are reduced, as Jews who are developmentally stunted, to the anticipatory Oriental position they at once epitomize and instantiate. Herder explains, for example, that the Hebrews were ruined in their education (*in der Erziehung verdarb*) (491; 263), which never attained the ripeness (*Reife*) (491; 263) of a political culture on its own ground (*Boden*) (491; 263).[34] This failure to develop is owing to the legal "dependence and order" (*gesetzliche Anhänglichkeit und Ordnung*) (491; 263) that prevents any "fruitful freedom of spirit" (*fruchtbare Freiheit des Geistes*) (491; 263).

This failure of the Jewish origin to develop, moreover, adversely affects the Christian-Western development itself. The writings (*Schrift*) of the Hebrews have served as "fetters" (*Fesseln*) (489; 261) for the nations who took them on, and the Hebrews' gift to other nations has turned into a poison: "For cannot even the holiest elements of nature become destruction and the most effective medicines become a creeping poison?" (*denn können nicht auch die heiligen Elemente der Natur zur Zerstörung und die wirksamsten Arzneien zu einem schleichenden Gift werden?*) (490; 262). The Jews are to blame for the fact that Christian worship has often assumed an "Oriental idiom" (*ihre Anbetung oft zu einem morgenländischen Idiotismus*) (489; 262). The structural reason for these appearances is that the development always realizes the origin both as origin and as falling away from the origin. That is, its debt to the origin can never fully be paid off, because it can never entirely give rise to that origin, can never appropriate and become the origin without regressing from the position of realization it wants to occupy, hence assuming a new debt to an external realization that it anticipates. Herder acknowledges this structure in the indirect form of an anti-Jewish disavowal:

> Thus the cruder nations of Europe became willing slaves to [the Jews'] usury [*daher denn die rohern Nationen Europa's freiwillige Sklaven ihres Wuchers wurden*].... It is undeniable that this extensive republic of clever usurers long restrained many a nation of Europe from exercising and utilizing its own industry and trade [*Unleugbar also hat eine so verbreitete Republik kluger Wucherer manche Nation Europa's von eigener Betriebsamkeit und Nutzung des Handels lange zurückgehalten*]. (490; 262)

There is nothing surprising about Herder's position here, because it is ideologically necessary that the alien origin fail to develop in order for the development to appropriate the origin, to take over the relay. But the fact that the origin is always thought to develop into the development itself—and how else could it get there?—means that development will always be affected by the origin's lack, or unrealized possibility, and thus derealized, dragged back, as it were, into the origin itself. First the Jewish-Christian relation lives out this problematic, and then the Oriental-Occidental one that, in modern historicist Orientalism, is based on it.

The Cycle of Chaos and Order—Linearized

So what permits development—origination itself—also prevents it. This structure is visible not merely in Herder's (relatively) concrete descriptions of the Eastern cultures but also in the conceptual aspect of his theory, when the opposition between chaotic origin and orderly development turns out to be reversible. And this occurs not only in the case of (Jewish) formal-juridical order as obstacle to development (a trait, moreover, that the Counter-Enlightenment links to the abstract formalism of Enlightenment in general, including its Kantian variant), but universally, in connection with the principle of light as principle of order itself. That is, Herder marks the element of light, which initially accounts for the ordering dimension of Jewish thought in his reading of Genesis, as an element of fire as well, and then more moderately as the nourishing *Urwärme* (or "primeval warmth"), which is in turn the chaotic creative element—or driving motive (*Triebfeder*) (410; 217) of life in its self-anticipating origination.[35]

This reversal leads Herder to argue—in his attempt to maintain the integrity of his argumentation—that within nature as a whole the organic forces shuttle continually back and forth between their chaotic unboundedness and the state of bound order.[36] Beyond this, in fact, the whole of nature passes from createdness qua order into chaos again, Herder seems to argue, as a whole.[37] But here, too, on the level of the whole or at least of the earth, as Herder immediately adds, the return to chaos will be followed by a renewal of ordered life, and the cycle starts again.

> That, however, such a work of art [i.e., nature as work] cannot exist forever, that the cycle that had a beginning has to have an end is in the nature of things. The beautiful creation works itself toward chaos, as it worked itself out of chaos. . . . Even the great organism of earth must thus find its grave, out of which, when its time comes, it will rise into a new shape. (410–11; 217)

Herder has thus now reconciled the irreconcilable tension between chaos and order, and their undecidable opposition, by turning it into a cyclical process.

But the cyclical interplay between chaos and order does not solve the problem of representing a pure origination; it endlessly repeats the two basic ways of failing to solve it. As Herder writes further on, perhaps in polemical response to Kant's polemic against his poetic excesses, but without really providing an argument that would strengthen his own case: "Abstractions provide a true original history of humanity as little as does the painting of the poets" (*Abstraktionen aber geben so wenig als das Gemälde der Dichter eine wahre Urgeschichte der Menschheit*) (415; 220). That is, neither abstract order nor concrete chaos yields "a true originary history of humanity."

And yet although Herder provides no conceptual solution to this problem, he does provide a historical-ideological one.[38] Circularity becomes linear and progressive—albeit not without logical tension—through the self-evident familiarity of typology. In the "Final Remark" to the *Ideas*, he asks, "How did Europe attain its culture and the rank due to it above other peoples?" The answer is: "Many common efforts, its own artistic industry" (*vieler gemeinschaftlichen Bemühungen, sein eigener Kunstfleiß*) (897; 309). Or again: "On activity and invention, on sciences and on a common, competitive striving is the lordliness of Europa founded" (*auf Tätigkeit und Erfindung, auf Wissenschaften und ein gemeinschaftliches, wetteiferndes Bestreben ist die Herrlichkeit Europas gegründet*) (897; 310). Activity yields order in the realization of the passivity of original chaos. Thus although Herder certainly notes some of the weaknesses of European manners and cultural institutions by comparison with some Oriental ones and although he is able to regret the subjugation of, for example, "unfortunate Hindus" with "peaceful institutions" (*arme Hindus . . . friedlichen Einrichtung*) (457; 244) by "covetous and cunning Europeans" (*geizig-verschmitzte Europäer*) (457; 244), he nonetheless accepts this as "the fate of peoples . . . nothing other than the order of nature" (*Harter Lauf des Schicksals aller Völker! und doch ist er nichts als Naturordnung*) (457; 244), which, of course, is the working out of the divine plan, not to worry.[39] Of the European empires established in the East, he writes:

> All news and wares that they bring us from there, are no replacement for the evils that they impose on a people that did nothing to hurt them. However, the chain of fate has been hooked up there; fate will dissolve it or extend it [*Indessen ist die Kette des Schicksals dahin einmal geknüpft; das Schicksal wird sie auflösen oder weiter führen*]. (457–58; 244)

Here, Herder accepts not happily but fatalistically the domination of the fatalistic Orientals by the actively self-emancipating Westerners. The latter are ostensibly able to dominate the Orientals, and also justify this dominion, because the Orientals lack the *Triebfedern*, or motivating forces, which, however, Herder elsewhere associates with the creative Oriental chaos itself. Through this fatalistic acceptance, and through his chaotic inconsistency, Herder places himself unwittingly in an Oriental idiom, parroting it like an imitative Chinese man or a parasitic Jew, according to his own derogatory characterizations. But he knows how to remove himself from chaos: namely, through the self-assertion of ordering more and more chaos (in both senses of the expression "ordering") with his (perhaps all too) good conscience.[40] Persisting passively in the disavowal of its own passivity, or inertia, which in Herder also implies maternal femininity, the West can only assert itself more and more violently or relentlessly against the various figures of that passivity. Of course, sooner or later—indeed at every point—the assertion will fail. But not without doing substantial damage in the process. Yet this is as it should be, writes the humanistic Herder. It's all part of the plan.

CHAPTER 2

Figuralizing the Oriental, Literalizing the Jew: From Letter to Spirit in Friedrich Schlegel's *On the Language and Wisdom of the Indians*

In this chapter, I illustrate the Orientalist application of medieval typology in German romanticism by examining crucial structural aspects of Friedrich Schlegel's treatise *On the Language and Wisdom of the Indians* (*Über die Sprache und Weisheit der Indier*) of 1808.[1] Although German romantic invocations of medieval typology in an Orientalist modality do not, of course, all take the exact form of Schlegel's argumentation and rhetoric, one could carry out readings similar to the following, with respect to a broad number of German texts, such as Novalis's *Disciples of Sais* and *Heinrich von Ofterdingen*, Achim von Arnim's *Isabella von Ägypten*, the work of the mythographers Georg Friedrich Creuzer and Joseph von Görres, and so on. My preference here has been to develop a close reading of just this one influential text by Schlegel, because to my mind the details count and because this very important text tends to be read in a rather cursory manner. My argument here is that Schlegel's paradoxically adulatory disparagement of ancient Indian culture in *On the Language and Wisdom of the Indians* must be understood as an attempt to confirm the historical-philosophical model of *figura* against his very acute sense of its radical instability. More specifically, Schlegel is trying to envision figural-literal unity as a Jewish-Christian unity under the sign of the literal truth of Christian spirituality. That is, he wants to construct somehow the total assimilation of (pre)figural letter to fulfilling spirit. In order to achieve this vision, Schlegel figuralizes ancient Indian culture, while he literalizes Jewish culture. He makes of ancient Indian culture a supplement—a replacement and repetition—of the Jewish, material (pre)figuration, in order to enable (and this means also to force) Jewish culture to disappear into what he construes as the literal spirituality of Christian inwardness.[2] The ancient Indian Orient accordingly represents, for what Schlegel conceives as a (Judaeo-)Christian Occident, both aspects of the Jew as seen from the structurally ambivalent standpoint of traditional Christianity. First, ancient Indian culture, like ancient Hebrew culture before it, is idealized as the original unity of figural and literal under the sign of the literal (i.e., spirit), for Judaism itself could never be taken to have (pre)figured Christianity if it were not construed as presenting in some sense precisely this unity. And second, the ancient Indian Orient is denigrated as the mere material figure of such unity, a unity now seen as having been literally realized in its spiritual truth by the (Judaeo-)Christian—and, more specifically, Catholic—Occident.

Before demonstrating this through a detailed reading of *Über die Sprache und Weisheit der Indier*, however, it is necessary that I first explain why Schlegel has a critical awareness of the instability of *figura*, and then where this awareness is taking him at the time when he composes the treatise on ancient India. Concerning the former: At least since Lessing, both the cultural identities of Jews and Christians and the conceptual identities of the figural (or rhetorical) and the literal (or philosophical) have been in an exacerbated state of crisis in German discourse.[3] In the ring parable of *Nathan der Weise*, as well as in other places, Lessing argued that faith was to be found—paradoxically—in works. In the Lutheran environment in which it was made, this argument was tantamount to suggesting that spirit was to be found in letter, thereby overturning Luther in Luther's name. As emerges from Schlegel's early essay on Lessing, Schlegel clearly feels from the later 1790s on that it is up to his generation to draw the consequences of Lessing's intervention.

Where, then, is Schlegel moving in his attempt to draw these consequences while composing the treatise on Sanskrit culture? As is well known, the text was written at a crucial turning point in Schlegel's career.[4] The displacement of Schlegel's trajectory in this phase of his life occurs, above all, on three interrelated levels: the political, the aesthetic-theological, and the erotic and/or familial.[5]

Friedrich Schlegel (1772–1829). Charcoal drawing by Philipp Veit (1793–1877). Circa 1810. Goethe House and Museum, Frankfurt am Main, Germany. (Bildarchiv Preussischer Kulturbesitz, Berlin/Art Resource, N.Y.)

(1) In terms of political orientation, Schlegel is in the process of turning back from a progressive to a regressive position. He is turning from a cosmopolitan republicanism, still sympathetic to many elements of the German Enlightenment, to an affirmation of reaction.[6] This will culminate, several years after Schlegel's composition of the text on ancient India, in his acceptance of a post as Metternich's secretary in restoration Vienna.[7]

(2) In terms of the relationship between aesthetics and theology, Schlegel's midcareer reversal involves a turn from the absolutization of the aesthetic to the aestheticization of the theological absolute, a turn that ultimately becomes radicalized as one, more simply, from aesthetics to theology.[8] Schlegel now exchanges the aesthetic sociality he has extolled through the period of the *Athenäum* and *Lucinde*—the witty play practiced by shifting and fragmentary constellations of partial individuals—for the organic communality of faith in the established church.[9]

How exactly are these first two levels of the displacement of Schlegel's discourse—the political and the theological—motivated and interrelated? For Schlegel, state and church are supposed to constitute a mutually complementary unity: Aristocratic society is to provide power (or figural, material form), while the church hierarchy is to provide meaning (or literal, spiritual content). In other words, Schlegel's political theology here is meant to be the political theology appropriate to the doctrine of *figura*. According to Schlegel's thought, in this phase of his career, church and state ought properly to function together to legitimate and delimit the monarchic center that marks their harmonious synthesis.[10] In opposition to Enlightenment figures such as Moses Mendelssohn, who argued in *Jerusalem*[11] that the church (as religion of reason) should be purged of all political power, Schlegel argues that the church must retain or rather regain such power in order to guide and limit the power of the state. Priests and warriors, in short, must balance each other in order to avoid the twin disasters of despotism and anarchy that impose themselves in an unpredictably alternating rhythm when modernity erases the power of the spirit and thereby radically emancipates political power. Medieval Catholicism, in the context of the feudal order, answers Schlegel's desire, at this point in his life, to reconcile knowledge with power, philosophy with rhetoric, and spirit with letter.

(3) But there is a further level on which Schlegel's career shifts at this point in his life, which I have called above "the erotic and/or familial." The change that occurs on this register does not involve the introduction of a new erotic relationship or familial situation, but merely Friedrich's displacement with respect to his wife, Dorothea Veit-Schlegel, née Men-

delssohn, and the converse: their displacement toward each other through an attempted mediation of sexual difference in purely religious-cultural terms. What effects this displacement, of course, is Friedrich's and Dorothea's common conversion to Catholicism, just a short while after she had converted from Judaism to Protestantism in order to marry Schlegel in the first place. On the one hand, the link thus established between Friedrich and Dorothea can be seen as having been entailed by Friedrich's theological-political turn; on the other hand, the desire for this link can be seen as having, in part, motivated the theological-political turn to the right.[12] In any case, and above all, the relation between Friedrich and Dorothea mirrors the internal structure of Friedrich's new theological-political orientation, for by converting together to Catholicism, Friedrich and Dorothea move onto the common religious-cultural ground of a neutral territory that mediates between the extremes of (his) Protestant spirit or meaning and (her) Judaic letter or power (for she remains psychically and socially marked by her Judaism, even if she has already converted to Protestantism). Indeed, once Luther's Reformation rebels against the church (now seen as the dead letter of the law) in the name of the pure spirituality of original Christian faith, Catholicism takes on the virtual significance of a synthesis of Judaism and Protestantism.[13] It appears to be both more spiritual than the Judaic letter and more material than the formlessness of Protestant spirit. It becomes, in short, a second Judaism, but this time a Christian one. On this ground, then, Friedrich and Dorothea can appear to bridge the gap of the sexual difference by bridging that of the Judaeo-Protestant difference. The harmonious agreement of the letter of the feudal state and the spirit of the medieval church hierarchy doubles as the harmonious agreement of Dorothea and Friedrich. No longer even attempting to affirm the undecidability of their difference as he had done in the name of wit in *Lucinde*, Friedrich decides in this later phase for their identity on the absolute ground of self-prefiguring, self-fulfilling revelation.

It is necessary to clarify how Schlegel's text on ancient Indian culture serves as a step in his politically, theologically, and personally implicated turn to medieval Christianity as the imaginary ideal of a spiritual fusion of letter and spirit. The text does so, problematically enough, by locating ancient India in the place hitherto reserved for Judaism, in order to free (and also to force) Judaism to be sublated into Christianity. The fact that Schlegel does indeed position ancient Indian culture as the originary (figure of the) unity of figural-material and literal-spiritual orders is already indicated by the title and structure of the treatise, on which, therefore, it behooves us to dwell briefly before launching into a detailed exegesis.

The title of the text—*On the Language and Wisdom of the Indians* (*Über die Sprache und Weisheit der Indier*)—explicitly states that it will divide itself into a study of the language (*Sprache*), that is the letter, and the wisdom (*Weisheit*), that is, the spirit, of the "Indier" under consideration. It seems as if the title were meant to indicate that the specific virtue of Indian culture is its capacity to contain—as in an originary unity—both language and wisdom, rather than only the letter (like the Jews) or the spirit (like the Christians). In short, it seems as if the ancient Indians embody for Schlegel the same balance he sees as having been achieved by medieval Catholicism between the extremes of letter and spirit.

The structure of the text, moreover, confirms the suspicions raised by its title about its thematic focus on letter and spirit, and it adds the synthetic third discourse of history to the list of principal terms *Sprache* and *Weisheit*. Specifically, the text begins by studying the Sanskrit language as the main evidence of the material existence of the people under consideration, and the first of its three books is accordingly titled *Von der Sprache*. It then goes on—in book 2, *Von der Philosophie*—to study ancient Indian *Weisheit*, the ideal essence of the ancient Indians, their mode of thought (*Denkart*). Finally, in book 3, Schlegel attempts to synthesize these points of view under the heading *Historical Ideas* (*Historische Ideen*), that is, the heading of a historicity marked by the privilege of the ideal, the philosophical, and so on.[14] Thus the treatise moves through language (as existence, or letter) to philosophy (as essence, or spirit) to historical ideas (as the synthesis of existence with essence, or again, as the synthesis of letter and spirit in the fulfilled promise of realized meaning).

Further, the three books unfold in a dialectical manner (as the famous tension between Schlegel and Hegel might prompt one to overlook). The thesis of the first is that the existence of the Indians is an essential existence, their real, material figurality an ideal, spiritual literality, their difference an identity. This is what it will have meant for Schlegel to posit that Sanskrit is an organic language. In an apparent symmetrical inversion of this thesis, the argument of the second book is that the essence of the Indians is an existential essence, their spirit a spirit of the letter, their thought properly a thought of its own disappearance. Concretely, this thesis takes the form of the claim that the Indian spirit is ultimately to be situated in the systems of emanationism and dualism, as we will see below. Finally, in the third book, Schlegel claims—somewhat surprisingly—that ancient Indian culture never really accomplishes, but only prefigures, the synthetic unification of the traits that the first two books have presented as a quasi-dialectical opposition. As he now argues, it is only in the Catholic Church, as an ultimate Judaeo-Christian synthesis, that the synthesis of essence and existence, the synthesis of meaning and figure, is actually achieved. Ancient Indian culture as "Historical Idea" becomes here a mere (pre)figuration of Catholic Christianity, which now appears as the sole fulfilled synthesis of identity and difference in the mode of identity.

In order to expose and problematize in some detail Schlegel's attempt to supplement the Jewish-Christian polarity with the Oriental-Occidental relation, I shall focus in the following first on Schlegel's formulation, in *Über die Sprache und Weisheit der Indier*, of the opposition between mechanical and organic languages; then on his development of this opposition in the discussion of ancient Indian philosophy; and finally on the realization of the Indian prefiguration as Judaeo-Christian spirit in the end of history.

Mechanisms of Organic Distinction

Schlegel opens his treatise by stating that there is a necessary relation, rather than a mere contingent similarity, between Sanskrit, on the one hand, and the Roman, Greek, Germanic, and Persian languages, on the other: "The agreement [*Übereinstimmung*] is therefore not an arbitrary one [*zufällige*] that could be explained on the basis of an inmixing [*Einmischung*] but rather an essential one [*wesentliche*] that points to common origination [*gemeinschaftliche Abstammung*]" (115). In staking a claim for such a necessary relation, Schlegel is alluding implicitly to the opposition Kant had drawn in the "Architectonics" section of the *Critique of Pure Reason* between internal relationship (*Verwandtschaft*) and external similarity (*Ähnlichkeit*) as a distinction between an accord of necessity (i.e., of essence) and an accord of chance (i.e., of mere existence).[15] But whereas Kant had invoked this opposition in order to differentiate between systematic and nonsystematic philosophy, that is, between the architectonics of philosophy as such and the mere rhapsody or aggregation of nonphilosophy, Schlegel applies it to the history of languages and peoples, and thereby essentializes history (or historicizes essences). What Kant supposes to distinguish between rationality and reality Schlegel imagines to distinguish between two forms of reality, the organic and the inorganic. Schlegel belongs in this sense to an idealist historicism.

But on what basis does Schlegel claim that this relation is necessary rather than contingent, essential rather than existential, an ideal rather than a material relation? Quite simply, the relation appears as a similarity of grammatical structure rather than as a similarity of the verbal roots that make up the elements of this structure. For Schlegel, similarity of structure indicates commonality of origin (*gemeinschaftliche Abstammung*) (115), and hence also commonality of essence or spirit, whereas similarity of roots indicates the belated intermingling (*Einmischung*) (115) of languages that have originated separately and that share a mere contiguity of material existence.[16] In other words, similarity of structure bespeaks identity, whereas similarity of content bespeaks difference. Or again, in terms whose contemporary sense we owe to Jakobson: Similarity of structure is metaphorical substitutability, whereas similarity of content remains marked by the distance of merely metonymical combination. Schlegel apparently presupposes from the outset that, in general, the binary opposition between the grammatical and lexical dimensions of language is so stable that there could be no contagious passage between the two. He apparently posits, in other words, that the border between the two is absolutely nonporous, that the grammatical rules, as the self-identical essence of the language, can be isolated absolutely from the self-differing existence represented in this schema by lexical material.

According to Schlegel, Sanskrit, Greek, Latin, Persian, and German have in common an "organic" structure, which he associates with community, identity, and essence. In turn, what makes other languages different from them—but also different from each other—is that these other languages share the "mechanical" structure of nonidentity: They are the languages of structural difference and inessentiality. Schlegel explicates this difference between organic and mechanical languages in terms of the difference between inflection and agglutination as types of grammatical structure:

> Either the auxiliary determinations of the meaning [*Nebenbestimmungen der Bedeutung*] are indicated through inner alteration of the root sound [*innre Veränderung des Wurzellauts*], through inflexion [*Flexion*]; or they are indicated through an added word of its own [*ein eignes hinzugefügtes Wort*], which already in and for itself means plurality, pastness, a future "ought" or some other relational concept of the sort [*Verhältnisbegriffe der Art*]. (153)

Inflected languages are self-same, literally flexing and bending their roots in order to vary the senses of these roots.[17] Their verbal elements do not need to go out beyond themselves, do not need to add further elements from without, in order to grow and to extend themselves across the infinite space of divergent connotations. Not only can any given inflected language thus express a broad field of meaning without becoming in any way separate from itself, but—astonishingly—this inflected language or language of identity can develop to the point of (apparently) becoming another language entirely without any essential break ever having occurred. All of the languages of identity constitute essentially a single, self-identical language. Because it is never interrupted by any meaningful discontinuities, and because discontinuation—disintegration or disorganization—is associated in this discourse with mechanism, which is in turn associated with death, this language excludes all death from itself.[18] Never allowing any essential interruption, this language is not just *an* organic language, that is, not just *one* particular organic language among others, but *the* one organic language of life itself:

> In the Indian or Greek language *every root is truly what the name says*, and like a living germ [*lebender Keim*]; for, as the relational concepts [*Verhältnisbegriffe*] are signified through inner alteration, free space for play [*freier Spielraum*] is given to development, and the fullness of development can extend itself indeterminately [*ins Unbestimmbare*].... But everything that comes forth in this way from the simple root retains still the mark of its kinship [*Verwandschaft*], coheres [*hängt zusammen*], thus they carry themselves mutually [*so trägt und erhält sichs gegenseitig*]. Hence on the one hand the richness and on the other hand the persistence and endurance of these languages, of which one can certainly say that they arose organically and form an organic weave [*organisch entstanden sein, und ein organisches Gewebe bilden*]; so that after millennia in languages that are divided by large countries one can often still readily perceive the thread that draws itself through the broadly developed richness of an entire verbal genealogy [*Wortgeschlechtes*] and that leads us back to the simple origin of the first root. In contrast, in languages that instead of inflexion use affixes [*Affixa*], the roots are not really that; no fruitful seed, but rather a mere pile of atoms, which every wind of chance can easily strew abroad or bring together; the cohesion [*der Zusammenhang*] is really none other than a merely mechanical one, through external attachment [*äußere Anfügung*]. These languages lack in their first origins a germ of living development; the derivation [*Ableitung*] always remains needy, and however much, afterward, the artificiality is intensified through the piling on of more and more affixes, the difficulty is only increased, rather than that true simple beauty and lightness would be achieved. The apparent richness is fundamentally [*im Grunde*] poverty, and these languages, whether raw or refined, are always heavy, easily confused and often further particularly characterized by a peculiarly arbitrary, subjectively strange and lacking character [*eigensinnig willkürlichen, subjektiv sonderbaren und mangelhaften Charakter*]. (157–59, emphasis added)

In the case of certain languages, and more specifically, in the case of their root words, word and thing, naming and origination coincide through a kind of repetition of Adamic-Christic-Paternal-Divine naming as creation or consummation of creation. Out of the self-grounding root of this fundamental word grows what it names, its own nominative creation-origination. A theology thus springs forth whose faith is invested, above all, in the self-unity of a fundamental, self-creative act that somehow, by means of some minimal distance, must crown the distinction between God and Nature, word and thing, by letting things be absorbed back into the words, or rather the single word, that give(s) them their being. This distance—the distance of a remainder left when things have disappeared into their words—is what will be cast out on—or cast out as—the nonorganic languages in which the roots, in the linguistic sense, are not natural roots, that is, languages in which things do not at any point correspond to their names.

Here, because continuity implies life, it is considered good, whereas discontinuity is bad because it means death. And Schlegel insists with a vengeance that this good continuity is to be unambiguously found in the place where it belongs. For example, even the apparent discontinuity both within and between inflected languages always boils down, for Schlegel, to an essential continuity. And conversely, the apparent identity that may seem, from time to time, to present itself in noninflected languages is ultimately an essential discontinuity. For him, in essence, the difference between organic, inflected languages and mechanical, noninflected languages is absolute, even if empirically (as he acknowledges) there exist stages of mediation that pass slowly from one into the other through mixing. Thus, while Schlegel unwittingly suspends—or disavows—the difference between identity and difference within both the organic and mechanical languages, he wittingly maintains it as the border between them (thus disavowing also their identity).

Indeed, Schlegel considers this difference between organic and mechanical languages to be so reliable that it must assert itself not only in terms of what the two types of language are, but also in terms of the different directions in which they develop. He posits that the organic languages originate, despite their living naturalness, in their greatest condition of "beauty and art of structure" (*die Schönheit und Kunst der Struktur*) (163). This beauty and art gradually dissolve as the organic languages revert to a natural condition. In contrast, the mechanical languages begin in naturalness and become more and more artificial as time goes on. They hide their internal self-difference gradually behind a facade of identity as their affixes increasingly melt together with the words to which they were originally added. Given that in this discourse nature is associated with the organic (or life), whereas artifice is associated with the mechanical (or death), we can read Schlegel's suggestion here in the following way: When he posits that the animate or living goes from artificiality to naturalness, this means that it moves from death to life; when he posits that the inanimate or dead goes from naturalness to artificiality, this means that it moves from life to death. Each term is involved in the other: Each is nothing other than a passage from the other to itself. In this way, the opposition thus already manifests its immanent breakdown.[19] The difference between identity and difference reappears within each term.

Although incessantly refusing to acknowledge—or, again, disavowing—its intrusive presence, Schlegel nonetheless responds to the threat of this disruption by attempting to exclude difference from identity, mechanism from organicity, at its temporal origin and at its temporal end. To begin with beginnings: When Schlegel thematizes the generation or origin of organic languages, he argues that their two dimensions arise out of a common root, which is itself neither linguistic root nor structure, but a kind of consciousness—*Besonnenheit* (169).[20] By arguing in this way, Schlegel implicitly and unwittingly acknowledges that there is a difference between the roots and the structure of even the organic language, the language in which roots and structure should, in principle, present themselves as one continuous weave of implications and explications. Even in the case of the organic language, roots and structure apparently need to be united beyond themselves in the common origin that comprises feeling and sense: "the roots and structure or grammar, both at once and united, for both arose of course out of the one and the same deep feeling and bright sense" (*einem und demselben tiefem Gefühle und hellem Sinne hervor*) (171). Whereas the language of life at first seemed to be that of origination, now it appears that this language in turn requires an origin outside of itself—namely, in pure feeling and sense—in order to be united with itself. The difference between the two aspects of language (roots and structure) might, of course, thereby appear to be successfully externalized, becoming now the difference between language and its origin. Even if one provisionally accepts this interpretation, however, the difference can still be seen as remaining immanent to the language, to the extent that it is a difference between a new avatar of the roots of the language (in feeling doubled by thought) and the structured totality of the language (i.e., the synthesis of its verbal roots with its grammatical structure).

Schlegel adds to the apparent success (and actual failure) of his attempt to reduce the internal difference of organic language to nought at its origin an attempt to reduce the same difference to nought at its end—at the point where the organic language turns into other languages that, for him, are nonetheless to be conceived as parts of itself. Indeed, it is to his credit that, having established the essential identity of the one language of life, Schlegel apparently feels nonetheless obliged to offer some sort of explanation as to how this one language comes to be empirically differentiated: How does there come to be at least an apparent difference between Sanskrit and the languages into which it unfolds? The origin of this apparent difference turns out—disappointingly, yet predictably—to be the languages of death, the mechanical languages of difference.

> All of these derived languages (as also the peoples themselves) have experienced a manifold and indeed in part entirely different inmixing of the foreign [*mannigfache und zwar zum Teil ganz verschiedene Einmischung des Fremdartigen*]. This necessarily had to estrange them even further from each other. I speak not only of those inmixings, like that of the Arabic into the Persian, [or] of the French into the English, where the penetrating words immediately betray themselves as foreigners because they do not fully melt into the grammatical form of the other language, but retain in part their own; examples that, moreover, offer a telling proof of the stubborn firmness of every originally noble, i.e., organically originated and formed language, and of how hard it is to suppress them even through the most violent inmixings. How entirely German has the fundamental character [*Grundcharakter*] of English remained, and how thoroughly different from the Arabic the fundamental character of Persian! I speak also of such inmixings as are still older and, even on the level of form, are still more melted [*verschmolzen*], because they took place at a time when the language was still youthful, more easily formed, more appropriative and productive, and therefore [these inmixings] are not so visible to the first glance as to analysis. (179)

The presence of deadly mechanism in the cultures of organic life, then, is due to the invasive presence of dead cultures, cultures of death, within the cultures of life.[21] More specifically, what tends to split the one language of life into a multiplicity is the entrance of foreign, mechanical words into the very grammatical structure of the organic. Where foreign words retain their foreign grammatical forms, they do not enter into the substance of the language, do not alter it, do not change it into a language different from before. But when foreign words take on the grammatical forms of the organic language, they introduce their foreignness into it and thus exile that language from itself, make it other than what it has been, in its essential structure. They alter, to some extent, its very grammatical core. Death enters into the one organic language to the extent that it becomes a multiplicity of languages. Thus contrary to Schlegel's stated intention, his theory of the differentiation of Sanskrit implies that mere verbal roots can indeed carry grammatical force. With the foreign word, a bit of the foreign grammar enters into the native grammar—otherwise, no essential or dangerous contamination would have occurred. The distinction between elements (or differences) and structures (or identities) of language must evidently be suspended, then, in order to be maintained in the form of the quasi-synonymous distinction between mechanical and organic languages. What this contradiction in Schlegel's argument illustrates is that the relationship between identity and difference is always either one of identity or one of difference and, at the same time, both. It is this undecidability that, in philosophical terms, Schlegel's text is above all struggling to deny. The Indian, Jewish, and Christian religious-cultural entities are mobilized in his discourse, then, as mere figures whose ultimate purpose is to carry out this struggle allegorically.

The Pantheistic Philosophy of the Orient as Materialized Spirit

Having concluded his characterization of Indian language, Schlegel proceeds, in the second book of his treatise, to consider Indian philosophy, or what he calls the Indian mode of thought (*Denkart* [197]).[22] In an inversion of what he has argued in the first book, he argues here that Indian thought, the essence of ancient India, is (or becomes) the existence it thinks. Indian thought posits in theory the necessary loss of thought into brute reality (the fall from grace), and then, in accordance with that theory, it actually falls, across time, into the pantheistic affirmation of that brute reality. It thus performs what it constates, exists in accordance with its essence, because its essence is the idea of the loss of essence. As one might imagine, Schlegel will ultimately have second thoughts about this argument, for how can essence become existence and still remain essence? How can spiritual identity become material difference and still remain spiritual identity, even if such identity consists in the narrative of its own undoing? But before tracing the emergence of Schlegel's reservations about his account of ancient Indian thought and of Indian culture as a whole, we have to traverse his account of the former, and because Schlegel's consideration thereof is dominated by his polemical opposition to the pantheism of his own day, it is perhaps useful to begin by recalling, briefly, the main contours of the pantheism debate that I have discussed above.

By the time Schlegel was writing the text on India, pantheism—associated with the work of Spinoza and most often considered to be atheism, materialism, and determinism—had been a scandalous topic in German letters for twenty-five years. It had been publicly under discussion ever since the 1780s, when the (anti)philosopher Jacobi had attacked the Enlightenment by claiming that the (recently deceased) exemplary representative of the Enlightenment, G. E. Lessing, had confessed shortly before his death to have been a closet pantheist. In response to this accusation, Mendelssohn had attempted to demonstrate, in the spirit of Enlightenment tolerance, the potential reconcilability of pantheism with theism. Indeed, Mendelssohn had argued in *Morgenstunden oder Vorlesungen über das Dasein Gottes* (*Morning Hours, or Lectures on the Existence of God*) that the difference between pantheism and theism cannot be decided or determined by human reason, due to the limitations language imposes on thought.[23] According to Mendelssohn, language does not allow us to distinguish between the identity of God and creation (which he construed as identity and difference, respectively), on the one hand, and the difference between God and creation, on the other. The distinction reduces, he had argued, to the distinction between prepositional expressions such as "inside" and "outside." And these expressions are merely metaphorical or indirect expressions for that which, in its literal being or reality, withdraws from direct determinability and denomination. How, indeed, could a finite understanding ever have proper knowledge of the relation between God and creation, infinite and finite, absolute and relative?

In stark contrast with Mendelssohn's position, Schlegel condemns pantheism as a nefarious doctrine precisely because it tends to efface the difference between identity and its difference. As he had needed to deny that the two overlap, in order to prevent organic languages from disappearing into mechanical ones, so here, again, Schlegel is compelled to deny this overlap in order to prevent the spirit of God from disappearing into the letter of material creation. But just as he had needed to assert the confluence of identity and difference within the organic languages, so here, too, he asserts this confluence in the form of the endurance of the identity of Indian thought even in its degradation or decadence into the radical difference that pantheism represents.

In order to describe the mode of thought characteristic of ancient Indian culture, Schlegel divides that culture into four philosophical-religious systems, which represent as many successive developmental stages. These four systems are emanationism, naturalistic materialism, dualism (i.e., the doctrine of the eternal struggle between good and evil, which take the form of the ideal and material principles, respectively), and monistic pantheism. For Schlegel, Indian philosophical-religious culture begins by situating the essence of things firmly in the ideal (seen as divine origin), and by characterizing all real (or material) existence as a falling-off from the ideal substance in which it originates, a substance to which, however, finite existence always ostensibly has the possibility of returning. After this period of emanationist idealism, there follows, according to Schlegel, a decadent period of primitive nature worship, in which Indian thought posits a radical materiality as the essence of things. The third period in the development of Indian culture accomplishes a kind of synthesis of the first two. Dualism—"the doctrine of two principles"—becomes predominant. This doctrine situates essence in both ideality and materiality, light and darkness, good and evil, life and death. More precisely, dualism situates the essence in the eternal struggle between these two principles, but in so doing it nonetheless does not become ethically neutral. It effaces neither the evil character of evil nor the ethical necessity of participating in this struggle on the side of the good. Finally, in the fourth period, this dualism decays into a monistic pantheism. According to Schlegel's presentation of these developments, the dualism of the doctrine of two principles privileges ideality over materiality in emphatically ethical terms, whereas the monism of pantheism privileges materiality over ideality and thereby entails a radical amorality.[24] Schlegel follows here in the tradition of Jacobi's Counter-Enlightenment attack on Lessing's ostensible Spinozism.[25] For Schlegel, at this stage in his development, pantheism is ultimately a materialism that tends to efface all distinctions between good and evil: Pantheism is ultimately on the side of evil (which in Schlegel's text is another name for difference or material existence), whose distinction from good (or identity or ideal essence) it effaces, thus reducing good to evil.[26]

Given this account of the four philosophical-religious perspectives offered by Indian thought, one must ask with which of the four the organic and mechanical languages are to be aligned. Clearly, the organic languages are to be associated with the systems of emanation and dualism, that is, with those systems that privilege the ideal, the light of the active spirit, and life. The mechanical languages, in turn, are to be linked with the systems of materialism and pantheism, that is, the systems that privilege the material, the darkness of passive nature, and death.[27] The surprising consequence of this unsurprising distribution, however, is that the mechanical principle appears here within the organic languages: The organic language par excellence includes within itself decadent doctrines and historical moments that manifest, on the level of content and meaning, the powerfully effective presence of this principle. We have already seen that contents (or roots) are not isolable from structure (or grammar). The mechanical doctrine of pantheistic materialism—as the self-affirmation of pure differential existence—cannot be prevented from affecting the essence of the language in which it is stated, even if the essence of that language—essence as such, which here appears as the emanationist version of the doctrine of original sin—predicts its own decay into the mere existence in which materialist doctrines encourage us to wallow or exult.

But Schlegel denies and disavows the presence of the mechanical in the organic. Both his critique of materialism and pantheism as forms of evil and his praise for the idealist phases of Indian thought as constituting the essence of that thought make more than sufficiently clear his will to destroy the mechanical principle and all that is associated with it. That principle—and the languages that embody it—represent for Schlegel evil itself. The identity of the light is not (to be) in any relationship of identity with the difference of the darkness it will have absorbed or annihilated in illumination. The identity that pantheism posits between identity and difference (or good and evil) amounts for Schlegel—arbitrarily—to the reduction of all identity to difference, to the ubiquity of differences as the ubiquity of death implied by the radical materiality of the mechanical.

Despite the various attempts on Schlegel's part to be fair and humane with respect to the languages and cultures outside the space of the one language of life, then, what emerges as the principal cultural-political implication of his linguistic ontology for both mechanical languages and pantheist-materialist doctrines is that these languages and doctrines are to be sacrificially destroyed as taking no part—i.e., destroyed in order to prove that they take no part—in the languages and doctrines of life.[28] After all, the essence of the apparent presence of difference (or evil) is an absence.[29] In order for the existence of the cultures of death to be brought into accord with their essence—that is, with their essential mechanical deadness—they would have to be annihilated, made dead, for the only proper form of existence of that which is essentially dead is its existence as death itself. This implication, of which Schlegel was doubtless not completely aware, constitutes the extraordinary danger, indeed the disaster, of his later thought as it appears in *Über die Sprache und Weisheit der Indier*.

Historicist Ideas: Figuralized Indians, Literalized Jews

I have thus far examined both Schlegel's characterization of the Indian language as radically organic and his attempt to isolate the radically organic strains of thought within Indian philosophical-religious traditions. I have read the section on language as positing an essentiality (or identity) of ancient Sanskrit and subsequent Eurasian existence (or difference), and I have read the section on philosophy as repeating this position in the form of what only seems to be its symmetrical reversal: the position of an essential existence. Further, we have seen how each of these positions is rendered impossible to the degree that it depends on the opposite it excludes. In each case, the synthesis of identity and difference under the sign of identity depends on their synthesis under the sign of difference, and the reverse. The suspension or denial of this mutual dependence or undecidability is indeed the impossible conceptual and imaginary task—the task of providing an absolute grounding of culture—that Schlegel's text sets out to accomplish. In the third book, *Historische Ideen*, the topic of history is introduced as the site of the completion of this task. History functions in this manner as the religious-cultural allegory of an ultimately total assimilation of existence to essence, of language to thought qua ultimate ideal ground. What one expects at this point, of course, is that Schlegel will conclude with some consideration of how language and thought (and their corresponding binary oppositions) are "one" in the history of Indian culture. Perhaps surprisingly, however, at the end of the third book he suddenly says that the history of Indian culture only prefigures this oneness, which is realized only by the Christian spirit into which the Jewish letter is sublated. The residual differentiation—which Schlegel has been attempting to expunge all along from the identity that ancient India, as organic principle, has been supposed to represent—now reasserts itself, as it always will. In order at once to allow for, and to ward off, this insistent reemergence of (ungrounding) difference within identity (qua ideal foundation), Schlegel now makes ancient India the mere (self-differential) prefiguration of spiritual identity. Christianity, into which, by contrast to Indian culture, Judaism can now appear to have been fully absorbed, becomes the (self-identical) fulfillment, the literal realization of this spiritual argument that I now examine.

Schlegel concludes his treatise with a chapter titled "Of the Oriental and Indian Studies in General and Their Value and Purpose" (*Vom orientalischen und indischen Studium überhaupt, und dessen Wert und Zweck*), which begins with the following passage:

> Now that we have shown and suggested the fruitfulness of Indian Studies for linguistics, philosophy, and ancient history, nothing would remain to be done except to determine the relationship between the Oriental mode of thought and the European one, and to present the influence that the former has had or should have on the latter. (295)

It is in this final chapter that Schlegel turns against ancient Indian culture, sacrificially identifying it with the letter whose unity with spirit it was supposed to realize, and so excluding it from the (Jewish-) Christian enclosure in which that realization is ostensibly achieved. In this turn, he anticipates, as it were, the more decisively negative view of India I consider below in Goethe and Hegel, whereas in the praise of India that governs most of the treatise prior to this point he lays some of the apparent groundwork for the hyperbolically positive view of India (at least concerning philosophy and religion) that we will encounter in Schopenhauer (and the Aryanist tradition). Let us see how Schlegel "argues" this turn.

First of all, according to Schlegel, the proper relationship between Oriental and Occidental thought is defined by the Holy Scriptures themselves. These mediate between the Occident and the ancient Orient: "The Holy Scriptures have become the actual link [*das eigentliche Band*] . . . through which also the European mode of thought and formation has connected up with Oriental antiquity" (295). It turns out, however, that the scriptures are the bond that connects European thought to the ancient Orient precisely insofar as the Orient is what mediates between "us" and the scriptures: "The opposite—i.e., error—shows us the truth in a new, still brighter light, and in general the history of the oldest philosophy, i.e., the Oriental mode of thought, is the most beautiful and instructive external commentary for the Holy Scriptures" (297). Ancient Oriental philosophy mediates between "us" and the scriptures, in turn, because it mediates between the Old Testament and the New. It does so by a kind of contrast: "The opposite—i.e., error—shows us the truth in a new, still brighter light." Since truth is self-identical spirit, whereas error is self-differential letter, Schlegel is arguing here that, against the foil of the letter, the spirit stands out more clearly. Now Schlegel claims that the tradition of ancient Oriental philosophy develops, but only in the crudest way, doctrines that are somewhat less crudely expressed within Judaism, and then quite properly expressed within Christianity. The radical difference between Oriental philosophy and the Christian tradition, combined with the analogies one can still draw between them, makes clear the essential unity of the Christian tradition, which absorbs the Jewish into itself through the easy translatability of Old Testament prefiguration into New Testament fulfillment.

Schlegel illustrates this notion with the Christian doctrines of the Trinity and the immortality of the soul. The sketchy, doubtful, figural presence of these doctrines in the Old Testament—Schlegel says that they are "more suggested and touched upon, than extensively and explicitly developed and set up as fundamental pillars of doctrine [*Grundsäulen der Lehre*]" (297)—comes to seem literal when compared with their Oriental versions, in which they are mixed up with the "crudest superstition" (*gröbste[n] Aberglauben*) (297). As the Old Testament anticipates the New (and thereby also European history up through romantic modernity), the Orient anticipates the Old Testament. By providing the Judaic (pre)figuration with a (pre)figuration of its own, the Orient makes the Judaic (pre)figuration already a kind of fulfillment and thus renders comprehensible the Christian fulfillment of the Judaic. The letters that are "indisch" (Indian) here anticipate those "jüdisch" (Jewish) ones they so closely resemble, in that each set of letters is too "irdisch" (earthly) for the spirit that will have escaped them at their origin and in their end.

According to Schlegel, then, the Indian texts serve to strengthen the bond between Hebrew prefiguration and Christian fulfillment, and hence to mediate between the two while holding the two apart:

> The comparison with the—in part—actually and—in part—apparently thus related mode of thought could, however, even serve to demonstrate in a historical and quite external sense that only one and the same intention, in the Old Testament and in the New, pervades and dominates the whole; it's only that what is there merely suggested and pre-figured [*vorgebildet*] appears here in its full glory. Therefore, the old Christian way of explaining the Old Testament must be the only correct one, and such it will be shown to be, even from without, through a complete knowledge of the history of the Oriental spirit. (299)

The Indian texts become the ground of our knowledge of essential identity (of identity and difference) as historically demonstrated by the disappearance of the Jewish into the Christian tradition. Difference is reduced to nought by the Christian self-identical spirit either by being cast out (as is ancient Indian culture) or by being absorbed (as is ancient Hebrew culture).

How, finally, does the determination of Indian culture as mediator between Jew and Christian affect that culture's status with respect to the mechanical-organic opposition? As the prefiguration of the identity between prefiguration and fulfillment, ancient India represents—at the end of Schlegel's account, and in contradiction to the starting point of his analysis—a merely mechanical version of the organic, that is, a mechanical composition of the mechanical and organic principles, which the organic principle actually fuses into a monadic simplicity. Being a merely mechanical version of the organic, ancient Indian culture now occupies the intermediate place between mechanical and organic, the place where death turns into life and life into death, difference into identity and identity into difference. In this sense, what takes the place of the early Schlegel's wit—or "chemical spirit"—in this text are the Indian texts themselves. Because they are situated on the border between identity and difference, the ancient Indian texts belong to the most uncanny zone of that self-differing difference from which Schlegel would like to exclude self-identical—that is, Christian, German—truth. Not only does Schlegel ultimately instrumentalize ancient Oriental culture in the service of the imaginary, ideological consolidation of (Judaeo-)Christian unity, but he ultimately places this culture in dangerous proximity to the purely mechanical cultures whose originary opposite it also ostensibly represents.

Accordingly, Schlegel intermittently criticizes ancient Oriental culture, indeed disparages it to the point of excluding it from the realm of the human. For example, despite his enthusiasm for the Oriental, Schlegel is able to say, in the context we have just been considering, that the religion of Fo (i.e., Chinese Buddhism) is to the Christian doctrine it resembles as the ape (*der Affe*) is to humanity (*dem Menschen*) (299), a figure that recalls the aping mimesis crucial to Herder's view of China, for example. Moreover, Schlegel asserts that although traces (*Spuren*) of truth can be found everywhere, the "coherence of the totality" (*den Zusammenhang des Ganzen*) and the "certain cutting away of all inmixture of error" (*die sichere Absonderung des beigemischten Irrtums*) can be found only in Christianity, whose truth and knowledge are beyond reason (301). The dispersed traces of truth, of course, provide truth in the mechanical and dead form of its difference and deferral, whereas truth totalized gives us truth in the organic form of its self-identity, its pure and radical vividness. As the place of mediation between mechanical and organic, dead and living, ancient Indian culture in particular is always in danger of becoming pure inessentiality, or death again. In short, the place of originary honor granted to ancient Indian tradition in Schlegel's text is in the end—like most places of originary honor, including that generally accorded by Christianity to the Old Testament—a dubiously honored place indeed.

Through Schlegel's own conversion, Catholicism will soon definitively occupy the position of the realization here anticipated by ancient Indian culture, the realization of the synthesis of the radical letter (of Judaism) and the radical spirit (of Protestantism) in a perfect balance nonetheless tipped from the beginning in favor of the spirit. As is well known, Schlegel soon aligns himself in Vienna on the side of the forces of the Restoration. Beyond his conversion and the displacement of the site of his ontotheopolitical investment to Vienna, however, the dangerous legacy of his precarious attempt to distinguish between different cultures and different languages on the basis of a distinction between organic and mechanical, living and dead, identical and different, will—unfortunately—survive. But what this legacy has taught us is that it is impossible, and therefore dangerous, to determine decisively binary oppositions such as those between the figural and the literal, difference and identity, or rhetoric and philosophy by reference to any cultural-historical allegory in which the terms of these binary oppositions would be personified by the figures of self-identically given, collective cultural subjects. The reality of such figures as figures is always the reality of their non−self-identity.

CHAPTER 3

Goethe's Orientalizing Moment (I): "Notes and Treatises for the Better Understanding of the *West-East Divan*"

> Mein Erbteil wie herrlich, weit und breit!
> Die Zeit ist mein Besitz, mein Acker ist die Zeit.
>
> How magnificent is my inheritance, far and wide!
> Time is my possession, my soil is time.
>
> —J. W. VON GOETHE, *West-East Divan*

The neo-Catholic Orientalism of Friedrich Schlegel constructs a typological narrative in which the Orient prefigures an Occident that, within itself, turns around a three-step sequence of Jewish-Protestant-(neo-)Catholic. This sequence is conceived in terms of an ontological-metaphysical rather than a chronological process, as I've spelled out above and in other writings on Schlegel. Goethe's very different approach to the Orient is dictated by his entirely different relationship to the topic of human history and, within human history, to religion. This very different relationship conditions in Goethe a turn to a poetic medieval Persia as his privileged Oriental interlocutor in the *West-East Divan*, and a repulsion from the protoromantic and romantic Indomania of Herder, Schlegel, and those who accompanied or followed them in that intellectual adventure (including August-Wilhelm Schlegel, of course, and the very different instance of Wilhelm Humboldt).[1] In this chapter and the following one I look at Goethe's relationship with the Orient, his sense of history (i.e., his brand of historicist metaphysics), and his relationship with typology (which links history with metaphysics) throughout the *West-East Divan* project. The first of these two chapters deals with the theoretical explanations he appended to the poetic cycle titled *West-East Divan* under the heading of "Notes and Treatises for the Better Understanding of the *West-East Divan*."[2] In the next chapter I lay bare the most crucial structures of the poems and the poetic cycle themselves. But before diving into that project, a few words on Goethe's relationship to history (and to its metaphysics).

History without Telos: How Radical Is That?

In various respects, Goethe's relationship with the theme and discipline of history is marked by a certain skepticism. First, Goethe is skeptical about the possibility of objective knowledge of history, insofar as it is based on human testimony.[3] Second, he is equally skeptical about the possibility of a scientific knowledge of history, in the sense of a knowledge based on a reliable application of mechanical causality to the narrative of human events.[4] Human events appear too strongly marked by chance, and too complicatedly overdetermined, for any linear modes of causal explanation.[5] Nor is Goethe sanguine about the possibility of discernible human progress on an optimistic Enlightenment model.[6] Hence, his approach to human history tends to favor subjective and individual generic perspectives on history: memoir, biography, travel descriptions, and so on. Despite his sometime tendency to suggest that nature is rule-governed, whereas human history is subject to chance and arbitrariness, Goethe's predominant pattern is to inscribe human history in nature, while in his approach to nature, he favors a description of appearances in the present over a natural-historical search for origins.[7] And, of course, such a descriptive bent is even more disinclined to teleology with respect to nature than with respect to humanity.[8] Goethe's focus on the perceptually given is so strong that Nisbet is prompted to speak of Goethe's "relative indifference to the temporal dimension" (*relative Gleichgültigkeit gegenüber der zeitlichen Dimension*) (30). Indeed, it is this apparent indifference to the temporal, or this focus on the present, that has made of Goethe, the historical skeptic, paradoxically one of the two pillars of historicist thinking, the other pillar being the perfection of teleology in Hegel, whom I consider in the next chapter. Goethe is the descriptivist of the individual (symbolic) phenomenon for whom each epoch is "immediate to God" (Ranke).[9] But does the individual, immediate moment just give itself to Goethe (or to anyone) as such? Is Goethe simply indifferent to the temporal dimension? Does he not rather struggle against it with something like every fiber of his anxiety-ridden being? Let us consider briefly and critically the account given by Ernst Cassirer in "Goethe und die geschichtliche Welt."

Cassirer provides a credulously sympathetic account of Goethe's relationship with history if there ever was one (and there have been plenty), which makes the impression of providing faithfully the picture that Goethe himself would have wanted us to receive. This means that it harmonizes all of the dissonance, resolves all of the tension in Goethe's relationship to history that render that relationship interesting and problematic. Yet in doing so it also quasi-inadvertently reveals this tension.

Cassirer quotes, for example, the very definitely relevant passage from *Dichtung und Wahrheit* in which Goethe says that he had a "feeling of past and present in one" (*die Empfindung der Vergangenheit und Gegenwart in eins*) (12), an intuition (*Anschauung*) which brought something ghostlike (*gespenstermäßiges*) into the present (*in die Gegenwart*) and which, while its effect was felicitous in poems, "at the moment when it expressed itself immediately on the edges of life or in life, had to seem to everyone inexplicable, perhaps unpleasant" (*im Augenblick, wo sie sich unmittelbar am Leben und im Leben selbst ausdrückte, jedermann seltsam, unerklärlich, vielleicht unerfreulich scheinen mußte*) (32).[10] The interpenetration of past and present, then, had a tendency to bring something ghostly into the present. When this occurred in the present of a life, that life then appeared divided between itself and its limit (*am Leben und im Leben*, Goethe writes), between its past and present, its objectivity and subjectivity, its death and life. In this situation, further, there emerges something inexplicable (*unerklärlich*)—that is, groundless—that is unpleasant (*unerfreulich*). The historicist collapse of past and present into one moment introduces, then, a dimension of ghostliness into the present moment itself.

Cassirer, however, disavows and tames this ghostliness—the temporal complication of the moment—in a number of ways. First, he makes this phenomenon a *Gabe*—a gift—of sight, whereas Goethe calls it a "feeling that was getting violently out of hand" (*Gefühl, das bei mir gewaltig überhand nahm*) (32), a feeling that was evidently not maintainable in the *main-tenant* of the moment of presence as *Vorhandenheit*. Second, Cassirer chiasmically smooths over the distance that inhabits the interpenetration of representation and presence in their guise as the polarities of the aesthetic and the historical, claiming that for Goethe the "historical grew immediately together with the poetical, the poetical immediately with the historical" (*wuchs ihm nun das Historische unmittelbar mit dem Poetischen, das Poetische unmittelbar mit dem Historischen zusammen*) (12). Thus, in the very moment, as it were, when Goethe speaks of an unsettling undoing of the moment, and of life interpenetrating disruptively with death, Cassirer speaks of a chiasmic totalization and organic fusion (*wuchs ihm . . . zusammen*) of history and poetry, reality and representation, object and subject, form and feeling, and so on. Nor does Cassirer reserve this gesture for his commentary on this particular passage from Goethe.

Indeed, Cassirer concludes the essay with a similar disavowal of the ungrounding complexity of temporality in Goethe. He emphasizes here that for Goethe history meant "no longer something that opposed the productive forces out of which he shaped his world" (*keinen Gegensatz mehr zu den produktiven Kräften, aus denen er seine Welt gestaltete*) (26), but rather "became a fundamental and original formative force that gave him the spiritual world as his own in its total richness" (*sondern es wurde selbst eine bildende Grund- und Urkraft, die ihm die Welt des Geistigen erschloß und in ihrem ganzen Reichtum zu eigen gab*) (26). Thus, for Cassirer, history is the origin and ground of a force that is at once the most proper force of the world and of Goethe himself, resolving passivity and activity in a timeless moment of pure presence, such that ghostliness is resolved into spirit itself.

As we will see, in the *West-East Divan* Goethe does approach the Persian historical object in this manner, that is, with the intention of realizing such a program, but as we will also see, the experience of the ghostliness of the present, which Goethe acknowledges and Cassirer pushes away, will haunt the *West-East Divan* project.[11] The celebration of the pure present is no less a denial of historical temporality than the celebration of teleological progress toward a goal, and it is no less dependent on typological thinking, albeit subject to certain displacements. The illusion of pure presence will be typologically organized by Goethe in the *West-East Divan* in two senses. First, typology will be doubled and reversed in two moments, each of which anticipates and realizes the other, fusing thus into the higher unity of the pure moment they are. Second, this general pattern will be construed as the realization that teleological typology itself has always anticipated. Aesthetics here supersedes teleology: Nonsupersessionist thinking supersedes supersessionism. In the next chapter we will see how Goethe constructs this performative paradox, specifically through his sustained poetic encounter with medieval Persian poetry in its complex mirror-relationship with his late love for Marianne Willemer. We will see there too how the organization of this paradox remains haunted by the specter of time as the promise of death.

Making a (W)hole in the Orient: *The* West-East Divan *Project*

In the "Notes and Treatises for the Better Understanding of the *West-East Divan*," appended to the 1819 first edition of this poetic cycle, which is Goethe's most important text on the Orient by far, Goethe wastes no time in getting to the point, beginning by quoting Ecclesiastes 3:1, "Alles hat seine Zeit!" (Everything has its time!).[12] And he goes on to characterize this as:

> A saying whose meaning [*Ein Spruch dessen Bedeutung*] one learns to recognize more and more in a long life; according to this saying, there is a time to be silent, another time to speak and this time the poet is deciding to do the latter. For if doing and effecting things [*Tun und Wirken*] are appropriate to earlier years, then reflection and communication [*Betrachtung und Mitteilung*] are fitting for the later years. I sent the writings of my first years into the world without a preface. . . . Now, however, I would like nothing to prevent the present little book [*gegenwärtigen Büchleins*] from making a good first impression. I have decided therefore to comment, to explain, to point out, with the intention that an immediate comprehension [*ein unmittelbares Verständnis*] should grow out of it for readers who are only minimally or not at all familiar with the East. (126)

The normative implication of the initial quotation, "Everything has its time," is evidently that things should happen at the right time. They should be done at the right place in time, and not elsewhere. They should be present to themselves in the present. And indeed, in order that this should occur, presence itself should not be divided from itself, but rather immediate, as Goethe hopes the understanding of his poetic text will be. In other words, if "everything has its time," this must above all not mean that everything is divided from itself by the temporal differentiation that splits presence into its anticipation and its realization, pastness and futurity. If everything has its time, this means that it contains its time and does not allow that time to gain ascendancy over it, to master it and potentially defeat it, to kill it by tearing it out of itself and putting parts or all of it elsewhere, as in a diaspora.

Further, it is here not just a question of time, or things in general in time, but explicitly also a question of activity and passivity. In the second sentence, Goethe invokes this conceptual opposition to distinguish between "doing and effecting things" (*Tun und Wirken*), on the one hand, and "reflection and communication" (*Betrachtung und Mitteilung*), on the other. Whereas Goethe associates action with youthful silence here, he associates the relative passivity of reflexion and communication with elderly loquacity. As an old man, Goethe will now speak, he says, at the right time, for the sake of the explanation of this most recent poetic cycle. But, of course, it is also as an old man that Goethe has just been writing the poems to be explained. It follows that he is in danger of doing, at least in part, in his own terms the wrong thing at the wrong time. Further, by adding the commentary to the poems, he is de facto trying to link activity to passivity such that the two will constitute a whole of spontaneous receptivity, of subject-objectivity. Moreover, silence and speech are respectively associated here (explicitly) with action and (implicitly) with passivity. It would not be illogical, however, to assume that silence relates to speech as linguistic inaction to linguistic action, and not the other way around. Hence, the relationship between passivity and activity is effectively (even if perhaps inadvertently) problematized here at the very start of the "Notes and Treatises" as entangled with the relationship between temporal punctuality and temporal disarticulation.

But I am not yet finished with these opening lines. For the sending out into the world of these poems—Goethe speaks here of sending poems "in die Welt" with or without explanation—implies a spatial movement of distantiation and differentiation, and consequently an exile of the subject from itself in writing. The commentary on these poems that constitutes the "Notes and Treatises" is meant to overcome this exile and distance, returning the poetic cycle to the inward place of its intentional origin, as to the knowledge base that informs the poems, and ultimately to the context to which they refer, the context of the transcendent origin as such, as we shall see below. The subjectivity of the poet (as the place of this transcendent origin) and the objectivity of the text should be kept, according to Goethe, in one place and time (i.e., the understanding of the text should be immediate). The distance between the authorial subject and the reading subject should be overcome.

Thus the problems of time and activity-passivity are complicated and overdetermined by the problem of space, a space between subject and world that is first of all a material space and secondly a hermeneutic one. The mutually implicated metaphysical motifs that we see at work in the initial frame Goethe establishes for the project of the "Notes and Treatises"—the unity of time in the eternal moment, the unity of space with itself, and the unity of action with passion—these motifs are, as I argue in what follows, the principal metaphysical motifs for the structure of the poetic cycle itself.[13] They structure the cycle in that their manipulation organizes Goethe's application and adaptation of figural interpretation to the East-West relation in general. However, before seeing in detail how these motifs, in connection with typology, determine the most important dimensions of the poetic cycle, we need to see how they structure the "Notes and Treatises." For it is in this supplement to the poems that Goethe provides the clearest view of the function of typological thought within the *Divan* project, as within his poetic dealings with the Orient in general. And Goethe's attempt to shore up the metaphysics of presence—as the spontaneous receptivity of subjective inwardness united with the outer world—is only fully comprehensible in terms of his continuing adherence to, and partial displacement of, the typological tradition.

What sort of commentary, then, does Goethe think will return the poetry to its time, its place, and its spontaneous receptivity? The project of returning the poems to themselves, to the time and spiritual place of their origination, to their self-presence—the project, in short, of preventing their reading or anticipatorily fulfilling it

> occurs in a certain cohesiveness [*Zusammenhang*], so that not disconnected [*abgerissene*] notes, but rather an independent [*selbständiger*] text should appear, which although treated only hastily and loosely connected, would nonetheless provide the reader with an overview and commentary. (127–28)

Goethe writes the "Notes" as a continuous text, in order to prevent disarticulation from entering at the site of unification of the poetic cycle with its meaning. The result is that, on the level of the text and its commentary, as everywhere else within the *West-East Divan*, it takes two wholes to make one: Doubling is the condition of unity. For this is how we acknowledge difference and teleologically disavow it at once, each term of the double functioning as the end of the other.

Accordingly, in his "Notes and Treatises," Goethe undertakes a sketch that is made up of two sequential parts. First, he adumbrates the (albeit episodic and digressive) narrative of an intellectual-poetic history of Oriental culture from its Hebraic origin down through the Arabs, the Persians, the development of Islam, and the medieval Persian poets. This narrative culminates in a summary of Goethe's own poetic cycle.[14]

Having written in the first half of the "Notes and Treatises" about the (poetic history of the) Orient itself, so to speak, as the referent and silent interlocutor of his own text, and then about this text (which thus appears as the last piece of Eastern literature, arriving from or into the West as its potential culmination), he now writes an extended discussion of the sources of his knowledge about this subject. The discussion begins with recent biblical criticism (which clarifies the ancient texts and history) and then proceeds to Western travelers' reports (which give us, he says, our best knowledge about the East since antiquity). After characterizing the most important travelers' accounts, Goethe tells us about recent Orientalist scholarship and translations. The "Notes" end with texts transported by the contemporary Persian emissary to the Russian court—as it were, the most recent document about the East, and evidence of the current direct communication between East and West—along with a couple of little poems, one of which is an apology for his own emissary's message, and another dedicated to Sylvestre de Sacy.¹⁵

In sum, the first half of the "Notes and Treatises" treats the Orient in historicopoetical terms, and the second half deals with Goethe's sources of knowledge on the Orient, the mediation between that Orient and Goethe himself. Goethe makes explicit the means by which the supplement is to achieve its goal of "an immediate comprehension" of the poems in the opening sentence of the last chapter, called "Final Conclusion" (whose pleonastic title itself rightly anticipates the reader's own impatience, thus highlighting again the problem of time and fleeting presence):

> To what extent we have succeeded in connecting the most original, distant [*urältesten, abgeschiedenen*] Orient with the newest and most alive [*den neusten, lebendigsten*], experts and friends will judge with indulgence [*Wohlwollen*]. (258)

Goethe indicates hereby his uncertainty and anxiety about whether he has accomplished such a seamless narrative, and he wards off that anxiety by telling the reader that he or she is either ignorant or an enemy if he or she points out the unseemly seams. But above all Goethe makes clear here that his intention has been just this: to link that ancient Orient with the modern Orient—the one that we can touch, as the letter from the Persian emissary demonstrates. The Origin and the End of cultural history, its Alpha and Omega (as he calls them in the poem to Sacy), should make up one continuous totality, one spiritual-human alphabet.¹⁶

Goethe in the Desert

I have thus far considered the goal of this supplementary doubling of the poetic cycle by its commentary—to return the poems to their immediacy in time, space, and activity-passivity—and the means to that end—the construction of a continuous (if internally doubled) narrative of the poetic history of the East and of the sources that give us access to this history (enabling its passage from East to West). I now look more closely at the text with which the second part of the "Notes and Treatises" begins: Goethe's reading of the wanderings of the Israelites in the desert.

Goethe's little piece of biblical criticism seems at first inappropriately or enigmatically placed in the "Notes and Treatises," as even so slavishly admiring an editor as Erich Trunz allows himself to point out (567). But we can recuperate its placement architectonically as Goethe's own contribution to contemporary historical biblical criticism. The piece belongs, that is, as an example, to his suggestion that we should search in such criticism for knowledge of the ancient East, preceding the discussion of the medieval travelers' reports. Moreover, because it opens the second part of the "Notes and Treatises" (the discussion of sources), Goethe's reading of "Israel in the Desert" functions as a double of the summary of the poetic cycle, with which the first part closes. The two together (the summary of the *Divan* and the reading of the Israelites' wanderings) are the two pieces of the hinge that connects the two halves of the "Notes and Treatises," the hinge that connects the Orient itself with our knowledge of the Orient, or the open border that allows one to pass smoothly into the other.

Before looking at Goethe's reading itself, however, it is necessary to look briefly at his characterization of the status of the Holy Scriptures and of biblical scholarship in this context. Otherwise, one is unable to understand what is at stake in his own contribution to such scholarship. The reason why such scholarship is important, Goethe asserts, is twofold. First, the Holy Scriptures make present (*vergegenwärtigen*) the "original conditions and gradual development of a significant nation" (*uranfängliche Zustände und die allmähliche Entwickelung einer bedeutenden Nation*). And second, the contemporary Orientalists—Goethe mentions Michaelis, Eichhorn, Pauls, and Heeren by name—are able to show us "more nature and immediacy" (*mehr Natur und Unmittelbarkeit*) in these traditional documents (*in jenen Überlieferungen*) than we would have been able to discover for ourselves (225). The Holy Scriptures function as the making present, the presentation, of origin and development, and not just of the origin and development of a significant nation, but of origin and development as such and in their unity, that is, of presence itself. Further, if (as the conceptuality of Western metaphysics prompts us to think) origin and development are always at odds—as eternity (or space) and time, structural synchrony and processual diachrony—then the task of grasping the presence of the origin and its development will require that we prevent this disjunction between structure and evolution from emerging, or that we undo it. If the commentators on the scriptures whom Goethe admires manage to return the scriptures to their nature and immediacy, at least tendentially, then this nature and immediacy imply the overcoming of that disjunction, for the essence (i.e., nature) at the origin is always potentially altered by its existence in time, and immediacy cannot be, wherever essence and existence fall away from each other. The Orientalists realize the scriptures, then, by returning the scriptures to their immediacy. They make a hole therein (pointing out the mediating internal distance that has entered and remained empty) that they also fill, in order to make the scriptures (once again) whole. How will Goethe's own reading of "Israel in the Desert" relate to this secular appropriation of the rhetoric of *figura*?

The Holy Scriptures represent for Goethe explicitly the pure origin, the "source waters" (*Quellwasser*) from which all of our wanderings in the Orient depart and to which they always return (27). The scriptures constitute the Orient as essential origin. But the grounding function of the scriptures is always in danger of being lost. Some groundlessness has entered, and some fundamental aspect has disappeared. We therefore have to free the scriptures from both of these occurrences through an appropriation that would rid the scriptures of what does not belong and return to them what they have lost:

> What will remain to us as ground, as primal material [*als Grund, als Urstoff*], of the four last books of Moses, since we find it necessary to recall some things that are forgotten there [*manches dabei zu erinnern*] and to get rid of some other things [*manches daraus zu entfernen*]. (207)

The realization of the scriptures, as the recovery of their grounding function, must be accomplished through the historical reading that Goethe will provide.

But what is the actual ground in or of the scriptures, which are represented here synecdochically by the story of the wanderings of Israel in the desert, the passage from Egyptian enslavement to the Promised Land, the Israelites' most proper ground (which story Goethe sees as the content of the four last books of Moses)? Goethe characterizes this passage as the struggle between disbelief and belief, a struggle that is the "authentic, only, and deepest theme of the history of the world and humanity" (208). But epochs in which disbelief triumphs, he tells us, are forgotten by future history. They are mortal, even if they show off (*prahlen*) with a false glory (*Scheinglanz*) for a moment (*einen Augenblick*) (208), which is here the noneternal kind of moment, the moment as pure disappearance.[17] In contrast, epochs in which belief triumphs live on as fruitful and inspiring (*herzerhebend und fruchtbar*) (208). So that which is alien in the origin, the aspect of the scriptural origin (which is properly "our" origin) that does not properly belong to it, is the element of disbelief. Even if belief does not yet here show itself "in its entire fullness" (*in seiner ganzen Fülle*)—that is, it is not *fulfilled* or *erfüllt*—it is nonetheless already here as the anticipation of its fulfillment, but continually hindered in its development by an abyssal element of disbelief. Goethe turns out to associate this element of disbelief—according to a familiar Lutheran motif—with the laws, not only because according to the principle of *sola fide*, laws are superfluous where belief is solid but also because like disbelief, the enunciation of the laws is what, for Goethe, repeatedly interrupts the narrative flow of the text. The story of the passage of faith toward its own self-fulfillment—the "progress of the story" (*Gang der Geschichte*)—is "constantly hindered" (*überall gehemmt*) by "innumerable interpolated laws" (*eingeschaltete zahllose Gesetze*) (i.e., laws whose infinity makes them nontotalizable, as Emmanuel Levinas would say)[18]—laws that are themselves for the most part groundless, for

> one cannot foresee the actual cause and intention, at least not why they were given in that moment [*in dem Moment*], or, if they are of later origin [*spätern Ursprungs*], why they are introduced and inserted here. (208)

The laws are groundless, and in the best of cases their connection with their contexts, with the time and place of their utterance, seems unmotivated. They appear in the wrong place and at the wrong time, slowing down the progress of the narrative (*jedes Vorwärtskommen*) (209). Appearing in the wrong *Augenblick* and inserted in the wrong place, the laws are situated in a time and place that is not their own; the time and place of the laws is improper, exiled and divided from itself. As a result of this constant interruption of narrative by the law (or of *aggadah* by *halacha*, as the Jewish tradition would put it, with a very different emphasis and interpretation), the narrative continuity gets lost and along with it the *Hauptzweck* (209), the final purpose or ground, which, according to Goethe, is the arrival in the promised land of the self of faith as touchstone of self-presence. Owing to this self-interrupting character, the very fundamental thread (*Grundfaden*) (208) of this story is disagreeable. Goethe refers to "the unpleasantness of this content, the confused fundamental thread that runs through the whole" (208) that makes us "unhappy and annoyed" (*unlustig und verdrießlich*). The thread of the story being one in which faith and law (and/or doubt) struggle with each other, this thread is woven of the ground, faith itself, and the ungrounding of that ground. In order to recover the *Grund* and *Urstoff* of the text, then, Goethe will have to get rid of that aspect of the "Grundfaden" that makes it no "Grund" at all, mixing it up with an *Abgrund*: the mortal and dis-Orienting element of a faithless obsession with the law.

Thus Goethe's project of recovering the ground in (and of) the Old Testament is "to carefully separate what is actual narration [*eigentliche Erzählung*] from teaching and command [*von dem, was gelehret und geboten wird*]" (209). The recovered continuity of the narrative will now be the universal content of the text ("what would be appropriate to all lands, to all ethical humans") (209), whereas doctrine and command (assuming, for example, against Mendelssohn, that the text contains a doctrine) is "what concerns and binds the particular people Israel" (209). Like Paul before him, Goethe will discover the ground of the scriptural ground, but as a writer, a storyteller, and/or as a metaphysical historicist, Goethe will situate the universality of faith in the symbolist-realist aesthetic of narrative continuity.

According to Goethe, this restoration of narrative continuity involves two components: first, the "development or derivation of the entire occurrence of this strange wandering from the character of the General, Moses" (*die Entwickelung der ganzen Begebenheit dieses wunderlichen Zugs aus dem Charakter des Feldherrn*) (209), and in this way the restoration of his dignity as leader, and second, the claim that the wandering (*Zug*) took not forty years but barely two. In fact it is the latter suggestion that makes possible the harmonization of the Israelites' wanderings with Moses' character, so the two aspects of Goethe's recuperation belong together. For Goethe, this abbreviation of the journey saves not only the honor of Moses but also that of the national God of the Jews (because God seems less brutal if he does not let them wander for forty years). To reduce the wandering (or *Zug*, which means also "train" or "trait," as in "character trait" [*Charakterzug*]) of the Israelites to the character of Moses is for Goethe to rehabilitate Moses as a leader (and also God as his leader in turn). The reality of wandering, or the wandering character of reality, is now explained by and as the intentional act of a (stable) character, a character with character.[19]

As the subjectivity of Moses subsumes or absorbs the objectivity of the Israelites' wanderings in the desert (or objectivity as a wandering away from subjectivity), so the reduction of the time from forty years to two years establishes an accord of time and space with themselves and with each other in the immediate. The biblical account was falsified, according to Goethe, in order to make the wanderings take the forty years dictated by the mystical significance of the number forty—arbitrary signification run amok. Additional stopping points were added to the original narrative in order to account for the fact that a journey of two years was supposed to have taken forty. But the additional points of passage are incoherent and undermotivated, according to Goethe, and in any case they don't add up to a plausible period of forty years. The result is a threefold disruption of the here and now. First, time and space do not cohere with each other, because a short distance here takes too much time to cross, so to speak. Second, space does not cohere with itself: Many of the cities in the list from chapter 33 of Numbers do not appear in the narrative accounts of the journey. And third, time fails to cohere with itself, because two years are stretched out into forty, as hesitation repeatedly interferes with the moment of action and decision.

The consequence of this derangement of space and time is that Moses' character in turn becomes incoherent: The man of action (*Mann der Tat*) (224), as Goethe sees him, acts like a man of passivity and hesitation. But "in such cases everything depends on personality [*Persönlichkeit*]. Character [*Charakter*] is based on personality, not on talents" (224). Goethe's reading thus saves the spirituality of Moses' personality, even if this spirituality remains within the limits of the anticipatory faith narrative of the Old Testament, where faith cannot be perfected "in its entire fullness" (*ganzen Fülle*) (208). Moses' image, which had been "entirely disfigured" (*ganz entstellt*) (224)—which means both displaced and distorted—by the interruption of the continuity of his activity, is restored to its "proper place" (*rechte Stelle*) (224).[20] By removing the spatiotemporal and subjective-objective disjunctions from the narrative, by restoring the continuity to the narrative so that it is no longer interrupted by law (as structure and doubt), Goethe recovers its ground—the ground of the original source—in its natural immediacy, the immediacy of each point in the narrative to itself as to the ones preceding it and proceeding from it.[21] He restores "the original, better" aspect (*das Ursprüngliche, Bessere*) (224), which has been "hidden, indeed disfigured" (*verdeckt, ja entstellt*) (224)—metonymically displaced—by "belated additions, interpolations, and accommodations" (224). The "inner, authentic primal and fundamental value" (*innerliche, eigentliche Ur- und Grundwert*) (224) arises, he says, in an "all the more lively and pure way" (*nur desto lebhafter und reiner*) (224), and this is what everyone wants and needs from the Bible (224).

The Jewish reading of the Bible, then, is for Goethe an exacerbatedly metonymic one: It displaces itself and operates by discontinuity. The Jews ruin the Oriental origin or ground that at the same time they are or (de)constitute. They (de)constitute the origin as loss of origin, the splitting of the eternal present into structure and narrative, eternal space (as represented by the laws) and linear time (as represented by narrative). This enables "us" to undo the displacement, to restore the origin to itself, to realize it, by restoring narrative continuity in its compatibility with space, here as the space referred to within the narrative (the space traversed by the time of the narrative itself). In this way, metaphorizing metonymy in all senses, Goethe attempts to accomplish the adjustment of time and space to themselves and to each other, so that action and passion, or intention and reality coincide in the pure here and now.

Goethe's Wanderings from the Bible to Persian Poetry

How does Goethe's reading of the Israelites' wanderings shed light on the relationship between his appropriation of the Orient of Persian medieval poetry, on the one hand, and the typological tradition, on the other? The answer to this question must take as its point of departure the way in which Goethe framed his insertion of the text on "Israel in der Wüste": "As all of our wanderings in the Orient have been occasioned by the Holy Scriptures, so we return to them always, as to the most enlivening, albeit here and there obscured source-waters [*Quellwassern*], which hide themselves in the earth, but then again reemerge pure and fresh" (207). Our wanderings in the Orient in fact (metaphorically) resemble their occasioning cause, their origin and end, since the synecdoche for the scriptures that Goethe has chosen is itself a text—the *Ur*-text of the Judaeo-Christian-Islamic world, no doubt—on wandering. "Our" wanderings in the Orient, then, are the mirror image of the Israelites' wanderings. To wander in search of a goal is to anticipate a realization or fulfillment. Further, the Israelites' wanderings constitute the passage specifically from enslavement to emancipation, and from heteronomy and self-differentiation in the land of the Egyptian master to autonomy or self-sameness in the promised land. Consequently, the wandering of the Israelites is a well-chosen synecdoche for the Old Testament from a Christian point of view (however partially secularized Goethe's position may be). The Israelites' self-anticipation, it would seem, anticipates "our" fulfillment of that self-anticipation in "our" own wanderings in the Orient. That is, Goethe's Orientalist works here replace or supplement traditional Christianity as the realization of the Old Testament text that wanders toward its own fulfillment.

Not unexpectedly, Goethe's Orientalist works realize this wandering as an at-home-ness, or what Levinas will call an "odyssey," as opposed to an actual wandering or exile, insofar as an odyssey is an always-Oriented voyage home. First, this is because in "our" wanderings through the Orient, according to Goethe, we return again and again, cyclically, to the biblical source; we are never radically off course or dis-Oriented. Even more extremely, in fact, we never leave it behind at all: The source to which we return again and again figures, by virtue of Goethe's synedochic selection, wandering itself. By wandering off from wandering, we remain as close as possible to it.

Second, the wandering of the Israelites that in "Notes and Treatises" synecdochically represents the source is, in his version, not finally a wandering at all, but a continuous narrative—they go as directly as possible to their goal—directed by a spiritual nature, the personality of Moses.[22] Further, it is the narrative of the development of a promise—God's promise to Abraham, then to Moses—that leads toward (and that is always already) its realization, the realization of the faith that is its core. The faith at stake here just happens to be, in Goethe's restoration, the faith in narrative, and the narrative of faith, as the incessant passage from an origin and back toward that origin. This circular narrative combines linear development with structure, or time with eternity (or space) in the form of the circle or cycle of its own movement, a movement that it gives to and takes from itself, in pure self-affection. Goethe's reduction of the discontinuous Old Testament narrative to its continuity functions to bring that narrative back to itself, to constitute the argumentative story of its return to itself.[23] This guarantees that the wandering "we" mirror (in "our" dealings with the Orient) is always one that remains at home with itself, self-same; it guarantees that the wandering of the Israelites (toward "us," the Christian West) never wanders off from itself (or above all from its goal, "ourselves"). In Goethe's secular and aesthetic (but not, therefore—as one can too easily forget—nonmetaphysical) appropriation of the typological tradition, the Old Testament anticipates its realization as the poet's wandering in the poetic traditions of the Orient, to which the anticipation leads by a continuous narrative down to Goethe (and so back to itself), as the course of the "Notes and Treatises" is to demonstrate.

Goethe, then, relativizes the importance of the Old Testament with one gesture (as he indicates, for example, when he calls the Israelites a "significant nation") while he absolutizes it with the other (calling it for instance "the source-waters" to which we return again and again, and so on). This duplicity illustrates the ambiguous or self-contradictory situation or predicament of modern Orientalism in general, at least through the long nineteenth century. The Bible is here (only) an Oriental text, and therefore (all of) the Orient, or (at least) the Oriental essence as such, must be the actual source of its transcendent authority; but what gives the Orient such authority is just the residual authority of the Bible itself.[24] According to this structure, wandering around in the Orient—that is, positing the Orient as ground of the transcendent authority of the West—becomes the contradictory realization of the sole authority of the Old Testament, one particular Oriental text as distinct from others. Orientalism in this sense ambiguously and ambivalently supplants and adds itself to—becomes the realization of—Christianity itself.

In terms of exactly this self-contradictory logic, Goethe's appropriation of the Oriental source is ambiguously and ambivalently adherent to, and divergent from (or in a state of wandering with respect to), the typological tradition. On the one hand, Goethe reasserts, if in secular and aesthetic terms, the privilege of the Christian West over the Jewish tradition whose culpably self-abandoned originality the Christian West would realize and recover. On the other hand, he relativizes the authority of the Judaeo-Christian tradition such that other Oriental texts can serve just as easily as the absolute source—here, medieval Persian poetry becomes his chosen source—and in so doing he questions even the Christian privilege. He grants the Persian source in some respects greater authority than the Jewish one—notably insofar as the Persian source is not seen even as a proleptic falling away from an ultimate Christian truth (or from itself as this truth). But further he grants the Persian poetic tradition even greater authority than the Christian tradition as well, insofar as the Persian source in the embodiment of Hafis is seen as possessing the universality of poetry, which—he argues in various poems—exceeds that of religion.[25] Even in the text "Israel in the Desert," when speaking of the Old Testament (and more narrowly of the last four books of the Pentateuch), he has called it "the Holy Scriptures" (207), suggesting that the source waters that anticipate "our wanderings in the Orient" (207) include implicitly or potentially the New Testament, as well.

Accordingly, with respect to Persian poetry, Goethe sees himself not as realizing its potential, but as rivaling it in originality, as mirroring its resourcefulness, which mirrors his in turn. If the two (West and East) are one in their separateness, this is because each manages to synthesize temporality and eternity, subjectivity and objectivity in equal degree, and also with equal difficulty.[26] The overcoming of temporal, spatial, and active-passive difference will not then openly take place at the expense of one of the two parties to the discussion.[27]

Nonetheless, the mutually rivalrous identification that Goethe tries to construct between himself and Persian poetry, as embodied in Hafis, is not devoid of the tension of figural interpretation, but rather comprises this tension symmetrically doubled: Each term of the relationship intermittently poses as both prefiguration and fulfillment of the other. The reversibility of these positions is made easier than it would be in any Judaeo-Christian cultural construct, because the Persians do not anticipate "us," nor do "we" anticipate them, at least not univocally.[28] Rather, for example, if religiohistorically they come after "us" insofar as Islam develops subsequent to Christianity, they come before "us" (now as Westerners and moderns) insofar as they are marked both as Eastern and as ancient and/or medieval.[29] Because of this reversibility in the temporal order and the relativization of linear progress that it implies, the reversibility in the order of figuration and literalization is more easily achieved, as we shall see in detail when we come to the poetry.

Further, because aesthetic discourse is less susceptible to the notion of progress than is theological, epistemological, or political discourse, by playing out the intercultural dialogue on the level of poetry, Goethe avoids having to deal seriously with the problem of the privilege, in terms of value, of religious or cultural identities. In the *Divan*, Goethe thus takes his distance from typology by displacing it with respect to the Persian Orient, but he maintains the typological relation of Christianity to the Jews as part of this structure, precisely because it is needed (and continues to function) to authorize the elevation of the Oriental to the status of ideal origin.

CHAPTER 4

Goethe's Orientalizing Moment (II): The Poetry of the *West-East Divan*

On the basis of the preceding discussion of typology and the metaphysics of presence in the "Notes and Treatises," we are now in a position to see how the poetry itself, the main body or act of Goethe's *West-East Divan*, belongs to the typological tradition but also displaces it. Goethe does not want to negate modernity and the discourse of the understanding (*Verstand*), as do some romantics, like Friedrich Schlegel, as we saw above. Indeed, Goethe indirectly attacks in the *Divan* Schlegel's successive overvaluation and undervaluation of the Orient in the form of ancient Indian culture.[1] He does not want to return to a discourse of positive religion, and certainly not that of medieval Catholicism. Nor does he idealize modernity or freedom (of the will), as the Enlightenment generation tends to do. Rather, in a manner akin to Spinoza, he defends something like the freedom from the illusions of freedom.[2] Instead of attempting to claim that it is in the Christian West exclusively that this freedom (from freedom)—or this synthesis of supersensuous and sensuous under the figure of eternal presence—has been realized, he attempts to establish a balance between the ancient Oriental origin and its Occidental culmination.[3] To some degree critical of both, Goethe does not try to sublate one pole through the other, but rather to sublate each through the other, to synthesize the two, each in the image of the other. The realization of Christian figural interpretation is now Orientalism as the wandering of the West into the East and vice versa.

Contextual Incoherence and the Divan

Before examining the ways in which Goethe attempts to restore presence in the poetry of the *Divan*, I must consider the context and point of departure he announces in the first poem of the cycle, "Hegire." This context is explicitly that of a radical lack of context, or *Zusammenhang*, the same context I posited in the introduction as that of modernity from late Enlightenment on. If only by virtue of the epoch in which he lives, the aging Goethe still shares the predicament of the young Wilhelm Meister: "denn es fehlte mir der Zusammenhang, und darauf kommt doch eigentlich alles an." All depends on contextual coherence or cohesion—*Zusammenhang*—because without such cohesion, the all disintegrates into infinite fragmentation. But cohesion is the ground Goethe's world lacks:

Nord und West und Süd zersplittern,
Throne bersten, Reiche zittern.

North and South and West are quaking,
Thrones are cracking, empires shaking.

The time and place in which Goethe finds himself are a time and place in which temporal (e.g., traditional) and spatial continuity are disrupted: "Alles hat seine Zeit!" precisely does not apply. Everything "here" is not in its proper place either temporally or spatially. Passivity and activity, moreover, are dis- or misaligned: Relationships of power and authority are disrupted. As he goes on to imply in the third stanza, one does not know how to recognize those forces subordination to which is actually self-affirmation; one serves instead the alien, subordination to whom cannot coincide with one's spontaneous will. The absence of the metaphysical cohesion or coherence of things—their capacity to be together in a unity of time, space, and (active-passive) event—is the form in which radical ungroundedness appears in this poetry. And this ungroundedness affects in turn the political, religious, familial, and philosophical orders.

Flüchte du, im reinen Osten
Patriarchenluft zu kosten,

Unter Lieben, Trinken, Singen
Soll dich Chisers Quell verjüngen.⁴

You must flee; the East will right you,
Patriarchs' pure air delight you;
There in loving, drinking, singing
Youth from Chiser's well is springing.

In the age of the French Revolution, the wars of liberation, and the coming Restoration of the European monarchies (and despite this Restoration), Goethe points to the East, in the very opening stanza, as a place in which to flee from the radical unsettlement of political and paternal-familial power and authority. The loss of religious faith and of philosophical certainty, moreover, emerge already in the second stanza to complete the picture of the shaky foundations of the present age, to which only a return to the "depths of the origin"—a wandering in the Orient—can provide an answer:

Dort, im Reinen und im Rechten,
Will ich menschlichen Geschlechten
In des Ursprungs Tiefe dringen,
Wo sie noch von Gott empfingen
Himmelslehr in Erdesprachen
Und sich nicht den Kopf zerbrachen.

Wo sie Väter hoch verehrten,
Jeden fremden Dienst verwehrten;
Will mich freuen der Jugendschranke:
Glaube weit, eng der Gedanke,
Wie das Wort so wichtig dort war,
Weil es ein gesprochen Wort war. (7)

Seeing rightly, seeing purely,
There I'll penetrate most surely
To the origin of nations,
When on earth the generations
Heard God's words as earthlings use them,
Did not brain-rack or confuse them.

When to fathers they gave honours
And rejected foreign manners;
I'll rejoice in youth's demotion:
Wider faith, narrower notion,

> Words weighed then as value's token
> Since the word was one that's spoken.

The Oriental origin of human races represents the stage of unity that is here figured in terms of youth and vitality (*verjüngen* [l. 6], *Jugendschranke* [l. 15]), but also in terms of the respect for paternal authority. It is situated, therefore, prior to the division between sensuous (*Erdesprachen*, which are moreover traditionally associated with youth) and supersensuous (*Himmelslehr*—tendentially the privilege of age), and thus faith is not separated from life nor philosophical reflection from sensuous perception.

Further, at the origin, which is neither simply young nor simply old, but both (each in continuity with the other), and where faith, in all of its dimensions, outweighs reflective analysis (*Glaube weit, eng der Gedanke*), leadership is still a dependable reality. Goethe figures the leader here as the leader of the trade caravan, wandering and yet at home, and as an aesthetic—and more specifically a poetic and/or rhapsodic—leader whom he evidently means here to embody:

> Bösen Felsweg auf und nieder
> Trösten, Hafis, deine Lieder,
> Wenn der Führer mit Entzücken
> Von des Maultiers hohem Rücken
> Singt, die Sterne zu erwecken
> Und die Räuber zu erschrecken.
>
> On the mountain's desolation,
> Hafiz, you give consolation
> When our guide, afraid of capture,
> High upon his mule in rapture
> Sings to set the stars a-blazing,
> Startled thieves with dread amazing.

The poetic leadership that Goethe wishes to reinstantiate comprises within itself epistemological and ethical leadership, because it is to be a unifying and unified one. Philosophical certainty is ensured and exceeded by aesthetic totality. This is what makes possible the philosophical books within the cycle, such as the "Buch der Betrachtungen" and the "Buch der Sprüche." Further, Goethe will argue, in complex ways throughout the cycle, for the ideal compatibility of aesthetic leadership with political, religious, and paternal authority. For even if the poet is figured as an exception to the regime of the law (cf. "Buch des Sängers" and "Buch Hafis"), the poetic exception is conceived as a necessary grounding of the ground, because the eternal present (in the here and now) that provides an absolute foundation qua absolute coherence of things is only possible as an aesthetic moment. The panic and/or anxiety of a leaderless situation—evidenced in the rhyming and alliterative "zersplittern" and "zittern" of the cycle's opening couplet—is here to be prevented or overcome by the poetic constitution of the eternal present because what splits apart and trembles within the leader, exploding "his" coherence, is presence itself.

In the remaining sections of this chapter, I examine how Goethe undertakes such a poetic constitution of the eternal present, or cohesion.[5] Before entering into the details of this examination, I indicate what I take to be the main three thematic levels on which Goethe concretizes his poetic constitution of presence, in order then to examine that constitution illustratively on each of these levels.

East-West, Feminine-Masculine, Man-Boy

There are three principal levels on which Goethe tries, through a dialectical structure, to concretize, elaborate, and illustrate—to prove poetically—the eternalization of the here as now. (1) On the macrological level he develops a cultural-historical allegory of East-West relations as embodied, above all, in the relationship between Goethe the poet and Hafis, his premodern Persian counterpart; (2) on the micrological level, he explores the erotic relationship between an older man (Goethe/Hatem) and a much younger woman (Marianne Jung-Willemer/Suleika); (3) and finally, as a kind of synthesis or confounding of these two syntheses, he presents the relationship between an older man (again, Goethe/Hatem) and a much younger man or boy (Saki), the figure of the cupbearer, or *Schenke*, whose name evokes the gift he embodies with particular explicitness. The young boy serves as something midway between an adult male poetic friend-rival and a younger female object of desire, thus effacing the gap and tension between the ego-libidinal and object-libidinal dimensions represented by the dialogues with Hafis and Marianne/Suleika, respectively. Goethe is compelled by the logic of his project to constitute the moment on all of these levels, because within the realm of poetic concretization the macrological and the micrological, the whole and the parts, must seamlessly cohere, and the division of the human into male and female must be relativized, in order for the homogeneity of the original ground to have been plausibly reconstituted.

The suggestion that these three levels are the most important of the cycle follows from my decision to grant a certain priority to the personified figures to whom Goethe dedicates particular books, and then to narrow the focus to the figures of Hafis, Suleika, and Saki. Although the question of the architectonics of the cycle could easily provide (and has provided), ample material for an entire essay of its own, let the following remarks suffice here to justify this way of limiting the present chapter.[6] First, not to have limited one's focus would have required writing an entire book on the question of typology and presence in Goethe's *Divan*, which would certainly have been possible (since these two topics in combination pervade the cycle, as well as the "Notes and Treatises"), but also perhaps superfluously exhaustive and repetitive, and in any case beyond the limits to be set to Goethe within the larger trajectory of this book. Goethe clearly links himself to the Orient not only by means of personifications with whom he can enter into imaginative dialogue, but also by other means. For example, he imitates and appropriates forms ("Buch der Betrachtungen," "Buch der Sprüche," "Buch der Parabeln"); he explores themes treated prominently in the Oriental cultures among which he is wandering ("Buch der Liebe," "Buch des Paradieses"), and he defends his hubristic poetic enthusiasm, by reference to the precedents of Hafis and other great Persian poets, against the moralizing tendencies of some of his contemporaries ("Buch des Sängers," "Buch des Unmuts"). As is highlighted in various poems (beginning with "Hegire"), however, the principal three thematic motifs of the collection are "loving, drinking, and singing," and these themes—modalities or metaphors of aesthetic transcendence—are most palpably presented through the personifications of Suleika, Saki, and Hafis. Indeed, the personality, as we saw above in "Israel in der Wüste," or the capacity to personify oneself, to be self-same, is what the metaphysics of presence is here to save. Even the discourses of politics, religion, and family, for example, turn around the possibility of a personal ruler, a personal God, and a father (or, for the matter, a mother) who can provide a substantial, personal foundation. The other books that turn around specific personifications, moreover, such as the "Buch des Timur," or the "Buch des Parsen," and even the "Buch des Paradieses," deal with the—already manifestly eternal— figures of nature and divine fire, and so all too obviously and easily engage the problematic of the eternal moment. Even if their detailed analysis in terms of this problematic would still be ultimately necessary and certainly productive, as my argument not only suggests but insists, they do not serve as well as the books on Hafis, Suleika, and Saki to illustrate the stakes and scope of Goethe's perilous wandering in the desert between enslavement to the disappearance of the moment and the promised land of eternity.

East-West Dialogue as a Figure of the Eternal Moment

I am arguing that the principal purpose of the geographical-cultural dialogue between East and West that Goethe constructs in this cycle is to establish the metaphysical illusion of this eternal present on the macrocosmic and public level of cultural history. Because the East counts as the past origin here while the West figures the future end of that past, the unification of East and West in the "Divan" figures the achievement or realization of an eternal (co)presence. The mechanism of this unification, or metaphorical totalization, is—as always in metaphorical processes—the chiasmic transfer (or gift and countergift) of spatiotemporal properties between East and West. Thus Goethe must posit that, paradoxically, the East is the future of the Western past (and not merely the reverse). He must show that the older is younger than the young, the young older than the old. There is perhaps no better place to begin to show how he operates this reversal of essential predicates than in the poem addressed to Hafis—Goethe's privileged synecdoche for the East and elective counterpart—titled "Unbegrenzt."

Unbegrenzt
Daß du nicht enden kannst, das macht dich groß,
Und daß du nie beginnst, das ist dein Los.
Dein Lied ist drehend wie das Sterngewölbe,
Anfang und Ende immerfort dasselbe,
Und was die Mitte bringt, ist offenbar
Das, was zu Ende bleibt und anfangs war.

Du bist der Freuden echte Dichterquelle,
Und ungezählt entfließt dir Well' auf Welle.
Zum Küssen stets bereiter Mund,
Ein Brustgesang, der lieblich fließet,
Zum Trinken stets gereizter Schlund,
Ein gutes Herz, das sich ergießet.

Und mag die ganze Welt versinken,
Hafis, mit dir, mit dir allein
Will ich wetteifern! Lust und Pein

Sei uns, den Zwillingen, gemein!
Wie du zu lieben und zu trinken,
Das soll mein Stolz, mein Leben sein.

Nun töne Lied mit eignem Feuer!
Denn du bist älter, du bist neuer. (23)

Unlimited
That you can never end—that makes you great;
That you cannot begin, that is your fate.
Your song revolves as vaulted constellations,
End and beginning are reiterations,
The import of the middle clear akin
To that which ends and as it did begin.

In you true source of joy and poetry shows,
From you unnumbered wave on wave outflows.
A mouth that's ready for the kiss,
Full-breasted voice which sweetness fills,
A throat that drink can never miss,
Good heart which always over-spills.

What though the whole wide world were sinking!
Hafiz, with you, with you and else none
I will compete! Let joy and pain
Be ours in common as twins are one!
Like you in loving, like you in drinking,
That shall be my pride, my life's sustain.

My song, let your own fire be ignited!
For you have old and new united!

The first thing to note about this poem is its apostrophic structure.[7] The address not only establishes a link between "Goethe" and "Hafis," new and old (or the other way around), as subject and object of address. Beyond this, in the final couplet, it also turns—apparently, although not unambiguously—toward itself, that is, toward the song itself as toward the vehicle and subject of the address to Hafis, thus reinforcing the fusion of subject and object, new and old (or the other way around). But I'll return to these final lines in a moment, after retracing the imaginative argument that leads to them.

The opening stanza posits that Hafis has no beginning and no end, that he escapes the temporal problematic of becoming and passing away. For the pure presence of the origin as such has no beginning or ending.

The middle, the border between beginning and ending, absorbs these two terms into its eternal—henceforth infinitely unbordered—presence. In connection with this transformation of linear time into cyclical time, the stanza accomplishes an imaginative overcoming of the distinction between East and West, as embodied by Hafis and Goethe, respectively, through the implied reversal of early and late, as follows. In his timelessness, Hafis is infinitely old and infinitely young at once. He is of our time and even our future as well as his own. The absolute youth of the Oriental origin is posited as an absolute old age. The Occident, older than the Orient in that it represents the Orient's aging, is consequently also younger than the otherwise absolutely youthful Orient. The Oriental Hafis and the Occidental Goethe are simultaneously younger and older than, and hence mirror, each other. The basis for their imaginative identification is established by their shared context of eternal presence.[8]

The second stanza begins with a spatial figure for the origin—a well or spring that recalls the *Quellwasser* of the scriptures from the "Notes and Treatises"—and labors to eliminate the separation of space from itself. Because the overcoming of spatial difference, which appears as a difference between subject and object, ultimately requires the overcoming of the active-passive opposition (so that subject and object converge), the stanza will also undertake the reversal of active and passive. Accordingly, the poet metaphorically identifies the source with a mouth that wants to kiss (an exteriority) and then immediately with the song of a breast or *Brustgesang* (a soulful, spiritual interiority). But to want to kiss is still to seek an outside, the inside of an outside—lips as borders—tendentially for the sake of its oral internalization. And conversely the breast is an external figure here for the most internal spirit. The last two lines of the stanza repeat this double attribution of an ambiguous externality and internality, as they emphasize the language of spontaneity and receptivity. Goethe associates the source with the receptive posture of thirst, and with the expressive, active stance of a heart pouring itself out. Taking and giving, as characteristics of Hafis, the Oriental source, bridge the abyss of difference between interiority and exteriority in a circular movement of receptive spontaneity.[9] Kissing mouth and singing breast are as one; the mouth receptively drinks while the heart pours itself out in song. The circular (trans)temporal movement between beginning and end is mirrored by a circular spatial movement between going out and coming in. If, furthermore, space is traditionally represented as an exterior condition of sense whereas time is construed as an interior condition (which Kant called an "inner sense"), then the ostensible overcoming (and actual disavowal) of the inside-outside spatial opposition implies the overcoming (or disavowal) of the space-time opposition. It seems that the pure self-affection of pure presence is all that remains.

Now that Hafis has become an absolute totality of spatiotemporal self-affection, one can easily comprehend and identify with Goethe's desire, expressed in the third stanza, to be "allein," both "alone" and "all one" with him, through a pantheistic double entendre common in the German literature of this period. The wish to share "pleasure and pain" with Hafis evokes again the pair of activity and passivity united in his self-affection. In their competition—*wetteifern*—which would be a mutual emulation, Goethe wishfully imagines and demands that they should be all-one—*allein*—identical in their desire to be identical. The identification of Goethe with Hafis ("Wie du"; "Like you") is that of the Occidental with the Oriental in the pure moment—the pure border—of eternal borderlessness.

Finally, in the last lines, when "Goethe" turns away from Hafis to address his song (or the song turns away to address itself [cf. the poem "Ginkgo Biloba" in the *Divan*]), he imitates with this self-referential gesture Hafis's circular self-totalization and paradoxically reinforces his identity with Hafis precisely by differentiating himself from him. When the poem closes with the line, "Denn du bist älter, du bist neuer," we can understand this in several senses. If this song is older than Hafis, it is because Hafis is radically new or young: The West represents the aging of the Eastern origin. If inversely this song is younger than Hafis, that is because the song has just begun as a Western song, whereas the Eastern song, and the great Eastern civilizations, have been around for a long time. Because both are the case (the song is both older and younger than Hafis), this ultimate line might be addressing itself with equal plausibility to Hafis or to Goethe's song. In this way, Goethe tries to perform the identity with Hafis to which he has thus far imperatively laid claim.

But two opposite perspectives do not necessarily constitute a single self-enclosed circle of meaning. Goethe does not so much bridge as disavow here the rift between the discontinuity and the continuity of future with past, the rift between the border of the present as separation and this same border as unification.[10] And we can read the persistence of this rift in certain aspects of the poem thus far passed over in silence. For example, if one's end is postponed into an infinitely distant future, while one's origin is pushed back into an infinitely distant past, then one is just as much without middle as all middle. The middle is nowhere. And if what it brings (line 5) is the same as what was at the (nonexistent) beginning and remains at the (never arriving) end, then it seems that what the middle brings—all that we have in the presence of Hafis and/or Goethe—is an endless anticipation and deferral of presence. In this sense, the fact that it is Hafis's "Los" never to begin could ironically (with or without Goethe's intentional control) signify as much as that he does not exist at all. It could well be, therefore, that the price of endless self-presence is this: *never to be*, other than in the form of an illusory solution and dissolution of temporal and spatial difference from the standpoint of an idealist metaphysics. Indeed, the fact that a fire can only either be extinguished by a watery source or perhaps manage to make the water evaporate, suggests that the two terms that constitute the eternal moment here—Hafis and Goethe, Orient and Occident, as past and future, inside and outside, passive and active—remain by their very positionally determined natures forever incompatible and at odds.[11] For the borders of the border not only expand infinitely but also contract infinitely so that what the border separates (that is, the spaces that border on it from either side) reduce it to nought, impinge on it from either side, without thereby unifying themselves (that is, these spaces) into the totality—here as now—of the one moment.[12]

Being as Presence in the Erotic Gaze

The tension we have seen here between the claim to achieve full presence, on the one hand, and the appearance of the impossibility of such presence, on the other hand, pervades also the love poetry of the *Divan* in and around the "Buch Suleika." In the face of the possibility of this impossibility, Goethe repeatedly invites the reader to identify with his claim to have overcome it, as our leader in the poetically intoxicating world of eroticism.

Let us begin with a poem in which Goethe represents the beloved as an illusory refuge from time, before moving on to those that disavow this insight for the sake of the reader's vicarious gratification. This poem appears in the "Buch der Sprüche," outside of the confines of the "Buch Suleika." Yet it illuminates the latter book not only through the forthrightness with which it marks full presence as impossible even in love, but also through the subtle ruse by which it then attempts to overcome this impossibility precisely by capitulating to it.

Was wird mir jede Stunde so bang?
Das Leben ist kurz, der Tag ist lang. (51)

Goethe's Orientalizing Moment (II)

> Why are each hour's apprehensions so strong?
> Our life is so short, the day so long.

The enigmatic anxiety of existence, of every hour, is here as if explained by the contradiction between the two ways in which time escapes our grasp. It disappears, slips through our fingers, moves too quickly relative to ourselves: An entire life passes in an instant. And yet it drags, moves too slowly: A day can seem like an eternity. According to this double movement, we fall behind our own time, or our time falls behind itself—life races through its course, as may be, before we are remotely ready for it to end—and we race out ahead of our time, our time anticipates itself—hence, the boredom or impatience of "der Tag ist lang." These two contradictory aspects of time are mutually intertwined, however, as each implies the other. To be behind oneself is to be out ahead of oneself, and vice versa. The pastness of the present moment and its futurity each entail the other.[13]

> Und immer sehnt sich fort das Herz,
> Ich weiß nicht recht, ob himmelwärts;
> Fort aber will es hin und hin,
> Und möchte vor sich selber fliehn.

> The heart forever yearns away,
> But if to heaven I cannot say;
> Longing away endlessly
> From itself it wants to flee.

The repetitive striving ("hin und hin") of the heart—its desire, or *Sehnen*—signifies in this context the movement of the inner sense, or sense of time, ahead of itself even as it falls behind itself.[14]

> Und fliegt es an der Liebsten Brust,
> Da ruht's im Himmel unbewußt.

> It flies to my beloved's breast,
> There in heaven unknowing to rest.

The resting of the heart, that is, of the sense of time, upon the breast of the beloved—as upon the maternal breast—signifies a return to the timeless origin in a (placeless) place or experience that presupposes the negation of consciousness, a place (the "Brust") where neither the spatial difference between inside and outside, nor the temporal difference between past and future, any longer obtains. The site of this negation, however heavenly, is also characterized as a flight—*fliehen, fliegen*. But Goethe cannot simply condemn such a flight, both because the entire collection begins with a flight ("Hegire") and (even more crucially) because the desire for refuge belongs to the very movement or ineluctable process of desire qua temporal existence itself. In accordance with this inscription of flight in the structure of temporal existence in general, the attempt to seek refuge upon the breast of the beloved is immediately followed by the forward movement of desiring time accompanied by its lag behind itself.

> Der Lebestrudel reißt es fort,
> Und immer hängt's an Einem Ort;
> Was es gewollt, was es verlor,
> Es bleibt zuletzt sein eigner Tor.

> The whirl of life may drag away,
> In One place still it longs to stay;
> And when all want and loss is past
> A fool it still remains at last.

This relentless movement of desire, backward and forward at once, in expectation and nostalgic recall, occurs evidently regardless of content. The specifics of desire's aim become ultimately a matter of indifference from the standpoint of the poem: The heart remains its own fool, or dupe, fooling itself ceaselessly, though never actually in the pure present, on the basis of its temporal structure. The "Ort" shifts, subverts, and anagrammatizes one's name as "Tor," the object of one's desire repelling and respelling itself as the "fool" one is.[15] But also perhaps as the gateway that consumes one's being (which "Tor," despite its masculine gender here, recalls, here as well as in *Faust*), as the gateway from one fleeting moment to the next. Giving up one's attempt to control one's own way of attempting to store and restore the moment—because one has recognized oneself to be a *Tor* whatever happens—one can now perhaps give oneself up to the always fleeting moment of the deluded attempt to restore the moment. One can now simply be in the moment of one's desires, one's foolish attempts to secure oneself in the (eternal) moment of the here and now. By capitulating to the impossibility of the moment, therefore, Goethe tries silently here to overcome this impossibility.

Despite the ruse that one can see at work there, the clear-minded analysis of the temporality of human being (and desire) in "Was wird mir jede

Stunde so bang?" does not bode well for the apotheosis of romantic love in the "Buch Suleika." Nonetheless, the opening poem of the latter book returns to some of the important motifs of that poem, as well as of "Unbegrenzt," but it attacks these motifs with imperatives and promises, attempting to resolve the problems constated elsewhere through the performance of their disavowal.

Einladung
Mußt nicht vor dem Tage fliehen:
Denn der Tag, den du ereilest,
Ist nicht besser als der heut'ge;
Aber wenn du froh verweilest,
Wo ich mir die Welt beseit'ge,
Um die Welt an mich zu ziehen,
Bist du gleich mit mir geborgen:
Heut' ist heute, morgen morgen,
Und was folgt, und was vergangen,
Reißt nicht hin und bleibt nicht hangen.
Bleibe du, mein Allerliebstes;
Denn du bringst es, und du gibst es. (62)

Invitation
Flee not from the day's distress:
For the day to which you've hurried
Is no better than today;
But if you stay here unworried,
Where I push the world away
So that I more World possess,
I at once will give you cover:
This day's now, tomorrow's other,
What's to follow and what's past
Neither pulls nor holds us fast.
Stay, my dearest of all that can be;
That's the gift you bring to me.

What the previous poem, "Was wird mir jede Stunde so bang?" determined as inevitable—trying to flee from the present moment (an attempt that the very structure of the present moment—as fleeting—forces upon the subject)—the poem "Einladung" directly forbids. In the first three lines, it enjoins the beloved to stay in the present. Subsequently, in the next three lines, it develops an extended condition the fulfillment of which it promises to reward in a particular way. The condition is that the beloved should happily remain in the present, where the poetic voice has paradoxically pulled the world of being to itself by getting rid of the world of time. (The use of "wo" ["where"] in line 5 strikingly turns the unstable time of a potential *Verweilen* into an eternally present, spatial place.) If this condition should be fulfilled—as if it were a matter of mere choice here—the poetic voice promises a state of *Geborgenheit*, or safety, which the poem appropriately states in the present indicative rather than the future, as it might have. This *Geborgenheit* amounts explicitly to the self-sameness of the present moment, sheltered from time's interruptive passages. The poem thus promises, in effect: If you stay in the present, with me, I will enable you to stay in the present. As usual, love is promising here what it does not have to give.

The poem promises being through love and commands it—"Bleibe du, mein Allerliebstes"—thus disavowing and belying the temporal and spatial self-separation the poetic cycle observes elsewhere. Consonant with the self-presence imagined here, the beloved is named in the neuter. Gender division is to be overcome in the moment of pure presence. At the same time, the beloved is designated as the one who brings and delivers the gift of an indeterminate "es" (or "it"). This gift is designated (through the "Denn" ["for"] in the last line) as the very ground of the command that the beloved stay.[16]

The poem argues, then, for the coincidence of self and other, past and future, passive and active, and masculine and feminine (both in the neutral of "Allerliebstes" and in the "es" with which Goethe rhymes it). Through imperatives and conditional clauses functioning performatively as promises, the poem urges on us and presents thereby as possible what the cycle also acknowledges to be impossible. It thus induces the structure of a kind of desperate desire in the reader, evoking the tragic pathos of a subjective necessity directed against an objective impossibility. But the "Buch Suleika" doesn't simply content itself with demanding and promising a metaphorical unification of past and future on which the *Divan* also states that it cannot deliver. Rather, it argues for this unification in manifold ways, above all through the dialectical manipulation of the same structure of young and old, before and after, that is at the basis of the West-East relation as sketched above. This manipulation occurs not only in the poetry itself about Goethe's relationship with Marianne Willemer but also in the structure of his "object-choice" itself, which (as is well known) occurred when Goethe was already under the inspiring influence of Persian poetry.

Consider the structure of Goethe's relationship with Marianne Willemer, née (of all things) "Jung."[17] She was twenty-nine years old when she met Goethe, who was then sixty-five. Willemer thus plays the youthful origin of the East to his aged end of the West, and this quite explicitly, of course, since Goethe posits his persona, Hatem, as an old man, while he situates Willemer's counterpart, Suleika, as a young woman. As soon as it is given, however, this structure starts reversing itself. For example, Goethe travels westward to see Willemer; to this extent, she, the representative of the youthful Orient, already functions as the aging West. The consequence is that the connotations of youthfulness are now also bound up with the West, the connotations of age with the East.

Further, the form of the relationship between Goethe and Marianne Willemer plays a role in the reversal of their positions. Goethe's love for her constitutes the subversion of Johann Jakob Willemer, who was at once her husband and a father figure, since he had first bought her from her mother as a "foster child" and subsequently married her.[18] By undermining the husband, who is at the same time a father-figure for the girl, Goethe puts himself—regardless of his actual age—into an adolescent position, repeating the oedipal subversion of the father, like his own Werther long ago. This puts Marianne Willemer in a quasimaternal position—because Goethe is subverting the paternal figure to gain access to the maternal one—even as Goethe is in a position equivalent to Johann Jakob Willemer's, as the substitute-father turned husband (or, in Goethe's case, lover). In this scenario, Marianne Willemer is both younger and older than Goethe at once, and the reverse, enabling the structural reversal of past and future into one another in the constitution of the eternal circular moment.

But the reversal only enables the effacement of difference up to a certain point. Because difference and distance implicitly remain and always (sooner or later) reassert themselves, even when the lovers are depicted as being together in the "here and now." Let us therefore look now at one further poem in the "Book of Suleika" where the being-together of the lovers is presented, and where, furthermore, this being-together is explicitly characterized as an *Augenblick* ("moment").[19] Even here, where it is a matter of the inversion of before and after (through the exchange of gifts), and not of their geographical-cultural correlatives, not only does the repetition of the origin condition the occurrence of the origin the first time around but also this repetition must itself be infinitely repeated in order to arrive at the origin of the true *Augenblick*.[20]

J. W. Goethe (1749–1832). Steel engraving based on pastel drawing by Ferdinand Jagemann. 1817. (Bildarchiv Preussischer Kulturbesitz, Berlin/Art Resource, N.Y.)

Freude des Daseins ist groß,
Größer die Freud' am Dasein,
Wenn du, Suleika,
Mich überschwenglich beglückst,
Deine Leidenschaft mir zuwirfst,
Als wär's ein Ball,

Maria Anna (Marianne) von Willemer (1784–1860). Pastel drawing. 1819. (Bildarchiv Preussischer Kulturbesitz, Berlin/Art Resource, N.Y.)

Daß ich ihn fange,
Dir zurückwerfe
Mein gewidmetes Ich;
Das ist ein Augenblick!
Und dann reißt mich von dir
Bald der Franke, bald der Armenier.

Johann Jacob von Willemer (1760–1838). Pastel drawing. (Bildarchiv Preussischer Kulturbesitz, Berlin/Dietmar Katz (photographer)/Art Resource, N.Y.)

Aber Tage währt's,
Jahre dauert's, daß ich neu erschaffe
Tausendfältig deiner Verschwendungen Fülle,
Auftrösle die bunte Schnur meines Glücks,
Geklöppelt tausendfädig
Von dir, o Suleika.

Hier nun dagegen
Dichtrische Perlen,
Die mir deiner Leidenschaft
Gewaltige Brandung
Warf an des Lebens Verödeten Strand aus.
Mit spitzen Fingern gelesen,
Durchreiht mit juwelenem
Goldschmuck,
Nimm sie an deinen Hals,
An deinen Busen!
Die regentropfen Allahs,
Gereift in bescheidener Muschel. (70–71)

Joy of existence is great,
Greater the joy at existence,
When you, Suleika,
Give me joy in excess
When you toss your passion towards me
As if a ball,
So that I catch it,
Casting it back again
Me, my dedicate self;
That is a moment true!

And then they tear me away from you,
Now the Frank, now the Armenian.
But it takes days,
Lasts years, for me to create anew
A-thousandfold your outpouring abundance,
To unravel my fortune's bright-coloured thread,
Thousands of fibres enwoven
By you, O Suleika!

Take in exchange now
Pearls of the poet,
Born in me by the dominant
Outsurge of your passion
And cast onto the foreshore
Of my desolate existence.
With pointed fingers
Nicely selected,
With gold of the jeweler
Threaded

>   Place them upon your neck,
>   Upon your bosom!
>   The drops of rain from Allah,
>   Matured in a shell small and modest.[21]

The moment of love is that in which the "ball" of their passion—a sort of spherical globe or earth—passes between them—passion being equated with the "dedicate self" qua entirely devoted ego. The "moment" of presence in the emphatic sense arises therefore through a kind of soul exchange: Through the mutual identification of the lovers with one another that overcomes the subject-object split. But this eternal "moment" is almost immediately interrupted by the necessity of Hatem—figured as a trader—to sell his wares, in the eastern (Armenier) and western (Franke) directions at once. The moment is torn apart in the direction of the past (of the Oriental sunrise) and the future (of the Occidental sunset).

After days and years, however, the cycle of the moment is repeated. Hatem gives Suleika back the fullness of her excessive gifts to him ("deiner Verschwendungen Fülle") as the pearl jewelry of poetry about pearl jewelry. Thus the sudden moment of mutual, passionate communication is repeated, after some temporal difference, as artistic re-presentation. But the repetition is not simply a second time, a "once again." For the "moment" is not only fleeting in the sense of short or (even infinitesimally) brief. Rather the gift of the present, which circles within itself, must (always) be repeated, the first passion of Suleika must be given back to itself (always) once again, in order to be there fully at all or to have been given. Indeed, the poem as a whole (or indeed the whole of the poetic cycle), which signifies itself through the "Dichterische(n) Perlen," functions as the countergift to the original gift of Suleika's passion, as if Hatem had not already thrown his "dedicate self" ("gewidmetes Ich") back to her.

>   Hier nun dagegen
>   Dichtrische Perlen,
>   Dir mir deiner Leidenschaft
>   Gewaltige Brandung
>   Warf an des Lebens
>   Verödeten Strand aus.

If the *Augenblick* of their love constitutes itself out of her (earlier) present to him and his (later, answering) present to her, then it is always already broken into its future and its past (as the interruption by the Frank and the Armenian already suggests). Furthermore, considered as a unitary moment, as a given one, it always needs to be given back to itself once again. Representation belongs to presentation as its constitutive completion or supplement, as the belated subject constitutively belongs to the object of his own experience. A process with no end in sight.[22]

The Cupbearer's Gift

Both the macrological account of the cultural-historical passage between East and West (personalized as Goethe's poetic friendship with Hafis), and the micrological drama of the erotic passage between the younger woman and the older man remain exposed to the impossibility of their metaphysical closure. As we have seen briefly in the case of "Unbegrenzt," one of the more important ways in which Goethe figures this impossibility is in terms of rivalry. In the case of the relation between Goethe and Hafis, one will recall, the rivalry between the two poets was supposed to be one of mutual emulation. There remained some question, however, as to whether the rivalry contained the potential for violent competition, as suggested by the incompatible images of fire and water. Further elaboration on this figure of rivalry is necessary here to introduce the discussion of the "Cupbearer's Book," where Goethe develops and attempts to contain the motif of rivalry in significant ways.

In the relationship between Hatem and Suleika, the problem of the noncoincidence of youth and age (i.e., of time with itself as presence), doubled by the problem of the noncoincidence of feminine and masculine, is signaled prominently by the enduringly intrusive presence of Joseph, the young beloved of Suleika in the Jewish and Islamic versions of the story. Despite Hatem's repeated exultation (beginning with "Daß Suleika von Jussuph entzückt war" [62], the second poem in the "Buch Suleika") over his perception that Suleika has preferred him to the more physically beautiful younger man or men whom Joseph represents, Hatem remains haunted by doubts that his gifts will be returned. He fears he is not actually in a position to return the gifts bestowed upon him, and so he fears the loss of these gifts in turn. These doubts emerge in the poem that begins as follows:

> Lieb' um Liebe, Stund' um Stunde,
> Wort um Wort und Blick um Blick;
> Kuß um Kuß, vom treusten Munde,
> Hauch um Hauch und Glück um Glück.

Love for love, hour for hour,
Look for look, and kiss for kisses;
Word for word, most faithful power,
Breath for breath, and bliss for blisses.

The poem's first four lines, gathered together by their a-b-a-b rhyme scheme, turn around a series of doublings that suggest the fusion of reciprocality and sequentiality. But its last five lines rhyme c-d-c-c-d, and so hesitate, as it were, anxiously on the c-rhyme, announced by the troubling term "Morgen" in line 5. Thus formally as well as explicitly they give voice to Hatem's worries:

So am Abend, so am Morgen!
Doch du fühlst an meinen Liedern
Immer noch geheime Sorgen;
Jussuphs Reize möchte ich borgen,
Deine Schönheit zu erwidern. (71)

So each evening, so each morrow!
Yet you fell my songs implying
Ever still a secret sorrow;
Joseph's charms I'd like to borrow,
To your beauty so replying.

Time—the time that disrupts the presence of the lovers to each other and to themselves—is inscribed here through the figure of the young rival, who as the young rival also threatens Goethe's possession of poetry or culture, insofar as he recalls Hafis's status as strong predecessor (*wetteifern* was the operative word in "Unbegrenzt," however underplayed). The spacing of time implies here also the timing of space (the distance between subject and object, between lovers, uncrossed except by a time always lacking), a space that the exchange of the gift of love cannot bridge, according to the poet's fears that it will be impossible for him to "reply" or "respond" (*erwidern*), that is, to give back the young beloved's beauty.

The cycle contains not only the rivalry between Goethe and Hafis within their male friendship, as well as the competition between Hatem and Jussuph for the affections of Suleika, but also a tension between the two main relationships: male friendship (in the public cultural realm) and erotic desire between male and female (in the private sphere). The ego-libidinal desire to be the other (the wish to identify with the rival poet) and the object-libidinal desire to have the other (or to possess sexually and romantically the object of love) potentially compete for the poet's attention. Each is a rival for the other, minimally in the sense that there would be a tension between work and love. But further, the other male poets are potential rivals of Hatem for Suleika's affections, just as Suleika becomes a potential rival of Hatem for the other poets' admiration or love. Indeed, even insofar as the two functions of poet and beloved are contained within the same person—in that Marianne/Suleika is in fact a poet as well as a beloved, and their relationship a love of poetry—at one moment Hatem doubts her faithfulness because he thinks the songs she is writing him must have been written by another man, since he didn't himself send them to her (and since in terms of sexist protocols he doubts her capacity to have written them herself). The woman becomes a rival for the man in his métier (and his relationship to men and to society) and for the man as lover at the moment when she absorbs the other man or men, or the poet-lover himself, into herself. (See "Ach, Suleika, soll ich's sagen?" and her answer "War Hatem lange doch entfernt" [78–79].)

On these three levels, then, the "rival" functions as a figure for the illusory hope of solving the problem of nonpresence. According to the logic to which this hope clings: If one can only get rid of the rival, one can have and be the object of one's desire, one's chosen touchstone of presence. In turn, as long as there is a rival, one has a good, graspable reason why the given relationship is marked by a lack of being or the lack of the other. It is structurally necessary, therefore, that the rival be absorbed or domesticated, but at the same time one always needs to hold onto the image of the rival in order not to have to confront the failure of (one's) metaphysical desire, of metaphysics or desire as such, to attain its fulfillment. Goethe pursues the project of such an absorption or domestication (an elimination and maintenance—in short, a sublation or an *Aufhebung*) in the "Cupbearer's Book"—*Das Schenkenbuch*—whose very name indicates that in the cupbearer it is a question of completing the gift of presence. And just in case one hadn't noticed that this book plays a particularly pivotal role, Goethe signals its exemplary and exceptional importance by inverting the syntactical order of the book's title: whereas in all of the other books, the title has the form, "The Book of X," here the title has the form "The X-Book."

In order to approach the function of rivalry in the "Cupbearer's Book," it is necessary to consider the most important general commonality between this book and the books of Hafis and Suleika: The cupbearer functions as a guarantee of presence in the overcoming of the distinction between time (with its linear spacing) and eternity (with its temporalized space). On one level, this occurs by way of the figure of the cupbearer's gift, wine itself, qua eternal. In "Ob der Koran von Ewigkeit sei?" for example, the poet raises the old question as to whether the Koran has existed for all eternity, but the poet is unable to attain certainty on this subject. In contrast, the poet is certain about the eternity of wine, even if (and precisely because) he expresses his certainty in a playful tone:

> Daß aber der Wein von Ewigkeit sei,
> Daran zweifle ich nicht.
> Oder daß er von den Engeln geschaffen sei,
> Ist vielleicht auch kein Gedicht.
> Der Trinkende, wie es auch immer sei,
> Blickt Gott frischer ins Angesicht. (90)

> But that wine from all eternity must be
> I've no doubts of any sort.
> And that created before angels it must be
> Is perhaps no mere poetic thought.
> In the drinker's sight, however it be,
> God's countenance is more freshly caught.

Wine, whose earthly sensuality is manifest, is what links the earthly with the divine, the temporal sphere with the eternal.[23]

But Goethe makes the link between the cupbearer and eternity also more directly, in that the drunkenness the boy purveys is what revives the old man's spirits and renews his youth.

> Trunken müssen wir alle sein!
> Jugend ist Trunkenheit ohne Wein;
> Trinkt sich das Alter wieder zu Jugend,
> So ist es wundervolle Tugend.
> Für Sorgen sorgt das liebe Leben,
> Und Sorgenbrecher sind die Reben (90).[24]

> To drunkenness all of us must incline!
> Youth is drunkenness less than wine;
> Age may its youth in drinking renew,
> Wonderful virtue so to do.
> Dear life for cares enough will care,
> And the grapes will all our cares repair.

The old man becomes young by drinking, while the young man who gives the old man drink and enables his rejuvenation is always already like a drunken old man. The old and young are collapsed into one age, one moment, by means of the give-and-take of alcohol.

This reversal of ages is completed and supported by another poem, a dialogue in which the Cupbearer—here named Saki after Hafis's cupbearer—speaks, and then the poet, Hatem, answers. The becoming-aged of the boy supplements here the becoming-youthful of the poet in the previous poem. The poem begins with the boy's consideration that the explosively unguarded bearing and behavior of the older poet when drunk is puzzling, in that it evinces less wisdom than youth itself displays:

Sag' mir nur, warum die Jugend,
Noch von keinem Fehler frei,
So ermangelnd jeder Tugend,
Klüger als das Alter sei. (96)

Tell me why is youth more skillful,
Prone to every fault we're told,
Lacking virtue, still all willful,
Why's youth cleverer than the old.

When drink makes the poet young, the young boy becomes older than he: smarter, wiser, more circumspect. Hatem agrees with the boy and underlines that poetry is betrayal (*Verrat*)—presumably betrayal of oneself as well as others—and that on earth it is deception (*Trug*) even if it remains a heavenly gift (*Himmelsgabe*). "Therefore, boy most dear and pleasant, / Stay forever young and wise" (*Eben drum, geliebter Knabe, / Bleibe jung und bleibe klug*) (97). Youth contains the extremes of itself and its opposite, wisdom, in a positive unity, while age contains the extremes as nonharmonized, as difference: earthly deterioration (betrayal and loss of control) in one place and spiritual power in another. Whereas the earlier poem emphasized how age can become youth, later earlier, through the presence of wine, this poem emphasizes that youth becomes age in the absence of wine. Youth is older than age in that it attains the balanced unity of mind and body that we would normally prefer to associate with maturity. Early and late meet together in the moment of their reversal of positions, even as the reversal retains the pathos of its impossibility (here in the figure of the debility of age).

Like the Persian poet and the young beloved woman, then, the cupbearer too is inscribed in the project of attaining stable, self-identical presence in the face of internally differentiated time, space, and causality.²⁵ This inscription itself already makes the cupbearer a rival of the other two figures, even as the rivalry of early with late makes itself felt within this book (as the exchange we have just considered demonstrates). But Goethe develops the theme of rivalry in this book much more explicitly than we have yet seen. First, Goethe sets up the cupbearer, in his love for the poet/Hatem, as Suleika's competitor for the poet's affections.

> Du, mit deinen braunen Locken,
> Geh mir weg, verschmitzte Dirne!
> Schenk' ich meinem Herrn zu Danke,
> Nun, so küßt er mir die Stirne.
>
> Aber du, ich wollte wetten,
> Bist mir nicht damit zufrieden,
> Deine Wangen, deine Brüste,
> Werden meinen Freund ermüden.
>
> You, with all your tawny ringlets,
> Get away you crafty Miss!
> When I serve my master's grateful
> So for that my brow he'll kiss.
>
> But for you, I'd like to wager,
> That won't satisfy you pests,
> You will make my friend exhausted
> With your cheeks and pressing breasts.

At the poem's conclusion, indeed, the cupbearer goes so far as to threaten to lie down on the poet's threshold to prevent the woman from sneaking back later. Goethe makes Hatem's young male rival "Jussuph" unthreatening by reimagining him (even if with a slight displacement of age toward childhood) as the woman's rival for the older poet's affection.

In turn, the poet replaces, or rather supplements, the young female object of his love with the young male object, making the beautiful male potential rival into the poet's object of desirous love.²⁶ The female object cannot injure him by turning away, for example, if the poet's love is actually directed toward the boy. So although Goethe tries to keep this book within the limits of a chaste form of man-boy love, he indicates the erotic dimension of the relationship with the cupbearer sufficiently, if discreetly, through repeated allusions to kisses the poet gives the boy (e.g., in "Eben das will ich behandeln" and in "Nennen dich den großen Dichter," 94 and

95, respectively), through the employment of the explicit language of love, and through the parallel established between Suleika and the boy, as in the following poem, in which the metaphysical problematic of presence emerges with useful explicitness:

> Jene garstige Vettel,
> Die buhlerische,
> Welt heißt man sie,
> Mich hat sie betrogen
> Wie die übrigen alle.
> Glaube nahm sie mir weg,
> Dann die Hoffnung,
> Nun wollte sie
> An die Liebe,
> Da riß ich aus.
> Den geretteten Schatz
> Für ewig zu sichern,
> Teilt' ich ihn weislich
> Zwischen Suleika und Saki.
> Jedes der beiden
> Beeifert sich um die Wette,
> Höhere Zinsen zu entrichten.
> Und ich bin reicher als je:
> Den Glauben hab' ich wieder!
> An ihre Liebe den Glauben;
> Er, im Becher, gewährt mir
> Herrliches Gefühl der Gegenwart;
> Was will da die Hoffnung! (94)

> Such a horrible creature,
> And all coquettish,
> World she is called,
> Deceptions she practiced
> Like the others who join her.
> Faith she took first away,
> Then came hope's turn,
> Now she was set
> After love—
> Then I got away.
> To secure for ever
> The treasure I'd rescued
> I shared it wisely

> Between Suleika and Saki.
> Each with the other
> Is zealous in competition
> To see which one gives the highest returns.
> And I am richer by far:
> My faith has been restored me!
> Her love the faith I believe in;
> He, by the cup, offers me
> The splendid sense of the present;
> What need then for hope there!

The poet has lost faith and hope, through the years of experience, to the world figured as an old woman, who thereby becomes perhaps the principal sacrificial victim of this entire cycle, as representative of the aging of the maternal origin. Finding himself now on the point of losing love as well, the poet has wisely divided his love between Saki and Suleika, making them into rivals for each other. They must now compete for his love, giving him more and more love back. His belief in their love provides him with the "feeling of presence" such that no hope is needed (and therefore no fear can enter, assuming that Spinoza—whom Goethe of course greatly admired—is correct in claiming that fear and hope always go hand in hand).[27] Fulfilled in the eternal presence of the present moment, the poet ostensibly feels no need of the future, like a Faust who would have attained to the "Verweile doch, du bist so schön!" ("Stay, thou art so fair!") The return of faith—with which, as we saw in the discussion of "Israel in the Desert," Goethe has been concerned from the start—occurs here as based on the sensuous-spiritual love of the young woman and the young boy. The "Love-, song-, and wine-drunkenness [*Lieb-, Lied- und Weines Trunkenheit*]" (92) is what gives Goethe back his faith, and the poetic cycle thus functions as the *Aufhebung* of Judaic wandering (in faith at war with doubt) into a faith no longer disfigured by the doubt about its own presence: its own "Splendid sense of the present [*Herrliches Gefühl der Gegenwart*]" (94).

But the faith here, associated with wine as what produces the feeling of presence, is made to seem a little bit desperate, a little bit illusory, as if the poet were protesting a little bit too strongly. (If one has to be drunk to have faith—one of the possible readings of "Er, im Becher"—then how strong is one's faith?) The negativity that we saw at work in rivalry, as a figure for the impossibility of presence, makes itself felt here, even if the poet tries to hold it at bay by displacing rivalry onto the figures of Suleika and Saki.

For example, in "Heute hast du gut gegessen" (95), the cupbearer brings the poet a dessert, in the slang of the time a "Schwänchen," which word leads him to call the poet a "Schwan" ("swan") an appellation that in turn leads associatively to the consideration that the poet could be singing his swan song:

> Doch vom Singschwan will man wissen,
> Daß er sich zu Grabe läutet;
> Laß mich jedes Lied vermissen,
> Wenn es auf dein Ende deutet. (95)

> But the song-swan men distinguish
> By its song that means it dies:
> Every song I would relinquish
> If your end it signifies.

If for the poet, Goethe, such a chain of poetic associations bespeaks anxiety about aging and death, coming from the mouth of the boy, it implies an entirely unbidden thought of the poet's death. Does the boy fear the poet's death, or does he wish for it, as in infantile or oedipal aggression, especially since the poet is in love with the woman, and so on? Indeed, if the young boy expresses here (under the erasure of reaction formation) the desired subversion of the older male, clearly Goethe shares this oedipalized hostility and expresses it on a number of levels and in manifold ways (e.g., ambivalently, through his very relationship with Marianne Willemer, as considered above). In this book, he does so by elevating wine to the status of an absolute. This move—even if it follows the historical Hafis—subverts the Muslim context of the poems, that is, the Islamic (paternal) law, which forbids the consumption of alcohol. But to see how negativity persists in this book, let us look, in conclusion, at the conclusion of the book itself.

What is the status of faith in presence as the "The Cupbearer's Book" closes? What was originally the final poem of the book is titled "Sommernacht," itself a dialectical figure for the fusion of summer—the height of presence between the beginning (spring) and the end (autumn)—and night—which suggests death or absence as the negation of presence.

> Niedergangen ist die Sonne,
> Doch im Westen glänzt es immer;
> Wissen möchte ich wohl, wie lange
> Dauert noch der goldne Schimmer?

> Though the sun has now gone under
> In the West there's still a blaze;
> How long will it last, I wonder,
> All that golden gleaming haze?

The poem begins with the poet's constatation that the origin—the sun—has set, and that its light remains visible now only in the West. This suggests that the West has become the realization of the Eastern origin, has taken on the relay of the light passing from east to west. Yet the prolongation of the origin in the shimmering of twilight in the West is of uncertain duration. The presence of the West is threatened already by its disappearance, by the inevitable passage of time. Realization and death go hand in hand as end and end.

The poem then goes on to propose a potential consolation in the face of this inevitable loss, in the form of what the boy says he has learned from the older poet. Speaking of the stars that are starting to come out, the boy says:

> Und das hellste will nur sagen:
> Jetzo glänz' ich meiner Stelle;
> Wollte Gott euch mehr betagen,
> Glänztet ihr wie ich so helle.
>
> Denn vor Gott ist alles herrlich,
> Eben weil er ist der Beste;
> Und so schläft nun aller Vogel
> In dem groß- und kleinen Neste. (97–98)
>
> And the brightest one is telling:
> "Now I'm shining appositely;
> With more light of God indwelling
> You would shine like me so brightly."
> For in God all things are splendours
> Just because he can't be bested;
> And we see now each bird slumbers
> In its large and small bed nested.

In line with the emphasis throughout on the notion of Islam as "devotion [*Ergebenheit*]" and *amor fati*, and also in line with a conservative tendency to rationalize injustice, this message functions above all as an answer to the anxiety of disappearance, the sense of finitude. Accept your place in things: Everything has its time and place. But this turns out not to be quite so easy, according to the poet's answer to the young boy. For whereas the boy tries to arrange a meeting with the poet at midnight (the time when the dying of the day circles back into its being reborn), in a kind of spiritual vigil beneath the stars, the poet explains that this is not possible and gives the boy different advice.

There can be no consoling meeting beneath the stars, because the dawn is coming to steal night away before it fully occurs, a dawn that is by no means merely benevolent. Rather, she—figured as Aurora here—threatens to seduce the boy, to steal his beauty. Time leaps ahead of itself such that the morning overtakes the night in order to annihilate youthful beauty. No place is secure from deadly differentiation—not even the night (despite the tradition of a certain counterrational fantasy that runs from the Novalis of *Hymns to Night* through the Wagner of *Tristan*, and so on). And nothing, not even the dawn (as privileged figure of origin), is completely devoid of the negative connotations of the erosion or loss of originariness (here, as the boy's youthful beauty). Hence, the poet advises the boy to go inside, and by implication deep inside himself, in order to hide from the dawn qua ravaging effects of time:

> Geh nur, lieblichster der Söhne,
> Tief ins Innre, schließ die Türen;
> Denn sie [aurora] möchte deine Schöne
> Als den Hesperus entführen. (99)

> Dearest son of all, retire
> Deep within, draw bolts across!
> With your beauty she'd desire
> You instead of Hesperos.

To hide within—that is, within the subjective space of interiority—in order to escape the objectively necessary seduction of time is a far cry from establishing a harmonious synthesis of outward and inward in an aesthetic transcendence of time, space, and causality. Moreover, for the man to be warning the boy against the woman, perhaps jealously, is a far cry from the goal of equipoise in the present, sovereign peace and calm. The poet is afraid of losing the boy as he is afraid of losing himself.

Rather than close the book on this note, Goethe added in the 1827 edition a pair of short poems, in which the boy speaks of having received, in conjunction with the poet's love, the perception of God's presence (*Gottes Gegenwart*) (99) in all elements. (This would imply a reconciliation, for example, between the fire and water whose relationship of tension was noted above with respect to the Goethe-Hafis relationship.) The boy then goes to sleep, and the poet/Hatem, meditating gratefully on what the boy has given him in turn, watches over the boy's sleep, which (we are told) will renew him. The fear of the boy's ravagement by time is thus replaced (or supplemented, or covered over) in this new ending by the peaceful vision of the sleep (or death) that enables his reinvigoration.

> Ich trinke noch, bin aber stille, stille,
> Damit du mich erwachend nicht erfreust. (99)
>
> I'm drinking on, but I am still, quite still,
> To keep me from the wakening joy of you.

The syntactically confusing last line clearly means (principally): "So that you do not give me the pleasure of awakening" (as in "damit du mich nicht, erwachend, erfreust"). Hatem here selflessly renounces his pleasure in the boy's company by letting him get the sleep he needs. But if we read the lines as saying, "So that you, by not awakening, give me pleasure" (as in "damit du mich, erwachend nicht, erfreust"), while they still say that Hatem is glad that the boy is sleeping, they now say also that Hatem takes pleasure in the boy's failure to awaken, rather than that he takes no pleasure in the boy's failure to awaken. But for Hatem to take pleasure in the boy's failure to awaken is for him to take pleasure in something that resembles the boy's death. (Hatem thus becomes the occasion for the return of an echo from the "Erlkönig.") The hostility of the boy toward the man is here very subtly answered by the man's figural (or unconscious or near) hostility toward the boy, despite the fact that the addition of these poems is evidently meant to cover over the fear of the boy's destruction (a fear that, itself, can be read also as the cover-up of a desire). The tension, in short, between early and late, before and after, reemerges here in the silence of the old man's vigil—or should we call it a wake?—over the boy's sleep. The tension between love and hate, positivity and negativity, faith and doubt, presence and its spatiotemporal and active-passive disarticulation—a tension that troubled Goethe in the Old Testament and rendered its narrative for him abyssal, "unpleasant and bothersome" ("unlustig und verdrießlich")—sustains itself throughout the *Divan*. If the poems try—time after time—to reassert that "everything has its time," the pathos that sustains them consists in the fact that they never quite manage to erase the inversion of this principle: time, and hence also space and the abyssal disjunction between spontaneity and receptivity, possess (and dispossess) everything in turn.

Excursus: Jussuph and the Question of Anti-Semitism in Goethe

A final, retrospective elaboration on the figure of Jussuph is necessary here, with mild apologies to generations of uncritical admirers of Goethe the world over. In the developments beginning with "Lieb' um Liebe, Stund' um Stunde," the figure of the younger rival signifies not just the possibility that the younger man could come between Hatem and Suleika, nor merely the problem of presence to which this possibility can be reduced. In addition, the younger rival recalls Judaism, the annoying predecessor, as becomes clear when Hatem's jealous worries about Jussuph's charms become the significant occasion for an anti-Semitic witticism on Goethe's part, a kind of disdainful swipe at the nonaesthetic Jews, one of very few remarks of its type in the *Divan* cycle, which is therefore worthy of some analysis.[28] This witticism prompts us to note that the figure of the youthful rival evokes and involves Goethe's ambivalence, as Christian subject, toward the Jewish tradition, an ambivalence that includes both certain implicit analogies and certain unbridgeable distinctions that can and must be drawn between this tradition and Goethe's own position.

Who, to begin with, is Jussuph, and especially at the moment when he fails to be recognized any longer by Pharaoh (the point at which Goethe began his investigation of the Old Testament in "Notes and Treatises")? First of all, he is the foreigner, the outsider, who has gained not only acceptance but great prominence as an assistant to the ruler of the native population. As the bourgeois outsider who has gained for himself something of the authority of an aristocrat among aristocrats, Goethe has every reason to identify with Jussuph's position, and perhaps to fear a common fate (in the sense of the cessation or withdrawal of recognition by the authorities). His—that is, Hatem's—rivalry with Jussuph is overdetermined in this sense as a rivalry with himself.

Furthermore, Jussuph is the interpreter of the dreams of the others, especially of those with whom he lives. Certainly, as the writer, Goethe is not just a dreamer but even more someone who gives meaning to the dreams (the unconscious desires, unspoken experiences, and so on) of his supporters and audience. In the *Divan* project (and especially in the "Notes and Treatises"), he could be said to be interpreting the dreams of the East.

Hence, he is a kind of dream-reader. This provides us with another parallel between his position and Jussuph's, another reason Goethe would have to be anxious about Jussuph's fate, and another reason why Goethe would want to disidentify with Jussuph (because he doesn't want to end up as the figure of the no-longer-recognized).

But to take this last point one step further, the interpreter of dreams is also the one who realizes or fulfills the prefigurations of others, insofar as he makes literal meaning out of the obscure figures of their imaginings. In this sense, Jussuph represents the Christian tradition, in which Goethe partly participates, as we saw above in the discussion of his biblical scholarship on the Israelites' wanderings. But Jussuph prefigures this Christian tradition from what is (from a Christian standpoint) arguably the wrong position. The Jew is not supposed to be the one who reads the gentiles' dreams. Rather, the Christian must read and master the Jew's dreams. Here, however, the Jewish prefiguration reads its Christian fulfillment, that is, its non-Jewish other. For even if, to be sure, the Egyptians are not supposed (from a Christian point of view) to anticipate the Christians, still the ("Egyptian") anxiety of the German-Europeans about the Jews living in their midst, and this in the early part of the age of Jewish "emancipation," is not to be missed when Goethe speaks in "Israel in der Wüste" about the brutal aggressivity of Moses and the tribe from which he comes, and about the uprising of the Israelites against the Egyptians: "The foreigner murders the native, the guest his host, and led by a cruel politics, one murders only the first-born" (212). The ancient proto-Jews appear as warlike and ungrateful guests who murder their hosts. Evidently, Christianity should take heed, lest it be mastered by its slave, even if its slave is dangerous principally in the form of the letter of language. But then again, the ungrateful guests (Jussuph and the others) here are also, as I've just indicated, in a position with which Goethe can identity in more than one way. The question raised by the identification, however, is whether one is absorbed, consumed by the other (in that he speaks and represents one's own truth) or the other way around (so that one becomes his actual realization). And Jussuph threatens to absorb Goethe (his authorial ground) in multiple senses. Figural interpretation is a question of survival, of the life and death of one's self-identity.

This is the situation that leads to Goethe's little anti-Semitic witticism two poems further on in the cycle. Given the complex combination of identification and disidentification between Goethe and the figure of Jussuph (and we haven't even considered the position of Jussuph as seducer) in the context of the tension between Jussuph (as Jewish dream-reader) and Christianity (as an interpretation of Jewish dreams), the course taken by Hatem's dialogue with Suleika immediately after the poem discussed above in which he expresses his desire to borrow the charms of Jussuph is not entirely surprising.

Suleika responds to the expression of this desire to borrow Jussuph's charms by saying that self-possession, which she also calls "die Persönlichkeit" (71), is the most important thing for human happiness. "One can lose everything, as long as one remains what one is" (*Alles könne man verlieren / Wenn man bliebe, was man ist*) (71). On the one hand, Goethe evidently agrees with this insofar as he has tried to save Moses' honor by reducing the latter's actions to his "Persönlichkeit," as to his (super)natural foundation, in the "Notes and Treatises." On the other hand, the desire to remain oneself is a desire that the poetic cycle problematizes in terms of time and change, separation from external context, and so on. Moreover, Goethe's/Hatem's essence, his value based on his self-sameness, is placed in doubt by the very figure of Jussuph. Hatem replies, in an evasion that transforms abjection into sovereignty, that his happiness is in Suleika, and in her way of expending herself on him. "If she ever turned away, that very moment I'd lose myself" (*Hätte sie sich weggewendet, / Augenblicks verlör' ich mich*) (72). The (eternal) moment would be lost to the (radically temporal, disappearing) moment in the (temporally disappearing, but decisive) moment in which she would turn away, like God turning his face away, according to the common scriptural image. Yet Hatem finds a way of imaginatively overcoming the potential loss of Suleika: He will simply "embody himself in the dear one, whom she caresses" (72). And this is where the anti-Semitic witticism appears:

> Wollte, wo nicht gar ein Rabbi,
> Das will mir so recht nicht ein,
> Doch Ferdusi, Motanabbi,
> Allenfalls der Kaiser sein. (72)
>
> I'd become, well not a Rabbi,
> That role's really not my best,
> But Ferdusi, Motanabbi,
> Or the emperor if pressed.

He would be willing to imagine himself, then, into the identity of anyone she might choose to love, for example a Persian poet, either the first great one (Ferdusi), or a poetic rival of Mohammed (Motannabi), who claimed to have said everything the prophet did, but to have said it more perfectly (that is, to have realized the prophet's prefigurations). Or to be the emperor would do. But what one would never like to be—the laughable as such—is a rabbi. One could consent to be an Oriental, even an Arab, indeed any rival at all—"the beloved, whom she caresses" (*den Holden, den sie kost*)—but not under any circumstance a Jew, not even a learned or honorable one. So why this sudden gesture of hostility toward the Jews, on the level of a relatively base form of offhand humor? Or how is it (over)determined, beyond the general anticlerical stance of Goethe, which does not fully account for it by any means?

We can interpret the gesture readily in terms of its appearance in the context of an anxiety toward youth, that is, toward what is earlier, an anxiety that is doubled by an anxiety toward what comes later. (Today's youth arrives later than today's aged, and to have come too soon, or to be now already too old, is to be—like the Jews in the negative sense—in the position of having been superseded.) In context, as we have seen, these anxieties are focused on the figure of Jussuph, who is—in more than one respect—an uncannily unapproachable or unachievable double of Goethe himself here. Goethe wants to avoid being like the Jew, who comes always either too early or too late. Yet he can and must identify with this position, both because he is like Jussuph in various respects, and because (as the cycle keeps showing) everyone is always too early and too late with respect to himself or herself, at all moments. For the only way of being on time—fully present—is to synthesize the positions of early and late. But this fusion can never occur, because neither of these positions is sufficiently self-identical to allow of its fusion with the other. Hence, Goethe rejects identification with the Jew because the Jew, in Goethe's (still Christian) discourse, represents the splitting of the present from itself into a "too early" and "too late": the obstacle to the fulfilled moment.

However, Goethe not only resembles but in certain respects wants to resemble, if not the rabbi, then what the rabbi is. For as Goethe shares certain traits with Jussuph, he also shares certain traits with a rabbi, and indeed he wants to possess these traits: He aspires to be the one who can teach us about, and who can master, the ancient Oriental texts, which are (by his own argument in "Israel in the Desert") always versions, as it were, of the Old Testament. In order to avoid this position, Goethe makes Jussuph the object of his rivalrous identification throughout the collection (as if to say: No, I am not he, I am not that!), and all the more insofar as the poet is positioned as seducer from "Hegire" on. To have chosen Jussuph instead of Moses as one's rival, moreover, puts Goethe once again at a distance from the rabbis, since if the rabbis themselves have a main rival, it is Moses himself, whose legislative activity they could be said to try to complete and outdo.

Finally, Goethe counts on his reader's, "our" everyday anti-Semitism to confirm the self-evidence of this "witty" gesture—*wo nicht gar ein Rabbi, / Das will mir so recht nicht ein*—through which he disavows his nonpresence, sacrificially putting the Jews in the position of the nonpresent (as the "too early" and "too late," as well as the splitting of body and spirit off from each other into dead letter and monotheistic God). In this expectation, Hatem's rivalry with Jussuph gives expression to Goethe's convoluted residual anxieties about Judaism as predecessor of Christianity.

The (W)hole Picture

As we have seen, Goethe's attempt to fill the void of absolute foundations—above all the threat of a vanished eternal presence—still makes use of typological arguments, but does so in a way that diverges from the more unambiguously teleological narratives of, for example, Herder and Schlegel. Goethe's application of typological patterns has two main aspects. First, as we saw in chapter 3, Goethe posits that his own Orientalist poetic experimentation, his own wanderings among Oriental materials, constitute the realization of the Christian realization of the Jewish source, which he understands as an essentially Oriental one. Goethe's occasional anti-Semitic remarks make clear that this claim to overcome Jewish temporal discontinuity, as discontinuity tout court, remains incompletely self-assured.

Second, within the poetic experimentation of the *West-East Divan* cycle, Goethe uses figural logic in both directions at once: to position the Orient as anticipation of the Occident, and vice versa. This double application of figural logic constitutes a poetic demonstration of an eternal moment of aesthetic fullness that combines cultural-political and erotic dimensions through homologies developed between these dimensions. By regarding with some suspicion the chiasmic structures that structure the eternal moment in the *West-East Divan*, we have discerned in Goethe an exacerbated tension. On the one hand, he generates aesthetic rhetorical artifacts that claim to fill the void of the moment by resisting its self-dispersion into futurity and pastness. On the other hand, albeit in an apparently inadvertent manner, he thematizes the very ineluctability of that void. This tension indicates the center and limits of his contribution to the German literary and philosophical encounter with non-Western cultures in his age. As we move to Hegel's philosophy of history, we will see similar anxieties with regard to the temporal rift that the Jews represent in Christianity as anticipatorily belated, but now in the context of an explicitly teleological program and in connection with ancient Indian and related figures of the origins of human civilizational history.

CHAPTER 5

Thresholds of History: India and the Limits of Europe in Hegel's *Lectures on the Philosophy of History*

> A Brahman may or must kill the chandala who would come too close to him and could stain him by touching him [*der ihm zu nahe käme und ihn durch Berührung beflecken könnte*].
>
> —G. W. F. HEGEL, "Über die unter dem Namen Bhagavad-Gita bekannte Episode des Mahabharata: Von Wilhelm von Humboldt"

> If thought [*das Denken*] is only true insofar as it is concrete within itself, then its characteristic determination is that pure universality, simple identity; the yogi, who sits there, inwardly and outwardly unmoved, and stares at the end of his nose, is that thought which has been violently held still and intensified to the point of empty abstraction. Such a condition, however, is for us a thoroughly foreign thing, a beyond [*ein durchaus Fremdartiges und Jenseitiges*], and would be brought much too close to us through the expression "thought," which is something very familiar in our minds [*würde uns durch den Ausdruck des Denkens, als welches uns in unserer Vorstellung etwas ganz Geläufiges ist, viel zu nahe gelegt*].
>
> —G. W. F. HEGEL, "Über die unter dem Namen Bhagavad-Gita bekannte Episode des Mahabharata: Von Wilhelm von Humboldt"

> The task of apprehension becomes at once all the more difficult, not so much because of a thorough difference of the Indian way of thinking from our own, as rather because this way of thinking communicates with the highest concepts of our consciousness [*weil sie in die höchsten Begriffe unseres Bewusstseins eingreift*], but in the wondrous depths, without being divided within itself, falls into the most degrading.
>
> —G. W. F. HEGEL, "Über die unter dem Namen Bhagavad-Gita bekannte Episode des Mahabharata: Von Wilhelm von Humboldt"

In the midst of this confusion the spiritual God of the Jews arrests our attention—like Brahma, existing only for thought, yet jeal-

> ous and excluding from his being and sublating all specificity of
> difference allowed freedom in other religions.
>
> —G. W. F. HEGEL, *"Vorlesungen über die Philosophie der Geschichte"*

According to a very simple but still far-reaching observation of Jacques Derrida's, the consequences of which he never tired of unfolding, with admirable if sometimes maddening tenacity: Any bordering frame that delimits an inside from an outside belongs simultaneously to both inside and outside, since it must be outside the inside and inside the outside.[1] The border is thus also inside and outside of itself; it is its own inside and outside borders. Moreover, each of these inside and outside borders of the bordering frame is constituted in turn ad infinitum by this self-displacing structure.

The understanding of this (il)logic or ill logic of the bordering frame—whereby it multiplies and crosses through itself, never entirely managing to be self-same—is crucial to an understanding of typology. As soon as one has formed the project of defining the human as spirit that has entirely liberated itself from matter—an anthropology that all typological metaphysics seems to share—the structure of the border produces the instability that typology is both meant to, and can never, resolve into a stable solution.[2] How is this the case?

Consider again in this context that typology in its most general form construes the passage—that is, the border—between matter and spirit as a tripartite structural process, from *littera* to *figura* to *veritas*, or preprefiguration to prefiguration to fulfillment, or—in the pre-Reformation mode—from pagan to Jewish to Christian, as from referent to signifier to signified. The middle term—figura, prefiguration, the Jew, or the signifier (as "dead letter" of the law)—functions as the border, limit, or threshold between the other two. It is the mediation that is supposed to separate them and hold them in relation to each other, such that a passage from one to the other can occur. But not a passage backward nor a precipitation forward, for either of these would signify the conflation of the one term with the other. The middle term in our example—in early Christian and medieval discourses this position is occupied by the Jewish border between pagan and Christian—is inside the pagan and outside the Christian. Hence, its overcoming of pagan materiality is incomplete. But the Jewish border is also inside the Christian and outside the pagan. Thus, it is taken to broach an overcoming of the pagan. The passage from pagan to Christian cannot do without this middle term, but the middle term always threatens the passage with breakdown or undoing. The Jew (along with various conventional translations as "dead letter" and so on) represents accordingly the threat of contagion and confusion of identities—Christians coming to seem pagans, pagans seeming Christians. This threat has appeared in many guises throughout the history of Christian (and for that matter pagan or secular) anti-Judaism. In sum: The structure of the mediating border as condition of the (im)possibility of the passage from one term to its complementary overcoming (most generally, from matter to spirit) belongs constitutively to all adaptations of typological thinking, including modern Orientalism. It does not belong merely to the medieval Christian construal of Christianity's relation to pagan and Jewish religious cultures. In every case, the border must be excluded from the spiritual term, even as this exclusion places it on the inside of the material term, outside of which it must remain in order to continue to function as the border between the material and the spiritual. If the border of the spiritual is not excluded from the spiritual, then it will exclude the spiritual from the spiritual itself. This untenable structure condemns typological thinking to an instability it can never master except by denial.

India as Prefigural Limit of History

In this chapter, I examine the structurally determined recalcitrance (or uncontrollability) of the mediating border in the grandiose expansion of typological thinking that is Hegel's *Lectures on the Philosophy of History*.[3] While considering the typological play of the border across the structure of Hegel's narrative of world history as a whole, I give special attention, as befits my theme, to his treatment of the "Oriental World." Within that world, I focus on the culture of ancient India in connection with that of ancient Judaea, both of which cultures play for Hegel particularly important (and problematically interrelated) mediating roles. I examine how and why Hegel tries to keep India (which he positions as the essentially Oriental limit between Orient and Occident) at bay. The complex situation of India simultaneously as center of the Orient and as threshold between Orient and Occident, I argue, is analogous in Hegel's text to the position of Judaism with respect to the pagan and the Christian worlds, and creates anxiety or panic in Hegel for analogous reasons. Jews are always more pagan—that is, even worse than pagans—because they pretend (and even seem) to have overcome the pagan position. Similarly, India introduces for Hegel the negativity of the material, the radically *prehistorical* (and non-Western), into the space of the historical (the Western).⁴ Because the border that mediates between Orient and Occident not only holds them apart but also draws them together into an uncanny identity, this line must function in Hegel as an object of extraordinary hostility.

The reason for which India—rather than any other Oriental culture, for example—has to play this role in Hegel's account is that, in this period, Sanskrit culture has come to provide, as this border, the very language—a dead language—from which the Western languages grow. In this respect, Sanskrit culture functions here like Judaism, which similarly provided the "dead letter" from which the spirit of Christianity was to have grown. The "dead letter" is the border because it broaches a language that exceeds pagan silence, or the mere noise of nature, without, however, arriving at the meaningfulness of a spirit that goes beyond natural materiality.

To further complicate matters, in Hegel these narratives—the Christian and the Orientalist—are articulated together, as we shall see below, not only metaphorically (by resemblance) but also metonymically. Judaism is placed within the Oriental origin, at its end (at least from one perspective), quasi-adjacent to ancient India, within the Persian Empire, and more precisely as the point of passage from the Oriental origin to the Occidental, Christian end. Although it comes after India in the historical sequence, however, it repeats significantly India's fate, whereby Hegel displaces what he has positioned as the break (or passage or limit) between East and West into the lesser position of the mere anticipation of such a break. Having considered the prefigural positions of India and Judaea with respect to the Occident as the realm of history, I complete the argumentative trajectory of this chapter by examining—with a view to the functioning of the limit at history's end—the repetitions of this Oriental prefiguration in its fulfillment as Western modernity, including the role of Islam in this fulfillment.

Before developing this argument, and within the context of this book, it is important to see at the outset how Hegel's aggressive polemic against ancient India is related to the general approaches to India taken by the other main authors considered thus far, especially Friedrich Schlegel. In particular, Hegel's attitude is overdetermined negatively by the enthusiasm for India common among the early romantics.⁵ Yet although he wants to situate India differently from the romantics, Hegel nonetheless has to take as his point of departure the historical linguistics they broach. His rejection of romantic Indomania, therefore, has to be carefully qualified, and his strategy has to involve subtle acknowledgments of the romantics' achievements.

To be sure, Hegel will tend to want to reject what his romantic adversaries idealize. These adversaries indeed prominently include Friedrich Schlegel, against whose *Über die Sprache und Weisheit der Indier* from 1808 Hegel explicitly polemicizes on more than one occasion. But as Dorothy Figueira has usefully recalled, they include also August Wilhelm Schlegel, whose Latin translation of the Bhagavad Gita appeared alongside the original in 1823; and even more important, Wilhelm von Humboldt, to whose addresses of 1815–16 (which defend both the Bhagavad Gita and A. W. Schlegel's translation) Hegel himself responds quite negatively, even if cordially, in a long review article published in 1827.[6] In distinction to the romantics, Hegel chooses to privilege Persia among the various Oriental cultures that present themselves to his view as candidates for the role of a positive Eastern origin of the West. He thereby places himself in a heterogeneous tradition that extends from Lessing to Goethe to Nietzsche's *Also Sprach Zarathustra*.

But Hegel's polemical treatment of ancient India does not constitute merely a blanket rejection of what his opponents, especially neo-Catholic romantics, hold in high esteem. After all, for example, Friedrich Schlegel ended up taking his distance from Sanskrit culture precisely in the name of his turn to Catholicism. Hegel could therefore easily have opposed Schlegel by promoting ancient Indian culture with respect to Christianity (as Schopenhauer does—see chapter 6). Rather, the key point is that by Hegel's time Friedrich Schlegel and subsequent philology had established as seemingly beyond question the importance of Sanskrit culture and especially Sanskrit language in the origination of the West out of the Orient. It is this incontestable elevation of Sanskrit (or at the very least of the Indo-Germanic predecessor to which it points) as linguistic origin that requires Hegel to struggle with the status of ancient India as limit or threshold of the West, as the new dead letter (or dead language) of the Western spirit. (And indeed, as we saw, Friedrich Schlegel had already positioned Indian culture as a prefiguration of the Western, Jewish, and then Christian heritage.)[7] In order to trace the implications of this struggle for Hegel's *Lectures*, I begin by reviewing the overarching structure of Hegel's narrative, specifically with a view to its typological schematization.

Typology as Organizing Structure of Hegel's Philosophy of History

As is neither surprising—in light of the preceding chapters, at least—nor to my knowledge generally appreciated in its significance, Hegel structures the course of human history as a grand series of interlocking typological steps. To attend to these steps is to become aware not only that Hegelian dialectics is typological, but that typology is "always already" dialectical. That is, it as it were anticipates dialectics. The triadic structures of typology are in evidence in the *Lectures on the Philosophy of History* on several homologous levels.

First, the prehistorical, absolutely nonhistorical realm—Africa (as well as the Native American cultures of the "New World," to which I return below)—functions as a kind of ultrapagan materiality. Hegel's racism is such as to prevent Africa from constituting what counts for him as a world at all. African "fetishism" is unredeemed (120–29; 91–99).[8] The overcoming of this materiality is prefigured then in the Oriental, Greek, and Roman cultures or worlds taken as a whole. And the fulfillment of this overcoming arrives with the development of the Christian, Germanic world. Hegel makes this structure explicit in the final section, where he argues that each phase of the Germanic world recapitulates one of the three worlds—Oriental, Greek, and Roman—that preceded it.[9]

Second, as the first point implies, the prefiguration comprises an anticipatory three-step passage from matter to spirit. The Orient functions on this level as a belated figure of the radical materiality of prehistory (or its repetition); Greece (pre)figures the overcoming of this materiality; and Rome realizes it, by achieving the passage to Christianity.

Third, because the Orient constitutes the point of departure for the overcoming of prehistory, whereas (according to some of Hegel's indications) the first truly historical, spiritual nation is ancient Greece, the Orient functions alone as the prefiguration of historicity, that is, of the overcoming of African materiality.[10] From this perspective, Greece and the subsequent empires (Rome and the Germanic, Christian world) function as its three-step realization—the West in its internal self-unfolding. The Orient is the not-yet but somehow (almost) already there of history, its complex beginning.

Finally, each of the three pre-Germanic worlds enacts within itself (like the Germanic world itself) a passage from *littera* to *figura* to *veritas*. In the Oriental world, which for Hegel comprises China, India, and Persia (in that order), India is situated in the position of the prefiguration. India therefore resonates with the position of the Jews in Christian culture (as well as with the Catholic position with respect to Protestant culture); as such, it unsettles Hegel's discourse.

Emancipatory Narrative as Theodicy

Before returning to consider more concretely the position of the Orient within this typologically overdetermined narrative, I wish to recall briefly some of the main conceptual—and more specifically political-theological—terms that organize it, insofar as the position of the Orient depends on these terms. First, Hegel understands world history as the "progress in the consciousness of freedom—a progress we need to know in its necessity" (*Die Weltgeschichte ist der Fortschritt im Bewußtsein der Freiheit—ein Fortschritt, den wir in seiner Notwendigkeit zu erkennen haben*) (32; 19, trans. modified). This progress is a progress in real freedom, as well as a development of consciousness (from the consciousness of an object, to self-consciousness, to the overcoming of the distinction between consciousness of an object and consciousness of self in absolute knowing), and an increasing liberation of consciousness itself (namely from an external object). As he tells us toward the end of the book, in a striking, indeed shocking and laughable formulation: "Man is not free when he does not think, for he relates himself then to an Other" (*Der Mensch ist nicht frei, wenn er nicht denkt, denn er verhält sich dann zu einem Anderen*) (521; 439, trans. modified). The course of history will take us from thoughtless immersion in materiality to the thinking that constitutes an uninterrupted spiritual domination of materiality, even as this domination involves a kind of acceptance.[11] For "as the essence of Matter is Gravity, so, on the other hand, the substance, the essence of Spirit is freedom" (30; 17, trans. modified).

Second, the philosophy of history constitutes for Hegel—and here he follows in the wake of Herder, to whom he, however, gives little credit—nothing less than an achieved theodicy.

> Our mode of treating the subject is, in this aspect, a Theodicy [*eine Theodizee*]—a justification of the ways of God—which Leibniz attempted metaphysically, in his method, i.e., in indefinite abstract categories—so that the ill that is found in the World may be comprehended, and the thinking Spirit reconciled with the fact of the existence of evil [*das Übel in der Welt begriffen, der denkende Geist mit dem Bösen versöhnt werden sollte*]. . . . This reconciliation can be attained only by recognizing the positive existence, in which that negative element is a subordinate, and vanquished nullity [*Diese Aussöhnung kann nur durch die Erkenntnis des Affirmativen erreicht werden, in welchem jenes Negative zu einem Untergeordneten und Überwundenen verschwindet*]. On the one hand, the ultimate design [*Endzweck*] of the World must be perceived, and on the other hand, the fact that this design has been actually realized in it [*in ihr verwirklicht worden sei*],

and that evil has not been able permanently to assert a competing position [*nicht das Böse neben ihm sich letztlich geltend gemacht habe*]. (28; 15–16)

God is justified by means of the demonstration of the "cunning of reason," and teleology accomplishes theodicy, on condition that one actually demonstrate this teleology in its realization from phase to phase across the main periods of history.[12] Accordingly, history is nothing less than the work of God, as Hegel reiterates in the final words of the *Lectures*:

> That the History of the World, with all the changing scenes which its annals present, is this process of development and the realization of Spirit—this is the true Theodicy, the justification of God in History. Only *this* insight can reconcile Spirit with the History of the World—viz., that what has happened, and is happening every day, is not only not "without God," but is essentially his Work. (540; 457)

The work of history is the work of spirit as God's work. Letter and spirit achieve their sublation into spirit in and as the course of history itself. History as work is God's freely self-given project.

Third, the progress of spirit toward freedom as God's work is to be grasped, according to Hegel, as a linear political-theological history of reigning cultural empires, empires whose main traits are legible in their state forms (their modalities of law-governed freedom) and in the religious formations that found these forms. The consequence of this position for the beginning (and end) of history is that where there is no state or religion properly so-called, neither is there history. Hegel's reasoning goes as follows. Freedom can develop itself only in or as the will, but the will is initially divided into a merely subjective will and a rational will. Only when the subjective and rational wills coincide to some extent can there be the beginning of a history. These wills coincide, however, only where there is an ethical whole. Such an ethical whole is for Hegel nothing other than the state.

> The subjective will has also a substantial life—a reality—in which it moves in the region of *essential* being [*im wesentlichen bewegt*], and has the essential itself as the object of its existence [*und das Wesentliche selbst zum Zwecke seines Daseins hat*]. This essential being [*Dieses Wesentliche*] is the union of the *subjective* with the *rational* Will: it is the moral whole, the State [*das sittliche Ganze, der Staat*], which is that form of reality in which the individual has and enjoys his freedom; but on the condition of his recognizing, believing in, and willing that which is common to the Whole.... In the history of the World, only those peoples can come under our notice which form a State. (55, 56; 38, 39)

G. W. F. Hegel (1770–1831). In his office. Color lithograph after a lost painting by Ludwig Sebbers. (Bildarchiv Preussischer Kulturbesitz, Berlin/Dietmar Katz (photographer)/Art Resource, N.Y.)

But the state, in turn, has its foundation in religion: "The State is the divine Idea as it exists on earth" (*die göttliche Idee, wie sie auf Erden vorhanden ist*) (57; 39). Religion is the "sphere in which a nation gives itself the definition of that which it regards as the True" (70; 50), a definition that becomes the foundation of the ethical whole that is the state. For in Hegel's view, worldly existence, as the temporal sphere, can gain legitimacy only if it is seen as an aspect of God, or part of God. "On this account it is that the State rests on religion" (70; 51). Or again: "The form of religion . . . decides that of the State and its constitution" (71; 51). The history of humanity, then, will proceed above all as a history of the interrelationships between state and religion in different cultural empires. The determination of the limits of history, its start and finish, will depend on the clarification of the start and finish of religion, and therefore also of the state. For only in the state, which is always at bottom a religious state, is freedom possible.

Excursus: The History of Panic— Angst- und Notgeschrei

But what if the state appears *not* to be founded on religion? What if the ground of the state seems to have fled? Strikingly, Hegel goes on, in the context we are considering (the introduction to the *Lectures*), immediately to consider in precisely such terms a certain worry present in his own day. Here, he indicates only, using an ambiguous subjunctive, that such a worry "would be" a very bad sign. A certain anxiety or panicky feeling is palpable as the background of Hegel's own emphatic claim that state-church unity has been perfectly achieved in the Lutheran Protestantism of modern Germany.

> If that outcry—that urging and striving for the implantation of Religion in the community—were an utterance of anguish and a call for help [*ein Angst- und Notgeschrei*] as it often seems to be, expressing the danger of religion having vanished, or being about to vanish entirely from the State—that would be fearful indeed—worse, in fact, than this outcry supposes [*so wäre das schlimm, und schlimmer selbst, as jener Angstruf meint*]; for it implies the belief in a resource against the evil, viz., the implantation and inculcation [*Einpflanzen und Inkulkieren*] of religion; whereas religion is by no means a thing to be so produced; its *self-production* (and there can be no other) lies much deeper. (71; 51–52)

To make matters worse, Hegel goes on immediately to polemicize against Catholicism for trying to separate religion from the state, an attempt he characterizes as "another and opposite folly which we meet with in our time" (71; 52).[13] Without the interpenetration of religion and state such as occurs in Protestantism the state would remain in abstraction and indefiniteness (*Abstraktion und Unbestimmtheit*) (72; 52). Thus Hegel finds himself face to face with the double danger of either assuming that the state has (currently) no foundation in religion or proposing that the state should have no foundation in religion. In either case, the danger of a state (i.e., an ethical totality) that is lacking transcendent foundations looms threateningly. And Hegel places his response to this situation into relation with a certain "Angst- und Notgeschrei"—a cry of anxiety or panic. We must not panic; we must not imagine that the state lacks a religious foundation, Hegel cries out, for I will not inculcate religion (*Inkulkieren* is Hegel's word), I will simply show that it inculcates itself! Hegel's philosophy of history—as the demonstration of the unity of state and religion in German Protestantism qua result and goal of universal history—appears thus as an attempt to conjure away this danger of groundlessness and its attendant anxiety, an anxiety faced with an abstract and indefinite world.

In order to strengthen this suggestion, before considering the Oriental world—which in Hegel bears precisely and explicitly the traits of such abstraction and indefiniteness—I would like to point to one further context in the *Lectures* where Hegel approaches the anxiety we have just glimpsed. This will enable us to see how panic explicitly enters into Hegel's text and to entertain the possibility that in thus discussing panic Hegel provides us with a useful frame for his own affect in relation to the abyssal passage(s)— and lack thereof—between the material and the spiritual that his dialectical narrative traces out.

It is through his reference to the Greek god Pan that in the section of the *Lectures* on ancient Greece Hegel explicitly yet indirectly avows the panic that, sometimes implicitly, signals the modern (as) encounter with the lack of absolute foundations. (I discuss Pan's philosophical namesake or echo, Indian pantheism, below.) In the section titled "Greek World," Hegel defines panic as a particular way in which one might respond to the materiality of nature, insofar as one takes nature to lack a spiritual ground. By defining panic in this way, he provides us with what we can see as an initial model or framework for the understanding of the affect that governs and accompanies his own philosophical response to the question of the limit between the prehistorical and the historical world. For this limit—the place where history is supposed to start—represents to Hegel the threat of being absorbed into an origin or a pre-origin that appears to him as the materiality of nature qua unreadable language. That is, Oriental—and more narrowly Indian—culture, in its imaginative richness and apparent opacity, appears to Hegel as quasi-unmasterable in terms of the Western concepts he has at his disposal and regards as properly his own. The Orient appears to him like a nascent language not yet endowed with sense: nature speaking without meaning. Because of the panic such a (not yet) language would evoke, Hegel must disavow and appropriate the Indian Orient as origin and newness of the West and Western language. In this process, the origin will have to be excluded from what it enables and already is.

The Greeks, however, constitute the first site of this appropriative exclusion. They represent thus the beginning of what Hegel thinks he realizes in his own thought, qua culmination of (Western) modernity. For Hegel argues that the Greeks not only master their own panic through understanding but master the Orient as well in the Persian Wars and then in Alexander's triumphant invasion (313–15 and 333–35; 256–57 and 273–74). They become thereby for Hegel the first properly historical people because they are the first properly spiritual one. In Greece, we are for the first time "on the ground of spirit" (*auf dem Boden des Geistes*) (275; 223, trans. modified), even if Persia (as we'll see further below) anticipates this historicity insofar as it represents the culmination of the Orient. Hence, I am anxious to suggest, Hegel's characterization of Greek panic displaces, names, and overcomes the panic that is at the abyssal foundations of his own discourse in the face of the Oriental source, especially the Indian, Sanskrit source (as well as its Jewish correlative) from out of which Hegel's own language (dis)avowedly flows.

Hegel mentions Pan in the context of his explanation of the Greek spirit as a whole. In this context, Pan represents more than just one given god. Rather, Pan condenses the essence of the Greek spirit, as the spirit that grounds history. History therefore begins—although Hegel for obvious reasons never quite puts it this way—in the panic embodied by Pan. The panic spirit is the very spirit that guides Hegel's undertaking as an attempt to disavow it. Without a proper grasp of the teleology of history that overcomes history's potential meaninglessness, we must necessarily dissolve in panic, as Herder also insisted.

So what is Pan, and what panic, for Hegel?

> The position of expectant listening, of attentive eagerness to catch the meaning of Nature [*Das ahnungsvolle, lauschende, auf die Bedeutung begierige Verhalten*], is indicated to us in the total image of Pan. Pan is in Greece not the objective whole, but the indefinite [*das Unbestimmte*], which is at the same time bound up with the moment of the subjective; he is the general shuddering [*der allgemeine Schauer*] in the stillness of the forests;

therefore he has particularly been honored in forested Arcadia (a panic terror is the usual expression for a groundless terror [*ein panischer Schreck ist der gewöhnliche Ausdruck für einen grundlosen Schreck*]). Pan, this one who awakens shuddering [*dieser Schauererweckende*] is then presented as a flute-player; it's not just a matter of an inner presentiment, but rather Pan can be heard on his seven-reeded pipe. In this, we have, on the one hand, the indefinite [*das Unbestimmte*], which, however, can be heard [*sich aber vernehmen läßt*], and, on the other hand, that which is heard [*das, was vernommen wird*], the subjective imagination and explaining that are proper to the one who is doing the hearing. In this way the Greeks listened to the murmuring of the springs [or sources: *das Gemurmel der Quellen*] and asked what that might mean; the meaning, however, is not the objective sense of the spring or source [*Quelle*], but the subjective one of the subject itself, which then raises the Najad to the level of the Muse. The Najads or the springs or sources are the external beginning of the Muses. . . . Everywhere the Greeks desire an interpretation and reading [*Auslegung und Deutung*] of the natural. Homer tells us [for example] . . . that while the Greeks were overwhelmed with sorrow for Achilles, a violent agitation came over the sea; the Greeks were on the point of fleeing in all directions when the experienced Nestor stood up and explained to them this appearance. (289–90; 235, trans. modified)

As this passage suggests, Pan is the personification not just of groundless terror but of the terror of groundlessness: an anxiety about groundlessness or the lack of contours, the undefined or borderless; a fear in the face of unexplainable or unexplained phenomena of nature and culture; a panicky flight "in all directions" from the alienness of things not grounded in our own explanations, as when "a violent agitation came over the sea." Not only external nature but also inner nature (the realm of dreams) as well as the received traditions from foreign lands constituted for Greece the objects of this desire to interpret, to put meaning into things.[14] The meaning the Greeks found in these sources, however, came from the Greek spirit itself: "This indeterminateness gained, however, a meaning only through the spirit that apprehended and interpreted it" (*dies Unbestimmte gewann aber auch erst eine Bedeutung durch den auslegenden auffassenden Geist*) (290–91; 236, trans. modified). This makes up the grandeur and the limitations of the ancient Greek world. But just as the Greeks want to place a spiritual foundation beneath what appears as groundless in order to master their panic, so Hegel wants to place such a spiritual ground beneath things as a whole, world history, a ground that is *Geist* insofar as it wills its own unfolding, *Geist* as an intentionality or final causality. The object of Hegel's own panic (or anxiety) in general is natural materiality—ultimately any object as such, in its very alienness from the subject. In his account of history, consequently, it is the border where the transition takes place from materiality to spirit that will become the enduring focus of this panicky affect, an affect that will often express itself through the rhetoric of a polemical aggression and dismissiveness. This border displaces itself into various forms, and at the limit it could be said to pervade the *Lectures on the Philosophy of History*. Still, the Orient in general and ancient India in particular (in proximity to ancient Judaea) has to function as its privileged figure to the extent that Sanskrit has come to seem in Hegel's times undeniably the linguistic basis, or "dead letter," of the West.

The Orient as Triple Border

For Hegel, three empires—China, India, and Persia—together broached the passage from a worldless world (i.e., a world without state, religion, or spiritual freedom) into a world properly so-called.[15] The latter will be a world in which ultimately state and religion, after being born in separating from each other, have become reunified—via the long path of history through Greece, Rome, and medieval Europe—in German Protestantism, where history in its most proper sense reaches its culmination and end. So how are China, India, and Persia positioned as a first dialectical progression on the way out of prehistory? And how does this dialectical progress represent Hegel's struggle with the border of history?

History begins for Hegel when peoples become capable of abstraction and thus pass beyond the level of myth. This capacity enables them to found a state upon the abstract discourse of law, thereby passing beyond the imaginary realm.

> We have to begin with the Oriental World, but not before the period in which we discover States in it. The diffusion of Language and the formation of peoples [*Völkerschaften*] lie beyond the limits of history. History is prosaic, and myths do not yet contain history. The consciousness of external existence first appears with abstract determinations, and when the capacity is present to express laws, then only enters the possibility of grasping objects prosaically. Since the pre-historical is what precedes life in the State, it lies beyond self-conscious life. (142; 111, trans. modified)

At this point of the inauguration of state and religion in abstract consciousness, the Oriental principle of the "substantiality of the ethical" (*Substanzialität des Sittlichen*) (142; 111, trans. modified) is situated. Here, there is an "initial seizure of the arbitrary will" (*erste Bemächtigung der Willkür*), which, however, immediately "sinks back into this substantiality" (*die in dieser Substanzialität versinkt*) (142; 111, trans. modified). Hegel mobilizes the concept of a unified substance in its Spinozan form—refunctioned here into a (non)foundation that excludes individual freedom or subjectivity—to characterize Oriental thought as a whole.[16] The Orient in general—here, as in Schlegel, but now in a much more differentiated way—is pantheistic. In the Orient, as in Judaism from the standpoint of traditional Christianity, the law rules the individual will as an "external power, such that all inwardness, reflexion, conscience, formal freedom is not present" (*alles Innerliche, Gesinnung, Gewissen, formelle Freiheit nicht vorhanden ist*) (142; 111, trans. modified). In the Orient, what is properly internal is made external—*das Innerliche [wird] äußerlich gemacht* (142; 111). Geist appears here only as natural: *natürliche Geistigkeit* (142; 111). For we are at the point of the passage from nature (or matter) to spirit, from the radical prehistory of Africa (and the Native American cultures) to the proper historicity of Europe. Religion and state are here still unified theocratically in a status of self-anticipation, as they have not yet separated one from the other in order to appear as such. "What we call God" (143; 112) has not yet appeared, because it has not yet separated from the world and become inward and supersensuous. It has not yet become an expression of our free subjectivity. The Orient is still heteronomous and *unmündig*, or immature, in a Kantian sense.[17] The passage beyond this immaturity on the threshold of history will require three steps, in accordance not just with Hegelian trinitarianism but with what underlies it: the structural necessity that the border be always supplemented by its own two borders. The problem will remain, however, that this supplementation is in principle endless and (so to speak) internally unstable.

In terms of logical categories, the way in which Hegel organizes the three-step progress of Orientality toward its own overcoming is by means of identity, difference, and their interrelationship.[18] Abstraction—which indeed, for Hegel, realizes itself only as the passage beyond itself to fulfilled concretion—requires not only the positing of identity, but the positing also of difference, and then the effacement of that difference in the realization of the identity between identity and difference. The birth pangs of abstraction, for the sake of which the Oriental world exists, will, therefore, include these three phases. The Oriental world will have to pass through identity, which Hegel associates with China, through difference, which he connects with India (e.g., in the caste system), and then through the unreconciled interplay of identity and difference, which he situates in the Persian Empire, a unified but culturally heterogeneous realm. But the question of whether identity and difference do not impinge on one another at every point in this trajectory will haunt Hegel's text and render his readings of each of these cultures and their progress problematically arbitrary in a way that he refuses to (or cannot) think. Let us look more closely at Hegel's characterization of this triple limit of history, then, in order to find out how he tries to manage the passage, and the prevention of the passage, from Africa into Europe.

Within the Oriental arrangement, China represents the culture of the Same, as that of radical materiality. The first and most extreme form of Orientality, the form of history closest to the dark abyss of prehistory, China is devoid of spirituality and inwardness. Indeed, Hegel characterizes China's not-yet religion as "magic" (*Zauberei*), thus connecting it with Africa, where magic stands in for a not-yet existent religion (167; 132). In China, the externality of the patriarchal state is so overwhelmingly present that there is no religion. The emperor is all to such an extent that this first state is not yet a state in the proper sense of one founded on religion. In lieu of the state, all of China is one very large family. And because there is no inwardness, no will or freedom (except as the emperor's freedom), there can be no development. In the case of China, its initial embodiment, the Orient is devoid of change: It is the eternal, static, material origin of spiritual movement itself: "the only realm of endurance in the world. Conquests cannot have any impact on such a realm" (*das einzige Reich der Dauer in der Welt. Eroberungen können solchem Reiche nichts anhaben*) (146; 115, trans. modified). The wall that China draws around itself is evidently perfect, impenetrable.[19]

In order to get started, then, even if it has already started starting in China, history will need more than merely the Chinese origin. The self-identity of China will need the self-difference of India to supplement its origination. In accordance with this need, Hegel explicitly characterizes both China and India as prehistorical history. They are "as it were still outside world history, as the presupposition of the moments whose bringing together first becomes its living process" (*gleichsam noch außer der Weltgeschichte, als die Voraussetzung der Momente, deren Zusammenschließung erst ihr lebendiger Fortgang wird*) (147; 116, trans. modified). That is, they are figurally outside history (as the origin that precedes it), but not literally outside (since that is where Africa lies, along with the Native Americans). Correspondingly, Persia must be figurally inside history, but also not yet literally, since that literal honor belongs to Greece first of all. If the border is inside and outside at once, then to split it in two and to designate each half as only "figurally," or "gleichsam," inside or outside is evidently one way of appearing to have at once acknowledged and solved the problem of the mediation. In fact, however, not only the problem of how to establish the distinction between the literal and figural here remains unresolved but also the problem of how to determine persuasively the border between figural inside and figural outside. As we'll see in a moment, Hegel does not consistently apply the "gleichsam," thereby indicating that the literal/figural distinction is not an entirely reliable one here. More important, therefore, is the latter division. Let us see, then, how Hegel will attempt to bring about this division between the Orientality that is inside history and the one that is outside.

If together China and India provide the preconditions of history, history itself (yet not quite literally itself, in accordance with Hegel's determination of the status of the Orient) emerges only with the entry of the Persian Empire, the first empire combining identity and difference and the first that has the good sense to pass away, thereby becoming (problematically) properly historical.

> Asia separates itself into two parts—Hither and Farther Asia; which are essentially different from each other [*Asien zerfällt in zwei Teile: in Vorder- und Hinterasien, die wesentlich voneinander verschieden sind*]. While the Chinese and Hindus—the two great nations of Farther Asia . . . —belong to the strictly Asiatic, namely the Mongolian Race, and consequently possess a quite peculiar character, discrepant from ours [*zur eigentlich asiatischen, nämlich zur mongolischen Rasse gehören und somit einen ganz eigentümlichen, von uns abweichenden Charakter haben*]; the nations of Hither Asia belong to the Caucasian, i.e., the European Stock [*zum kaukasischen, d.h. zum europäischen Stamme*]. They are related to the West, while the Farther-Asiatic peoples are perfectly isolated. (215; 173)

Once again, Hegel mobilizes the language of literal and figural here, but now to posit that China and India are literally, properly Asian (*eigentlich asiatischen*), whereas the Persians are literally European, even if they remain (by implication) figurally Asian. The anchor of the literal, proper meaning or essence, its foundation here, is the "natural" concept of race.[20] In accordance with this racial literalism, Hegel draws the line between Europe and Asia, as between history and prehistory. Further, this line functions as one between the properly human and the inhuman. In Persia, a European still feels at home (*einheimisch*) and encounters "European dispositions, human virtues, and human passions" (*europäische Gesinnungen, menschliche Tugenden und menschliche Leidenschaften*) (215; 173). In crossing the Indus, he encounters "the highest contradiction. . . . With the Persian Empire we first enter into the context of History. The Persians are the first historical People; Persia was the first empire that passed away" (*dem höchsten Widerspruch. . . . Mit dem persischen Reiche treten wir erst in den Zusammenhang der Geschichte. Die Perser sind das erste geschichtliche Volk, Persien ist das erste Reich, das vergangen ist*) (215; 173, trans. modified). In addition, this racially literalist anthropology of the historical and Western is overdetermined by the opposition between stasis and developmental movement.

> While China and India remain static and prolong a natural, vegetative existence up to the present [*statarisch bleiben und ein natürliches, vegetatives Dasein bis in die Gegenwart fristen*], this land is subject to developments and revolutions, which alone betray a historical condition. The Chinese and Indian Empires can only in themselves and for us come into the context of history [*in den Zusammenhang der Geschichte kommen*]. Here, however, in Persia, the Light first arises, which shines and illuminates something other than itself, for first Zoroaster's light belongs to the world of consciousness, to spirit as a relation to something other. . . . The principle of development begins with the history of Persia, and therefore Persia constitutes the literal beginning of world history [*den eigentlichen Anfang der Weltgeschichte*]. (215–16; 173–74, trans. modified)

With Persia, then, we enter history, as coherence of context—*Zusammenhang*. History appropriates and contextualizes the prehistorical and not yet properly coherent context of its origination. (See chapter 7 for my discussion of Kafka's implicit but precise critical response to this motif of coherence and/or context—*Zusammenhang*—as touchstone of the properly historical in "The Great Wall of China.") Persia is on the inside of this context of history, whereas China and India are on the outside, pure and simple.

But if China and India belong together as the broaching of identity and difference, respectively, nonetheless India is the closest to Persia in geographical and dialectical-developmental terms. Hence India constitutes at this juncture the outside border of the border between the inside and outside of history. To what extent and in what manner will Hegel manage to maintain its exclusion from the inside (of the) boundary of history?

The problematic character of India's position is revealed in an initial way by this: Hegel has elsewhere indicated that China is static whereas India represents pure movement. But in the passages we've just considered, he places India with China on the side of stasis as opposed to the developmental dynamism of Persia.[21] Persian dynamism, as opposed to the static character of the extrahistorical *Hinterorient*, is hard to distinguish from the principle of *Unruhe* (or "disquiet") that India opposes to Chinese lack-of-movement. Similarly, the synthesis of identity and difference that is not yet a synthesis (for Persia does not yet achieve the synthesis) is difficult to distinguish from the (Indian) operation of a principle of difference in unsynthesized oscillation with identity. That is, given that difference cannot be present without some relation to identity, how can India fail to bear an essential resemblance to the Persian interplay between identity and difference? (Indeed, likewise, the difference between China's "identity" and India's "difference" is at best quantitative, not qualitative. The limit shifts.) But in order to do justice to Hegel's attempt to determine India's position on the border of history and to see exactly how both identity and difference are in play there, I turn now to his more detailed discussion of Indian culture per se.[22]

India as Differential Limit

On the site of India, Oriental prehistory—which excludes "us" because it is "our" no longer accessible origin—threatens nonetheless to gain access to Occidental history. It comes near to us, enters into our very neighborhood. And conversely, Occidental history risks being dragged back down there into the endless, yawning night of African prehistory: or again the place of spirit caught in the endless birth-trauma of history, the never-ending passage from the materiality of nature to itself, as spirit itself.

In what terms, then, other than through the claims of race, does Hegel argue for India's position outside the (Western) fold of history, even though India's ancient language, Sanskrit, provides the grounds of the Western languages? The polemical description of India through which Hegel justifies and carries out the exclusion or casting-out of India constitutes the attempted exclusion precisely of exclusion itself, or of a certain haunting specter of exclusion as (self-)exclusion.[23] Hegel excludes India as a figure for exclusion, a figure for the (self-)exclusionary differentiation of the border as such.[24] For what does a border or limit do, if not differentiate, and what is differentiation—recall that India is for Hegel the realm of difference—but exclusion of one thing from another? Yet in line with the self-displacing character of all limits, differentiation also includes what it excludes (as excluded). It is exactly this structure—the inclusion, by exclusion, of what it still excludes—that Hegel attributes (and sacrificially so, ridding himself of this good riddance) to the Indian culture as its essence. Hegel, therefore, includes exclusion (qua India) in his narrative in order not to exclude it, but he includes it as excluded. If China represents inclusion and Indian exclusion excludes inclusion, then with Persia history begins by including exclusion as excluded.

Now let's see how this occurs in Hegel's text, in which at certain points the signifier for exclusion—*Ausschließung*—will play an important role. The overarching achievement and limitation of Indian culture, as Hegel sees it, consists in the partial, therefore still abstract, interiorization of the utterly external laws of Chinese culture. Ancient India posits the "unity of subjectivity and being or [the] idealism of existence" (*Einheit der Subjektivität und des Seins oder [den] Idealismus des Daseins*) (175; 139, trans. modified). That is, Indian culture begins to create a space for subjectivity; it broaches an interiority. But this unity of subject and object within the subject, this "idealism of existence," remains an "idealism of the imagination devoid of concepts" (*ein begriffloser Idealismus der Einbildung*) (175; 139, trans. modified). To be sure, Hegel grants, concepts do come into play—"the thought plays its way into the picture" (*der Gedanke als hineinspielend vorkommt*) (175; 139, trans. modified)—but concept and image, or general and particular, are united only by chance—"in a chance unification" (*in einer zufälligen Vereinigung*) (175; 139, trans. modified). They have no coherently articulated relationship, and the image reigns, along with its exteriority.

Thus, the Indian spirit dreams. This spirit presents itself as "God in the intoxication of his dreaming" (*Gott im Taumel seines Träumens*) (175; 139, trans. modified). The problem with dreaming, however, is that it undoes the distinction between outside and inside that the idealism of existence began to set up by positing the world as an essentially interior world. As Hegel understands it, when one dreams, one fails to recognize the difference between oneself and the world around one as an objective, rationally differentiated context. Hegel suggests, then, that ancient Indian culture immediately effaces the distinction it also draws between external existence and inward essentiality, or substance and subject. "In the dream, the individual ceases to know himself as *this*, excluding the objects across from it" (*In dem Traume hört das Individuum auf, sich als* dieses, *ausschließend gegen die Gegenstände, zu wissen*) (176; 140, trans modified). The Indian is always both the particular (as externality) and the universal (as inwardness) at once, but also neither, or always one and then the other, because Indian culture does not articulate fully the one level with the other, repeatedly drawing the distinction and then revoking it, in an unregulated and incoherent manner:

The dreaming Indian is therefore all that we call finite and individual, and at the same time—as infinitely universal and unlimited—a something intrinsically divine [*alles, was wir Endliches und Einzelnes nennen, und zugleich als ein unendlich Allgemeines und Unbeschränktes an ihm selbst ein Göttliches*]. (176; 141)

Indian culture is in this sense a pantheism, but specifically a "pantheism of the mere imagination, rather than thought" (*Pantheismus der Einbildungskraft, nicht des Gedankens*). The conflation of finite and infinite does not amount to a mediation, so that the extremes remain distinct, though also identical; the result is a (dis)continuous and unregulated oscillation between empty abstractions and blind images. In place of an articulated relationship between universal and particular, one finds the meaninglessly precipitous positing of their identity. The Indian spirit is lost (*verloren*) (177; 141) in its dreams, "thrown back and forth" (*hin und her geworfen*) (177; 141) by them, as natural entities inflate themselves into gods, while gods reduce themselves to mere particulars, becoming "bizarre, confused, and ridiculous" (*bizarr, verworren und läppisch*) (177; 141).

We can see here that in India the principle of difference asserts itself through the differentiation of the identical, but also the principle of identity as identification of the different (an element that Hegel wants to downplay in order to reserve the interplay of identity and difference for Persia, in a move I problematized above). Difference in India is bad or limited for Hegel because while it excludes one thing from its other, it cancels itself out, allowing one thing to fall into the other as the border between them becomes a border within each. India appears from this point of view as the land of the borderline.

The same abstraction and the same obstruction of abstraction appear on the level of the politics that this pantheistic metaphysics entails. The gesture toward a subjective position here makes it possible for Hegel to characterize the movement from China to India as one from identity to difference:

> The next degree in advance of this Unity [beyond China] is Difference, maintaining its independence against the all-subduing power of Unity [*daß der Unterschied sich hervortut und in seiner Besonderheit selbständig gegen die alles beherrschende Einheit wird*]. (180; 144)

Yet the differentiation India introduces remains too abstract, because not abstract enough, limited, still bound up with the gravity of natural unity. For ancient Indian society limits itself to the differentiations of the caste system, a social system based on merely natural distinctions, in the sense of "dead," material nature. The particular does not differentiate itself as free subjectivity from the substantial unity at the center of things, but only as massive class differences. These differences have their origins not in the free subjectivity of individuals (181; 145), as will begin to emerge with Persia (and be more realized in Greece), but rather in mere birth (182; 145). The difference between nature and spirit collapses when the differences the society establishes (as caste categories) remain limited and determined by where one is born. In the caste system nature avenges itself on spirit.

Whereas properly organic life requires for Hegel mediated identity of identity and difference, both China and India fall short of such a requirement, short of life, and so short of history. They do so because (ostensibly) China involves only identity, India only difference, including the nonmediated, differential identity of identity and difference; in contrast, the mediation of identity and difference ostensibly begins in Persia. (Recall that for Schlegel Indian culture, as rooted in Sanskrit, represented the self-anticipation of the organic.) The reason that spirit as history and history as spirit are not born in India, then, is because India never gives birth to anything beyond birth. Life falls there back into death, Hegel writes, prevented by its adherence to mere life from being born as something more than life.[25]

> Yet the distinctions which these imply are referred to Nature [*diese Unterschiede fallen in die Natur zurück*]. Instead of stimulating the activity of a soul as their centre of union, and spontaneously realizing that soul—as is the case in organic life—they petrify and become rigid, and by their stereotyped character condemn the Indian people to the most degrading spiritual serfdom [*versteinern und erstarren sie und verdammen durch ihre Festigkeit das indische Volk zur entwürdigsten Knechtschaft des Geistes*]. (181; 144)

In the caste system, then, as in the pantheistic metaphysics that is supposed to ground it, difference suspends itself. In the caste system the fact that the differences remain naturally determined signifies that they fail to provide a place for the assertion of individual freedom and subjectivity against the One substance, whereas this is exactly their destined function: "They have not arisen out of free subjectivity" (*aus der freien Subjektivität hervorgegangen*) (181; 145, trans. modified). In this sense, they fail as differences. They exclude nature (the nature of the One substance) only in order to include it.

Thus, they end up excluding the subjectivity that they meant to include or even embody. The exclusion begins as a particular one, but gradually it

Thresholds of History: Hegel 151

reveals itself to be universal in the sense that all subjectivity is closed out. The manifest scandal of the exclusion of the outcastes is first of all an occasion for Hegel's indignation.

> This caste [of the Chandalas] is excluded [Sibree puts here "excommunicated"] and detested; and are obliged to live separate and far from association with others. The Chandalas are obliged to move out of the way for their superiors, and a Brahmin may knock down any that neglect to do so [*ausgeschlossen und verhaßt, muß abgeschieden wohnen und fern von der Gemeinschaft mit anderen. Einem Höheren müssen die Tschandalas aus dem Wege gehen, und jedem Brahmanen ist es erlaubt, den nicht sich Entfernenden niederzustoßen*]. (183; 146, trans. modified)

But even beyond this scandal, the existence of the caste system poses to the individual the continuous danger that one might be excluded from one's own caste, and so from the society at large. If a Brahman or indeed a member of any caste transgresses (*übertritt*) (192; 153) the laws and prescriptions of his caste, then he or she is "automatically excluded from his or her caste" (*von selbst aus seiner Kaste ausgeschlossen*) (192; 153, trans. modified). Finally, this danger of exclusion by means of transgression of limits is always already realized, for Hegel, in Indian culture by virtue of the fact that the caste system itself, as determined by birth, excludes subjectivity, or difference, from itself (although it initially broaches or includes such difference).[26] Yet Hegel himself, as we have seen above, establishes what amounts to a global caste system on the basis of what he sees as the "natural" category of race, the differences between African nonhistory, Mongolian (Chinese and Indian) pre- or protohistory, and European historicity.[27] So here, as Hegel falls into an identity with it, India becomes a kind of outcaste—don't come too close!—at once for its racism and for its race, in a contradiction or hypocrisy the tension of which Hegel perhaps registers in the very vehemence of his polemical language.[28]

What are the specifically political implications of the caste system, its consequences for a possible state? The implications of the caste system for the state-form in India are similar to those of the patriarchal system of identity in China, but in the opposite form.

> In India, there is this initial inwardness of imagination [*Innerlichkeit der Einbildung*], a unity of the natural and spiritual, in which neither nature as a rational world nor the spiritual as that self-consciousness which opposes itself to nature exists. Here opposition in principle is lacking [*fehlt der Gegensatz im Prinzip*]; freedom is lacking both as a will that exists in itself and as subjective freedom. Hence, the proper ground [*der eigentümliche*

Boden] of the State, the principle of freedom, is not at all present: there can therefore not be a proper State. . . . If China is all State, then the Indian political being is only a people, not a State. (201; 161, trans. modified)

In China, there cannot really be a state because there is nothing but the state (qua patriarchal family). In India, there cannot be a state because there is only religion, but a religion that is none, for subjectivity is voided by virtue of absorbing everything into its dreaming self.

As there can be no state in India, we already know that there can be no religion. For when present, religion necessarily provides the foundation of a state. We nonetheless need to consider briefly, for the sake of what follows, Hegel's characterization of the closest thing India has (in his view) to God, namely Brahma. Although Hegel grants that "it is . . . difficult to discover what the Hindus understand by Brahma," because we tend to impose our own conceptions, he nonetheless concludes that

> we should call Brahma the pure unity of thought in itself, the God that is simple within himself [*Nach der Übersetzung in unseren Gedankengang ist also Brahman die reine Einheit des Gedankens in sich selbst, der in sich einfache Gott*] (195; 156) . . . substance in its simplicity, which by its very nature expands itself into the savageness of diversity. For this abstraction, this pure unity, is that which lies at the basis of all other things, the root of all determinacy [*die einfache Substanz, welche sich wesentlich in das Wilde der Verschiedenheit auseinanderschlägt. Denn diese Abstraktion, diese reine Einheit ist das allem zugrunde Liegende, die Wurzel aller Bestimmtheit*]. (195; 156, trans. modified)

Because India is the realm of difference, this abstract unity expresses itself in sensuous multiplicity—reminiscent of Spinoza's substance and its modes, but also more generally of the Jewish God: too abstract and too material at once—where the sensuous multiplicity is disjoined from the one substance, so that "the concrete content is spiritless and savagely strewn about" (*der konkrete Inhalt geistlos und wild zerstreut*) (196; 156, trans. modified), like a dead letter. The result is a duplicity of abstract unity and abstract sensuous particularity to which correspond two paths, both equally despicable for Hegel. On the one hand, there is the path of the "abstraction of pure self-suspension" (*Abstraktion des reinen sich Aufhebens*) (196; 157, trans. modified), the self-negation of self-consciousness and/or suicide. On the other hand, there is the path of immersion in natural sensuality, as the "suspension of the consciousness of differentiating oneself from naturalness" (*das Bewußtsein des sich Unterscheidens von der Natürlichkeit sich aufhebt*) (197; 157, trans. modified). In Indian religious practices per se, then, we have again the incoherent oscillation between the particular and the universal that is inscribed for Hegel in pantheistic Indian metaphysics. India is differentiation and delimitation that fails to delimit, the (universal) framing that falls into an identity with what it frames (i.e., the particular) and the (particular) image that falls out of its own (universal) framework as that framework itself.[29]

Disavowing Sanskrit, Foreign Mother Tongue of the Western Mind

Having shown in outline how Hegel frames India as differential framing, I would now like to examine his acknowledgment and disavowal of the status of India as the linguistic ground of the Western language(s). As I argued above, this status of India as linguistic ground constitutes Hegel's most important reason for determining India—rather than, say, China or Egypt or Persia—as the Oriental origin of Europe (and thereby excluding India from Europe itself, which then ostensibly develops out of, and realizes, that origin). Furthermore, the status of India as Sanskrit basis for—or dead letter/language of—the Western languages is one of the most important traits India shares with Judaism, its predecessor as mediating origin (which I return to consider in the next step of my argument).

As I indicated above when introducing Hegel's concept of history, Hegel insists that history begins only with the state, rather than with less systematically organized structures. While making this claim, however, and repeatedly thereafter, Hegel is forced to acknowledge (but just as soon to disavow) the importance for history of the fact that Western languages arise out of the Sanskrit origin, as had been known widely in German intellectual circles at least since Friedrich Schlegel's work *On the Language and Wisdom of the Indians*:

> Peoples may have passed a long life before arriving at this their destination, and during this period, they may have attained considerable culture in some directions. This pre-historical period [*Vorgeschichte*]—consistently with what has been said—lies outside of our plan; whether a real history followed it, or the peoples in question never attained a State constitution. It is a great discovery—as of a new world [*wie einer neuen Welt*]—which has been made within rather more than the last twenty years, respecting Sanskrit and the connection [*Zusammenhang*] of the European languages with it. In particular, the linkage of the German and Indian peoples has been demonstrated, with as much certainty as such subjects allow of. . . . In the connection [*Zusammenhang*] just referred to, between the languages

of peoples so widely separated, we have a result before us, which proves the diffusion of those nations from Asia as a center, and the so dissimilar development of what had been originally related, as an incontestable fact, not as an inference deduced by that favorite method of combining, and reasoning from, circumstances grave and trivial, which has already enriched and will continue to enrich history with so many fictions given out as facts. But that apparently so extensive range of events [*Jenes . . . so weitläufig scheinende Geschehene*] lies beyond the pale of history [*außerhalb der Geschichte*]; in fact preceded it. (82–83; 59–60, trans. modified)

Hegel grants here—at least verbally—that the discovery of the importance of ancient Indian language and culture for Western languages and cultures belongs to a certain kind of *Geschichte*, and also to that which has happened, "Jenes . . . Geschehene"—a word obviously and intimately related to the word *Geschichte*. He grants further that there is a connection, cohesion, or coherence at stake here—*Zusammenhang*—that cannot be denied. Yet—whether it is because his doctrine that history begins with the state requires it, or because his very desire to keep the development of Sanskrit (into other languages) outside the sphere of history requires that history begin with the state—this occurrence of the spread and transformation of Sanskrit must nonetheless lie outside of history properly so-called.[30]

To keep this development out, Hegel designates it as a natural phenomenon, in line with the notion that the Orient is characterized by a still-natural spirituality.

Externally, India sustains manifold relations to the History of the World. In recent times [*neueren Zeiten*] the discovery has been made, that Sanskrit lies at the foundation of all those further developments which form the languages of Europe [*daß die Sanskritsprache allen weiteren Entwicklungen europäischer Sprachen zugrunde liege*]; e.g., the Greek, Latin, German. India, moreover, was the center of emigration for all the Western world [*der Ausgangspunkt für die ganze westliche Welt*]; but this external historical relation is to be regarded rather as a merely natural diffusion of peoples from this point. (177–78; 141–42, trans. modified)

In his attempt to relativize the originality or originarity or radical newness of India, Hegel makes the development of Sanskrit and the spread of Indian cultural influences a matter of mere externality, of the "natural diffusion of peoples." He thus restricts it to the material surfaces of the world, instead of including it in the spiritual depths.[31] This mere externality and natural character accrue to the Sanskrit language not only despite but also owing to the fact that it lies at the ground (*zugrunde liege*) of "all further development of European languages." For Enlightenment and post-Enlightenment modernity is characterized here as "the newer times"—*neueren Zeiten*. The newness or grounding originality of India must be mitigated if the realization of newness, the event of newness as such, is to appear in modern Europe. (I return to the "newness" of modernity below when I consider the realization of the prefigural threshold[s] of history.)

It is in line with this discursive imperative to minimize India's originarity that Hegel characterizes the importance of Sanskrit's influence not only as natural and external but also as abstract, in opposition to the concreteness of what comes after. The abstract materiality of India—derived from the traditional Christian notion of the abstract materiality of (ancient) Judaism—applies to Sanskrit's influence as to the "dead letter" of Jewish legalism from which it derives:

> Even if in India the elements of further developments could be discovered, and even if we could find traces of their being transmitted to the West, this migration is nonetheless so abstract [*so abstrakt*] that that which can be of interest to us in later peoples is no longer that which they received from India, but rather something concrete [*ein Konkretes*] that they have formed for themselves and with respect to which they did best to forget the Indian elements. (178; 142, trans. modified)

Abstract materiality, further, calls to be rightfully supplanted by concrete spirit because, in its very materiality (in Hegel's view), it is radically passive and therefore without value in itself. The value that apparently comes from the origin actually comes from elsewhere. What is apparently proper to the origin, in actuality belongs to the originated (i.e., to what emerges from that origin). For India has been passive rather than active—it has not been value-positing—as is demonstrated by the fact that it has been conquered and exploited. In this view, Hegel echoes Herder. For the idealist-realist universe—where what is true is real and what is real is true, or where what is possible realizes itself—to be defeated is to deserve to be defeated. It is to have earned defeat through the weakness or sin of passivity, an anticipatory heteronomy. It is to have failed to maintain one's freedom through the incessant, uninterrupted thinking that, for Hegel, prevents one from entering into a relation (of dependence) with an other.

> The spread of Indian culture is prehistorical [*vorgeschichtlich*], for History is limited to that which makes an essential epoch [*eine wesentliche Epoche*] in the development of Spirit. In general, the diffusion of Indian culture is only a dumb, deedless expansion, i.e., it presents no political action [*nur eine stumme, tatlose Verbreitung, d.h. ohne politische Handlung*]. The people of

India have achieved no foreign conquests, but have been on every occasion vanquished themselves. And as, in this silent way, Northern India has been a center of natural emigration, India as a *desired* land forms an essential moment in the whole of History [*Indien überhaupt als* gesuchtes *Land ein wesentliches Moment der ganzen Geschichte*]. (178; 142, trans. modified)

Whereas India itself does not properly belong to history, the desire for India, or India as desired or sought, constitutes an "essential moment in the whole of History."[32] And the desire has been for the most part successfully achieved:

There is scarcely any great nation of the East or of the modern European West that has not acquired there a smaller or greater piece of land. . . . It is the necessary fate [*das notwendige Schicksal*] of the Asian Empires to be subjected to the Europeans, and China will one day have to submit to this fate as well. (178; 142, trans. modified)

India becomes historical, along with the rest of the Orient, only in being appropriated by the (colonialist) day to which it gives rise.

Judaea as a Persian India

The position of India is analogous to that of Judaism in Hegel first of all to the extent that Sanskrit is the dead language that gives rise to our living languages, much as the Hebrew Bible and its Talmudic extensions constituted the dead letter out of which the living Christian spirit was to have resurrected itself. Beyond this, when the Persian Empire arrives to inaugurate history by completing the Oriental World and anticipating the Greek World, Hegel places ancient Jewish culture within the general category of Persia and bestows upon it the preliminary spiritualizing position that, within this empire, corresponds to India's position within the development of the Orient as a whole.[33] Let us rehearse these basic determinations to clarify the analogy.

In general, the Persian Empire provides the mediation between universal and particular, identity and difference, under the figure of the religion of light (in its struggle against darkness). The universal as light bestows itself on the particulars that are now both clearly separated from it, and also connected to it, in that the light enables them, across their distance from the source, to grow and flourish as they lift themselves up, resisting the gravity of materiality, back toward that source itself. Light is the universal that has now become an object freely posited by subjectivity. As a universal that is poised on the limit between nature and spirit, light is the most spiritual mode of nature imaginable. Its mediating force enables the universal and the particular, the identical and the different, to communicate across the distance it opens and is.

But the Persian light realizes itself only through a process involving the participation of specific cultures that reside, on Hegel's account, essentially within it. The principle of light "unfolds itself" (245; 198, trans. modified) into three main phases. First, the sensuous dimension asserts itself in Babylonia and Syria. Second, the spiritual dimension develops in two forms: the Adonis-worship of the Phoenicians, where there is an "initial consciousness of concrete spirit" (245; 198–99, trans. modified), and "the pure and abstract thought among the Jews" (245; 199). Of these two forms, Hegel summarizes that the first (the Phoenician) lacks the unity of the concrete, and the second (Judaism) lacks concreteness itself.

As Hegel provides separate headings only for "Persia," "Syria and Semitic Western Asia," "Judaea," and "Egypt," in the chapter "The Persian Empire and Its Constituent Parts," placing the Phoenician Adonis cult within the "Syria and Semitic Western Asia" section, the Adonis cult is evidently less important for Hegel here than the religion of ancient Judaea. Also he elsewhere says that Phoenician culture is not really spiritual, because it is still excessively bound up with nature (241; 195). In the following, therefore, and in accordance with the priorities dictated by the current argument, I focus on the delineation of the Jewish religion.[34] Nonetheless, it is important to note in passing why the Adonis cult is connected with Judaea here under the heading of spiritualization. Namely, the Adonis cult plays out the death and resurrection of the God, and so represents a kind of premature anticipation of Christianity.[35] It is as if, in the Phoenician cult, the appearance of the Jewish God were already accompanied by the potential to become the appearance of Christ.

Finally, in the third main phase of Persia, Egyptian culture develops the task of the unification of these elements (the sensuous and the supersensuous), a task that it delivers as the sphinxlike riddle of itself to Greece, which will first accomplish this task (if, of course, only in an initial form to be completed by Rome and Christian Europe).[36]

The outlines of the analogy are initially clear: Within Persia, China is recapitulated in Babylonia and Syria; India is recapitulated in both Phoenician and Hebrew cultures; and Persia itself is recapitulated in Egypt, or as Hegel puts it, Egypt accomplishes the internal transition to Greece, whereas the Persian Empire as a whole accomplishes the external one (146; 115). Given this initial analogy between the positions of India and Judaism, as two different forms or levels of the introduction of spirit into a material world, it will not be surprising that when Hegel presents the Jewish God, this God is explicitly likened to the Hindu God, or Brahma, and this in various contexts. Thus:

> In the midst of this confusion [of the Persian Empire], the spiritual God of the Jews confronts us—like Brahma, existing only for thought, yet jealous and excluding from his being and sublating all the specificity of difference that is set free in other religions [*tritt uns der geistige Gott der Juden entgegen, der wie Brahman nur für den Gedanken ist, doch eifrig, und alle Besonderheit des Unterschiedes, die in anderen Religionen freigelassen ist, aus sich ausschliessend und aufhebend*]. (146; 114, trans. modified)

The Jewish God is like Brahma in that it is a God of (or for) pure thought, but in an even more radical sense than the Indian God. It excludes all difference more radically than the Indian universal, since in India the universal became all particularity, as well as the reverse, whereas in Judaea all particularity effaces itself before the one universal. And through this difference, as well as the similarity or identity, Judaism becomes (at least for the moment) not the outside limit of the limit between East and West, but the limit itself, the site of the break.[37] Judaism constitutes within the Orient the limit between the Indian outside of Europe and the Persian inside.

> If the spiritual in the Phoenician people was still limited by the natural side, among the Jews it shows itself entirely purified; the pure product of thought, thinking-itself [*das Sichdenken*], comes to consciousness and the spiritual develops itself in its extreme determination against nature and against unity with the same. We saw earlier the pure Brahma, but only as the general being-of-nature, and specifically such that Brahma does not himself become an object of consciousness; we saw it become among the Persians an object of consciousness, but in sensuous intuition, as light. But the light is now Jehova, the pure One [*das reine Eine*]. Thereby the break occurs between East and West; the spirit descends into itself and grasps the abstract fundamental principle as the spiritual. Nature, which in the Orient is Primary and the Foundation, is now suppressed to become mere creature; and spirit is now Primary [*geschieht der Bruch zwischen dem Osten und dem Westen; der Geist geht in sich nieder und erfaßt das abstrakte Grundprinzip für das Geistige. Die Natur, die im Orient das Erste und die Grundlage ist, wird jetzt herabgedrückt zum Geschöpf; und der Geist ist nun das Erste*]. (241; 195, trans. modified)

The Jewish God is again said to be very much like the Indian one, "das reine Brahman," who was characterized in the passage we considered earlier as "the pure unity of thought within itself" (*die reine Einheit des Gedankens in sich selbst*) (195; 156, trans. modified).[38] The only difference, as Hegel spells out here again, is that the Jewish God does not step forth from his isolation into the infinite variety of natural finitude but remains a spiritual object, withdrawn from nature and its multiplicity. The Jewish religion draws a line between the universal and the particular that nothing, it seems, can cross. In this sense, Judaism establishes the break between East and West, because spirit is now radically separated from nature.[39]

However, the limitations of the Jewish innovation place it, in some respects, on the far (i.e., Eastern) side of the break between East and West. First of all, Hegel's emphasis on the exclusive—*ausschließend*—character of Jewish religion, even if he employs it to differentiate the Jewish religion from the religion of Brahma, also recalls a certain aspect of the Indian world that he saw as placing it outside the fold of European spirituality. Although the *Ausschließung* in India pertained first of all to the Chandalas, then to the castes in general, ultimately it implied there, as we saw, the exclusion of the subject from the difference that was meant to serve the emergence of freedom. The exclusion of particularity, and so of all other religions (and of their inclusions of particularity), from the Jewish God turns out to constitute simultaneously an exclusion of the free subject from this God, which is fundamentally the same exclusion that bothered Hegel in India. Concerning Judaism, he writes:

> This great principle is, in its further determinateness, the *excluding* unity [*das* ausschließende *Eine*]. This religion must necessarily attain the moment of exclusion [*das Moment der Ausschließung gewinnen*], which essentially consists in the fact that only the one people knows the One and is recognized by Him. (241; 195, trans. modified)

Further, the Jewish religion does not have "the lax good-naturedness" (of thinking all religions are equally true), in that it "absolutely excludes" (*Diese schlaffe Gutmütigkeit hat die jüdische Religion nicht, indem sie absolut ausschließt*) (242; 196, trans. modified). Or again: "In general Jewish history has sublime traits; it is only rendered impure by the sacralized exclusion of the spirits of other nations" (*große Züge; nur ist sie verunreinigt durch das geheiligte Ausschließen der anderen Volksgeister*) (244; 197, trans. modified). The exclusion of nature from God implies the exclusion of other religions, because everything other than this God is untrue ("Only the One . . . is the Truth" (*Nur das Eine . . . ist die Wahrheit*) (242; 196). The resultant service to this One reintroduces, however, the lack of freedom that it discovers everywhere outside the One:

> The subject as concrete subject does not become free, because the Absolute itself is not grasped as concrete spirit, because spirit still appears as spiritlessly posited [*als geistlos gesetzt erscheint*]. . . . [The subject] remains therefore strictly bound to the service of ceremony and law, whose ground [*Grund*] is pure freedom as abstract. The Jews have what they are through the One; thereby the subject has no freedom for itself. . . . The State . . . is inappropriate to the Jewish principle. (243; 196–97, trans. modified)

The spirituality of ancient Judaism ultimately falls, through the very radicality of its abstractness, back into the materiality it shuns. The outside border of Judaism, materiality, becomes its inside qua dead letter of the law: ceremonial works. The lack of freedom thereby entailed ensures that Judaism remains also in principle stateless, as did India, whose religion was likewise characterized as mindlessly ceremonial.[40] Hence despite the "break" that it establishes between East and West, Judaism represents not the limit between East and West, but the outside limit of that limit, as did India, if on a slightly different level (i.e., in a displaced repetition). The passage from East to West will occur by way of Egypt, which incipiently synthesizes the spirituality of Judaism with the sensuality of Babylonia/Syria under the heading of the Persian light.

In terms of the (il)logic of the limit in general, the reason for this development is clear. Since the limit between East and West always becomes the inside limit of this limit, to allow Judaism to remain the break between East and West would carry the danger of allowing Judaism to become the very constitution or inside of the West. The consequence of this development would be doubt—and the attendant anxiety—as to the self-constituting character of Christian-Germanic Europe. Hence the limit must once again be redetermined as its own outside limit, just as India could not be allowed to assert itself as an Eastern ground of the West, thereby alienating (or excluding) the West from itself in its very foundation. The anxiety of exclusion, of being excluded—*ausgeschlossen*—from oneself, from self-determination, from a groundedness in oneself, requires that the excluding One—*das ausschließende Eine*—or identity as difference, be excluded, included as excluded, in the Oriental anticipation of the passage from Orient to Occident.

Sunrise "for the First Time Again": Modernity as Realization of the "Time of the New"

I began by considering, with reference to the instability of the border in general, the typological structure, the organizing theological-political concepts, and the panicky affective overdetermination of Hegel's *Lectures*. I then examined the structure of the Orient as a triple border between the nonhistorical and the historical. And we went on to see the analogously prefigurative positions of India and Judaea in Hegel's attempt to present this border as what transforms the nonhistorical into the historical while keeping the former out of the latter, including it as excluded.

It remains for me to show, as we move toward the conclusion of this chapter, how Hegel figures the ultimate realization of this (Indo-Judaic) prefiguration in his presentation of the arrival of history at its end in Christian-Germanic modernity. Appropriately, and indeed predictably, it is in this moment of realization that the Oriental figures of sunrise and the allied concept of the new obtrusively return in Hegel's text. Whether he can manage to master this return, so that it constitutes neither a mere repetition of prematurity nor a confession of belatedness, is the main question to consider in this discussion. In advance, it makes sense to suspect that he cannot. For as he both inscribes in his project and wants to avoid or deny, there is an ambiguity about the end—*Abendland* (or "the West" qua "Land of Evening") as arrival and as *Untergang* (or "descent"): presence and disappearance.[41] The moment of realization will tend to appear as its own outside edge, as too late, and therefore also as too early for the next repetition of the arrival of being, or the coming into presence of history. Because Hegel will figure the Christian-Germanic world not only as modernity, or more literally as "Time of the New"—*Neuzeit*—but also as "New World"—*die neue Welt*—one must begin here by examining what he means by "New World" more generally, and consider how Hegel relates this extension of Europe, this post- and also pre-European phenomenon (the New World), to his conceptions of European history and Oriental (especially Indian) proto-history. Once again, it is a question of how an outside edge or threshold of history relates to its inside.

So what is the "New World" for Hegel? Hegel determines the New World, in the sense of America, on the one hand, as the place of what he considers to be the utterly uncivilizable Native Americans and, on the other hand, as the site of the European colonial offshoot or "land of the future" (*das Land der Zukunft*) (114; 86), which he also calls a "land of desire" (*ein Land der Sehnsucht*) (114; 86) for Europeans "bored by the historical storeroom of Old Europe" (*alle die, welche die historische Rüstkammer des alten Europa langweilt*) (114; 86, trans. modified).

> America is hence the land of the future [*das Land der Zukunft*], in which in times that lie before us, for example in the struggle between North and

South America, the world-historical importance shall reveal itself; it is a land of desire [*ein Land der Sehnsucht*] for all those who are bored [*langweilt*] by the historical storeroom of Old Europe. Napoleon is supposed to have said: "This old Europe bores me." America has to cut itself off from the ground [*von dem Boden*] on which until today world-history has played itself out. What has occurred there up till now is only the echo of the Old World [*der Widerhall der Alten Welt*] and the expression of a foreign liveliness, and as a land of the future [*ein Land der Zukunft*] it is of absolutely no concern to us here; for we are concerned in history [*nach der Seite der Geschichte*] with that which has been and with that which is—in philosophy, however, we are concerned with that which has neither merely been nor merely still will be, but rather with that which *is* and eternally is, with reason [*weder nur gewesen ist noch erst nur sein wird, sondern mit dem, was ist und ewig ist, mit der Vernunft*], and with this we have plenty to do. (114; 86–87, trans. modified)

Insofar as it is not simply nothing—the place of the extrahistorical Native Americans, for whom Hegel reserves his only polemic more derisory than his dismissal of African culture—America is only "the land of the future." The futurity of America places it beyond the purview of history. For history is concerned "with that which has been and that which is" (*mit dem, was gewesen ist, und mit dem, was ist*) (114; 87). Since philosophy, in turn, is concerned with "that which has neither merely been nor merely still will be, but rather with that which *is* and eternally is, with reason" (*was weder nur gewesen ist noch erst nur sein wird, sondern mit dem, was ist und ewig ist, mit der Vernunft*) (114; 87, trans. modified), without bothering with the futurally transient he has plenty to do (*damit haben wir zur Genüge zu tun*) (114; 87). The things that have been and are, in connection with eternal presence qua reason, are the concern of a philosophy of history. Since America is the merely futural, in contrast, it is of no concern here.

And yet, not only must America qua future, in principle and necessarily, affect and interest Hegel's philosophy of history, displacing it at some future point retroactively—and Hegel knows this well—but Hegel also connects America for historical reasons explicitly with the external origin of history that keeps threatening to become its internal origin, its very self. For example, Hegel calls America not just "the land of the future" but also a "land of desire," while he will call India "the land of desire": "It has always been the land of desire and appears to us still as the realm of wonders, as a magical world" (*Es ist immer das Land der Sehnsucht gewesen und erscheint uns noch als ein Wunderreich, als eine verzauberte Welt*) (174; 139, trans. modified). There is evidently a danger—even in Hegel's text—of confusing America with the presence of the origin and the origin of presence as site of the (eternally) new, a danger analogous to the danger of considering India itself to constitute such an original presence and present origin. Hence there is also a danger of confusing America with India, as indeed occurred at the moment of its "discovery." What comes after the end—America—and what comes just before the beginning—India, as immediately prior to Persia—are equally the limits of history that we should not confuse with history itself, nor with each other. Yet Hegel underlines precisely this danger when he characterizes the discovery of Sanskrit as the (false) discovery of a "new world," in a passage I cited earlier but must briefly discuss now.

The context, as one may recall, was Hegel's disavowal of Sanskrit as origin. He wrote in the passage cited that the "discovery" of Sanskrit as the basis of the main Western languages was greeted like the discovery of a new world (*wie einer neuen Welt*) (82; 60).[42] His polemical point in this context, however, was to emphasize that the world being discovered was precisely not a New World at all, at least not in the sense in which a New World would be a world of the new, an originating ground. After all, the "discovery" of the New World took the form of a confusion between America and India. The discovery amounted to a failed attempt to rediscover the Old World of India qua New so as to appropriate it, to transfer its original riches—both material and spiritual—to the European qua site of the new. The East Indies turned out to be the mere West Indies; the origin was not situated where it was thought to have been found. And yet the new "discovery" continued to draw people on into the land of futurity as into the space of desire for presence qua freedom. (The opposite of boredom, or *Langeweile*, would, after all, be the *Kurzweile*, whose absolute form is the infinite brevity that stills time, the eternal moment or presence itself that Goethe also sought.) Similarly, the great discovery (*große Entdeckung*) of the Old World in the form of Sanskrit language and culture, although it appears to be a discovery of a New World, of the very Newness of the World, in fact is not. With India, we do not discover a New World, a world as good as (it is) new, but only an Old World, a dead language. Where we think we are discovering old newness, we are only discovering new oldness.

The rediscovery of ancient India, in short, should not blind us to the fact that the real (or realized) New World—even if Hegel also calls Europe "Old" on occasion—is the "modern"—or *Neuzeit*—world of Europe, as the "Germanic" world.[43]

> The Germanic spirit is the spirit of the New World [*der Geist der neuen Welt*], whose purpose is the realization of absolute truth as the infinite self-determination of freedom, of that freedom which has its absolute form itself as content. . . . The Christian world is the World of completion [*Vollendung*]; the principle is fulfilled [*das Prinzip ist erfüllt*], and therewith the end of days has become full; the idea can see in Christianity nothing that is still unsatisfied. (413; 341, trans. modified)

As the spirit of the New World, the Germanic spirit extends itself over that world. It thereby appropriates both the forward movement of history (or the future) in advance and the origin of the West in Sanskrit culture, which appeared like a New World but turned out to be only an old one. The actual New World, as a world of the new—the incessant dawning of presence—is neither the (absolute) past nor the (absolute) future, neither the Oriental East nor the American West, but the modern world, the world of the (absolute) now—"Neuzeit" in Christian, Germanic Europe.[44] The reason why neither India nor America is the New World is that the New World is German, Christian Europe.

As always, the realization of this realization will take three stages. It behooves us to consider these three stages briefly, since it is in key moments of this trajectory that not only the term *new* but also the figure of sunrise, the Oriental image par excellence, plays a prominent role. It is only by examining these resurgences of the figure of the newly rising sun that we can come to critical terms with Hegel's presentation of the modern, Germanic, Christian world as appropriation and realization of the Orient.[45] We will see here that the final sunrise bears a troubling resemblance to the situation—African, Native American, Oriental, and Indo-Judaic—before the first sunrise.

The first period of the Christian, Germanic world lasts from the beginnings of the Germanic nations in the Roman Empire until Charlemagne. It is the time when the Christian church and the state develop in relative independence of each other. The second period extends from Charlemagne to Charles V. This is the epoch when the relation between church and state develops as a contradiction. The third extends from Charles V and the Reformation through the Enlightenment and the French Revolution until Hegel's own time. In this phase, the reconciliation between church and state completes itself.

Hegel establishes the three phases of the Germanic world in relation to two sets of analogies: a Christian, trinitarian conception and a world-historical schema. In Christian terms, we pass from the period of the father, to that of the son, to that of the holy spirit. In world-historical epochal terms, the first of these Germanic periods recalls the world of Persia, being a period of "substantial unity"; the second bears comparison with Greece, as a period of "particularities" and "differences"; and the third resembles Rome, as a rule of "universality" but here in the mode of "self-conscious thought" (417–18; 345–46).

Initially conspicuous in this setup are two ways in which Hegel keeps China and India at bay. First, the Orient boils down here to its Persian culmination (in accord with Hegel's view that China and India remain outside of history). Second, in connection with the absence of China and India, one notes that Hegel does not mention the sense in which the three periods of Christianity correspond to China, India, and Persia, respectively. In our context, this suggests that we should be particularly curious about the passage or limit between the second period of Christian history and the third, with a view to the former period's potential role as outside limit of Christian history. For it is with this second period—the Middle Ages—that we have a figure analogous to India (and therefore once again to Judaism).[46]

Indeed, our curiosity is not disappointed, for it is with the arrival of modern Christianity at the end of the second period that Hegel goes back to the imagery of sunrise, emphasizing thus that the appropriation of the Orient is realized in modernity. The third section of part 4 on the Germanic world, titled "Die neue Zeit" ("Modern Times," or "The New Time"), begins with the Reformation, which Hegel introduces as "the all-transfiguring sun that follows upon the dawn at the end of the Middle Ages" (*die alles verklärende Sonne, die auf jene Morgenröte am Ende des Mittelalters folgt*) (491; 412, trans. modified). The *Morgenröte*, or dawn itself, signaling the "end of the middle ages" (i.e., of the second period in Germanic history), comprises three traits: the "restoration of the sciences, the blossoming of the fine arts, and the discovery of America and of the path to East India." These three traits, Hegel says, are

> to be compared with the dawn [*der* Morgenröte *zu vergleichen*] that, after long storms, for the first time again signals a beautiful day [*zum ersten Male wieder einen schönen Tag verkündet*]. This day is the day of universality [*Allgemeinheit*], which finally breaks in after the long night of the middle ages (so terrible and so rich in consequences), a day characterized by science, art, and the drive to discovery, i.e., by the most noble and highest things, which the human spirit, having become free through Christianity and emancipated through the Church, presents as its eternal and true content. (491; 411, trans. modified)

As the dawn of humanity occurred in the Indian Orient's differentiation of identity, so the dawn will appear "for the first time again" in the end of the middle ages that coincides with the return to India in its Eastern reality and its Western simulacrum.[47] The morning will appear "for the first time again" in the moment when Christianity manages to totalize the world from India to India and so, apparently, to master the external limits of the beginning and the end of its becoming.

But "for the first time again"—*zum ersten Male wieder*—what could such a phrase signify? Is it the inside or the outside limit of history that we encounter with this sunrise? Is it history itself (the inside) or still its not-yet or already its no-longer (outside)? The question seems undecidable, but Hegel cannot have it both ways if he wants the Reformation to constitute "die alles verklärende Sonne" ("the all-transfiguring sun") as fulfillment of the principle or ground. Let me detail this undecidability briefly.

The first possible reading is that with this new sunrise we return to the beginning, repeat the beginning. This reading would be reminiscent of Nietzsche's "wohlan, noch einmal" ("well then, once again")—his affirmation of the eternal return—but it is clearly not what Hegel has in mind, for such a return would signify that this new sunrise is once again merely anticipatory, giving rise to an insufficient sun. The implication of such a realization would be that it is either always too early—that history never begins (if even the real beginning simply recapitulates a not-yet)—or always too late—that the not-yet is always already an already, or even an already-no-longer, that history began (and perhaps ended) even before it began.

The second possible reading, the one Hegel requires, is that this time the sunrise appears as the first time. It truly presences or presents the sun, rather than merely anticipating a day to which it cannot immediately give rise, a day it is not yet and cannot itself become. On this second reading, history is actually, truly beginning, finally, with the Reformation.

Yet even as Hegel must insist on this second reading of "zum ersten Male wieder," the phrase does not admit of any decision on the first or second of its readings. The emphasis on the Reformation as inaugurating the realization of the *Neuzeit* qua time of the new—qua eternally new presence of the interpenetration of subject and object, arrival of the concrete as such—requires that the first reading not haunt the second one, but such a haunting cannot in fact be excluded. I will consider two forms in which this haunting occurs. In the first case, the Oriental sunrise and its sunset recur within the Germanic world in the form of Islam and the

Crusades, at the conclusion of which the West takes its leave of the Orient once again, a leave that coincides with the sunrise at the end of the Middle Ages. In the second case, the sunrise of the Enlightenment asserts itself in the French Revolution, but with problematic results. These two late sunrises are closely related, moreover, as we shall see, through the motif of terror—a motif not without relation to that of the panic guiding our trajectory here, the panic of being haunted by an impossibility of acceding to, or even identifying, one's proper ground or origin.

Grave Developments: Islam and Terror from the Holy Land to Paris and Beyond

What is the place or role of Islam in Hegel's philosophy of history? During the first period of the Germanic world, Islam arises as a principle of radical monotheism, abstract universality, of the "integration of the whole" (428; 356, trans. modified), which opposes the dominant tendency within the Christian world in this period, a tendency toward particularity, the fragmentation of the world into "chance dependencies" (*zufälliger Abhängigkeiten*) (428; 355, trans. modified).[48] Islam—or what Hegel mostly calls "der Mohammedanismus," in line with a tradition drawing unflattering parallels between Mohammed and Christ that Edward Said insightfully and usefully problematized—effects a "Revolution of the East" (*Revolution des Orients*) (428; 356), which

> destroyed all particularity and dependence and completely enlightened and purified [*aufklärte und reinigte*] the heart [*Gemüt*], in that it made only the abstract One into the absolute object and in the same manner made the pure subjective consciousness, the knowledge of only this One, into the sole purpose of reality—making the relationless into the relation of existence [*das Verhältnislose zum Verhältnis der Existenz*]. (428–29; 356, trans. modified)[49]

The development of Islam is akin, Hegel writes, to Jewish abstract monotheism, in which alone the "principle of simple unity raised itself into thought" and which alone honored "the One, who is for Thought" (429; 356, trans. modified). But Islam is more radical: It purifies Judaism of its exclusiveness, its residual particularism. In this sense, it finishes the destruction and overcoming of Judaism necessary to the installation of the world hegemony of Christianity. The One in Islam is more properly spiritual than the One in Judaism, but because in Islam subjectivity disappears into this One, its absolute object, the One remains still abstract and the subject still unfree (429; 356).

These characteristics (the abstractness of the absolute and the unfreedom of the subject) still tie Islam, however, not only to Judaism, but also to the Hinduism that, on Hegel's account, resembles the latter. Hence, Hegel is compelled to state explicitly at this juncture what nonetheless differentiates Islam from Hinduism:

> But Mohammedanism is not the Indian, Monkish absorption [*Versenkung*] in the absolute, but rather subjectivity is here lively and infinite, an activity which, stepping into the worldly, only negates the latter, and is only effective and mediating in service to the imperative that the pure honoring of the One should exist. (429; 356–57, trans. modified)

Yet this distinction remains problematic to the degree that subjectivity is here active only in order to annihilate or suspend the world—"in reality nothing should be solid" (430; 357, trans. modified)—and that the greatest honor is dying for the faith (430; 357), so that a certain suicidal tendency, a desired self-negation of the will in the face of an abstract absolute, like that of the Hindu monks, is present here in Hegel's account of Islam. Like ancient Indian culture, Islam introduces relentless abstract differentiations, borders without border: It undoes all identities, as a process of limitation that itself has no limits, producing a worldless world of formless forms, like the desert itself in which it arose, an image Hegel exploits to develop his account of Islam. The shifting sands of the world become an object of "indifference" (the Muslim is "gleichgültig dagegen" ["indifferent to it"] [431; 358]), but fixed forms become the object of aggression because the only thing that should exist is the abstract universality of the One as object of thought. An endless differentiation of all identities serves the one negative Identity, the abstract Universal, much as was the case in ancient India, and also in Judaea.

Hence it is not surprising that Islam, as repetition or resurgence of the abstract absolute, should involve for Hegel a kind of panic. The enthusiasm for the abstract is what Hegel calls the "fanaticism" of Islam: "This enthusiasm was *fanaticism*, i.e., an enthusiasm for an abstract thing [*ein Abstraktes*], for an abstract thought, that relates only negatively to what is" (*der negierend sich zum Bestehenden verhält*) (431; 358, trans. modified). And this fanaticism, in its negativity with respect to life, as service to a foundation that unfounds and confounds all that it founds, is terror, as

Hegel asserts, comparing the "Revolution of the Orient" with the French Revolution: "*La religion et la terreur* was the principle in this case, as with Robespierre, *la liberté et la terreur*" (431; 358).[50] Forcing an abstract God upon the world is like forcing an abstract notion of freedom upon the world. The impositions imply two different forms of the same abstract universality, two different effacements of the concrete particulars of existence. In both formations, the subject terrorizes others, and lives itself in terror, or panic, because it attempts (in vain) to make an abstraction the foundation of all concrete existence, of the very existence which that abstraction simultaneously negates.

But not to worry: The anxiety-inducing natural spirituality will once again give way to meaning. Owing to its one-sidedness, the "fanatical" service to abstraction in Islam leads—here, as in various ways in both India and Judaism—to its reversal and overturning. To be sure, Islam is for Hegel a revolution that leads to great achievements, incomparable heroism, intensely inward poetry, imaginative arts, and scientific progress (432–33; 358–59), especially during the dynasties of the Abassid caliphs. In this sense, the "Revolution of the Orient" indeed is a sort of sunrise. But the refusal of fixed forms means that Islam remains unstable in the world, and when stability arrives, with the Ottoman Empire, this is already predicated on the cooling off of the "fanaticism" (433; 360) of Islam. With fixed forms of life and institutions of power, the equivalent of the dead letter of the Jewish law and the natural differences of the Indian caste system asserts itself. Here, however, materiality takes the form of sensuous self-indulgence:

> The Orient itself, once the enthusiasm gradually had disappeared, sank into the greatest vice, the ugliest passions became dominant, and since sensuous pleasure already lies in the first formations of the Mohammedan doctrine itself and is established as reward in Paradise, such pleasure now took the place of the fanaticism. Today . . . Islam has already long since disappeared from the ground of world history and stepped back into Oriental complacency and quietude. (434; 360, trans. modified)

The abstraction of the Islamic Orient thus eventually reverses itself into its opposite: debased materiality, stagnation, and death.

But the appearance of Islam will have served a crucial purpose for the development of the modern West, as arrival and end of history. Here, as when Greece absorbed Oriental wisdom, Christianity absorbs the high culture of Islam. Just prior to the inevitable fall of the Islamic Orient (the regression to its inherent materialism), the West takes up the relay by way of the Crusades, appropriating the sciences and arts, including philosophy, that have blossomed (433) in the high period of the Abassid Caliphate.

> In the struggle with the Saracens European bravery had idealized itself into beautiful, noble Knighthood; science and knowledge, especially philosophy, came from the Arabs into the Occident; a noble poetry and free fantasy was ignited amongst the Germanic peoples in the Orient, and thus Goethe also turned to the Morning-Land and produced in his *Divan* a chain of pearls that outdoes everything in inwardness and fortunate fantasy [*die an Innigkeit und Glückseligkeit der Phantasie alles übertrifft*]. (433–34; 360; trans. modified)

The culmination (441; 366) of the Middle Ages in the Crusades—which is the point where the dawn of the Orient in its Islamic repetition passes its gift of origin to the Occident as high culture of arts and sciences—is also the moment when the Occident *breaks* (as in a repetition of the Judaic *break*) with the Orient and, breaking itself, issues in the sunrise that is the end of the Middle Ages. Let us see how this occurs.

In seeking to (re)gain possession of the grave of Christ in the Orient, the Christianity of the Crusades was attempting to appropriate the spatially situated sense-certainty of God as "this" (468; 390), as concrete materiality (467–70; 389–92). "But in the grave lies the actual point of reversal; it is in the grave that all of the idleness of the sensual goes under or sets" (like the sun: *untergeht*) (471; 392, trans. modified). Christianity found "its ultimate truth" (471; 393), namely, "the principle of your religion you have not in the sensuous, in the grave with the dead, but in the living spirit amongst yourselves" (471; 393, trans. modified). The dead letter of Christ's place of burial must be renounced. In losing the Holy Land after having regained this grave and its disappointing emptiness, Christianity discovers the truth of its radical spirituality (472; 393). The "this" is not sensuous at all, but the "spiritual being-for-itself of the person" (472; 393, trans. modified). Subjectivity finally comes to its rights.

> The Occident *took leave* of the Orient at the Holy Grave forever [*Das Abendland hat vom Morgenlande am Heiligen Grabe auf ewig* Abschied *genommen*], and it grasped its principle of subjective infinite freedom. Christianity never again stepped as a whole onto the stage of history [*als ein Ganzes aufgetreten*]. (472; 393, trans. modified)

The ultimate failure or disappointment of the Crusades becomes already the splitting of the church (into outward and inward), that is, ultimately the Reformation, which announces itself in the end of the Middle Ages with the rise of the arts and sciences and the noble Orders of Knights and pious Orders of Monks, a rise occasioned by the passage of Arab Muslim high culture to the West.[51] The West thus appropriates not so much the grave of Christ as the spirit of (Western) Greek philosophy from the Arab Muslims, in accordance with the notion that the prefiguration belongs always already to its realization (476–77; 397–78).

What the West renounces in renouncing the East, taking leave of the East, is the materiality of the empty grave, or of the grave as emptiness, the dead letter of materiality as the principle of the Other of the West, the materiality into which high medieval Muslim culture will soon fall as into its own essence. The "break," or *Bruch* (241; 195), from the East to the West—which was originally established by the Jewish monotheistic invention, then repeated in the Arab Muslim radicalization, but never really achieved by either of these anticipations—is now made finally by Christianity in its turn away from the grave of the materiality of the East at the end of the Crusades. Indeed, the very term *break* returns here as well: "The spirit, un-satisfied in its desire for the highest sensuous presence, threw itself back within itself [*hat sich in sich zurückgeworfen*]. An initial and deep break occurred [*Es ist ein erster und tiefer Bruch geschehen*]" (474; 395, trans. modified). The break from the East that (almost) occurred with the ancient Judaic religion, and before that with ancient Indian difference, and again long afterward with the Muslim "purification" of Jewish monotheism, prolongs itself in the (still) "initial" break that occurs when Christianity turns (anew) inward after the successful failure of the Crusades. And this latter break in turn prolongs itself in the slow rise of sciences and arts and the world-exploration encompassing India and America that constitute the dawn at the end of the Middle Ages. But if the sun of the Reformation is supposed to arise through an origination of daylight that is no longer susceptible to collapse back into its essential night of materiality, if this dawn is supposed to be in some sense an ultimate dawn (as the realization of the destiny of humanity toward the consciousness of freedom), then the temporal logic of the prolongation of becoming must no longer operate here. And yet manifestly this logic, the (il)logic of the border, is still at work. Moreover, it will continue to be at work in the realization of this ultimate realization, the very French Revolution to which Hegel likened the Islamic "Revolution of the Orient" that therefore anticipates it, including what we will see to be its belatedly still anticipatory character.

Specifically, in the third chapter (or the ostensible realization) of the section on the "new time," or modernity, titled "The Enlightenment and the French Revolution" (the first two sections of the chapter are "The Reformation" and "Effects of the Reformation on the Constitution of States"), Hegel calls the French Revolution "a magnificent dawn" (*ein herrlicher Sonnenaufgang*) (529; 447). The sun, it seems, just keeps on rising.

> Never since the sun had stood in the firmament and the planets revolved around it had it been seen that man stood on his head, i.e., on Thought, and built up the world of reality in accordance with the latter [*daß der Mensch sich auf den Kopf, d.i. auf den Gedanken stellt und die Wirklichkeit nach diesem erbaut*]. Anaxagoras had been the first to say that *noos* governs the world, but not until now had man advanced to the recognition of the principle that Thought should govern spiritual reality. This was thus a magnificent dawn [*daß der Gedanke die geistige Wirklichkeit regieren sollte. Es war dieses ein herrlicher Sonnenaufgang*]. (529; 447, trans. modified)

Although Hegel perhaps minimizes the importance of this sunrise, in contrast to the sunrise of the ending Middle Ages, by calling it "a" dawn, not "the" dawn, it remains unmistakably the case that the "zum ersten Male wieder" repeats itself here again, as it were within the prior repetition (modernity as Reformation). Evidently, the French Revolution repeats the beginnings of humanity—as the progress in the consciousness of freedom—that have begun (only without beginning) in the Orient—China, India, Persia—and again in Islam. The dissolution of the Middle Ages just prior to the Reformation realizes itself, then, in the French Revolution, repeating itself there "for the first time again," and leading to the German state of the postrevolutionary period, in which the progress of history comes to a kind of conclusion.[52]

But precisely to what kind of conclusion does the French Revolution lead? Is the reconciliation, or *Versöhnung*, there totally total? Or only partially total? In short: How total is total? At the end of his discussion of the process of the French Revolution, Hegel writes of a "collision" (*Kollision*) or "knot" (*Knoten*), a "problem . . . where history stands and . . . which it will have to solve in future times" (*dieses Problem ist es, an dem die Geschichte steht und den sie in künftigen Zeiten zu lösen hat*) (535; 452, trans. modified):

> The main one-sidedness remains, that the general will is also supposed to be the *empirically* general will, i.e., that the individuals are supposed to rule as such or at least participate in the government [*daß der allgemeine Wille auch der empirisch allgemeine sein soll, d.h. daß die Einzelnen als solche regieren oder am Regimente teilnehmen sollen*].
>
>   Not content that reasonable rights, personal liberty, and freedom of property, are in force, that an organization of the State exists and within it circles of bourgeois life which themselves have business to perform,

that rational individuals have an influence upon the people and that trust reigns within the people, *liberalism* opposes to all of this the principle of the atom, the individual will; everything is supposed to occur through its express power and express consent. With the formal mode of freedom, with this abstraction, they let nothing solid in the way of organization arise [*setzt der Liberalismus allem diesen das Prinzip der Atome, der Einzelwillen entgegen: alles soll durch ihre ausdrückliche Macht und ausdrückliche Einwilligung geschehen. Mit diesem Formellen der Freiheit, mit dieser Abstraktion lassen sie nichts Festes von Organisation aufkommen*]. Freedom opposes itself immediately to the particular rulings of the government, for they are the particularity of the will, thus arbitrariness [*besonderer Wille, also Willkür*]. The will of the many brings down the ministry, and that which has been the opposition steps in now to govern. But the latter, insofar as it is now the governing party, has once again the many against it. And so the movement and unquiet continue. This collision, this knot, this problem, is where history stands and that which it will have to solve in future times [*Diese Kollision, dieser Knoten, dieses Problem ist es an dem die Geschichte steht und den sie in künftigen Zeiten zu lösen hat*]. (534–35; 452, trans. modified)

Where, then, does the "herrlicher Sonnenaufgang" of the French Revolution lead? It leads to the still unsolved problem of how to link the particular will with the general will, how to articulate the one with the many, substance with subject, identity with difference. That this remains the problem to be solved "in future times" is certainly an astonishing statement to read toward the end of Hegel's *Lectures*, in the section on the culmination of history, its arrival at its full presence! Indeed, this is all the more the case as Hegel makes history as such depend on the existence of states, and makes it begin to begin with the rise of the Oriental quasi states, defining the state precisely—we saw this toward the outset—as the articulation of the individual with the general will.

From this perspective, on the one hand, it appears as if history has not quite started even when it is most fully present, in the arrival at its end, when state and church are supposed to have been entirely achieved and mutually reconciled. On the other hand, since the situation of India was one in which difference was at odds with identity, a situation characterized by the "Unruhe" (or "disquiet") of which Hegel speaks again here concerning the post–French Revolutionary conjuncture of his own day, it seems as if history had perhaps already realized itself in ancient India, at what was supposed to be the outside limit of its origination, the almost but not quite yet of the origin. Finally, since Hegel says that this problem of the mediation between individual and general will is a problem for the future of history, it seems as if its solution will be the task of America. For America is the "land of the future," a future which, it now appears, consists in the possible origination of history through the overcoming of "this collision, this knot, this problem." The outside limit of history at its end appears to double as the inside limit of its still-future (mere) possibility.

Perhaps what Hegel's *Lectures* finally nolens volens tell us about history is that if history is full presence as the overcoming of the distance between particular and general (or reality and its representation, or spirit and letter), history has always already started (because there is some relation bridging these distances) and never yet started (because the relation is a relation without relation: it doesn't overcome the rift). Where we live-and-die, in the (non)present of the limit between these two, is always in memory of and in desire for history, way back there up ahead to come. The starting of history is therefore a start(l)ing—an interruption—of the start itself. The starting starts. This situation, however, cannot produce the narrative of appropriated origination that Hegel desires, his own textual and philosophical "land of desire." Hegel's project stumbles on the threshold, the unmastered problem of the limit, despite his energetic (and fascinating) application of typological thinking to the whole of world history as he conceived it.

From Hegel to Schopenhauer: The Assumption of the Indian "Origin"

In the development of German historicist metaphysics in philosophical, philological, and literary writing about the Orient from Friedrich Schlegel on, the resistance to the philologically or language-historically induced threat of Western culture's regression back into its Eastern and more specifically Sanskrit origin—resistance to the danger of coming to seem to oneself a mere belated metaphor of the Orient—receives its most well known and perhaps grandest philosophical formulation in Hegel's philosophy. In Hegel, the resistance takes the form of the positing of a barrier between East and West at the limit between ancient Indian and ancient Persian cultures, a limit that repeats itself on "higher" levels in ancient Judaea, in Islam, in the Crusades, in the French Revolution, in America, and—at the limit—all across the surface of Hegel's text. In this privilege granted to the Persian East as the beginning of the beginning of the West (a privilege that remains despite the repetitions), Hegel is in partial solidarity with Lessing, Goethe, and Nietzsche. (Nietzsche will formulate this preference, through the persona of Zarathustra, in consistency with his rejection of Schopenhauerian philosophy.)

When Hegel's philosophical hegemony begins to fade, however, the opposite strategy will become prevalent, in the form of the Aryan myth. For this myth undertakes the enthusiastic assumption of the Indian origin as an origin in an essentially (always already) Western East. This Indian origin will then stand opposed to what will be regarded as the essentially Eastern (hence radically foreign, nonappropriable) East of Semitic cultures. Schopenhauer's philosophy, as we will see in the following chapter, accomplishes this shift very early already in its main philosophical outlines, although the Aryan myth will require the entire nineteenth century to solidify itself as a racist anti-Semitic ideology with significant—horrendous—political potential.[53] In the development of the Aryan myth, the relativization, rejection, or exclusion of ancient Indian culture as beginning or foundation of the West will give way to the absolutization, embrace, and inclusion of this culture as origin. This will occur largely because of the philosophical difficulties that attend the former strategy (that is, exclusion, etc.) in the face of the prestige of historical linguistics as the master discourse of cultural historiography, and more specifically in the face of the internal development and proliferation of Sanskrit studies. If Sanskrit founds "our" (Western) languages, might we not constitute a mere fall away from their literally spiritual ground? Schopenhauer will claim as much, replacing the (still optimistic) Hegelian evening of realization with the (pessimistic) realization of an originary night. Pursuing a strategy no less problematic then Hegel's, though in important respects its inversion, Schopenhauer will argue that "we" must return to the ancient Indian ground by purifying Christianity of the Jewish contamination that places "us" in a diasporal relation to this ground, as I show in the following chapter.

CHAPTER 6

Taking Up Groundlessness, Fulfilling Fulfillment: Schopenhauer's Orientalist Metaphysics between Indians and Jews

> There lives only in the innermost depths of his consciousness the wholly obscure presentiment that all this is indeed not really so strange to him, but has a connexion [*Zusammenhang*] with him from which the *principium individuationis* cannot protect him. From this presentiment arises that ineradicable dread, common to all human beings . . . which suddenly seizes him, when by any chance they become puzzled over [*irre werden am*] the *principium individuationis*, in that the principle of sufficient reason in one or other of its forms seems to undergo an exception [*eine Ausnahme zu erleiden scheint*]. For example, when it appears that some change has occurred without a cause, or a deceased person exists again; or when in any other way the past or the future is present, or the distant is near. The fearful terror at anything of this kind is based on the fact that they suddenly become puzzled over [*irre werden an*] the forms of knowledge of the phenomenon [*Erscheinung*] which alone hold their own individuality separate from the rest of the world. This separation, however, lies only in the phenomenon and not in the thing-in-itself; and precisely on this rests eternal justice. In fact, all temporal happiness stands, and all prudence proceeds, on undermined ground [*auf untergrabenem Boden*].
>
> —ARTHUR SCHOPENHAUER, *The World as Will and Representation*

> Historical subjects have a decidedly detrimental effect only when they restrict the painter to a field chosen arbitrarily, and not for artistic but for other purposes. This is particularly the case when the field is poor in picturesque and significant objects, when, for example, it is the history of a small, isolated, capricious, hierarchical (i.e., ruled by false notions) obscure people, like the Jews, despised by the great contemporary nations of the East and of the West. . . . [It] is to be regarded generally as a great misfortune that the people whose former culture was to serve mainly as the basis [*Unterlage*] of our own were not, say, the Indians or the Greeks, or even the Romans, but just these Jews.
>
> —ARTHUR SCHOPENHAUER, *The World as Will and Representation*

Schopenhauer occupies a very important but also ambiguous place in modern Orientalist metaphysics. To circumscribe his place, I begin by delineating three interrelated displacements he effects within the German (and more broadly the European) philosophical tradition.

First, he makes explicit like no philosophical thinker before him (with the possible complex exception of Schelling) the confrontation with groundlessness that occasions modern Orientalism.[1] Indeed, at least up to a certain point, he is capable of affirming and assuming this groundlessness in its necessity. Let me expand on this point briefly before proceeding.

Schopenhauer assumes or accepts groundlessness under the figure of the will. The will is the essence of things—the *Ding an Sich*—and it is the ground of appearances—it is the will to appearances—which arise out of it insofar as it is subjected to the principle of sufficient reason, the (mere) form of appearances. But in itself, prior to the application of the principle of sufficient reason, the will is groundless: It has no origin, end, form, or meaningful content. It is pure hunger, striving, struggle, desire without possibility of satisfaction. Because it seeks always to fill the lack that constitutes it—the lack that is the ground of its own groundlessness—the will is the endless and groundless search precisely for a ground.

The foundation that the will seeks would further comprise precisely its fulfillment, for the will has to be understood, in temporal terms (i.e., in its ineluctable appearance as representation or "Vor-stellung"), as an endless (and retrospective) anticipation, in figural terms as (metaleptic) *prolepsis*: the prefiguration of a fulfillment that can never (re)arrive. Accordingly, Schopenhauer literally and repeatedly insists that the will can find no fulfillment, or "Erfüllung."[2]

This brings us to Schopenhauer's second radical contribution, entailed by the first. The assumption of eternal groundlessness, which cuts off all possibility of fulfillment or realization, in principle makes impossible all typology. It renders questionable, for example, at once the Orientalist reference to the East as to a transcendent-historical ground of the West and the typological appropriation of that ground for the West qua realization. This implicit delegitimation of the typological model of prefiguration and fulfillment (wherein, as Erich Auerbach shows, historical reality and the donation of meaning coincide) follows logically from Schopenhauer's willingness to wrestle in a serious way with groundlessness as such. For an eternal lack of transcendent foundations means quite simply that fulfillment as cessation of striving is no longer an option, or at any rate that fulfillment is no longer quite what it used to be. Prefiguration and retrospection become ubiquitous—they come to pervade the self same instant, rending it into multiply separated renditions of itself. Typological relations complicate themselves, in principle, out of existence. This second contribution occurs, then, on the level of (biblical) hermeneutics, but it therefore affects also, of course, the ideologies of religious history and modern racism that depend on this hermeneutics.

The third aspect of Schopenhauer's intervention that one must stress here occurs on the level of the philosophy of history, especially in its Hegelian lineage, which is still in the process of articulating itself as Schopenhauer contests the adequacy of its foundations. Schopenhauer's move at this level affects the ideologies of concrete cultural history within this philosophy of history as well as, conversely, the philosophy of history that influences in turn these ideologies. Although his thought develops in an Orientalist age—marked by various Indomanias and Egyptomanias, preferences for Persians, and so on—more than any other modern Western philosopher before him, Schopenhauer is able to see the Oriental thought he most admires—ancient Indian thought—as the equal of any Western philosophical achievement. This indication of the limits of Eurocentrism follows from Schopenhauer's implicit critique of the prefiguration-fulfillment model—as the contrast with Schlegel's text on the Indians and with Hegel's *Lectures on the Philosophy of History* illustrates nicely. To see the Indian East as always already leading toward its fulfillment in the West, for example, would require that Schopenhauer place himself above the East. But this is precisely something that he is in principle disinclined to do, even if he struggles against this disinclination, as we shall see. Finally, this third insight reinforces the first: Schopenhauer's idealization of ancient Indian pessimism, his view of it as the ne plus ultra of philosophical achievements, strengthens his commitment to the notion of the groundlessness of the will. Ancient Hindu thought confirms Schopenhauer and guides him in his strictly philosophical explication of that problem: the articulation of the (Leibnizian) principle of sufficient reason with a revision of the Kantian transcendental account of experiential possibility-conditions.

These three Schopenhauerian gestures or displacements, then, hang together tightly, in a certain *Zusammenhang*. The positing of an abyss at the ontological origin, the questioning of typology, and the recognition of ancient Indian thought beyond the purview of Eurocentrism (at least within certain limits)—these three points cohere in Schopenhauer's oeuvre such that to unsettle one is to unsettle them all. They are also points, however, that challenge Schopenhauer himself. For Schopenhauer is not quite ready to yield to the victor—his own innovations—the more traditional stance that constitutes his point of departure.

Acknowledgment of an irrecoverable loss of foundations, first of all, does not go without saying. Second, the renunciation of two thousand years of Western, Christian orientation in *Heilsgeschichte* is difficult to undertake in one go. And third, the loss of Europe as center of authority implies for Schopenhauer his own superfluity, the nonnecessity of his precise way of putting things—an implication hard for any philosopher to accept, as we have seen also in the case of Hegel. It is not my intention, of course, to make excuses here for Schopenhauer's shortcomings or lapses in rigor. Rather, the point is to understand them. For Schopenhauer's influential contribution to the metaphysics of Orientalism and Orientalist metaphysics can best be measured and described as the tension between his positive—and indeed (in the etymological sense) radical—contributions and his own resistance to them.[3]

Accordingly, in what follows I consider interrelated aspects of Schopenhauer's work—linked contexts of systematic discussion—in which he contradicts and disavows each of his three main contributions. (1) The first of these is Schopenhauer's doctrine of salvation, the negative telos of all striving, the end as both curtailment and goal. I suggest here that the very notion of a possible negation of the will-to-live disavows or denies the groundlessness of the will in a problematic way. (2) Next, I consider the tension between Schopenhauer's sense that Indian philosophy cannot be outdone and his rather different claim that his philosophy grasps the ancient Oriental wisdom in its most proper form.[4] Wherever Schopenhauer wants to privilege his own specific articulation, to return with a difference is to posit oneself as the fulfillment of the foreign anticipation of one's own thought.[5] (3) I then consider four contexts in which Schopenhauer has explicit recourse to—depends on and refuses or fails to mourn—typological ideology. Like the notion of the self-negation of the will, this recurrent recourse to typology disavows the implications of the doctrine of the will-to-representation as infinite deferral of fulfillment. Consideration of these contexts demonstrates that Schopenhauer's invocation of typology is not incidental to his philosophical project, isolated in the sphere of his politics of religion or his privately held stereotypical beliefs about given religious groups. Rather, it organizes his entire conception of the relationship between his philosophical achievement and the philosophical tradition. (A) The first of these contexts is Schopenhauer's (philosophico-politically weighted) history of positive religion, or his theological ideology, and in particular his construal of the relationships between Indian, Jewish, and Christian traditions. (B) Second, Schopenhauer problematically invokes typological motifs and notions of a self-grounding absolute within his argument for the separation of church and state, which doubles as an argument for the separation of philosophy from religion, and which begins, in addition, to envision the politicization of Schopenhauer's own thought. (C1) Third, Schopenhauer orients or positions his entire (ethical) philosophy with respect to the previous history of all ethical philosophy by means of a key reference to typology. (C2) Finally, and more specifically, Schopenhauer again invokes the typological model from an explicitly Christian identity-position in order to construct his relationship to pantheism in particular, and more narrowly still to Spinozism. Here we arrive at the end of the more strictly philosophical trajectory within this book, which runs from Spinoza to Schopenhauer.

In each of these invocations of typology, Schopenhauer positions the Jews as the representatives of the law (viz., the law of representation, the principle of sufficient reason), a law he hopes to overcome so as to achieve redemption, by sacrificially casting its representatives out. Schopenhauer's realization of the Indian origin, then, will proceed—not surprisingly from this historical distance, but at a level of philosophical complexity and involvement that we perhaps rarely appreciate or adequately comprehend—by way of a sacrificial exclusion of the Jews.

I Know There Is Radical Absence, But Still

Schopenhauer's description of the world as representation haunted by lack implies the impossibility of fulfillment in a transcendent presence, hence the impossibility of any ultimate foundation. However, the normative implication he draws from this description—the moral of his story, or rather his eudaemonistic ethics of world-renunciation—disavows this impossibility. To renounce the world is to escape the directionlessness, formlessness, causelessness, and emptiness of the will. The exceptional status of the momentary renunciation in aesthetic contemplation becomes the rule that replaces all rule with radical freedom in the saint's sustained self-negation.[6]

Schopenhauer's gesture of disavowal here entails not only that the self-negation of the will contradicts the depiction of the world as a will that groundlessly grinds on, but further that this self-negation necessarily contradicts itself. For the negation of the will is always haunted or doubled by an identification with the will as self-affirmation: The negation is always carried out in the name of an affirmation of what one is—of the freedom and autonomy that only escape from the will can achieve—but what one

Arthur Schopenhauer (1788–1860). Daguerreotype. Between 1855 and 1860. (Bildarchiv Preussischer Kulturbesitz, Berlin/Art Resource, N.Y.)

is, is at the same time always will, and freedom can characterize only the will. One still affirms oneself in self-denial (as indeed Nietzsche, and the Kafka of "A Hunger Artist," later well understood). Perhaps this structural inseparability of the negation of the will from its affirmation explains why Schopenhauer says that the negation of the will is not something one can ever conquer or achieve once and for all, but that one must always re-achieve it, again and again (497; 391). Nonetheless, Schopenhauer also repeatedly claims that the achieved self-negation of the will can coincide with itself, that it is absolutely distinct from the will's affirmation. In doing so, he denies and loses touch with what may have been his most important philosophical contribution: the theory of the world as representations marked by radical lack (similar to what Lacanians will later call the lack of the Other). It follows that Schopenhauer was a bit too optimistic about the possibility of separating pessimism from optimism, as indeed he was optimistic in envisioning the possibility of any pure self-negation of the will whatsoever (even if only as an exceptional metaphysical state).

Schopenhauer's disavowal of the absence of a foundation occurs not only explicitly, through his eschatology of world-negation, but also implicitly, on the level of ideologies of religious identity. Notably, he disavows this absence through the way in which he positions his thought with respect to the various traditions that precede him. For these traditions are in his discourse inextricably philosophical and religiocultural. He positions himself, moreover, explicitly in terms of the tradition of figural interpretation by repeatedly characterizing his position with respect to a given predecessor as the equivalent of the New Testament with respect to the Old.

Fulfilling Fulfillment

Merely by claiming both to effect a return to the ancient Oriental truth of nonfulfillment, and to provide this ancient truth with its most perfect articulation, Schopenhauer lays claim to the fulfillment of the (fulfilled) truth of nonfulfillment. He thus implicitly invokes typology in the very moment of its overcoming, even when he doesn't explicitly allude to the typological tradition. More concretely, he reenacts the Eurocentrism that his high respect for Indian philosophy placed in question. Yet in Schopenhauer's own terms, to lay claim to the fulfillment (or even to the possibility of the fulfillment) is always an optimistic move. Here, too, then, denying obstinately his own analysis of the will as "unergründlich," Schopenhauer is optimistic about his own fulfillment (and therefore grounding) of the truth of pessimism. Perhaps this accounts for the reader's nagging sense of the silliness of Schopenhauer's insistence on the superiority of his philosophical position over those of others, the puerile character of his insistence on its proper literality.

As we shall continue to see below, moreover, this performative contradiction significantly overdetermines Schopenhauer's anti-Semitism (and the converse). Evidently, somebody will have to enable Schopenhauer to purge his pessimism—and infinitely so—of the ineradicable fault of optimism that not only the claim to have returned to the wisdom of the East (which is the wisdom of the impossibility of any such return) but also, as we saw above, the very hope for a possible negation of the will continue to reveal as integral and crucial aspects of Schopenhauer's own discourse. This "somebody" will be the "Jews" in this discourse, through which Schopenhauer does his part to lay the apparent foundations for the Aryan Christianity that will play such a terrible role from the late nineteenth through the first half of the twentieth century, and especially, of course, in the 1930s and 1940s. The Jews will function in Schopenhauer as the ground of the loss of the ground (of groundlessness). But one can see much more clearly the way in which Schopenhauer positions himself as fulfillment of the Indian origin, itself always already fulfilled, if one considers this positioning in the more concrete terms of Schopenhauer's characterization of the principal players (or counters) in his typological schema, which I now consider.

And Around We Go, or Back to Typology—Indian, Jewish, Christian

In his construction of the history of positive religion, Schopenhauer positions himself as fulfilling Christianity—fulfilling fulfillment—by enabling its return to the higher truth of ancient Indian culture (from which Christianity ostensibly stems). This truth was originally uttered prior to the intrusive infusion of Indian culture with the Jewish culture that, for Schopenhauer, poisoned the pessimistic well of Indian wisdom with its optimistic remedy. Let us unpack this position while attempting to specify its precise relationship to the typological schema.

In Schopenhauer's thought, the ancient Eastern origin appears as split into two extreme forms, the Indian origin (as "our" origin) and the Judaic debasement of that origin (as the alienation of the ground).[7] Schopenhauer constructs Judaism as a derivative of a Zoroastrian Persian dualism that itself would derive from the Indian source (more specifically Schopenhauer cites the Indian monism of Indra). On this account, Judaism becomes a debasement, indeed a radical reversal, of the Indian origin of truth, which truth is already at the start the complete realization of its own potential.

> Judaism has as its fundamental characteristics [*Grundcharakter*] *realism and optimism* which are closely related and are the conditions of theism proper.

For the latter regards the material world as absolutely real and life as a pleasant gift bestowed on us. Brahmanism and Buddhism, on the other hand, have as their fundamental characteristics *idealism and pessimism*, for they assign to the world only a dreamlike existence and regard life as the consequence of our guilt. In the doctrine of the Zendavesta whence, as we know, Judaism has sprung, the pessimistic element is represented by Ahriman.[8]

Judaism arises (or rather falls) out of Zoroastrianism (itself already partially fallen away from Hindu origins) by taking Ormuzd, the principle of light, as Jehovah, while it subordinates to him Ahriman, the principle of darkness, as Satan. And in turn, "Ormuzd is itself another term for Indra" (402; 369). Judaism functions as the radically fallen form of the Persian Wisdom that goes back to the Indian source.

Christianity begins to rediscover Indian wisdom, but it only achieves a partial return to this source. It is composed of Indian wisdom propped—like ivy upon an alien pole, says Schopenhauer—inappropriately onto a Jewish support. "Christ's teaching . . . has sprung from Indian wisdom" (415; 380), and "in the New Testament the spirit of Indian wisdom can be scented like the fragrance of a bloom which has been wafted over hills and streams from distant tropical fields" (416; 381). Although he does not provide a detailed trajectory for Indian philosophy from its place of origin and into the Christian worldview, Schopenhauer does allow himself to speculate somewhat (shamelessly), surmising, for example, that perhaps "Jesus was educated by Egyptian priests whose religion was of Indian origin and from whom he had accepted Indian ethics and the notion of an avatar" (418; 383).

One can describe Schopenhauer's displacement of figural interpretation readily in terms of the ultimately threefold schema of typology I have developed elsewhere at length.[9] (See the accompanying illustration, "The circuit of negative fulfillment in Schopenhauer.") In terms of that analysis, Schopenhauer appears as a very particular example of the "pagan Protestantism" I see as structuring in crucial ways German *Geistesgeschichte* subsequent to the main phase of romanticism and prior to the rise of philosophical-literary-artistic modernism. In Schopenhauer's case, the narrative (and dialectical) logic—the circuit of fulfillment—runs as follows. Cultural history, or the path of the Idea (of the abyssal character of things), starts with the literal, spiritual fulfillment (in ancient India). The path passes regressively, then, to the anticipation of the anticipation, or the prefiguration of prefiguration (Judaism, with ancient Persia as the culture of transition, the inauguration of the fall into optimism), which represents

Taking Up Groundlessness: Schopenhauer

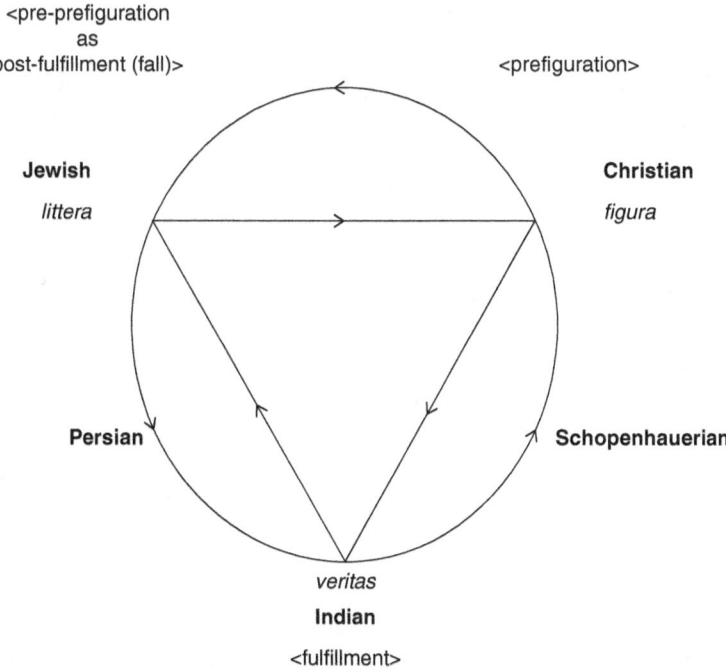

The circuit of negative fulfillment in Schopenhauer

a radical materiality into which humanity will have descended. The path of culture returns then in two steps to the fulfillment at the origin (which is, of course, qua will, entirely timeless). First, culture steps up its spirituality so as to shed the negativity of the Jewish letter—here the negativity of the positive (attitude), which translates as the deadness of the materially given, of mechanism, and so on. The result of this partial shedding of the letter is Christianity.[10] In the subsequent, culminating step, one ascends out of Christianity into the pure negativity, hence—because the terms are reversed in Schopenhauer—the pure positivity of the Indo-Germanic origin, ancient Sanskrit culture. This last movement of ascension would be the one Schopenhauer's thought ostensibly enables (and so also constitutes) as the passage from the Christian hybrid back to the purity of the Indic beginning. (Insofar as he occupies this position, Schopenhauer appears here, from his own point of view, as providing a radical inversion of the Persian contribution.) And this last step must consist, finally, in the negation of the Jewish contagion, that is, of the very idea of a possible fulfillment, of hope:

the liquidation of the contagion of hope embodied in the Jewish conception of law (and in the representativity that this implies).[11]

Thus, in this displaced repetition of the typological schema, Judaism appears not yet as the prefiguration of the return but as the radical fall away from an Oriental (Edenic) Indian origin, but a radical fall that prefigures the prefiguration itself. Christianity functions there as the partial and still prefigurative return or resurrection of this origin, with the twist that the origin is here a pessimistic one, the fall away from it the plunge into a false optimism. And Schopenhauer's own philosophy will complete and realize this partial return.

In order to gain a clearer sense of the (sacrificial) rationale for this envisioned negation or liquidation of (Jewish) optimism, it is crucial to consider further the position of the Jews as fall of the origin (which is complicated here by Schopenhauer's reversal of the positions of fallen and risen). In fact, not only is Judaism essentially fallen, but the only aspect of it that is not fallen, for Schopenhauer, is the narrative of the fall. Judaism falls insofar, and only insofar, as it does not fall (into the narrative of the fall).

> From the Old Testament there is nothing corresponding to this ["spirit of Indian wisdom" quoted above] except the Fall which had to be added at once as a corrective to optimistic theism and to which the New Testament was attached. For the Fall is the only point which offers itself to the New Testament and on to which it can hold. (416; 381)

Strikingly, however, in Schopenhauer's rewriting of the myth of the fall, Judaism stands for Satan, or woman, because it is responsible for the fall. (In causing the fall, Judaism causes the birth of Satan, namely by distinguishing him from God.) Schopenhauer must consequently extirpate from Christianity the "Jewish optimism," the Satanic negativity that he blames Judaism for causatively extirpating (thus causing our fall away from the Indian origin, causing our fall from the fall). Schopenhauer himself thus remains in what he considers a "Jewish" position in his very polemic against Judaism for having put "us"—the Christian West—into a Jewish position. This ensures, however, that the polemic will never come to an end.

Similarly, Schopenhauer's polemic against the Jews explicitly situates them as the one exception to the rule that all peoples believe in an afterlife, and even in metempsychosis.[12] Yet he fails to note that this makes the Jews not necessarily more optimistic than the rest about the current life, but certainly more pessimistic about the possibility of redemptive fulfillment in the afterlife (as the "wandering Jew"—to whom I return—and his repudiation of Christ threateningly suggest). Schopenhauer's optimism about the possibility of redemptive self-negation therefore contrasts starkly—both in and against his own terms—with Jewish pessimism. This contrast exacerbates Schopenhauer's need to rid his discourse of its extimate "Jewishness."

From Typology to the Saint as Philosopher King, or The Jew as Figure of Language

In order to gauge the economy of ideology and insight in Schopenhauer's oeuvre, one needs to know how his views on religiocultural history express themselves on other levels of his thought. I consider next the level of his minimalist but nonetheless fleetingly adumbrated vision of the way in which his philosophy might come to intervene in the world. Schopenhauer argues for the separation of church and state (and concomitantly for the separation of philosophy from religion) as an intermediate step toward the establishment of a properly philosophical basis for an eventual political reorganization of the state. Here, Schopenhauer's reliance on the typological tradition provides him with a ready scapegoat, enabling him to cast aside structural uncertainties his own philosophy uncovers and encounters, by designating them as due to a historically contingent accident—Jewish influence. Specifically, the separation of church from state, as he conceives it, ends up depending on the possibility of separating truth—the signified thing-in-itself—from language, or signifying representation. Schopenhauer must therefore disavow the fact that such representation is necessary for the (indirect) presentation of meaning. He must deny the fact that the possibility-condition of the signified is also its impossibility-condition: the signifier itself (or "die Welt als Vorstellung"). Here, too, in line with a long and problematic tradition, the path of this disavowal will be the polemic against the Jews.

Schopenhauer argues explicitly against the linkage of politics with religion in both of its major historical forms. He is against founding the church on the state: He opposes established religions on the post-1648 model of *cuius regio, eius religio* ("whose realm, his religion"). But he also argues against any neo-medievalizing attempt—like the one the later Schlegel and the Novalis of "Christianity or Europe" envision—to found the state on the church.[13] In fact, in this respect he is an adherent or descendant of the Enlightenment (and he prefigures, as it were, the Freud of *The Future of an Illusion*). He argues that it should be possible to establish an ethical discourse that has nothing to do with positive religious points of reference. Such an ethical discourse would have nothing to do with the pretense of revelation, which Schopenhauer characterizes (recalling a Lucretian and Spinozan tradition and anticipating Nietzsche) as the priestly manipulation of the people. In this sense, he represents the secularist position in favor of the separation of church and state, and he explicitly suggests that the progress of science will inevitably lead to the withering away of religion.

However, Schopenhauer also entertains arguments in favor of the unity of religion and politics. In the opening dialogical section of "On Religion" (chapter 15 of *Parerga and Paralipomena* II), Schopenhauer pits Philalethes, the secularizing philosopher (who most closely resembles his own position elsewhere), against Demopheles, a kind of cultural conservative or perhaps communitarian, who defends religion as a socially and politically necessary popular metaphysics. The dialogue's literary and philosophical strength, such as it is, consists in the fact that there is some limited degree of parity between the two interlocutors. To Philalethes' suggestion that we should "leave everyone to form for himself his own creeds" (372; 343), Demopheles responds: "That, indeed, would be a fine business! [*Das würde etwas Schönes werden!*] A whole people of metaphysicians, explaining things by the light of nature, quarreling with one another, and eventually beating each other up!" (372; 344). Through this response, Schopenhauer makes room in his text for the suspicion that separation of church and state could tend toward a Hobbesian war of all against all, pitting each individual's private absolutes against those of all the other members of the society. The separation of state from church does not suffice to separate power from belief; it does not purify belief of the violence that inhabits and distorts it. Violence reemerges on a newly chaotic, individualized level when the individual becomes the sovereign who possesses the right to determine the religion of his or her own domestic state of one. For Demopheles, religion can never be separated from politics qua play of power, violence, and opacity. The only thing that the ostensible separation achieves is a displacement of the level on which the politics plays itself out. Consequently, Demopheles argues that one should consciously cultivate the interpenetration of church and state.

As is crucial for what follows, Demopheles bases his argument for public religion on the figural status of such religion. Public religion gives people a common representation of absolutes whose meaning they can all interpret differently while agreeing about its meaningfulness. Public religion ensures through this shared representation a minimal communal cohesion and human solidarity. To be sure, Demopheles acknowledges that religion is always an allegorical or mythical—a figural and indirect—presentation of more general truths.[14] Further, he grants that religion can maintain itself only by falsely claiming to provide a literal presentation of these truths. Nonetheless, he insistently argues that public religion serves both communal unity within the state and morally righteous behavior.

Schopenhauer counters Demopheles' proposal, however, by having Philalethes demonstrate its impossibility. Philalethes argues not just that public religion—or unification of state and church—is undesirable, but that it cannot be achieved. He does not merely point to the manifold political destabilizations, genocidal horrors, and moral hypocrisy that are often occasioned by public religions and myths. Going further, to demonstrate the impossibility of public religions he attacks Demopheles' affirmation of their figurality, from which Demopheles had derived their usefulness in satisfying the metaphysical need of the masses. Philalethes, the philosopher, suggests that to place figures, or simply representations, where truth should be is to do violence to religion. It is to efface—to suppress and risk the destruction of—the philosophical thought to which religion aspires. In short, to unify politics and theology is to efface theology, and so also to fail to unify them. An example of this effacement is the way in which early religious training paralyzes (356; 329) the best minds so that they become dogmatically obstructed.[15] To require that beliefs should conform to a particular discursive and ceremonial shape is to limit beliefs to the point of wiping them out. It is to adhere to a dead letter. This is the death of religion, as opposed to its realization in true philosophy. The politicization of religion leads to its death, for Philalethes and to a great extent also for Schopenhauer, if one can judge by his emphasis in other texts on the necessity of secularizing thought.

The two positions on church-state relations base themselves, then, on two different views of figural language in relation to truth. Philalethes, the defender of church-state division, thinks that figural representation effaces the literal truth of things as they are. Demopheles, the defender of church-state unity, thinks that figural representation is of crucial importance because it gives us all we can have of an absent truth (or sense), even if in an indirect, partial, and mediated form. The first rejects mediation; the second accepts it.

Ultimately, however, their differences concern not just figural language in general but more specifically two distinct attitudes toward catachresis. And this should not surprise us, since representation becomes radically problematic (and performative) only at the point where it introduces something new—substituting itself for an absent reality. Answering Philalethes' charge, Demopheles says that public religion "takes the place of pure philosophical truth which is infinitely difficult, and perhaps forever impossible, to reach" (363; 335). (And we will see in the discussion of pantheism below how, in spite of his intention to provide a literal formulation of the "thing-in-itself," Schopenhauer has recourse to the catachresis of will, thereby fitting—uncomfortably—Demopheles' definition of religion, as opposed to philosophy.) Philalethes responds sardonically (and figurally—nolens volens playing the game), that religion does this as "a wooden leg takes the place of a natural one" with the difference that "a natural leg was there before the wooden one, whereas religion has everywhere taken a head start from philosophy [*überall der Philosophie den Vorsprung abgewonnen hat*]" (363; 335), springing ahead on a false leg. For Philalethes, religion is an anticipatory, prefigurative prosthesis of philosophy. Demopheles grants the prosthetic character of representation, yet insists on the necessity of the prosthesis as a catachresis: "All this may be true; but for the man who has no natural leg, a wooden one is of great value. . . . Man's metaphysical needs positively demand satisfaction because the horizon of his thoughts must come to an end and cannot remain unbounded" (363; 335). In short, if one does not have the thing in itself (or nature), representations (as artifice) can come in handy. Yet this consideration does not entirely allay Philalethes' concern that to purvey truth mixed with lies is continually to endanger truth: "Truth in the dress of the lie," he says, is a "corruptive alliance" (*verderbliche Allianz*) (361; 334). For him, separation of religion from politics (and of philosophy from religion) means and requires the separation of ideal signified from material signifier. For Philalethes, the separation of religion and politics stands for the possibility of the attainment of literal, spiritual truth beyond the letter.[16] As we will see below in the discussion of pantheism and Spinozism, Schopenhauer can never quite come to terms with the fact that the very notion of the thing-in-itself as will is precisely a catachresis. Instead, he insists that the will is the immediate object, and therefore immediately accessible to us as thing-in-itself. Just so, here his Philalethes cannot come to terms with the catachrestic character of any discourse on ultimate things.

We see here, then, that the question of church-state unity or division (and at the same time of the identity or difference of philosophy and religion) depends on that of the unity or division of the signified/signifier couple. Political theology depends here on semiological and rhetorical presuppositions. The politics of positive religion comes down to the question of the status of representations with respect to insight into things in themselves. But the result is that the question of the division or unification of church and state becomes an undecidable antinomy as soon as one synthesizes the insights of Demopheles and Philalethes beyond the limits of each of their positions, as the dialogue form itself prompts us to try to do.

To the degree that representations are necessary, that is, to the extent that meanings are necessarily clothed in arbitrary material forms, there is both politicization of religion and at the same time its falsification, the obstruction and loss of truth, as well as the unleashing of violence that such obstruction and loss entail. For the necessity of representation does not do away with its impossibility. Knowledge fails to come into existence as such because belief is carried away by power. The politicization of religion or unification of church and state doubles, therefore, as a division of church and state, if only in the negative sense that the church disappears because spirit has vanished from the scene of the signifier (or representation).

Conversely (i.e., beginning with the opposite premise), if one could possess the ideal truth beyond all representation, one could divide church from state, emancipate knowledge from violence, and free philosophy from religion. It might then be possible, in the case of the exceptional advent of a philosopher-king, to unify the human community around this truth without obscuring it: "But if, as the rarest of exceptions, a philosopher ascends the throne, there arises the most embarrassing disturbance in the whole comedy" (394; 362). The philosophical achievement of religion would enable a politicization of religion in a positive sense hitherto unknown on earth, a unification that would be nonviolent: political rule guided by the truth of the groundlessness of the will and the desirability of its (self-)negation. Here, Schopenhauer's argument in favor of separation of church and state becomes a vision of (if not quite an argument for) the founding of the state on the philosophical essence of religion. The manner in which Schopenhauer envisions or imagines the political consequences of his pessimism begins to appear, if in a still sketchy or hazy way, in the form of the philosopher-king's disruption of the "comedy" of the collusion of cynical rulers with manipulative priests whose authority is based on X or Y ostensible revelation (393–94; 361–62).

In sum, and to restate the dialectic of this antinomy more simply in terms of its basis in language: If one unifies signifier and signified, one separates them (the signified is effaced or repressed), but if one separates them, one ends up unifying them (the signified erects a signifying representation of itself as a church or philosophy founds an institutional politics). Hence, what appears to be responsible for the irresolvability of the theopolitical problem—language itself—will have to go away. One will need to get rid of the connectedness of meaning to signifiers that, however, are disconnected from them, related to them only figurally, at a distance of nonrelation and impropriety.

In Schopenhauer, as so often elsewhere in Western texts since Paul, this goes by way of the polemic against the Jew as figure of the necessity of figures, as privileged representation of representation as such.[17] As the representatives of the "dead letter," the Jews represent the fact that signifying mediation fails to mediate, that is, fails to produce immediacy—that representation is always only representation, not presence. They represent the fact that not just the ignorant masses but the philosophers, too, are missing the natural leg, and have to stand on the wooden one, perhaps on two wooden legs, legations and delegations of pure representation. Schopenhauer makes this point—blames representation on the Jews—in many ways. I briefly consider four of them here: his characterization of the Jews' relationships with place, nation, God, and nature.

Concerning place: Schopenhauer quotes with uncritical approval the conventional image of the Jew as "eternal [or wandering] Jew, Ahasverus," of which Schopenhauer says that he is "never at home, never foreign" (283; 262). It can readily be seen, however, how this exiled status describes representation itself—*Vor-stellung*—both in Schopenhauer's sense and more generally. As the Jew is always equally at home ("never foreign"), yet always equally in exile ("never at home"), at once proper and improper, so representation is always the allegorical appearance of the will, but always at a distance, as are figures in relation to their improper sense in general.[18]

In terms of the question of nation, the Jews represent in negative terms both the unification and the separation of state and church, the effacement of spirit by the signifier and the undesirable drifting of meaning away from all signifying material. And because they make up one cultural entity—the Jews = the Jews—they represent the bad unavoidability of the reversal of each of these poles into its opposite, the theopolitical antinomy that is inseparably a rhetorical-semiological one. On the one hand, the Jews appear for Schopenhauer as embodiments of the principle of theocracy that he explicitly disdains. Judaism is at once a national identity, or political entity, and a religion. It is a theocracy. Consequently, in accordance with his conviction that fusion of church and state annihilates religion, Schopenhauer argues that Judaism is not a confession at all, that is, not a religion but a nation only. On the other hand, if the Jews place their faith at a distance from the states in which they reside, as Schopenhauer likewise stresses, then they also function as an exemplary model of the separation of church and state, which Schopenhauer also, implicitly and ultimately, wishes to overcome, even if while replacing the church of religion with that of philosophy. Indeed, since the Jews have persisted as a religious grouping without any state over the last two thousand years—as a kind of ghost (a traditional notion Schopenhauer at one point perpetuates)[19]—they represent the separation of church from state, the radical autonomization of religion, in an exacerbated way. But because the Jewish people exhibits loyalty to the religiously defined group, it functions equally as a painful reminder that the separation of church and state tends to reverse itself into its opposite. The political space—exercise of public power—tends to reconstitute itself on the level of the ostensibly privatized religion. In sum, the Jews represent the inseparability of the unification of church and state from their separation, because the Jews represent the inseparability of the unification of the signified and the signifier from their disjunction, the uncanny interpenetration of these two extremes.

Third, while Schopenhauer says that they do not constitute a confession, but only a nation, he nonetheless makes the Jews responsible for nothing less than theism qua monotheism. Here too the allegory of language will not be hard to discover. Schopenhauer claims that "monotheism and Judaism" are "convertible terms" (*Wechselbegrifffe* [285; 262]) and speaks of "Jewish theism" (398; 365) and of the way in which "theism is weighing like a nightmare on all spiritual . . . philosophical strivings and constraining" (356; 329) them. Further, he speaks of "monotheism" (389; 358)—explicitly Judaism and its two branches, Christianity and Islam—as being responsible for all of the fanaticism and violent excesses of religion. This includes those excesses that have taken the Jews as their object, such as the expulsions from Spain and the exterminations related to them (386; 356), which Schopenhauer surprisingly regrets while nonetheless hereby making the Jews responsible for their own persecution. The intolerance of monotheism, however, is here linked to what Schopenhauer situates as its core idea, that of the jealous God. For this God constitutes an absolute that is defined as nonrepresentable and at the same time as given in a specific set of representations of its nonrepresentability—the law. The monotheism thus made responsible here for the effacement of religion by politics is nothing other than the duplicity of signification, as a process in which representations at once cannot achieve the presentation of spirit or meaning and cannot avoid claiming to do so.

Finally, Schopenhauer at once criticizes the Jews for falsely and arbitrarily separating animals from humans and for giving off a "foetor Judaicus," or Jewish smell.[20] The contradiction inherent in this position is patent and self-intensifying. The Jews' smell evidently makes them like animals. The fact that Schopenhauer thereby wants to separate them off from the human into the animal realm, however, puts him into what he designates as the position of the Jew: He is fallaciously making distinctions of essence between animals and humans. Thus Schopenhauer must push the Jews away, purify himself of "Judaism," with ever renewed vehemence.

The semiological parallels of this critique of Jewish anthropocentrism appear as follows. If Jewish thinking separates animals from humans, then evidently it does so in terms of a material/spiritual split, an attempt to separate spiritual humanity from material animality, or in linguistic terms to separate the ideal signified from the material signifier. This is Jewish abstraction, its radical monotheism. But it is also, of course, exactly what Schopenhauer himself wants to do, and what—from another perspective that typology dictates—the Jews precisely do *not* do, to the extent that, according to the "dead letter" charge, they are excessively bound up with the material. Both the abstraction of language and its materiality, and above all the uncontrollability of their disjointed indistinguishability, are associated here, sacrificially, with the Jews.

The entanglement of Schopenhauer's own positions with those that he wants to designate and cast out as Jewish continues both to drive his resentment of the Jews and to prevent him from plausibly making them responsible for the ills of being-in-language that he wishes to solve for philosophical and politico-religious reasons. The typologically structured disavowal of the groundlessness of representation, then, governs his polemic against the Jews in the context of his discussion of church and state, a discussion whose goal is to draw out the theopolitical implications of his ethics. I now turn to that ethics itself.

Schopenhauer as the First Christian Philosopher: The Ancient Indian Fulfillment of Christian Ethics

Strikingly, Schopenhauer reasserts the typological paradigm at exactly the moment when he characterizes his own ethical position with respect to the entire tradition of ethical thought that precedes him. In one of the paragraphs from *Parerga and Paralipomena* in which Schopenhauer elaborates on his doctrine of the affirmation and negation of the will-to-live, he claims that his ethics stand in relation to all previous ethics in European philosophy as the New Testament in relation to the Old Testament.

> My ethics is related to all the ethical systems of European philosophy as the New Testament to the Old, according to the ecclesiastical concep-

tion of this relation [*im Verhältnis des neuen Testaments zum alten; nach dem kirchlichen Begriff dieses Verhältnisses*]. (340; 314)

Schopenhauer's philosophy is thus, he says, "die eigentliche Christliche Philosophie" (341)—"the Christian philosophy proper" (315)_and all philosophy prior to his appearance on the scene boils down to "mere Judaism (plain, despotic theism)" (341; 314). As the Greeks—with the notable "Ausnahme," or exception, of Plato—are optimists (let us imagine in passing Nietzsche's apoplexy upon reading such a claim), it seems that for Schopenhauer Jewgreek is Greekjew, but since Christianity is Hindu in inspiration, the affinities between Greek and Jew in no way suggest that there is a significant, much less fundamental, affinity between Christian and Jew.

But how does Schopenhauer justify his claim that his ethics relates to all the others as New Testament to Old? The relation between the New Testament and the Old turns here around the traditional Pauline opposition between grace and law. Schopenhauer repeats that grace, which frees one from the law through faith, love of neighbor, and self-denial, leads to redemption, whereas the law does not. The mediator who is the center of the New Testament enables salvation, whereas the works of the Old Testament do not. Because Schopenhauer's ethics turns around the negation of the will-to-live rather than what he calls "merely moral virtues" (*bloß moralischen Tugenden*), he is the first in the West to go back to the East and hence back behind works. This ethical development he takes to be the "sensu proprio" of the passage (*Übergang*) from Old Testament to New.

Of course, this proper, or literal, sense of the passage from Old to New is also the proper sense of the passage from the figural to the literal meaning of the will or testament of what will have been the self-negated subject. As Schopenhauer argues in other sections of the chapter "On Religion," and as I have indicated, philosophy supplies the literal fulfillment of religion's allegories. For example:

> The common error of both [rationalism and supernaturalism in scriptural interpretation] is that in religion they look for the plain, dry, literal and unvarnished truth [*die unverschleierte, trockne, buchstäbliche Wahrheit suchen*]. But only philosophy aspires to this. Religion has only a truth that is suited to the people, one that is indirect, symbolical, allegorical [*eine indirekte, eine symbolische, allegorische Wahrheit*]. (425; 389)

And lest one imagine that philosophical literalization is not fulfillment, Schopenhauer suggests that if philosophy could one day express the "nackte Wahrheit" (as he himself claims to do):

> Then truth in a simple and intelligible form would naturally drive religion from the place which the latter had so long occupied as a deputy [*vikarirend eingenommen*] but had in precisely this way kept open for the former. Religion will then have *fulfilled* its mission [*ihren Begriff erfüllt*] and completed its course; it can then dismiss the race that it has brought to years of discretion [*Mündigkeit*] and itself expire in peace; such will be the euthanasia of religion [*die Euthanasie der Religion*]. (365; 337)[21]

It is worthy of note here that, since religion is the not-yet of philosophy just as Judaism is the not-yet of Christianity, the "euthanasia of religion" carries the echo here of the "euthanasia of Judaism" (but also more distantly that of the "euthanasia of Christianity").

What the New Testament does for the Old, then, Schopenhauer's philosophy will do for all previous philosophy, and for Christianity itself, which has not yet become truly Christian, that is, Indian, by going beyond itself to become philosophy. He will achieve Christianity and religion at once qua philosophy by providing "Grund, Zweck, und Ziel" (341)—"ground, purpose, and goal" (314)—as the Old Testament and all prior ethics do not. His thought provides us, he says, with a ground in the specific sense that it provides "the metaphysical ground [*den metaphysischen Grund*] of justice and love of other humans" (314; 341)—that is, a certain becoming-transparent of the principle of individuation (or the principle of sufficient reason and the appearances it occasions). This *durchschauen*, or "seeing through," of the principle of individuation is the cause or origin of the sense of justice and love of other humans in the sympathetic understanding that we are all *one* on the level of the will. And Schopenhauer's philosophy also gives us a purpose and goal in the form of the negation of the will-to-live "to which these [that is, justice and love of other humans] must lead in the end if they are perfectly (or completely) achieved [*vollkommen geleistet*]" (314; 341). The fulfillment of justice and love of humans, or sympathetic identification, is tantamount to the arrival at the goal of the negation of the will-to-live, which negation signifies redemption, or *Erlösung*. As we see here, then, the language of foundation—as efficient and final causality—constitutively organizes the claim to provide the "authentic Christian philosophy," the realization of the Christian realization of the Jewish will and testament in the ethics of world-renunciation.

Through an imperceptible, infinitesimal displacement—that from "gänzliche Verleugnung seiner selbst" (340) (or "complete denial of oneself" [314]) to "gänzliche Verleugnung seiner selbst"—we can perceive the doubling of denial in Schopenhauer's would-be Christian sense by the

Freudian notion of denial. "Verleugnung" in this Freudian sense—as the disavowal of a lack already acknowledged, the "I know well . . . but all the same," of the perverse moment—functions here in the "disavowal of the self" as the disavowal of the inscription of the self in a law of individuation and desire marked by radical lack. Self-denial is here the denial of the constitutive situatedness of the self in a world of representations in turn haunted by a certain absent excess.

By virtue of this disavowal, Schopenhauer thinks he becomes the exception to the rule that all philosophy will be what he considers "Jewish" philosophy. He becomes the only—the first—philosophizing non-Jew that the West has ever known: the only one who has overcome the unfreedom or enslavement to the (always Jewish) law of the principle of sufficient reason, or egoism. As such, he is capable of leading, that is, of functioning as the sovereign leader, or *Führer*, insofar as he can guide us—the word he uses in this context is "hinführen" (341; 314)—along the path (or "Weg") of the negation of the will-to-live, the negation of the value of life, to the redemption that it realizes.[22]

Schopenhauer's Pessimism as Fulfillment of Spinoza's Pantheistic Optimism

Schopenhauer concretizes the way in which his—first-ever Christian!—ethics distinguishes itself from all previous—Jewish—ethics by determining explicitly his relationship to pantheism, and more specifically to Spinozism. Pantheism and Spinozism are of crucial importance to Schopenhauer for at least three reasons. First, the post-Kantian philosophical debates Schopenhauer regards as contemporary are all bound up with Spinozism, ever since the earliest phases of the pantheism panic.

> In consequence of Kant's criticism of all speculative theology, almost all the philosophizers in Germany cast themselves back onto Spinoza, so that the whole series of unsuccessful attempts known by the name of post-Kantian philosophy is simply Spinozism tastelessly got up, veiled in all kinds of unintelligible language, and otherwise twisted and distorted. (58; 644)[23]

Second, as excommunicated Jew and free-thinker, and as the author of the *Tractatus Theologico-Politicus*, Spinoza—Benedict or Baruch?—challenges the Christian, Western philosophical tradition to rethink what "Jewish" and "Christian" mean. Third, the pantheism that the "Oriental" Jew Spinoza is commonly thought to have introduced into the Western tradition has already, and long since, become the stereotypical image of "Oriental" thought within philosophical and philological circles by the time Schopenhauer begins his career.[24] Given his embrace of Asian and especially Indian philosophy, Schopenhauer is compelled to work out the relation between himself and both pantheism and Spinozism in order to clarify his systematic standpoint.

Accordingly, Schopenhauer situates his discussion of the relationship between his philosophy and pantheism and Spinozism in no less important a place than the very last section of *The World as Will and Representation* (at the end of volume 2), titled "Epiphilosophie." He says here: "My teaching . . . is related to Spinozism as the New Testament is to the Old" (59; 644). How does he argue for this typological placement of his work with respect to Spinoza's, and how does this argument relate to the abyssal question of foundations? I begin with Schopenhauer's account of pantheism in general.[25]

Schopenhauer opens the "Epiphilosophie" precisely by posing the question of the status of the world-will with respect to ultimate foundations. He then goes on to distinguish his thought from pantheism (and Spinozism) in terms of the difference between his way of (not) grounding the world (qua will) and the pantheistic and Spinozistic ways of trying and failing to ground the world—in God and substance, respectively. Schopenhauer asserts here that he does not claim to have explained the ultimate grounds of the will. Rather, in Kantian terms, he claims to have stayed with the surfaces, the "facts of outward and inward experience" (54; 640) and shown their "true and deepest connexion" (*den wahren und tiefsten Zusammenhang derselben*) (54; 640). Instead of going beyond "possible experience" (640), he has been "content to comprehend the true nature of the world according to its inner connexion with itself" (*begnügt sich also damit, das Wesen der Welt, seinem innern Zusammenhang mit sich selbst nach, zu begreifen*) (54).[26] Schopenhauer emphasizes the internal coherence of the world—its *Zusammenhang* with itself—as opposed to a notion of ground in which one thing would find its ground or cause in another thing outside itself. (As in Schlegel, Goethe, and Hegel, the notion of coherence, or cohesion, functions in Schopenhauer, at this juncture, as a crucial way of conceiving immanent foundations. In the next chapter, we will see how, in contrast, Kafka develops a parodic fictional critique of *Zusammenhang* in its Orientalist context.) In accordance with Schopenhauer's doctrine of the principle of sufficient reason, the possibility of an external ground is applicable only to the phenomena of the world, that is, to the world of representations, not to the world as will, in the sense of the world as totality of beings/Being.

> To all such questions [of the "ultimate grounds" (*letzten Gründen*) of the world] the reply would have to be, first, that the expression of the most universal and general form of our intellect is *the principle of sufficient ground or reason* [*Grund*], but that, on this very account, this principle finds application only to the phenomenon, not to the being-in-itself of things; but all whence and why rest on this principle alone. (55; 641)

In this sense, the will is indifferent to grounding: It is neither grounded nor is it susceptible to grounding. Its nongroundedness is not like the nongroundedness of phenomena: It is not a privation of ground, not an insufficiency, but rather a sufficiency of nongroundedness. This structure accords well with the structure of perverse disavowal that Octave Mannoni has unfolded with respect to superstitious disavowal of demystifications in terms of the utterance: "I know well . . . but all the same. . . ." Schopenhauer knows well that the will is ungrounded, but all the same, it is grounded within itself, as self-coherence, or *Zusammenhang*.

And yet Schopenhauer's ambivalence and uncertainty about this sufficient nongroundedness of the will appear in two ways that require mention here. First, on the one hand, the will is designated as the essence of things, while on the other hand, Schopenhauer still worries the question of the essence beyond this essence. The essence of, or beyond, the essence of the world, he says, is not accessible to us: "The essence of things before or beyond the world, and consequently beyond the will, is not open to any investigation, because knowledge in general is itself only phenomenon and therefore it takes place only *in* the world" (56; 642). Schopenhauer here delineates "the limits of my philosophy and of all philosophy" (56; 642), repeating the Kantian move with respect to something like a thing-in-itself of, or beyond, the thing-in-itself.

But Schopenhauer's ambivalence shows itself secondly in that the reason why the will has to be suspended is that it is groundless, without any final purpose (and the ground of a will has to be a finality). This is why it entails endless and senseless suffering. The insufficiency of the nongroundedness of the will appears therefore in the imperative of its renunciation. Hence, the will is, on the one hand, by a certain perverse rigor, indifferent to grounding, and on the other hand, in necessity of grounding, which takes place by means of its (self-) negation. Schopenhauer's desire both to ground and not to ground the will in something outside it (even if that something is called "coherence"—*Zusammenhang*) will cause him to have difficulty distinguishing himself from pantheism and Spinozism as neatly as he would like. Fulfillment—with and against Schopenhauer—is not always as fulfilling as one might have imagined.

Schopenhauer has begun the "Epiphilosophy" with the discussion of the world's potential foundations because he wants to distinguish his version of the essence of the world from the pantheist and Spinozist versions. He wants to distinguish the will from God (in the case of pantheism in general) and from substance (in the case of Spinozism in particular). To state this difference, Schopenhauer asserts that he offers an immanent (54; 640) theory only, whereas these other cosmologies are transcendent—they go beyond the phenomenal world, or what Schopenhauer here calls *natura naturata* (a term Spinoza had employed), to explain its origin in a ground outside of it, called "God" or "substance." Schopenhauer's theory is immanent, he claims, because it is frankly anthropocentric and not theocosmological, as are both pantheism and Spinozism.

> From the most ancient times, man has been called the microcosm. I have reversed the proposition, and have shown the world as the *macranthropos*, in so far as will and representation exhaust the true nature of the world as well as that of man. (57; 642)

The grounding of the will in its "internal coherence," then, is—with and against Schopenhauer—its grounding in humanity, its understanding precisely in terms of the catachrestic figure, which is at once a personification, of the will. More narrowly, the place at which the will coheres with itself is in its negation, where its self-affirmation and its self-negation (contradictorily) coincide (as I argued above). If the pantheists reduce all possibility to the world, whereas Schopenhauer includes within the realm of possibility the will's self-negation, as he asserts, then it is precisely in this marginally extraworldly or extrasecular negation, where the will's full realization occurs, that its grounding in its coherence and in its anthropomorphic character are achieved, precisely beyond the world, on the verge of its disappearance.

We are compelled, therefore, to wonder whether Schopenhauer's way of distinguishing himself from pantheism succeeds, or whether he is not rather realizing pantheism not so much by going beyond it as by contributing another version of it to the history of philosophy. Again, does not the sanctioning of a place beyond the world in its negation, as a place that nonetheless belongs to being, correspond to the pantheistic sanctioning of a ground of the world in God? In each case, one is transcending the groundlessness of the world by arbitrarily positing a stable place that exceeds it. If Schopenhauer cannot reliably distinguish himself from those who provide a ground that is not one, then how will he escape from the abyss that he everywhere at once acknowledges and, in his optimistic and messianic hope of redemption, disavows? In order to suggest that this question remains a rhetorical one, I examine Schopenhauer's presentation of the distinction between his own position and Spinozism. He treats Spinozism here as a special case of pantheism, although in his analysis it takes the form of the opposite of pantheism in important respects.

Thus far Schopenhauer has laid out the main terms in which his philosophy distinguishes itself from pantheism: It provides a more limited grounding than does pantheism, a grounding more human and subjective in its orientation, and so more reliable—grounding through the implicit rhetoric of a catachrestic and anthropomorphic synecdoche (the [human] will as the whole). He now goes on to distinguish his thought from Spinoza's more particularly. He feels he must do so because (as I indicated above) following Jacobi, he sees all post-Kantian philosophy—what we know as German idealism—as one or another form of Spinozism. And manifestly Spinozism is a kind of optimism, because we are encouraged by Spinoza to affirm this world, loving its divine necessity, and to assert ourselves within it, even while tempering our passions. Here, then, is the point at which Schopenhauer boldly claims: "My teaching . . . is related to Spinozism as the New Testament is to the Old" (59; 644).

The Old and New Testament—two different "testaments" or "wills" (willing and willed doctrines of the will)—have in common the same "God-Creator" (59; 644). Just so, Schopenhauer and Spinoza share the same "world" that "exists . . . by its own inner power and through itself" (59; 644). Further, as the two testaments understand this God differently, so Spinoza and Schopenhauer interpret this world-substance in different ways, specifically with regard to its value.

Spinoza's world is self-affirming:

> With Spinoza, his *substantia aeterna*, the inner nature of the world, which he himself calls *Deus*, is also, as regards its moral character and worth, Jehovah, the God-Creator, who applauds his creation, and finds that everything has turned out excellently, *panta kala lian*. . . . All was very good. (59; 644)

Spinoza's substance is the old Jehovah, albeit "deprived" of all "personality" (59; 644).

In contrast, Schopenhauer argues, his own "world"-concept does not coincide with Jehovah but with "as it were the crucified Saviour, or else the crucified thief, according as it is decided" (59; 645). As a result, his ethics "is in accord with Christian ethics, and indeed with its highest tendencies, as not less with the ethics of Brahmanism and Buddhism" (59; 645). In other words, Schopenhauer's world negates itself, as God negates himself, crucifying himself in the figure of his Son.

Despite Spinoza's optimistic fault, however, he remains for Schopenhauer "a very great man" (60; 645), as indeed he must if Schopenhauer wishes to maintain that he himself is the realization of what Spinoza initiated. Spinoza's greatness consists, however, in a (merely) negative achievement, the undoing of the Cartesian dualisms of mind/matter and nature/God. Yet the monism of substance does not suffice to ground the specific nongroundedness of the world. Spinoza's achievement is only "negative," then, because the mere equation of world with God does not suffice to "explain" the world. "For to call the world God is not yet to explain it" (*Denn die Welt Gott nennen heißt nicht sie erklären*) (60; 645). Spinoza only anticipates an appropriate explanation of the world that Schopenhauer claims he has achieved.

But how can Schopenhauer have "explained" the world if he hasn't been able to ground it in any way in anything outside of itself? Moreover, his own account tends to be phrased in terms of a *Verständnis* or *Verstehen*, as Rüdiger Safranski has observed.[27] In this sense, Schopenhauer manifestly provides no explanation in the sense of "Erklärung." The problem here—the problem with which Schopenhauer is struggling in the entire "Epiphilosophy" chapter—is that in accordance with the principle of sufficient reason (in conjunction with the principle of noncontradiction), neither an explanation nor the lack of an explanation of the world is satisfactory. If the world is left ungrounded/unexplained, it needs a ground; but if it is grounded, and therefore necessarily grounded in something outside of itself (even if one calls that something the *Zusammenhang* or internal coherence of the world), then this ground in turn requires some sort of grounding. There seems to be no way of preventing the mind from asking after the foundation of the world as will, even when it tells itself it can never answer this question.

In response to this double inadequacy, Schopenhauer argues in the final turn of his argument that his position constitutes the *Aufhebung* of the opposition between these two strategies, in the forms of Spinozist rationalism and of the anti-Spinozist counterrationalism of Friedrich Heinrich Jacobi, who was the main opponent of Spinoza's philosophy in late eighteenth- and early nineteenth-century Germany. Jacobi and those akin to him,

Schopenhauer recounts, refused to "confess" neo-Spinozism (*sich zum aufgekommenen Neo-Spinozismus zu bekennen*) out of the fear of fatalism. They refused to reduce the world and the "critical situation of the human race in it" (60; 646, trans. modified) to some "necessity" that cannot be explained any further. Instead, they reduced the world to "the free act of will of a being existing outside it" (60; 646) in a symmetrical reductiveness that, to his credit, Schopenhauer finds no less problematic. To ground the world in necessity or freedom, in mechanical or final causality, is equally untenable: In the former case, one leaves the world without any meaningful ground whatsoever, and in the latter, one grounds it in something—a transcendent, divine will—that is itself groundless, unexplained. (We can see here that Schopenhauer is implicitly and, it seems, unwittingly, assimilating to each other pantheism and Jacobi's anti-Spinozism, since both reduce the world to God.) In place of these two inadequate solutions, Schopenhauer summarizes his own position as the following, which he conceives as the third possibility:

> The act of will, from which the world springs, is our own. It is free: for the principle of sufficient reason or ground, from which alone all necessity has its meaning, is merely the form of the will's phenomenal appearance. Just on this account, this phenomenal appearance is absolutely necessary in its course, when once it exists. In consequence of this alone can we recognize from the phenomenon the nature of the act of will, and accordingly *eventualiter* will otherwise. (60; 646)

Schopenhauer proposes that "our will" is the origin of the world, but that this free will becomes subject to the principle of sufficient reason when it affirms itself. Freedom thereby turns into necessity, life into death, spirit into the dead letter of the world of appearances, *Vor-stellungen*. Through this little narrative of the becoming-physical of the metaphysical (i.e., the will), Schopenhauer aims to combine freedom with necessity, Counter-Enlightenment with Enlightenment (and implicitly pantheism with Spinozism), and to point the way out of necessity back into freedom, the way of the self-negation of the will, through which it refuses to appear and thus refuses to subordinate itself further to the law of its own form, the principle of sufficient reason.

How, then, finally, is Schopenhauer's answer to the question of the grounding of the world conceivable as the "fulfillment" of Spinoza's answer? Since Schopenhauer has already indicated that the fulfillment is rooted in Christology, what exactly is the Christological structure or meaning of the self-negation of the will? The sovereign limitlessness of the will is always doubled or haunted by the absolutely servile, endless limitedness of the phenomenon into which the will constitutively and incessantly transforms itself. For the will is the will to appearances. The father, then, becomes the son (the world of representation grasped by the saint as unworthy of persistence), who annihilates and is annihilated by the father (the will) insofar as he annihilates himself, thereby saving himself from endless annihilation. This is the ultra-Christian and therefore ultimately also would-be Hindu logic through which the will-to-life or the will-to-appearances crucifies itself—suspending itself as the law of the principle of sufficient reason—in order to attain to the grace of emancipation from the doomed hopefulness of longing. Through this self-negation, the will attains to a kind of fullness beyond fullness, a fullness reached paradoxically but also conventionally by the negative way of greater and greater emptiness. *Die Wüste wächst* ("the desert grows"), as Nietzsche's vexing and vexed translation will have it almost three quarters of a century later.

Beyond and through the Christological structure of the will's self-negation, when Schopenhauer says that his thought relates to Spinoza's as New Testament to Old Testament, he means principally three things. (1) Spinoza's Jewish optimism is here overturned by a pessimism that returns the myth of the fall from grace to the fundamental and totalizing status it enjoys in Hindu thought (i.e., the appearance of the world as fall). The accident becomes the paradigm, but also its overcoming: The exception becomes the rule in the (bad) reality of the world as well as in its (good) negation, in the form of Jew and saint, respectively. The optimistic Western Jehovah is replaced by the pessimistic Eastern Christ. (2) At the same time, Schopenhauer claims to go beyond Spinoza by getting rid of God, proposing an immanent reading of the world in place of the reading that, in Spinoza, remained still all-too-transcendent, despite Spinoza's efforts to think divinity and nature together. As the Jewish God is too "abstract," the Christian God-as-Man properly concrete, so Spinoza's solution and its mirror-image, the pantheistic Counter-Enlightenment, are too "abstract," always one-sided, but Schopenhauer's solution is dialectically self-mediating, despite Schopenhauer's hatred of Hegel. (3) Finally, whereas Spinoza replaces freely willed creation with mechanical necessity, prefiguring the overcoming of the senseless irrationality of such an act of creation, Schopenhauer is able to synthesize mechanical necessity with freedom in order to go beyond the limitations of both, realizing a higher freedom, the freedom from freedom (and its opposite) that is attained at the pinnacle of the will's self-negation. In this concluding chapter of *The World as Will and Representation*, volume 2, the metaphysical disavowal of endless nonfulfillment or desire (that is, the vision of an eventual self-negation of the will) coincides with the reinstallation of the typological political theology of fulfillment. This takes place despite the inconsistency of such a political theology (or politics of religion, or religiocultural ideology) with the view of representation that underlies it, where representation is determined as the endlessly anticipatory (and retrospective) appearance of radical lack or desire.

The Bifurcated Oriental: The Indian as Sovereign Saint, the Jew as Homo sacer

In conclusion, what does Schopenhauer's ambivalence about his radical contributions to the history of philosophy, hermeneutics, and philosophy of history finally mean for the notion of the Oriental in Schopenhauer, and for his "Orientalism"? As we have seen, the Jews and Indians remain in his text two extremes of the "Orient" that are not permitted to come into contact with each other. The Jews function as the foreign extreme, the Indians as the native extreme, the part of the alien origin that is always already "our" origin, the Other as appropriable origin of the Self-Same. Schopenhauer writes in the *Parerga and Paralipomena* that the Jews "are and remain a foreign Oriental people, and so must always be regarded merely as domiciled foreigners" (*sind und bleiben ein fremdes, Orientalisches Volk, müssen daher stets nur als ansässige Fremde gelten*) (286; 264). While the Jews remain a "foreign, Oriental" people, the Indians—and especially the ancient Indians, are somehow not foreign, though no less Oriental. In order to be appropriated, the origin we have outside ourselves must always be divided from itself into the one that is properly our own and the one that is alien.

Schopenhauer's division of the Oriental origin into alien and familiar enables him to find a place in which to situate that aspect of grounding that ungrounds what it grounds, the place of the interpenetration of grounding and ungrounding, on the border where both come undone. This helps lay a "foundation," as epistemologically shaky as it will be performatively real, for the Aryan myth that will nourish the growth of German fascism and the ideological legitimation of its unspeakable horror one century on.

In terms of sovereignty and exception, the sovereign (as saint, or Indian) is always haunted in Schopenhauer by its identity with the emergency itself (or the *homo sacer*, here the Jew) that it characterizes as what interrupts its own state. Schopenhauer's saint is (the negation of) the Jew, who in the death camps will be transformed into the horrifying essence of nonessence she or he here represents: the will as "hungry": a human being in the process of being starved and worked to death.

PART II

How Not to Appropriate Orientalist Typology: Some Modernist Responses to Historicism

CHAPTER 7

Dialectical Development or Partial Construction?: Martin Buber and Franz Kafka

> Whereas history teaches us that at each time something different has been, philosophy endeavors to assist us to the insight that at all times exactly the same was, is, and will be. . . . The Hegelian pseudo-philosophy that is everywhere so pernicious and stupefying to the mind, the attempt, namely, to comprehend the history of the world as a planned whole . . . a crude and shallow *realism* is actually at the root of this. . . . What history relates is in fact only the long, heavy, and confused dream of mankind.
>
> —ARTHUR SCHOPENHAUER, *The World as Will and Representation*

> Once the belief in a divine purpose in social existence declined with the increasing secularization of thought in the nineteenth century and the triumph of naturalism, the philosophical foundations of the historicist faith in the harmony of power and morality lost their credibility.
>
> —GEORG IGGERS, *The German Conception of History: The National Tradition of Historical Thought from Herder to the Present*

As we have seen, across the long nineteenth century, German intellectuals such as Herder, F. Schlegel, Goethe, and Hegel develop modern, historicist Orientalism. Schopenhauer in turn, among others, calls ambivalently for an end to it.[1] In widely diverse philosophical, literary, and philological manifestations, the historicists apply figural interpretation to the project of positing and appropriating an Oriental cultural and metaphysical origin of the human spirit. Instead of being ungrounded by being grounded in what is outside of oneself (and what may itself lack substantial foundations), one is now grounded in oneself to the degree that one has appropriated the outside ground as one's own. Indeed, I believe this is not just a German phenomenon, although it is particularly pronounced in German texts due both to the harsh isolation of spirit from letter in the Lutheran tradition down through its inversion in Lessing, and to the peculiar position of the German cultures in Central Europe, never securely Eastern or Western even within the European frame of reference. However, the demonstration of the links between typology and historicist Orientalism on a European scale, including English, French, and other national literatures and philosophies goes beyond the limits of this book.

In this chapter and the following one, I sketch how, in selected instances, European (in the event, Austro-Hungarian Jewish) modernism responds to this historicist tradition. What is of particular interest and value in the modernist epoch regarding the question of Orientalism is the way in which some important writers question and even disarticulate the historicist tradition, while they keep a certain distance from its Enlightenment (and structurally preoccupied) forerunner and rival. Nonetheless, of course other members of the modernist generations remain to a greater extent caught up in the typological modalities of historicist teleology or in Enlightenment structural models. It is this tension in the period that I illustrate in Part II.

The most important intellectual-historical background of the high modernists' positions on the Orient is in methodological terms the "crisis of historicism." When the teleological foundations of historicism begin to crumble in the late nineteenth century, its relativist tendencies emerge, placing its value in question.[2] Whereas the first historicists, during the Counter-Enlightenment, invoked history so as to avoid the perceived nihilism of abstract reason, historicist relativism now seems nihilistic in turn.[3] At the same time, the artificiality of Enlightenment formalist rationality is widely regarded as problematic, despite and across the neo-Kantian and early phenomenological developments in academic or university philosophy.[4] As I show here, the modernists who develop a critical (or postcritical) take on Orientalist historicism accordingly tend to interrogate both the dialectically developmental versions of typological thinking and the static, structural, or architectonic accounts of reason against which these narrative modes reacted from the Counter-Enlightenment on. As instances of this more (post)critical stance, I consider in this chapter works by Franz Kafka and in the next, Sigmund Freud. As a more traditionalist foil against which to read Kafka and Freud, I begin here with the relatively early Martin Buber. In a few notes, I discuss in chapter 8 works by Thomas Mann and Fritz Lang, the former a more (post)critical type, the latter perhaps somewhat less so, at least in the film I consider, *The Indian Tomb* (*Das indische Grabmal*). Obviously, there are Jewish and Christian cultural producers on both sides of this divide between (more) skeptical and (more) dogmatic approaches to Orientalist motifs in the first half of the twentieth century, and in fact most thinkers and writers straddle the divide to some extent. The early Buber, with whom I begin the discussion of the modernists, remains essentially faithful to the Hegelian dialectical mode in the structure of his thinking about Orient and Occident, while he diverges from Hegel in the specifics of content (i.e., the order and meaning he gives to the cultures he considers).[5] Before discussing Buber, however, I need to recall briefly some of the main outlines of Hegel's construction of the Orient, with particular emphasis on the relative positions of the Chinese and Jewish cultures within that construction. It will then be possible to compare and especially to contrast the positions of the modernists with the Hegelian culmination of teleological philosophy of history.

The Hegelian Orientation

As shown in chapter 5, within the Hegelian Orient—which comprises China, India, and Persia—it is China that takes the first step, or rather no steps whatsoever, for to Hegel China represents stasis itself. China functions as the anticipation of the Indian anticipation of the Persian fulfillment of the Oriental anticipation of Greece. Within this arrangement, China—which will be important for both Buber and Kafka—represents not just the principle of stasis but (consequently) also the culture of radical materiality and externality. China is devoid of spirituality and inwardness. It is "the inward made outward" (*das Innerliche äusserlich gemacht*) (142; 112, trans. modified). China is the eternal, static, material origin and other of spiritual movement itself: "the only realm of endurance in the world. Conquests cannot have any impact on such a realm" (*das einzige Reich der Dauer in der Welt. Eroberungen können solchem Reiche nichts anhaben*) (146; 115, trans. modified). The wall that China draws around itself is evidently perfectly impenetrable, something Kafka will present rather differently, as we'll see below.

At the end of the Oriental trajectory, in contrast, the Persian Empire is the first empire that combines (Chinese) identity with (Indian) difference and that has the good sense to pass away, thereby becoming properly historical.

> With the Persian Empire we first enter into *the context* [*Zusammenhang*] of History. The Persians are the first historical People; Persia was the first empire that passed away. (215, 173, emphasis added, trans. modified)

And within the Persian Empire, it is Judaism that accomplishes an anticipatory negative reconciliation between matter and spirit.

In the midst of this confusion, the spiritual God of the Jews confronts us—like Brahma, existing only for thought, yet jealous and excluding from his being and sublating ("abolishing") all the specificity of difference that is set free in other religions. (146; 114, trans. modified)

Because this Jewish reconciliation synthesizes matter and spirit in purely spiritual terms in the form of the Old Testament God, it represents for Hegel the very opposite of the Chinese god/emperor. Indeed, Hegel explicitly contrasts the materialized substance of Chinese with the spiritualized substance of Jewish culture in order to clarify initially what Chinese culture is all about. Speaking of the patriarchal Chinese emperors, he writes:

> The universal will enacts itself immediately through the individual: the latter has no knowledge of himself in opposition to substance, which it does not yet posit as a power standing over against him, as, e.g., in Judaism the jealous God is known as the negation of the individual. In China, the universal will immediately commands what the individual is to do, and the latter complies and obeys with proportionate renunciation of reflexion and personal independence. (152; 120, trans. modified)

Although it is the opposite of the Chinese, the Jewish *Aufhebung* of difference does not yet quite accomplish itself—and so it still merely anticipates Greek plasticity.

Nonetheless, it is explicitly with the arrival of the supernatural light of the Jewish God, "the pure One," that we enter history as Occidental history: "The break between East and West thereby occurs; the spirit descends into itself and recognizes the abstract fundamental principle as the spiritual" (*Dadurch geschieht der Bruch zwischen dem Osten und dem Westen; der Geist geht in sich nieder und erfasst das abstrakte Grundprinzip für das Geistige*) (241; 195, trans. modified). How, then, do modernist texts conform to, or diverge from, the outlines of Hegel's dialectical-typological account of Oriental origination? Let's begin with the Jewish modernist context.

The Jewish People as Aufhebung *of East and West: Martin Buber's Appropriation of Hegelian Dialectics*

> None of the great religious doctrines arose in the Occident; the Occident stands receptively opposite them. It processes what the Orient offers it.... It never managed to erect the seamless world of a divine doctrine on a transrational and unshakable ground.... What is it that Europe lacks, that it always needs, and that it can never create out of itself? ... What it

lacks is the exclusivity of the message of the true life, the inborn certainty of that one thing necessary. It is this that exists creatively in the great doctrines of the Orient and only in them. They posit the true life as the fundamental metaphysical principle, derived from nothing else and to be traced back to nothing else: they teach the way. (56–57)[6]

By the early twentieth century, the increasingly racist opposition between the Indian and Jewish (or Aryan and Semitic) poles of the Orient had become a concrete danger for European Jewry (not to mention the rest of Europe) in the face of the European right wing, even if fascism had not yet become a party-political reality.[7] This ethnic-racial opposition is always entangled, moreover, with its implicit reversal, that is, with the identity of the Aryan and Semitic terms, whether the opposition appears in its Schlegelian, Hegelian, or Schopenhauerian and subsequently Aryanist modalities.[8] In fact, the violence it generates is linked to this very entanglement. First, by virtue of having spoken and written in Sanskrit, the ancient Indians become the inheritors, within modern Orientalism, of the role played within the medieval Christian world by the Jewish "dead letter" qua language/origin of the West. (We saw this with striking clarity in the texts of Schlegel and Hegel.) The analogy between Jewish and Hindu here enables, complements, and undermines their opposition. Second, and precisely against this background, when the later nineteenth-century Aryanists vehemently oppose Aryan to Semite, it is in order to situate themselves— imitatively and enviously—in the position of the origin that has come to be marked as simultaneously Jewish (or Judaeo-Arab) and Hindu, Semitic and Aryan, each always in virtual conflation with the other. The protofascist and fascist Aryanists therefore want to become and be the (opposite of the) Jews, to appropriate the position of self-anticipating realization, by getting rid of the Jews, with whom they surreptitiously identify.[9]

Thus a "Jewish" thinker and writer in German (and European) modernism finds himself or herself in one of two positions. He or she is either simply and explicitly relegated, insofar as Jewish, to the garbage-dump of history (in terms of Hegelian-style supersessionist histories); or she or he is, even more aggressively, blamed for turning Christianity away from its pure ancient Indian roots (in a Schopenhauerian or otherwise Aryan Christian mode), the latter a variation on blaming the Jews for the death of Christ/God. Any modernist German-Jewish thinker and writer is consequently compelled to respond to the complex entanglement of "Jewish" and "Oriental" in his discursive environment.[10] The modern German Jew is someone whose very mother tongue (a medieval German derivative,

Yiddish, that has recently retransformed itself into German, the language of a Mitteleuropa on the indeterminable border between East and West) makes him or her both a model for, and an instance of, the Oriental. Such a subject evidently has to try to grasp this discursive complex and determine it in some way or be buried figuratively and perhaps also literally by its implications.

To illustrate this subject position, numerous versions of the Jewish-Oriental conjunction from this modernist epoch might be cited. For example, Karl Wolfskehl, Jakob Wasserman, and Hans Kohn all constructed positive images of the "Oriental Jew" in the influential anthology *Of Judaism* (*Vom Judentum*) of 1913.[11] Of the thinkers who participated in such developments, none was more importantly influential than Martin Buber, especially through his discourse "The Spirit of the Orient and Judaism" ("Der Geist des Orients und das Judentum"), pronounced in 1912 before the Bar Kochba Society in Prague and published in 1916 in the polemically titled collection, *Of the Spirit of Judaism* (*Vom Geist des Judentums*).

This text is quite sensitive to the problems of Western hegemony and domination in the East, and it even privileges Oriental values over Occidental ones as capable of providing metaphysical foundations. But the text is much more than a defense of the Orient against Occidental colonialism.

Buber begins by referring to key German cultural authority figures—Herder, Goethe, Novalis, and Görres—as support for the idea that the Orient is "one" (*eine Einheit*) in having a unified core of spirit (*einigen Kern des Geistes*). He argues that it is the reality of spirit (*die Wirklichkeit des Geistes*) that makes the Orient a single unified organism (*Organismus*) "standing across from the West with its own right to exist" (*der dem Abendland in eignem Recht gegenübersteht*) (46–47). This idea, he argues, has been lost by the "race theory of our age" (46). In other words, turning modernist vitalism against its most reactionary racist forms, Buber starts out by negating the Aryan-Semitic distinction, without mentioning it directly by name.[12]

Having begun by insisting on the spiritual unity of the Orient, Buber will go on to argue that the Jews are the last or most belated Orientals. That is, they are the last Orientals to experience a cultural-religious efflorescence.[13] He will also argue that they are at once the most Oriental of all Orientals and (by an apparent paradox) completely familiar with the West.[14] The Jews are familiar with the West both because of their long Western diasporal experience and because Christianity itself remains essentially an offshoot of Judaism, matters to which I return below.

By positioning the Jews in this manner, Buber attempts to subvert negative Western stereotypes of Jews as Orientals—whether as surpassed (in the optimistic-progressivist Christian and then Hegelian narrative) or as needing to be excised from the properly Aryan Christian body (in the pessimistic narrative of regression à la Schopenhauer). He undertakes this subversion by appropriating the characterization of the Jew as an Oriental, while reversing the negative evaluative dimension this characterization entailed. In addition, at once strategically and idealistically, Buber wants to provide support here for a certain mode of Zionism through the idea that the Jews still belong in the Middle East. And finally he argues that the West should affirm this effort, because it is the destiny of the Jews to reconcile East with West. But in order to gauge more precisely Buber's gesture, we have to look more closely at its form (or method) and content.

First of all, Buber constructs here a miniphilosophy of history that is methodologically reminiscent of Hegelian dialectics. He develops the conceptual opposition between East and West as a temporal sequence, then resolves the opposition, envisioning the (re)establishment of a harmonious world totality through the *Aufhebung* that the Jews constitute. Second, on the level of content, Buber reverses and displaces the Hegelian polarities. Buber sees the Eastern sensibility as characterized precisely by its inwardness, *Innerlichkeit* (49), which is exactly what Hegel denied that the East can possess in its extreme or pure form (China), as we saw. And Buber associates the West, as epitomized by ancient Greece, with the objectivity or *Gegenständlichkeit* (49) that is opposed to inwardness. In accordance with dialectical patterns that have been updated in Bergsonian terms, Buber construes the inwardness of the East further as a motor sensibility, centrifugal in its direction, and therefore, we can infer, as expressive.[15] In contrast, Buber characterizes the West as a sensory attitude, a centripetal force, and hence a mimetic position (47). The Eastern sensibility is temporally focused, attentive to occurrence, action, relationship, and movement; the Western mind is spatially fixed on figure (*Gestalt*) or image (*Bild*), the latter conceived in its objective isolation and stasis under the dominion of the gaze. The Oriental experience is one of groundedness, whereas the Occidental experience lacks foundations. (See the passage quoted as epigraph to this section of my argument.)[16] The next question is how Buber reconciles these two diametrically opposed tendencies.

Having opposed the practical, engaged, passionate, and self-grounding East to the theoreticist, disengaged, cold, and ungrounded West, Buber constructs the Jews, at the end of the Orient and the beginning of the Occident, as the culture that knows how to undo the division, or *Entzweiung*, of the world within the *Entzweiung* of the subject. (*Entzweiung* is, of course, one of the key Hegelian words here.) The Jews undo this

Entzweiung through decision: "In decision, the divided world de-cides itself unto unity" (*In der Entscheidung entscheidet sich die entzweite Welt zur Einheit*) (54). Decision—which Buber marks as quintessentially Jewish by reference to the Jewish concept of a return to piety or *teshuvah* (*Umkehr* in Buber's German)—functions further as the *Aufhebung* of the division into subject and object, and therefore also into Oriental subjectivism and Occidental objectivism.[17]

The motif of Jewish decision, however, is for Buber a radicalization of the tendency toward realization that characterizes all Oriental cultures. Through this motif, Buber inverts the typological pattern according to which the East provides the potential that is realized in the West. For example, Buber writes that in Oriental cultures "the unified world is not supposed to be merely conceived, it is supposed to be realized—and here all great Asiatic religions and ideologies encounter one another" (50). It is precisely the fulfilling life (*dem erfüllenden Leben*) that is the Eastern path, or *Weg* (50).[18] The ground that the East provides for the West is not a ground of potential but one of realization.

Buber connects the "decision" of *teshuvah* to the path of Eastern religions, notably Taoism, by way of the Jewish emphasis on law. More specifically, he likens the Jewish *halachah*, the Law, whose signifier is rooted in the verb "to go" or "to walk," to the Chinese *Tao*, or way—*die Bahn*.[19]

As an achievement of the Eastern way, the path of decision itself becomes the sublation of the self-grounding East and the ungrounded West in an even deeper foundation, a kind of metafoundation. For Buber claims that more than any other Oriental path the Jewish path is susceptible of unification with Western modes of thought, precisely because it is already unified with Christianity, in that Christianity is an extension of the Jewish tradition.[20] But the reason why Christianity is an extension of Judaism—which boils down to the answer to the question as to why Judaism was able to influence the West more than other Oriental doctrines—is the universality of Judaism's ethical message: It speaks as an ethics not just to the learned elite but to all. Thus, the two principles of Judaism that were attractive to others—its "openness to all" (*Alloffenheit*) and its "orientation toward the positive deed" (*Richtung auf die positive Tat*) (57)—were the traits that made it capable of influencing the West so profoundly. By arguing in this way, Buber takes back up into Judaism the two traits Paul wants to claim for Christianity—universality and the notion of the sinner as the one who cannot do what he knows he should (which Buber reinflects as *Entzweiung* that can be undone through right action). On the site of this decisive path, between an Orientality the Jews achieve in its purest form and an Occidentality whose foundations they have laid in grounding Christianity, the Jews are poised to facilitate a world-wholeness and world-healing for which the global East-West conflict cries out as the solution to its divided sufferings.

But for the Jews to be able to play this unifying role, according to Buber, they have to return to their Oriental souls, that is, to their own foundations, for the ground (*Grund*) of the Jewish Oriental is the soul: "This ground is the soul of the Jew himself. For the Jew has remained an Oriental" (*Dieser Grund ist die Seele des Juden selbst. Denn der Jude ist Orientale geblieben*) (62). Yet in order to return to this soul the Jews have to overcome diaspora and return to their cohesion or coherence with their natural, literal ground, or context. The soul can be the grounding path only if it can walk on the real ground that is its proper home. Writing about the diaspora, Buber explains: "All creation took its force and form from the organic cohesion with this earth. And now this cohesion was torn: along with it the inner cohesion of the Jewish spirit was torn" (*Alles Schaffen nahm seine Kraft und seine Gestalt aus dem organischen Zusammenhang mit dieser Erde. Und nun wurde dieser Zusammenhang zerrissen, mit ihm zerriss der innere Zusammenhang des jüdischen Geistes*) (60). As a result of this lacerating loss of the natural context in the land, the Jews became "a nomadic people" (*ein Nomadenvolk*) (60), like the northern nomads that the Chinese in Kafka's text "The Great Wall of China" will try—in vain or superfluously—to hold at bay, as we will see below. Hence the Jews need to return to Jerusalem, the "gateway of the peoples. Here is the eternal passage between Orient and Occident" (*das Tor der Völker. Hier ist der ewige Durchgang zwischen Orient und Okzident*) (65).

Buber's gesture comprises, then, a complex combination of impulses, which we can reduce in summary to two main tendencies. On the one hand, in a very traditional (Western) metaphysical sense Buber indulges—along with many other Zionist thinkers, as is well known—in a negation of medieval, Talmudic Judaism.[21] This negation is based on (modern, Christian) organicist ideals of wholeness (the harmonious fusion or balancing of spirit and body envisioned in the aesthetics of grace since the late eighteenth century at least), especially as Herderian, Hegelian, and Wagnerian versions of the metaphysics of national spirit linked to land. Further, Buber reorganizes Hegelian dialectical figures in a chauvinistic and manifestly ideological, not to say grandiose way so as to make the Jews appear as the *Aufhebung* of East and West.[22] In this respect, he appropriates typological Orientalism by assimilating himself to a displaced version of his own making.

On the other hand, Buber's analysis is ethically defensible and appropriate in two important respects. It staunchly defends the Middle East and Far East against Western colonialist and supersessionist exploitation (although he essentially passes over Islam in silence in this text). And also, more specifically, he defends the Jews against the various denials of their cultural right to exist in the historical present and future. Further, he is correct, as we can perhaps see more clearly today, to insist that many of the world's geopolitical and religiopolitical woes can be addressed only to the extent that the East-West conflict is addressed and solved, and he is astute to recognize the dangerous potential of this conflict:

> Today Jerusalem is the gateway of the peoples in a still heavier, still wider, still more threatening and promising sense than before. It is necessary to seek the salvation or healing of Jerusalem, which is the salvation or healing of the peoples [*Heute ist in einem noch schwereren, noch umfänglicheren, noch drohungs- und verheißungsvolleren Sinn Jerusalem das Tor der Völker. Es gilt das Heil Jerusalems zu suchen, welches das Heil der Völker ist*]. (65)

Despite the nationalist and religious pathos resonating there, Buber's message about the world-political importance of the Middle East is certainly neither entirely wrong nor wrong-minded. Nor is he entirely wrong to seek out elements in the Jewish tradition that are linked to its historical existence among ancient Eastern, non-European cultures. In this respect, he *refuses* typological Orientalism. The metaphysically based, messianic optimism of Buber in the age of the "Asian crisis" (*asiatischen Krisis*) (64) and of the troubled European "Jewish question" leading up to World War I contrasts, however, sharply and importantly with the less metaphysical, more pessimistic, indeed nihilistic, approach to the same problems provided by Franz Kafka.[23]

The Great Wall of China as Foundation of the Tower of Babel: Kafka's "System of Partial Construction" between Structure and History

"Fundamentally, of course, I'm Chinese" (*Im Grunde bin ich ja Chinese*), Kafka wrote.[24] The striking contrast between Kafka and Buber in their general orientation, as it were, as well as in their approaches to the Orient is already summarized well by a brief aphorism from Kafka's *Nachlaß*: "There is only a goal, no path [*Weg*]. What we call path is hesitation [*Zögern*]."[25] But having already thus arrived at our goal of grasping the relationship between Kafka and Buber, the only thing that remains for us to do

Martin Buber (1878–1965). During unrest in Palestine, Buber is seen in a white suit, boarding an armored bus in Tel Aviv. 1937. (Bildarchiv Preussischer Kulturbesitz, Berlin/Walter Zadek (photographer)/Art Resource, N.Y.)

Martin Buber (1878–1965). In the rearview mirror of a bus in Tel Aviv. 1937. (Bildarchiv Preussischer Kulturbesitz, Berlin/Walter Zadek (photographer)/Art Resource, N.Y.)

is evidently: to hesitate. Thus, in this section I follow a *path* through some of Kafka's work that will clarify Kafka's relationship not only to Buber and to Hegel before him but more generally, on the one hand, to the entire historicist Orientalist tradition, and on the other hand, to the anticipatory critique of that tradition in the Enlightenment. This path takes us through

Franz Kafka (1883–1924). Circa 1918. (Bildarchiv Preussischer Kulturbesitz, Berlin/Art Resource, N.Y.)

Franz Kafka (1883–1924) in context: The Alchemistry (or Goldsmith) Alley, northern view, in the Castle complex of the Hrdcany, where Kafka lived during the winter of 1916/1917, when he seems to have written "The Great Wall of China." (Bildarchiv Preussischer Kulturbesitz, Berlin/Stiftung Deutsche Kinemathek, Berlin/Hans G. Casparius, 1931 (photographer)/Art Resource, N.Y.)

Kafka's short text, "The Great Wall of China" (*Beim Bau der chinesischen Mauer*), written in early 1917, and some closely related fragments.[26]

Like so many other Kafka texts that concern separation and connection, from the first collection *Betrachtung* to the very last stories, "The Great Wall of China" refers throughout to its own possible relations with its various contexts, especially, of course, the Orientalist one.[27] The motif of the wall alludes continuously to the relationship between text and context. Kafka concretizes text here as the Chinese national subject or ego, and context as the northern nomadic enemies of China. In terms of the relatively proximate historical resonances (or context) of "The Great Wall of China" as defined by Kafka's concerns, publishing venues, and so on, the relation between China and the northern nomads evokes those between Europe and the nomadic Jews, on the one hand, and inversely those between the Jews and the northern, Germanic Europeans, on the other hand. The West-East relation presented as an eastern southern-northern relation is thus overdetermined here in two directions by the Jewish-European one. Before returning to these cultural political specifics and to the text's relations with the Orientalist traditions, however, I consider its implications for acts of self-delimitation and self-appropriation, separation and connection more generally.

According to the model that Kafka's text proposes: How does a subject relate to its context, to the outside, to the other in which it can always find itself lost? It does so first of all—as Freud later spelled out in the *Ego and the Id* (1923) and elsewhere, and as Benjamin further explored in his essays on the perceptual conditions of modernity—by building a wall, a protective limit around itself for self-defense. And of course *Selbstwehr* (Self-Defense) was the very name of the Jewish journal in which two of Kafka's Chinese fragments first appeared. Such a limit is the condition of the possibility of any subject's existence as a separate subject, and thus also of any relation between that subject and its henceforth distinct, surrounding contexts. And the outside of the subject appears in principle as a nomadic world with respect to the subject itself qua home and at-homeness. The process of building the wall of China, then, allegorizes (and ironizes) here—among other things but perhaps above all—the development of the structure (and/or the structure of the development) of such a subject as separate from, and embedded in, its context.

I discuss below the development itself, the method (or path) through which the Great Wall in Kafka's text was built—"the system of partial construction" (*das System des Teilbaues*)—which is precisely not coherent or contextual (*nicht zusammenhängend*), and which more than half of the text attempts to ground, or *untermauern*. I also consider below the internal structuring limit, that is, the emperor who centers the realm as its sovereign subject. For now, let me consider what kind of relation with the outside is enabled by this wall, which is, again, the externally structuring limit of the (national) subject, China.

The main trait that should attract our attention in this connection is lack: The wall seems to have holes—*Lücken*—although we cannot be sure, because there are holes, the narrator tells us, in our knowledge of whether it has holes.

> Of course, in this way many large holes [*Lücken*] arose, which were only slowly filled in later, some even first after the building of the wall had already been announced as completed. Indeed, there are supposed to be holes that were never filled in; according to some they are much larger than the constructed parts, which is however a claim that possibly belongs to the many legends that have arisen around the construction, and that cannot be checked by any individual human at least with his own eyes and his own measure [*Maßstab*] due to the extension of the construction [*Ausdehnung des Baues*]. (65)

Hence, the wall's existence implies the possibilities of relation and nonrelation, without resolution of the uncertainty. Indeed, like any wall, this wall connects its inside to its outside while separating the two; it establishes the relationship it disrupts through the disruption itself. A wall with holes in it—virtual holes—is perfectly suited to concretize this situation.

In accordance with this paradoxical relation-without-relation, the narrator characterizes the wall, given its mode of construction, as both useless (because a relation with the outside is forever maintained) and superfluous (because there is never any relation anyway). On the first point:

> Not only can such a wall not protect, but what there is of it is in perpetual danger. These blocks of wall left standing in deserted regions could be easily pulled down, again and again, by the nomads, especially as these tribes, rendered apprehensive [*geängstigt*] by the building operations, kept changing their encampments with incredible rapidity, like locusts, and so perhaps had a better general view [*Überblick*] of the progress of the wall than we, the builders. (65–66)

The wall keeps letting the others, the nomads, the placeless and improper aliens in; it can never fully come into existence to hold them at bay. And the brief text "Ein altes Blatt" ("An Old Manuscript")—which can be regarded as an extension of this text, according to Kafka's own method of "partial construction" (to which I will return in a moment)—develops this thought more fully, in that it describes the situation of the emperor's city as overrun by northern nomadic soldiers.[28]

Still, at least in the village of the narrator, the Chinese not only have never seen these nomads, but

> if we remain in our villages, we shall never see them, even if on their wild horses they should ride as hard as they can straight toward us—the land is

too vast and would not let them reach us, they would end their course in the empty air [*in die leere Luft werden sie sich verrennen*]. (294)

Hence, there is no relation between the interior and the exterior of the nation, subject, or text. The nomads can never get in. The wall of difference would be absolute even if no wall were built.

But the situation is not exhausted by the contradictory constatations of ineluctable relation and its equally unavoidable absence. Despite the superfluousness of the wall, and because of the continuing threat of its uselessness, one still evidently has to (or ought to) build a wall. For a wall is being built, and the narrative respects its necessity even as it fails to attain any satisfactory ultimate explanation of that necessity. Separation from context remains an imperative or desideratum. Conversely, despite the wall's uselessness and because of its superfluity, Kafka's narrator implies that one should try to be in a relation with one's context, as long as it is the right one: hence the emphasis on solidarity between the builders, on community, and so on.[29] Because you are radically in relation, you need to resist the nonrelation that remains; but because you are equally not in relation, you need to resist the relation that exists. The paradoxical double imperative follows, in short, from the paradoxical double constative. The text reminds us, then, not to imagine that any *Zusammenhang*, either an internal coherence—be it formal or conceptual—or an external (e.g., historical, developmental) context, can provide a stable ground or foundation for its reading or its existence. Each ground both ungrounds and abandons the other.

How does this meditation on separation and connectedness shed light on historicist Orientalism, as a typological appropriation of original context, and on Kafka's own possible separation from such appropriation? If one is always both in one's context and at a distance from it, as Kafka has just suggested, so that text and context each infinitely unground the other and leave it in suspension, then one cannot ever expect to arrive at an ultimate appropriation of one's context. I cannot grasp the other to make it mine, either because it is too far away or because it dominates my attempts to delimit myself against it: In either case, this other, who represents—qua nomadic—the strewing of identity, exceeds appropriation. There can be no question of my making myself the literal realization of any identity that it—the (nomadic) other—would prefigure. Still, the appropriative endeavor continues. And if Kafka himself cannot appropriate typological appropriation, he will remain exposed to the possibility that such appropriation, and the Orientalist tradition it helps define, if not appropriates, then continues to affect and harrass, his own borders. Indeed, these are the two senses of the title of Part II of this book, "How Not to Appropriate Orientalist Typology": how to take one's distance from it and how one might fail to take one's distance from it. In order to see more specifically how Kafka's text relates (and does not) to the dialectical typology of historicist Orientalism, it is necessary to consider how it relates (and does not) to Hegel's method (and to his specific approach to the meaning of China in the process of world history), as well as to Hegel's Enlightenment forebears.

Consider Kafka's opening:

> The Great Wall of China was finished off at its northernmost corner [*nördlichsten Stelle*]. From the southeast and the southwest it came up in two sections that finally converged there [*wurde der Bau herangeführt und hier vereinigt*]. This system of partial construction [*System des Teilbaues*] was also applied on a smaller scale by both of the two great armies of labor, the eastern and the western. It was done in this way: gangs [*Gruppen*] of some twenty workers were formed who had to accomplish a length, say, of five hundred yards of wall [*eine Teilmauer von etwa fünfhundert Metern Länge*], a similar gang built another stretch of the same length to meet the first [*baute ihnen dann eine Mauer in gleicher Länge entgegen*] . But after the junction had been made the construction of the wall was not carried on from the point, let us say, where this thousand yards ended; instead the two groups of workers were transferred to begin building again in quite different neighborhoods.... Now one would believe from the start that it would have been more advantageous in every way to build the wall continuously [*zusammenhängend*], or at least continuously within the two main divisions.... But how can a wall protect if it is not built as a continuous structure [*zusammenhängend*]? ... Nevertheless, the task of construction probably could not have been carried out in any other way. To understand this we must take into account the following. (65–66)

More than half of the text, then, if not the entirety, goes on (ironically) to try to ground this groundless mode of construction of the grounding wall, to give this noncontextuality at the basis of all context a context that is coherent. What does all of this have to do with Hegelianism and/or with Kantian Enlightenment?

The first Hegelian motif that finds itself explicitly displaced in this passage is nothing less than the *dialectical method itself*, which, as we saw in chapter 5, is itself a grand and grandiose realization of typological reasoning, the construction of a narrative of world history through the development of oppositions out of previous syntheses in a continuous coherence of context, or *zusammenhängend*. Needless to say, what is surprising here is not that Kafka differs from Hegel, but that he so explicitly provides an alternative—self-ironizing but also posed as necessary—to what are obviously Hegelian terms. Kafka's principle for the construction of the Chinese identity through its walling in, the "System des Teilbaues" (289), is precisely and specifically *not* dialectical in a Hegelian sense. The synthesis of thesis and antithesis, eastern segment and western segment of wall, does not function as a new thesis, to be answered by an antithesis in turn, for one does not continue to build on the end of the thousand-meter units. Rather, the new thesis arises at an arbitrarily determined elsewhere that has no connection with the point of the prior synthesis. The dialectic is interrupted every step of the way and the place of its renewal does not cohere or belong in the same context with—*hängt nicht zusammen mit*—the place of its previous breaking off. Not only do "many large holes"—*viele grosse Lücken*—arise through such a method, as I indicated above, some of which may have been filled in only after the claimed completion of the wall. (This suggests that the moment of the wall's completion is deferred beyond itself.) In addition, "we" think there may be some holes left, although there are holes in our knowledge of whether or not there are holes, whether or not the stories of still existing holes are simply legends, which arise because we cannot get an image of the wall in its entirety. So the coherence of the wall, its finished totality, remains in doubt as a result of its very nondialectical method of construction.

This brings us to the question of Kantianism and Enlightenment structural thinking in general. Should we conclude from its anti-Hegelianism that the architectonics of Kafka's Chinese Wall are more closely allied with the architectonics of Enlightenment rationality in a Kantian mode?[30] In one sense, this seems to be the case, for as in the Kantian sublime, especially the mathematical sublime, the wall is not perceptually totalizable: We are told that there is no "Maßstab" that could measure its greatness. It is quasi-infinite: The allusion to the mathematical sublime is unmistakable.[31] Unlike the Kantian sublime, however, this failure of imagination hardly gives rise to a discovery of our supersensuous destiny. It does not yield to a systematic architectonic whole that would provide a rational foundation in terms of which one could orient oneself. Rather, it remains bound up with the merely rhapsodic or aggregative ongoing attempt to wall ourselves in from the nomadic "sensuous diversity of the manifold," or, alternatively, from the endlessly strewn multiplication of reasons for its own failure.[32] If the first context into which one fits and which one must appropriate is that of one's bordering limit, the universalizable limit of the "one," the context of China (as of any subject) is the very noncontextuality or incoherence of its non–self-appropriated definition. Kafka's text manifestly ironizes rational architectonics qua self-limiting critique just as much as it does the developmental narratives of the post-Enlightenment philosophy of history.

As a consequence of Kafka's fictionally nonfictional account—in which identity constitution or self-grounding appears as a "system of partial construction," and where identity arises as a strewn and incoherent construct not susceptible of dialectical totalization—a number of further displacements of Hegelian world history ensue in Kafka's text. These displacements concern the content of China's identity. First, China is now neither purely static nor developmentally progressive; it is infinitely on the way to its identity. That the northernmost point has been announced as finished (*beendet*) (67), for example, does not necessarily mean that work on the wall is finished, especially since we are told that the filling of gaps in the wall may have continued after its claimed completion. Yet China is not arriving here at this structured identity in any great hurry. Temporality—a point that will recur below—is nonlinearized.

Second, even the eastern status of China has become uncertain in Kafka's text. The northernmost point is reached from both the southeast and the southwest; and eastern and western armies of Chinese masons are each subdivided into many discontinuous pairs of eastern and western workers. Finally, these workers slide laterally, over time, into new positions as they move from job to fragmentary job. The difference between East and West inhabits in a multiple and nonhierarchized way both East and West within the radical East that is China.

Third, Kafka collapses the opposition Hegel posited between Chinese and Jew into a ghostly quasi identity, a textual fact that Clement Greenberg, Robert Alter, and others have observed, although not perhaps finally placed in its proper context, so to speak.[33] The use of the building of a wall around China to allude, in part, to the Jewish motif of the building of the traditional oral law as a fence around the written law—introduced by Rabbi Akiva in Mishna Avot—brings together the Hegelian beginning and end of the Orient, homebound stasis and diasporal drift, excessive materiality and overblown spirituality, in a way that resembles Hegelian thinking even as it escapes the specifics of his system.[34] In this way, Kafka's text reveals—parodically and not by mere (dialectical) opposition—the nonnecessity, indeed the arbitrariness, of the *Zusammenhänge* that Hegel establishes.

Having indicated two important levels—namely, method and content—on which Kafka's text critically displaces the historically distant Hegelian approach to the Orient, it will be useful—for the sake of circumscribing

Kafka's specific intervention in his own context, as it were—to characterize Kafka's text also in terms of how it—at least implicitly—appropriates (and does not) Martin Buber's dialectical approach to the Orient, which it seems Kafka may well even have heard as a lecture in Prague. The best way of approaching the relation of Kafka to Buber on the question of the Orient is to consider how the two longest and principal parts of Kafka's text—other than its final section, which I consider below—hang together (or do not).[35] By the two main parts of the text, I mean: the part we've already considered, where the narrator tries to justify or ground the "System des Teilbaues" (i.e., the system of the construction of the ground—or unifying reason—in piecemeal fashion); and the part where he considers the relationship between the Chinese and the institution—or *Einrichtung*—of the emperor, which I consider now.

The relation between emperor and wall is fairly clear, if one can risk such a statement with respect to any Kafka text. The wall functions to protect the inside of the national subject from the outside, constituting that inside in the process; the emperor functions as the most interior or central point within the interior of the national subject, from whom the command to build the wall may seem to issue. (I don't say it does.)[36] The text itself, however, is narrated from the standpoint of a member of the people, who is neither as external as a nomad nor as internal as the emperor. This text is topically or tropically divided, therefore, between a centrifugally, outwardly focused tendency, and a centripetally, inwardly directed one. Whereas Buber explicitly constructs East as centrifugal and West as centripetal, Kafka splits his text about China down the middle, the one part looking out to ponder relations with the outside, the other looking in and questioning its *Zusammenhang* with the inside. Kafka's extreme East, as exemplified by the narrator's gaze, is both centrifugal and centripetal, in Buber's terms Oriental and Occidental at once.

Moreover, the two directions are difficult to separate, quasi-identical, despite their opposition. Notwithstanding the radical interiority of his position with respect to the Chinese national subject, the emperor qua absolute interior is exterior to the people: They are divorced from his presence in a radical, hyperbolic, parodic, and almost surrealistic manner, despite their desire to follow his dictates. They worship and obey an emperor long dead, scoffing at people silly enough to believe that the one who happens to be the present emperor is actually alive, and so on.

But here the outside is also the inside. That is, we are dealing not only with this exteriority of the center (embodied by the emperor) with respect to the people.³⁷ In addition, and conversely, the text confronts us with the inexcludable character of the exterior—the northern nomads—as considered above. Moreover, the "System des Teilbaues" makes the lower leaders, who are sent from site to site, into nomads themselves, thereby inadvertently importing the nomadic exterior.

By disrupting the outside/inside opposition in this way, Kafka's text renders impossible the essentialisms through which the dialectical narratives of Buber and Hegel cohere within themselves, narratives that depend on and maintain this opposition, even if they also sublate it in a series of syntheses. In the oscillation between the wandering off of the center and the becoming-central of wandering, there is no room for the identification of any *Innerlichkeit* with any particular individual or collective subject whatsoever, along the lines of Buber's association of Orientality with inwardness. Nor can one say that the inwardness has become entirely outward here, as Hegel said of China: Distance interposes itself in Kafka's text between individual subjects and the exterior will of the emperor—they lead "a to some extent free, un-dominated life . . . not at all unethical (or without customs), but a life that stands under no present law" (*ein gewissermassen freies, unbeherrschtes Leben . . . Keineswegs sittenlos . . . doch ein Leben, das unter keinem gegenwärtigen Gesetze steht*) (298). Nor finally is there any ideal or pacifying resolution or *Aufhebung* of the opposition between the two conditions of inwardness and outwardness. For the Chinese still try here to keep the nomads out, and they still try to live in accordance with the emperor's decrees, with respect to which one is "hopeless and hopeful" (*hoffnungslos und hoffnungsvoll*) (76).³⁸ Hopeful, one awaits a message from the emperor that is meant for oneself—hence, the emperor remains one's own interiority. But hopeless, one knows the message will never arrive— for that interiority is exterior to oneself, part of one's infinite and infinitely alien context and not of oneself. Kafka's text evades not only the ideology of inwardness common to Buber and Hegel, but also the synthetic telos of Orientalist dialectical typology in general.

In accordance with this reticence with respect to resolution, Kafka's text sustains indecision throughout the second part of his text, as he did in the first part concerning the grounds of the "System des Teilbaues" through the multiplication and mutual suspension of determinations of these grounds. So if Kafka sustains the path of decision in a Jewish sense as Buber had construed it, he does so only through the resolute decision in favor of indecision, hardly what Buber has in mind, because indecision does not achieve unity. In the second major segment of his text, Kafka supports indecision ultimately through an indecisive decision to suspend only for the time being—*vorderhand*—the investigation in which it is involved.[39] But the specific juncture at which this occurs requires brief discussion, because the passage concerns the metaphysical foundations of (the Chinese) ethnic community.

The narrator has designated this segment on the emperorship (*Kaisertum*) at the outset as concerning one of the most indistinct (*allerundeutlichsten*) institutions of China, the grounds (*Gründen*) (73) of whose unclarity he is trying to clarify. He now concludes this section with the indication that the people's unclear conception or perception (*Auffassung*) of the emperor is partly owing to the government's failure to make it clear and "immediately and continuously effectual" (*unmittelbar und unabläßig wirkte*) to the people all the way to the borders (*Grenzen*) of the empire; and partly due to the "people's weak imaginations and faith" (*Schwäche der Vorstellungs- oder Glaubenskraft beim Volke*) (78). Regardless of its basis, this (failure of) conception, as an incapacity of the people to represent the emperor clearly to itself, is nothing less than the "ground on which we live" (*Boden auf dem wir leben*) (79), in that it is "one of the most important means of unification of our people" (*eines der wichtigsten Einigungsmittel unseres Volkes*) (79).[40] Not only does the narrator call it this ground, or *Boden*, but he also uses another term for ground, *Grund*, four times in the direct run-up to this claim, highlighting thereby by antiphrasis or parody the very uncertainty of the grounding of this unity (or of the unity of this grounding). Specifically, he claims to know that the particular or local unclarity about the imperial presence is indicative of a universal or pervasive unclarity throughout the empire on the basis (*auf Grund*) of his wide reading, and on the basis (*auf Grund*) of his observations, and in summary again on the basis of all of this (*auf Grund alles dessen*) (78). He adds that there is everywhere a "certain common fundamental trait" (*einen gewissen gemeinsamen Grundzug*) (78) shared by the different conceptions of the emperor in different regions. And finally, the narrator closes the section by leaving the grounding of the weakness of this ground (*Boden*) in suspension, out of fear of undermining the ground that remains, however unstable it may be:

> To thoroughly ground a critique would be not to unsettle our conscience, but rather—much worse—our legs. And therefore I do not want to proceed further, for the time being, with this investigation.
>
> *Hier einen Tadel ausführlich begründen, heißt nicht an unserem Gewissen, sondern was viel ärger ist an unsern Beinen rütteln. Und darum will ich in der Untersuchung dieser Frage vorderhand nicht weiter gehn.* (79)

And thus the ground of the community, in its failure to represent to itself its internal ground or limit (the emperor), is left ungrounded. The ground of its indeterminacy remains indeterminate and undecided.[41]

Excursus on a Brief Excursus—Concerning Babel

If Kafka's narrator *were* to question this ground, however, as the text suggests it will *not* do for the moment, it would presumably be to say not that the people should have a more distinct representation of their leader but that the use of any representations for the purposes of a people's unification (or for any unified purpose) will undo itself in its own ungrounding dispersion. Indeed, he has already effectively argued this, in his discussion of the Tower of Babel, in the first main segment of the text (and related fragments), on which it will be useful to touch before concluding the discussion of Kafka. The narrator refers to Babel in a very funny, brief commentary on a book he claims to have read, which had supposedly argued that the failure of the Babel-tower project was due to insufficient foundations (*der Bau an der Schwäche des Fundamentes scheiterte und scheitern mußte*) and that "the Great Wall would now comprise a secure foundation for a new Tower of Babel. Thus, first the wall and then the tower" (*erst die große Mauer werde . . . ein sicheres Fundament für einen neuen Babelturm schaffen. Also zuerst die Mauer und dann den Turm*) (69). This conception, which recalls Orientalist fantasies from Leibniz to Hegel, alludes conceptually to the typological passage from prefigural foundations to fulfilled structure, and turns this entire tradition to ridicule. For the narrator confesses his puzzlement over the incomprehensibility of building a tower on top of a wall, and when he tries to read this theory allegorically—"That must have been meant in a figural sense" (*Das konnte doch nur in geistiger Hinsicht gemeint sein*) (69)—passing from literal to figural meaning, he remains confused by the enduring literalism of the building of the wall and the plans for the tower. Concluding this excursus, he says that there was much "confusion of heads then" (*Verwirrung der Köpfe damals*) (70), a trope on *Sprachverwirrung*, the standard German term for the "confusion of tongues" resulting from the biblical Babel's destruction. He hereby inscribes the Chinese narrative into the biblical one, and vice versa, performatively confusing one narrative with another. The narrator then explains the failure of both projects in terms of the claim that the unification of humans around one purpose inevitably leads to the dispersion, and not only of the collectivity but of "das menschliche Wesen" (70)—the human being and its essence itself.⁴² As with the attempt to wall out the nomads—and this is the point—here too unification leads to multiplicitous dispersion, identity to difference, appropriation to self-expropriation.⁴³ Where appropriation and expropriation imply each other, endlessly and without sublation of the opposition, progressive dialectics in general and Orientalist typology in particular are certainly no longer possible.

The Father's Final Silence

Given Kafka's resolute maintenance of indecision on grounds concerning the internal and external limits of the empire—the emperor as center and the wall as periphery—and even on the positions of these limits relative to each other, it is appropriate not only that the text wanders off nomadically into related fragments on the Chinese Wall and on the Tower of Babel, but that it closes, if it closes, with words from the father that, in the manuscript, are precisely *crossed out*.⁴⁴ In this way, the text's final words are both put into the father's mouth—who appears here as mediator between public and private, outside and inside, and as a privileged figure for the Chinese principle itself in its Hegelian determination—and prevented from emerging from that mouth by a movement of crossing out. On the one hand, this is not surprising, given Kafka's well-known tortured mixed feelings about paternal figures—constantly shifting between hatred, fear, resentment, envy, and admiration—manifestly in evidence everywhere from the "Letter to the Father" to "The Judgment" and so on across his writings. And on the other hand, we have no hint as to why he crosses out these last words of the text known as "The Great Wall of China," and whether or not he meant to insert later a revised version of the brief speech here. What *do* we know about this textual passage?

In this final paragraph of the text, the narrator recounts his childhood memory of the arrival of the imperial messenger with news of the building of the wall. This account is replete with grotesquely exaggerated, silly, and parodically Orientalist descriptions of Chinese phallic paternal attributes: the father stroking his long, thin pipe, the father's beard jutting into the air, his ponytail ("an object of respectful fear for the children") (79) hanging down, and so on. More generally, the text describes the way in which the boatman arrives and whispers the imperial news into his father's ears; then it pantomimes briefly the exchange between the father's unbelieving response and the messenger's attempts to persuade him. Finally, the father stands on the threshold of the home (between inside and outside) to announce the news, which evidently brings together wall and emperor as telos and arche, outer and inner, but the text simply breaks off with "My father thus said approximately" (*Mein Vater sagte also etwa*) (80)—and silence. The stricken passage appears as crossed out in the wonderful manuscript-facsimile edition of Roland Reuß and Peter Stengle, which I cite without including corrections within the text:

> *Ein fremder Schiffer—ich kenne alle, die gewöhnlich hier vorüberfahren, dieser aber war fremd—hat mir eben erzählt, dass eine grosse Mauer gebaut werden soll um den Kaiser zu schützen. Es versammeln sich nämlich oft vor dem Kaiserlichen Palast die ungläubigen Völker, unter ihnen auch Dämonen, und schiessen ihre schwarzen Pfeile gegen den Kaiser.* (111)[45]

The Schocken edition of *The Complete Stories*, printing this last part of the text separately as "The News of the Building of the Wall: A Fragment," gives the full stricken passage without indicating that it was crossed out:

> An unknown boatman—I know all those who usually pass by here, but this one was a stranger—has just told me that a great wall is going to be built to protect the Emperor. For it seems that infidel tribes, among them demons, often assemble before the imperial palace and shoot their black arrows at the Emperor. (249)[46]

Having reconstructed the situation, and in the attempt to make some sense of this concluding cancellation of the father's speech—if that is what it is—I would underline first that the father is presented here as a doubter or unbeliever, for he doubts twice the messenger's news of the building of the wall (*der Vater die Nachricht nicht zu glauben schien . . . der Vater noch immer nicht glauben konnte. . . . Der Vater stiller wurde*) (79). And we note further that in his crossed-out announcement the father says that the wall is to be built to protect the emperor because "the unbelieving peoples" (*die ungläubigen Völker*—not "tribes" as the Schocken translation renders it but somewhat more familiarly "peoples") (Reuß and Stengle, eds., 111; Glatzer, ed., 249) are gathering before the palace and shooting their black arrows at him. So the (family) father has his doubts about the (imperial) father's project to protect himself from those who have their doubts about the (imperial) father's projects. But the family father and the imperial father are to function as mirror images of each other. The figure of the father thus doubts and threatens (thereby) his own project to defend himself against those whose doubt threatens his security, to whose number he evidently belongs.

That this figure's speech is both written down and then crossed out—with a single diagonal line running from the lower left to the upper right of the paragraph, which leaves the writing entirely legible—certainly seems appropriate both to the speech in particular and to the ending of this little text as a (non)whole, "very characteristic of the people's conception" (*für die Volksauffassung sehr bezeichnend*) (80), as the narrator puts the sense (*Sinn*) of the father's words before they (dis)appear. The message of the necessary nonarrival of the (emperor's) message (or the intentional ground) at its destination—published separately in Kafka's lifetime (in the *Country Doctor* collection as "An Imperial Message"), but part of "The Great Wall of China" in the manuscript—has been delivered earlier in the text.[47] But in effect, it also concludes the text, with the lacking (or self-cancelling) ground of a paternal logos, in the interruption of the text's narrative self-grounding through arrival at an end that would also be a beginning. For here the beginning of the building of the wall, in the people's internalizing response to their leader's expressed intention, interrupts itself as the text (inconclusively) concludes.

CHAPTER 8

The Dreamwork of History: Orientalism and Originary Disfiguration in Freud's *Moses and Monotheism*

> Hardly do I open my shop in the morning twilight, and I see already the entrances to all of the streets that lead into the square occupied by armed men. Yet it is not our soldiers, but rather evidently nomads out of the north. In a manner incomprehensible to me, they have penetrated into the capital, which is however very far from the border. . . . It is a misunderstanding, and we will be destroyed by it.
>
> —FRANZ KAFKA, *Beim Bau der chinesischen Mauer*

> We live in a particularly remarkable time.
> [*Wir leben in einer besonders merkwürdigen Zeit*].
>
> —SIGMUND FREUD, *Der Mann Moses und die monotheistische Religion*

> The disfiguration of a text is similar to a murder. The difficulty lies not in carrying out the deed, but in hiding its traces. [*Es ist bei der Entstellung eines Textes ähnlich wie bei einem Mord. Die Schwierigkeit liegt nicht in der Ausführung der Tat, sondern in der Beseitigung ihrer Spuren*].
>
> —SIGMUND FREUD, *Der Mann Moses und die monotheistische Religion*

> Every event rather appears to be overdetermined.
> [*Vielmehr scheint jedes Ereignis überdeterminiert zu sein*].
>
> —SIGMUND FREUD, *Der Mann Moses und die monotheistische Religion*

The invasion of barbaric nomads from the outside might be construed as having been a relatively metaphorical matter for Kafka, although he wrote about them during World War I and had his own extensive and painful personal experiences with invasion by the Other, including the tuberculosis that would be diagnosed several months after he composed the Chinese Wall texts.[1] But the invasion is for sure a politically, militarily acute reality for Freud when, in his last Vienna years (from 1934 on) and then in exile in London after the *Anschluß*, he writes *Moses and Monotheism*, his major contribution to the ongoing debates in Orientalist studies. At this point, Freud is losing his Viennese home, the "home . . . where [psychoanalysis] was born and grew up,"[2] and where—compared with the fascist threat—even the inimical Catholic Church has begun to appear in a friendly light (504). During the gradual approach of his necessary departure from Austria and immediately afterward, Freud contemplates a grandiose metaphor for his life trajectory: the departure of the Israelites from Egypt, their exodus from their exilic home toward another home, which from the start recedes into the indeterminate distance of a promise and a law of how to live in the meantime, or *vorderhand*, as Kafka had put it.

But although Freud obviously goes back in this text to his own cultural origins and personal history—pondering why the Jews have been able to survive for so long, asking why they have attracted such hatred, and other related questions—he ultimately places his main emphasis on something else. He focuses, I argue, on the paradoxical notion of the origin as a loss of origin, and on the link between this originary loss and the emergence of language for the psyche (or the emergence of the subject within language). (I demonstrate this below principally by following the obsessive motif of "distortion" or "disfiguration" [*Entstellung*] in this text within the larger context of Freud's thought as a whole, especially *The Interpretation of Dreams*.) Indeed, monotheism, and then Judaism, are important for Freud ultimately because for him they commemorate this (loss of the) origin of the human with what he finds an admirable though still inadequate degree of explicitness.[3] It is in Freud's theorization of this (loss of) origin that his significant displacement of historicist, typological Orientalism consists, a displacement that has correlatives in Kafka's intervention that I will note below. In other words, while leaving behind Vienna and the realities of Nazi-dominated Austria, Freud also flees and sheds certain of the conceptual foundations of that Austria (and all of Europe and the West more generally): the fundamental Christian narrative, and especially the medieval typology or figural interpretation that underlies this narrative. While doing so, further, Freud flees—and kills, and mourns—the modern Orientalist narrative that developed as a displaced repetition of this typological scheme especially from the eighteenth through the nineteenth centuries and on into the twentieth.

Destabilizing the Identity of Typological Terms

In an initial and anticipatory approximation, we can see that a number of Freud's main gestures in this text on the mass psychology of religious history disrupt and destabilize the religiocultural identities on which Judaeo-Christian typology is based. To start with Jewish identity, as both the self-sameness and the traditional meaning of "the Jewish": The text famously opens with the attempt to establish that Moses was an Egyptian. Freud claims, moreover, that the Mosaic God was not even invented or discovered by Moses but was the God of the Aton religion initiated by Amenhotep IV, later renamed Ikhnaton. According to Freud and his main sources this God, the first properly monotheistic deity, grew out of the sun worship in Egypt, in part as an effect of the imperialistic successes of the Egyptians.[4] Reigning over a multiplicity of lands, the Egyptians had to establish their God as the One universal God reigning over the multiplicity of other gods, and the abstraction from the sun to a purely spiritual instance enabled this transition.[5] Freud's account of this process situates in the Egyptian Empire a development similar to the one Hegel associated with the Persian Empire in his *Lectures on the Philosophy of History*.

Freud thus begins by making both the founder of Judaism and the inventor of monotheism Egyptian, that is, pagan, while explaining monotheism partly as the result of imperialism. Needless to say, these are not points of view common among, or flattering to the views of, traditional Jewry— for Abraham doesn't invent monotheism; he responds to God's call. And this alienation applies to the entire spectrum of Jewry, from orthodox to essentially secular, since even the latter generally presuppose that Moses is an Israelite. So the first identity Freud's analysis unsettles is Jewish identity, and especially Jewish narcissism or pride, as attached to the notion that Jews discovered monotheism (this notion itself a displacement of the idea of chosenness).

But traditional Christian self-conceptions are no more secured by this Egyptianization of Moses than Jewish ones, because Judaism ceases here to be even the site of the prefigurative invention of monotheism. Nor is Freud supporting—needless to say—Aryan Christianity theories. For these theories on the extreme right had been arguing since the mid-nineteenth century, as supported by Schopenhauerian and Wagnerian metaphysics, that Christianity comes out of an originary monotheistic impulse rooted in India and germinating within ancient Sanskrit texts. On this level of Freud's text, a pagan instance invents its monotheistic opposite. And this pagan instance is not in any sense Western or even South Asian rather than African, as in so many accounts Martin Bernal cites (where Egypt is replaced by India).[6] Exile from Egyptian exile here starts within Egypt itself; it is an Egyptian exile in principle, or spirit, or genius. And in addition, Freud sees Christianity as realizing Judaism only to the (limited) degree that it (indirectly) acknowledges its complicity in the murder of the primal father it repeats (I return to this below), not exactly what the Church Fathers seem to have had in mind.

Finally, even the identity of the pagan is here dislodged. First, the Egyptian invention of monotheism is of mixed authorship, in that Freud suggests Syrian influences are also present, and so on. Second, this invention constitutes in Freud's account a symptomatic formation that in turn recalls (as will Christianity)—in the displaced form of a denial—the (murder of the) primal father at the threshold of the human. That is, the invention of monotheism itself, wherever it can be said to have occurred, is only the derivative aftereffect of a primal event—the abyssal ground of civilization itself—that, as Freud also says, had to occur innumerable times ("ungezählt oft wiederholt worden ist" [529]) before it became an institutionalized reality. And the polytheism that preceded this monotheistic invention was itself the repetition of a phase in the mourning over this primal event—the (murder of the) primal father—hence anything but neatly self-identical. In fact, Freud pushes back the traditional pagan term, conceived (within Judaism and Christianity) as preceding the key step in the development of spirit, into a prehuman realm prior even to the development of the primal father horde itself, for as soon as we have the father horde, the developments of spirit, human society, and religion have simultaneously been broached.

Freud thus reduces Christian typology—the history of full presence qua Christian (and Western)—to the non–self-identity of a repetitive origin that is the violent suppression of violence (in the murder of the primal father). Each of the typological terms—pagan, Jewish, and Christian (and their later Orientalist avatars)—is involved intimately with the others in this repetition.

But before we can grasp precisely the structure and sense of what Freud puts in place of typology, a number of preliminary steps must be taken. First, it is necessary to retrace briefly in literalist terms his narrative of the origin and development of society. Second, it is important to recall, again in a literal-minded way, his narrative of the origination and development of religion. Third, I develop a reading of these two narratives together as a two-step allegory of the development and coming to (limited) self-awareness of humanity, insofar as humanity is inscribed in linguistic disfiguration. After sketching, fourth, the motif of disfiguration (*Entstellung*) across Freud's text, I return to Freud's specific intervention in the Orientalist tradition, and the question of its enduring importance, despite the problematic and dated, easily dismissed levels or aspects of his late texts on Moses.

Grounding and Grunting: The Origin of Society out of the Primal Horde

For Freud's account of the biopsychosocial origins of humanity, as presented in *Totem and Taboo* in 1912–12 and recalled in *Mass Psychology and the Analysis of the Ego* in 1921, Darwin's description of original humanity as "primal horde" forms the point of departure.[7] At this stage, each small horde is led by an all-powerful and tyrannical father, the strongest male, who exiles all other male rivals, including all of the sons, in order to possess all of the women for himself. This is a Freudian equivalent of the construction of the Tower of Babel or the Chinese Wall in Kafka: the construction of the self-identical. (I return to this below.)

Subsequent to this initial organizational step, which constitutes the formation of patriarchal despotism, the next step in the development of humanity involves the murder of the primal father by the combined forces of the sons. After fighting each other for a while to determine who will be the new tyrant, the sons finally get smart and decide that it's better if no one has a *jouissance*-monopoly: Each takes a little bit of *jouissance*, but renounces all the rest. They accept the lot of the grunt, so to speak, as the *Grundlage* of society. The incest taboo and its attendant exogamy arise: All the males decide that they will not fight each other for the familial women and therefore that they will accept (in his absence) the dead father's (former) monopoly on the familial women, but only on condition that all accept that monopoly equally. Matriarchy intervenes in this period, Freud assumes (following Bachofen to some degree), such that the mothers regain some of the power previously held by the fathers.[8] Although relatively happy about this arrangement, the sons also feel guilty about the father's murder, regretful because they loved and still love him ("Ordnung ist das halbe Leben" ["Order Is Half of Life"]), as the German saying has it). The tyrannical moral conscience—or superego—of the self-limiting, "good" brothers derives from the initially (literally) cannibalistic internalization of the father. It is a compensatory identification with him in an idealized form. The father now both protects and brutally excludes them from their own experience and impulses in their own minds. The father becomes the internal principle of mediation and displacement. The ego ideal shared by all of the brothers gives them a common trait, the basis and center of their (collective) identity. Over time, after the matriarchal latency period, the patriarchy returns, but in a milder form, displacing the matriarchy and giving a now self-limiting role to paternal power in reality, as controlled by the idealization and inwardization of that power through the internalization of paternal figures.[9]

The result of this process of civilization for religion is as follows: The core of what will later be religion is formed by two operations. First, one identifies with the father as one's own ideal, that is, with an idealized father, or with the rule of the ideal (and the concomitant intention to renounce one's own tyrannical will). And second, one identifies with the other members of the group through this commonly assumed ideal.[10] Identification, as the love for the primal father that remains when hatred has run its course, is the birthplace—the origin and essence—of religion. And conversely, religion is the religion of identity. Or at least so it seems.[11]

Religion as Return of the Repressed Origin: From Totemism to Christianity

How does religion develop out of the identification with the murdered father that completes the founding of human society? Given the foundation of society in the violent suppression of its founding violence, religion develops as the reflection of this foundation (in both the moment of the primal father-horde and the moment of the brother-horde) on the level of consciousness. But this reflection is always marked by some degree of opacity, because it is a symptomatic repetition (i.e., a return of the repressed). The stages of the development of religion are those of an increasingly clear consciousness of human society's origin, but here the increase is never entirely assured. Hence the teleological view of religious history—the history of revelations that reigns, for example, in the idealist tradition after Lessing from Herder to Hegel—is no longer tenable or in any way guaranteed. Further, whereas in idealism the advance of consciousness is an advance in the consciousness of freedom, the advance of consciousness in Freud is an advance in the consciousness of the murder of the primal father, that is, in consciousness of limitation (or mediation) as the result of the violent suppression of original violence. I shall review here briefly the stages of this religiohistorical development from totemism to Judaism to Christianity, according to Freud's account (531–39).

Totemism is the first religion, according to Freud and the anthropologists he follows. In totemism, on this (currently widely discredited or revised) theory, an animal is worshipped as sacred representative of the clan, and periodically consumed in the "totem feast," where the animal functions as a replacement for the primal father consumed long ago. In the next step, the deity becomes gradually humanized. When patriarchy reinstalls itself in moderated form, mother-goddesses emerge as figures of mourning for the now diminished power of the mothers. And male gods appear likewise, initially as figures of the mother's favorite son, but always also as indirect reminders of the dead, displaced, internalized father.

The next step, the invention of monotheism, is understandable as a fairly explicit return of the primal father's recognition, prior to his murder and consumption:

> It is the religion of the primal father, and the hope of reward, distinction, and finally world sovereignty is bound up with it. The last-named wish-phantasy—relinquished long ago by the Jewish people—still survives among their enemies in their belief in the conspiracy of the "Elders of Zion." (108)

But the return of the primal father as religion of the father occasions, not surprisingly, the return of his murder, and so Moses is put to death by his rebellious people. One does not want to relive or to be reminded of either the absolute dominion of the primal father or his murder, so one rids oneself of the reminder, here the messenger Moses, acting out rather than remembering and working through. Indirect evidence of this murder of Moses is available, according to Freud (and Ernst Sellin, as well as Goethe), in the murmuring of the Israelites against Moses, their continual relapses into idolatry, their lack of confidence in the Mosaic God, Moses' failure to reach the Promised Land, and so on.[12] The cycle of the origin of society and "morality and law" (530) is repeated thus within the development of Judaism. The Jewish people absorbs within itself, in the wake of Moses' death and the repression of his monotheism, a Midianite volcano god—Jahve. But over time, Jahve is fused with Adonai. And finally, Adonai, the Egyptian Moses' monotheistic God, with his emphasis on the ethical renunciation of drives, returns to the forefront of Judaism, as the murdered father is remembered once more, internally resurrected.

But for Freud, Judaism does not consciously recall or acknowledge the murder of the primal father. This work of memory, this lifting of repression, awaits the invention of Christianity, and in this work consists Christianity's progressive dimension. For Christianity recalls the murder of the primal father (in the indirect form of the notion of original sin), and it atones for the murder indirectly, by way of Jesus, the son who dies (for all the other sons), so that they, that is, we, may live. But if, on the one hand, Christianity acknowledges the murder whereas Judaism denies it, on the other hand, Christianity repeats the murder of the father by murdering the father-religion, Judaism, and replacing it with the son-religion, Christianity itself. It accuses the father-religion—both a religion of the father and a religion in the father's position—of murdering the father-qua-son and thus in its turn avoids responsibility for the murder of the father, or the repetition of violence in the suppression of violence. Failing in this way to do justice to the father and to the necessary (if necessarily ambivalent) love of the father, it returns (to some degree) to polytheism and so represents for Freud a regression. This is the role of "Paul, a Roman Jew from Tarsus" (534), and the inventor of the typological relationship between Judaism and Christianity. For Paul "was a man with a gift for religion, in the truest sense of the phrase. Dark traces of the past lay in his soul, ready to break through into the regions of consciousness" (534–35).

The Origin of Humanity as Origin of the Logic of Representation

Having recalled in outline Freud's account of the origins of human society and their reflection in religious history, I still need to do one more thing—namely, read the text interpretively—before taking up again the question of how Freud displaces typology. Specifically, I need to show how Freud's account of the origins of human society functions as an allegory of the (loss of the) origins of the logic of representation. Freud's text's plausibility and significance, I think, emerge only when our reading accedes to this level of the more abstract signification in his account of the origins of society. On this level, an allegorical sense links his account in form to idealist philosophies of history, despite other differences, and even if such philosophies are generally loath to acknowledge their allegorical character. But the differences are crucial, and Freud's materialist allegory constitutes a critical response to such idealist philosophies of history.

From this standpoint, the primal father signifies—personifies—the logical or metalogical principle of identity, which underlies the personal principle of identity. After all, the primal father creates by force a unity out of a dispersed multiplicity. His violence is the violence of the reductive identification and internalization (or externalization) of difference. (In terms of Kafka, he is a one-man wall of China, but also a nomadic barbarian.) Accordingly, the murder of the primal father dramatizes the notion of the differentiation of identity, the emergence of difference as such, as the explicitly posited antithesis of identity. In consuming the body of the father, further, the brothers perform the absorption of identity into difference, that is, the dependence of difference on identity, for there can be no differentiation without self-identical terms that are differentiated one from another. (The brother-horde is the Freudian equivalent of Kafka's method of partial construction, dispersion in the service of concentration.) Of course, the converse is also true: Identity depends on difference, and, indeed, even the primal father creates the difference between his horde and the others, everything on the outside of his horde. In this sense, the murder of the primal father is immanent in the primal father himself—the primal father completes himself in being murdered by his sons. And the murder, consummated in the consumption of the father (a very good way of "hiding the traces"), culminates in the creation of a representation—the father as idea, and as basis for the identification of different subjects, their common ego ideal. Even more generally, however, the story of the primal father's murder and internalization allegorizes the emergence of identity, difference, and a certain vexed and nonharmonious combination of identity and difference, as the constitutive emergence of representation. Further, Freud renders through the motifs of murder and forgetting a certain ungraspability of this emergence. But how do we get from identity and difference to representation or language as such?

Representation identifies the disparate while maintaining its difference, substitutes while combining. For example, a common noun refers to the multiple objects it names as if they were all one object, although we know they are not. Recall that, in Roman Jakobson's work, the two principles of language appear as metaphor and metonymy, the rhetorical names for the logical or metalogical terms, identity and difference.[13] And, of course, Jacques Lacan develops at length Jakobson's suggestion that the metaphoric/metonymic poles be brought into correspondence with Freud's terms for the dreamwork.[14] In turn, applying this tradition to the reading of *Moses and Monotheism*, we can see that the story of the emergence of society out of the primal horde and the brother-horde doubles as the story of the emergence of representation out of the principles of identity and difference. Since humanity seems—at least for a psychoanalytic anthropology—to require both society and language—that is, the reality of common existence and its constitutively supplementary doubling by representational communication—it is hardly surprising that Freud's

Sigmund Freud (1856–1939), with his two chow-chows on his apartment balcony. Circa 1930. (Bildarchiv Preussischer Kulturbesitz, Berlin/Stiftung Deutsche Kinemathek, Berlin/Hans. G. Casparius (photographer)/Art Resource, N.Y.)

story of human origins can be seen to combine both of these dimensions. But even more to the point, Freud explicitly (although somewhat indirectly) connects the genesis of society with the genesis and/or learning of language itself. Namely, the childhood situation of trauma with which he compares the early civilizational trauma of the primal father and his murder occurs in the "time of beginning linguistic capacities" (*Zeit der beginnenden Sprachfähigkeit*) (522), and again "in the age of barely attained linguistic capacity" (*im Alter der kaum erreichten Sprachfähigkeit*) (527), or again "at a time, when the child was hardly capable of language" (*zu einer Zeit . . . da das Kind noch kaum sprachfähig war*) (574). Freud does not, to be sure, ever go so far as to state directly the correspondence between the learning of language and the particular scenario of patriarchal unity and fraternal (and maternally mediated) multiplicity. Perhaps this is because he is still attached to the hope for an empirical historiography of human origins. Nonetheless, he does place the linguistic and paternal traumas in immediate juxtaposition, metonymically supplying an account he is unwilling to provide in metaphorical terms.[15]

It follows from this allegoresis that the history of religion, as a becoming conscious of the murder of the primal father, now doubles as a becoming conscious of the origin of language. This is also a becoming conscious of the loss of that origin, both because the primal father suppresses the "Real"—whatever (dis)order will have come before—and because his presence and his murder are at best only indirectly accessible. This (loss of) origin, moreover, is simultaneously the (lost) origin or cause of the inaccessibility of pure presence, and therefore the (lost) origin or cause of distortion, or disfiguration. For the movements of identification and differentiation that constitute it—allegorically dramatized as the primal father's violence and the counterviolence of the brothers—can never shed the violence that is part of their makeup. To be sure, their makeup also includes eros as love—which appears in Freud's text as love for the father, the father's love for his children, the mother's love for the sons, and so on. And indeed, eros is the very principle of identification, or the creation of larger and larger wholes, according to *Jenseits des Lustprinzips* (*Beyond the Pleasure Principle*). But the flip side of love is death. The gap between identity and difference can neither be reliably closed nor reliably kept open if representation is to occur. Religion thus registers in a distorted way the ongoing origination of language (and sociality) qua distortion. Religion is the distortion of distortion, the disfiguration of disfiguration.[16]

What justifies such a reading of Freud's text? Freud's text supports such a reading, of necessity somewhat obliquely, through its discussion of "distortion," "defacement," or "disfiguration"—*Entstellung*—one of the most important motifs in this work, and not just here but also in Freud's text as a whole, as demonstrated by its prominent role as a concept (and chapter title) in *The Interpretation of Dreams*, "The Dream Distortion" (*Die Traumentstellung*).[17] Let us recall briefly its appearance in that text of 1900 before considering its presence in *Moses and Monotheism*.

The Freudian meaning of *Entstellung* in general, based on its position in *The Interpretation of Dreams*, is that unconscious processes can appear on the conscious level only by passing through *Entstellung's* filter, that is, by way of language, which involves significant loss.[18] Language disfigures the unconscious in its presentation.[19] The principal mechanisms of the dreamwork, and so of the *Entstellung* of the dream content in its presentation as dream surface, are condensation and displacement, or metaphor and metonymy, or—in their (meta)logical translation—identity and difference. *Entstellung* is thus the result of the operation of identity and difference on reality. Or again in a Lacanian idiom we might say that *Entstellung* is the result of the operation of the Imaginary dimension—the violent movement of identification—and the Symbolic dimension—the idealizing translation of the image into a signifier (here, the father as symbol rather than as reality)—on the Real, which latter constitutes the immediacy of presence, the originary escapee or lost object. (This reality—or rather Real, in Lacanian terms—cannot strictly be situated inside or outside the subject because to situate it thus we need to apply to it the language of identity, difference, language in general.) *Entstellung*, then, as it appears in *The Interpretation of Dreams* and thence more broadly in Freud's oeuvre, is the functioning of representational disfiguration as the struggle between identity and difference, substitution and combination, or ego libido and object libido.

But how does *Entstellung* function, narrowly and specifically, in the context of *Moses and Monotheism*?[20] The main explicit role Freud reserves for *Entstellung* here is that of the distortion of the record of scripture and oral tradition in the effacement of the traces of the murder of the primal father, and then (of) the murder of Moses, as well as of his Egyptian origins, and so on.[21] *Entstellung* thus serves—or rather is—repression, but at the same time, as repression, it is imperfect: It leaves traces, and the repressed returns. Language writes, or representation inscribes, its negativity, leaving it as a positive residue. Like (or rather as) language in general, disfiguration manifests and hides (itself) at once.[22]

Further, disfiguration is violent. Freud says that it not only hides the murder but that it is *like* murder, and precisely in terms of the common difficulty of hiding the traces of its own violence. "The disfiguration of a text is similar to a murder. The difficulty lies not in carrying out the deed, but rather in getting rid of the traces" (*Es ist bei der Entstellung eines Textes ähnlich wie bei einem Mord. Die Schwierigkeit liegt nicht in der Ausführung der Tat, sondern in der Beseitigung ihrer Spuren*) (493). The figure of this comparison, moreover, performs what it is talking about, since the figure itself is a distortion and a violence (for, of course, in many ways the mere distortion or disfiguration of a text is not at all like a murder). The hyperbolic dimension of the figure thus does violence in the name of the reduction of violence, like reading to correct a distortion, and above all like the murder of the primal father at the hands of the brother-horde. *Entstellung* is "like a murder" because it is here the repetition in miniature of the murder it means to hide. And more generally, *Entstellung* is "like a murder" because it is the violence of the primal father—taken together with the violent suppression and consumption, or *Aufhebung*, of the primal father by the brother-horde—that is the figure for *Entstellung* itself, an *Entstellung* of *Entstellung*, as the disfiguring power of language in general. So the violence of the primal father and brothers figures the loss of the unconscious (or of what Lacan will call *jouissance*) and its return in language (including the body of language and the language of the body). While struggling against the disfiguration of the historical memories he means to reconstruct, Freud makes manifest that the reconstitution of the (loss of the) origin—the double (loss of the) origin of the primal father's self-assertion and negation—is itself the reconstitution of the originary scene of disfiguration. In the beginning (of humanity) was disfiguration.

How and Why Freud's Text Exposes Itself as Necessarily Disfigured

But why struggle in language against disfiguration, if disfiguration is language itself? Is Freud not caught in a contradiction here, if indeed I am not disfiguring him by suggesting he equates all representation with disfiguration? The very term *disfiguration* (or *distortion* or *displacement* or *de-positioning*—other possible translations of *Entstellung*), implies the possibility of a nondisfigured, undistorted, nondisplaced truth that the universalization of disfiguration seems to belie. Perhaps our very notion of disfiguration is disfigured here. A credulous ethics of truthfulness, it appears, runs counter to a skeptical epistemology. However, we can resolve—that is, make more acceptable—the contradiction if we consider Freud's double commitment: to the claim that we live in a world of reality (or nature), and to the claim that we live in a world of dream (or culture); or, for example, to the view that the ego (which speaks) provides access to reality (as *Realitätsich*), and to the view that the ego is an instance of repression (Lacan will call this aspect the imaginary "moi"). Thus, if language represses, it also conveys (something); if repression is ubiquitous, it is never total. This is why Freud implies—or says in disfigured ways—that disfiguration is everywhere (in culture) and still struggles against it, turning language against language's turning away from what it names, its ground in intentional subject and/or referential object. Far from merely being unscientific, Freud needs to work not only with but also against the very principle of noncontradiction.

It remains necessary to indicate how disfiguration appears intermittently in *Moses* as coterminous with language, other than insofar as the father-horde and brother-horde can be read as allegories for metaphor and metonymy. The reader will doubtless find it helpful to see some signs in *Moses* of Freud's awareness both of his own implication in disfiguration and of its more general presence, beyond intentional dissimulations. And indeed Freud does highlight and repeat in many different ways his anxiety concerning the possible unfoundedness of his assertions, and therefore their distorting violence, both as would-be referential statements about the world and as expressions of his own intentions. He thus ironizes his own text in various ways, directly and indirectly in relation to the problematic of *Entstellung*. That is, he suggests that his own text, too, may well belong to a universally human realm of disfiguration he nonetheless keeps working against.

To begin, recall that Freud initially had given his work the subtitle "An Historical Novel" (457). This already indicates his uncertainty about the status of his claims, as fictional or historical, subjective or objective, figural or literal.[23] And all the more so, in that "Moses an Egyptian" turns largely around the "family novel of the neurotic" (and Otto Rank's extensions of this notion). Freud is manifestly aware that, on some level, he is writing his own family novel here. But not only does Freud indicate that he is unclear about how the subjective and objective dimensions of his discourse may hang together.[24] He indicates repeatedly the distortional disruptions that unground his text both in its historical dimension (with reference to historical reality) and in its personal dimension (with reference to his own intentionality).

Focusing initially on the question of historical foundations: In the introductory section of part 2, "If Moses Was an Egyptian," through the famous figure of the "iron image with clay feet" (*ehernes Bild mit tönernen Füßen*) (468) Freud expresses his anxiety that his work may lack solid foundations, an anxiety he links here with a suggestion of pagan idolatry.[25] The lack of foundations, which would imply the distorted character of Freud's text, is further linked in this passage to the image of exposure, which evokes the myth of the exposed baby Moses that Freud has discussed at length in "Moses an Egyptian."[26] To quote the passage somewhat more fully— Freud feels strongly "the warning not to expose [the insights that follow from the supposition that Moses was an Egyptian] to the critical attack of the environment [*dem kritischen Angriff der Umwelt auszusetzen*] without sufficient foundation [*ohne sichere Begründung*] like an iron image on clay feet" (468). (Of course, Freud will immediately go on to do just this.) But just two sentences before, Freud had spoken of how "the interpretation of the exposure myth linked to Moses [*die Deutung des an Moses geknüpften Aussetzungsmythos*] compels us to conclude that he was an Egyptian" (468). Thus, the word for *exposure* appears here once with reference to Moses, once with respect to this work. The work, Freud's baby, or Freud *as* baby, is figured not just as idol but as Moses, the object it treats hence self-reflexively in this respect. But this is not supposed to be a simple work of art, and Freud will be exposed to criticism if his historical account has an inadequate referential and historical basis. The implications of separation (as birth or castration) and abandonment that belong to the myth of exposure (e.g., 462–63) are now carried over to Freud and his work, exposed as it is to annihilation (this its Nile) at the hands of critics (internal or superegoic) who would understand it as illegitimate distortion. Since the unconscious is for Freud not representable by language, it is reasonable that he would be writing in such a way as to suggest that to take a position verbally on (the) historical reality (of the unconscious) will expose one to the claim that one is doing so without adequate basis, that is, that one is disfiguring or displacing the matters at hand.

But Freud does not only try to come to terms with the fact that all representation (including his own historiographical essay) may operate at a distance from its ostensible referential foundations. He also considers the sense in which any work of representation (even if it were meant to be a pure fiction or a purely subjective utterance) must also diverge from its intentional ground in the subject. One way in which he does so discreetly is by indicating in various ways that his work is out of sync with his own intentions. For example, he writes in the second preface to part 3: "Now as then I feel uncertain [*unsicher*] in the face of my own work [*angesichts meiner eigenen Arbeit*]; I miss the consciousness of unity and belonging-together that should obtain between the author and his work" (507). Interestingly, his reflections here run counter to Freud's attempt to rehabilitate a kind of teleology in terms of a doctrine of the will that is not reconcilable with his own thought of the unconscious. For one of the major thrusts of Freud's

Moses texts is to argue that Moses creates (as the "great man") the Jewish people.[27] But at the same time these texts repeatedly encounter the impossibility of replacing teleology with some form of the great man's will to power. Not only does Freud also credit the Jews with responsibility for accepting Moses' monotheism (and thus he does not give sole credit to Moses). And not only does the repressed that returns in Moses (as commemoration of the murdered primal father) return despite his will or talents, and not just because of them. Further, here Freud encounters the rift between subjective intention and work that is induced by the disfiguring function of language. Like Moses, Freud finds himself slow of tongue.[28] And he finds also that if works alone cannot save, belief remains hard to come by.[29]

Freud develops this notion of the rift between author and work further in such a way as to suggest, in the rhetorical mode of litotes, its human universality and ineluctability. For example, in the introductory remarks to the second section of part 3, "Summary and Repetition," he indicates that although he tried to leave the work unpublished, it "tortured him like an unredeemed spirit (or ghost)" (*sie quälte mich wie ein unerlöster Geist*) (550). The dead letter or the work lives a life of its own here and haunts the living, like a "wandering Jew." Similarly, Freud says in this same preface (and here is the understatement) that "the creative force of an author [*Schöpferkraft eines Autors*] unfortunately does not always follow his will; the work turns out [*das Werk gerät*] as it can, and places itself across from the writer often [*stellt sich dem Verfasser oft . . . gegenüber*] as independent, indeed as alien [*wie unabhängig, ja wie fremd*]" (551). According to these remarks, Freud's work is in exile with respect to its own author, a foreigner outside the grounding power of his intentional will, a spirit without spirit, or the spirit of the letter itself, not a dead letter but a living or at least an undead one. The work disfigures his intentions, (mis)placing itself across from him—*sich ihm gegenüberstellend*. To be sure, Freud makes the passage seem both socially and logically acceptable (even to himself) by softening (and disfiguring through understatement) his claims here. On the one hand, he points to the contingency of a work whose failings he regrets. It is as if this work *should* obey his will, and he is sorry that it doesn't. The failure appears due to some contingent neurotic compulsion, to the degree that Freud stresses the repetitive motions of the death drive. He explicitly regrets here that the text contains too much repetition (550–51). On the other hand, this failure is recuperated first by virtue of the fact that Freud indicates that this often happens, implying that it's not such a terrible thing, and second by virtue of the romantic aesthetics of unconscious genius that implicitly turns his failings into inspiration here. He says that "the creative force . . . does not always" follow the author's will, and that it even often stands opposite the author as a strange being. But the sentence also contains the phrase "the work turns out, as it can" (*das Werk gerät, wie es kann*) (551), which may suggest that this alienation of the work from the author is neither something that means failure, nor something that is somehow okay as an exception, or occasionally hyperjustifed by genius, but rather something *that happens necessarily and always*. It is as if Freud's litotes ceases in order to allow a universalizing claim, potentially hyperbole, to set itself out. Freud's exception would then exemplify the norm. Neither is the dead letter simply dead, nor is it simply alive (e.g., with "my" intentions). The work(s) of representation are unredeemed, as distant from presence—of subject (or meaning) and object (or reference) alike.

To summarize these observations: Always necessarily in a mediated manner, Freud repeatedly places the text of his "historical novel" within the context of a universal disfiguration, a universal exposure both to the loss of original presence (subjective and/or objective) and to its inevitable and partial, fleeting and incalculable returns. Often linking disfiguration with exposure, he tries to understand the implications, for human beings, of being in the distorting field of language. But before returning to the question of Freud's intervention in, or appropriation of, typological Orientalism, I find it important to consider one final form in which disfiguration and exposure are interwoven in Freud's text, a striking concretion that has a grotesquely interesting evocative force, namely the figure of "leprosy" or "Aussatz": "The so frequent insult in ancient times, that the Jews were 'lepers' [*die Juden seien 'Aussätzige'*] (cf. Manetho) must have the sense of a projection: 'They hold themselves so far from us, as if we were lepers'" (552). Freud's explicit point here is simply that the Jews were hated because their sense of chosenness, their pride in their elevated "Vorstellung" of God, made them seem (or indeed be) arrogant. But the signifier for lepers—*Aussätzige*—connects the Jews with a form of disfiguration (the disease itself) that is a disfigured mode of exposure (*Aussetzung*), and a form of disfiguration the specter of exposure to which is terrifying, as a virtual exposure to death. The Jews are evidently associated with disfiguration here, as Freud says, because they make the others feel like they are subject to disfiguration. In turn, however, this is directly connected—as Freud fails to spell out—to what makes the Jews feel superior, namely a notion of the one invisible God, which entails the notion that all representation of the Real is disfiguration. So with and against (or beyond) Freud on this point, it is not just the Jews' arrogance that makes the others feel disfigured but their doctrine of representation as disfiguration, which is the doctrine that makes them proud in the first place. Freud, in his turn, adheres to this doctrine, albeit in an atheistic mode, but attributes its discovery first to the Aton religion, the Egyptian Moses, and so on, and then traces it back to the origin of humanity in the primal father's murder and in its correlative, the arrival of language as the traumatically disfiguring reduction of the Real to the interplay between metaphoric and metonymic principles. That is, Freud corrects the connection of the Jews with the disfiguring power of language—propagated by Judaism in one sense and distorted in turn by Christianity in a different sense (while being turned against the Jews)—by replacing it with an account of humanity as constituted by the birth of disfiguration—that is, representational mediation—well before the earliest monotheists (wherever they came from) began to get an antimagical grasp on the necessity and limitations of such mediation.[30]

Typology in the Context of Originary Disfiguration

Given this reading of Freud's account of humanity's origins as those of language as disfiguration, how does typology—Judaeo-Christian and Oriental-Occidental—look from the standpoint of *Moses and Monotheism*? We can now see that Freud replaces an interest in prefiguration and fulfillment, as guiding concepts for an understanding of religiocultural history and civilizatory progress, with trauma and repetition of the trauma in the symptomatic return of the repressed. And if the figure—*typos*—was always a traumatic strike or stroke, its fulfillment had the sense of overcoming the trauma, not repeating it. In contrast to the typological universe, Freud lives in a world where there is no absolute fulfillment, where the fulfillment endlessly anticipates itself. One might say: in a world of desire. And in Freud the category of the pagan disappears, as I noted above, into the prehuman. That is, all that is human—however "primitive" it may be—is understood as participating in the repression (or language use) that is all we have left of revelation. Our (de)formalizing allegorical reading—perhaps a kind of post-Hegelianism without dogmatic teleology, totality, or historical realism—suggests further that the original trauma is that of the emergence of identity, the One, which indeed anticipates the overcoming of an indeterminate or nonrational multiplicity. The repetition occurs as the supplementation of identity by difference, which fulfills identity by completing it with its other, at the same time repeating the trauma or violence of identity in a mode of denial.[31]

Freud articulates this unmasterable structure of anticipatory trauma (of identity) and its ironic fulfillment as repetition (in difference) on at least three principal levels. First, the primal father's self-positing violence anticipates his fulfillment in his murder, his negation, which repeats his violence in suppressing it. Second, the murder of the father, which establishes the self-identity of the brother-horde as a unity, anticipates its self-differentiation through the internalization of the father as conscience, which divides the subjects from themselves. Guilt fulfills the deed and repeats it as violence of the subject against himself or herself qua autonomy. Third, the origin of society and representation, hence disfiguration, in the drama of the primal father, his murder, and his internalization, anticipates the many religions that fulfill it, as return of the repressed, always in an incomplete and violently erotic form.

But—to conclude—does Freud envision no telos or hierarchy of values? Is there no passage from the symptomatic return of the repressed to sublimation? And if not, how are we to make sense of Freud's parti pris for the progress in spirituality he sees in monotheism, however ambivalently and cautiously he may outline this progress in the face of the German fascist regression to "nearly prehistorical barbarism" (*nahezu vorgeschichtliche Barbarei*) (503)?[32] Freud does see something like the entirely unassured telos of a potential endless striving in the recognition and assumption of one's responsibility for the "murder of the primal father," that is, the acknowledgment of one's necessary implication in a language of disfiguration, an unmasterable interplay of identity and difference that prevents the unmediated access to the Real, or God (whom Kant still characterized ontotheologically as "the most real Being"). And if Freud reads Judaism as tending in this direction, as a culture of exile from the Real, he also exiles himself from this—identitarian, or culturally nationalist—attempt in various ways in the text. Because he understands that the assumption of responsibility begins with the first and every imposition of any ordering sense, and—this aspect of analysis is indeed interminable—never ends.[33]

Excursus: Edward Said and the Identity of the Different, or Freud in Palestine

> Identity cannot . . . constitute or even imagine itself without that radical originary break or flaw which will not be repressed.
>
> —EDWARD SAID, *Freud and the Non-European*

This brings us to a particularly painful and difficult, because history- and pathos-laden, contemporary context for rereading Freud's text on Moses, the context of the Israeli-Palestinian conflict. This conflict appears here as one between two supposedly Semitic groups who struggle together in vain to achieve separate sovereignty or self-determination, as well as the international status of the good Semite. Both of these groups function essentially in the same identitarian terms Freud (among others) encourages us to renounce, however regretfully or reluctantly we may do so and however much such a renunciation might leave traditional political discourses of self-determination in disarray. I close by comparing and contrasting my own reading of Freud's text with the reading proposed by Edward Said in his lecture *Freud and the Non-European*.[34] Such a comparison and contrast will help us see how the continuing force of discourses of sovereignty as self-determination (i.e., self-grounding) imposes some limitations on Said's understanding both of Freud's text and of the structure of Orientalism. These limitations include the difficulty Said has—entirely understandable (to understate the matter), given the ongoing Israeli-Palestinian conflict—in fully appreciating the extent to which anti-Judaic and Orientalist traditions are mutually entangled, especially in the modern period broadly conceived.[35] To be sure, on more than one occasion Said discusses "the connection . . . between Islamophobia and anti-Semitism" ("Orientalism Reconsidered," 207).[36] But oddly, especially given the importance of Erich Auerbach for his work, Said does not make the connection between figural interpretation and anti-Judaism, anti-Islamism, or Orientalism more broadly, even though one of the guiding notions of *Orientalism* is what Said rightfully considers the dehumanizing and maddening tendency of Orientalist discourse to see the Orient as having no right or capacity to speak for itself. (Of course, Auerbach never makes any of these connections either, at least not in print.) This tendency is precisely an aspect of typological thinking, as well as its modern, historicist extensions, but Said doesn't quite see it. Although he does suggest that historicism and imperialism (and Orientalism) are somehow linked together, he can still speak of figuralism as follows, in his discussion of Auerbach's essay on that subject:[37]

> Auerbach, I believe, is bringing us back to what is an essentially Christian doctrine for believers but also a crucial element of *human* intellectual power and will. In this he follows Vico, who looks at the whole of human history and says "mind made all this," an affirmation that audaciously

reaffirms, but also to some degree undercuts, the religious dimension that gives credit to the divine.[38]

The comments that one would expect at this point, concerning the role of *figura* in historicist Orientalism, do not materialize.

The reason why it might be productive to develop here a critique of Said's misreading of Freud is because left alone, that misreading (and its underlying tendencies, which are more generally present in Said's critical oeuvre) can contribute, albeit in a small way, to the infinitely larger forces that conspire to keep (especially Israeli) Jews and Arab Palestinians locked in senseless struggle not only over territory but, within that struggle, for recognition by the West as the morally superior and therefore assimilable, that is, "good" (Western) Semites. Underestimating the inextricable intertwinement of modern anti-Judaism and Orientalism makes it easier for both parties to fail to grasp the commonalities in their destinies within (or in relation to) the history of European Christendom, including especially its modern, colonialist formations.

Said reads Freud approvingly in several respects. For him, Freud admirably acknowledges both that Judaism has non-European (Egyptian) roots, and more broadly that "Semites" were neither European nor nonassimilable to Europe, viewing "Moses as both insider and outsider" (*Freud and the Non-European*, 16). That is, Freud implicitly refuses to "erect an insurmountable barrier between non-European primitives and European civilization" (19). In connection with this refusal, Freud questions the sense and limits of his own Jewish identity from a secular perspective. He refuses to make "any doctrinal attempt . . . to put Jewish identity on a sound foundational basis" (45), and he therefore tends toward a diasporalism with regard to cultural identity in general. For all of this, Said praises Freud, and argues that "official Israel" has repressed Freud (44).

However, Said criticizes some aspects of Freud's work. He indicates, although forgivingly, that Freud's general educational and cultural horizon is Western, and that in this connection his main interests in the ancient world concern Greece, Rome, and Israel, with the exceptional addition of Egypt. Somewhat less forgivingly, Said takes Freud to task for what he considers Freud's attempt to inscribe Judaism into a European identity in the face of the spreading anti-Semitism of Freud's day. And here is where some important misreading occurs.

Said finds this attempt in Freud's discussion of anti-Semitism, or "the issue of the non-Jew, which Freud treats lackadaisically late in *Moses and*

Monotheism" (38). Said goes on to consider Freud's responses to three bases of anti-Semitism: the views that the Jews are "foreigners," that they are "different from their hosts," and that "they defy oppression" (39). Said focuses on the first two of these, saying that they amount to "variations on each other" (39). As we will see, Said distorts Freud rather strikingly, in an interpretation that leads Said to argue, in fact, that the Jews are foreigners in the Middle East. This result, in turn, begins to make clear why Said is troubled by Freud's discussion here and why he acts out with particular aggression and sloppiness at precisely this point.

The first misreading comes as follows. Said argues that Freud dismantles or demystifies the first excuse for anti-Semitism by indicating that the Jews had been in Europe since the Roman times. "As for the charge of Jews being foreigners (the implied context is, of course, European), Freud is dismissive of it, because in countries like Germany, where anti-Semitism is pervasive, the Jews have been there longer, having arrived with the Romans" (39). In order to make this polemical gesture—"the implied context is, of course, European"—Said simply ignores Freud's text here (and paraphrases it inaccurately). For Freud's text first makes a generalization that would include, for example, the Middle East, and second, specifies the case for Cologne, which he calls specifically an *example*, but which is a reasonable one since, after all, in the late 1930s, Freud's most immediate concern is German anti-Semitism. I give Katherine Jones's English translation, the edition Said refers to in general in this text, but which Said does not quote in this context. Freud writes:

> The most fallacious is the reproach of their being foreigners, since in many places nowadays under the sway of anti-Semitism the Jews were the oldest constituents of the population or arrived even before the present inhabitants [the actual German says: "the Jews belong to the oldest parts of the population or were in place earlier"—*gehören die Juden zu den ältesten Anteilen der Bevölkerung oder sind selbst früher zur Stelle gewesen als die gegenwärtigen Einwohner*]. This is so, for example, in the town of Cologne, where Jews came with the Romans, before it was colonized by Germanic tribes. (115, 538)

So here, Said makes Freud's frame of reference European and takes him to task for it, whereas the passage in Freud explicitly has a wider frame of reference.

But now addressing Freud's answer to the second of the two reasons for anti-Semitism under consideration, that the Jews are "different," Said writes: "Freud backhandedly says that they are not 'fundamentally so,' since they are not 'a foreign Asiatic race, but mostly consist of the remnants of Mediterranean peoples and inherit their culture'" (39). Oddly, Said omits from the quotation the phrase "as their enemies maintain," which comes just after the phrase "Asiatic race." The effect of the omission is to turn what is, at least first of all, a mention or indirect quotation in Freud's speech into a usage of the term "Asiatic race," to which Freud would now be signing his own name. Said then says, in a tone of annoyance:

> In light of Freud's early harping on Moses's Egyptianness, the distinctions he makes here strike me as limp: both unsatisfactory and unconvincing. . . . I am convinced that Freud was aware that simply saying of the Jews that they were the remnants of Mediterranean civilization, and therefore not really different, is janglingly discordant with his show of force about Moses's Egyptian origins. Could it be, perhaps, that the shadow of anti-Semitism spreading so ominously over his world in the last decade of his life caused him protectively to huddle the Jews inside, so to speak, the sheltering realm of the European? (39–40).

So the Jews were non-European in the face of Nazi Europe—for whom "Jews were foreign, and therefore expendable" (40)—but then they tried to become European and effectively did so after the war, as a European Israel meant to "hold non-European indigenous peoples at bay" (42).[39] And Freud is already, despite his stronger insights, part of this movement. The "relevant non-Europeans" after 1948 were then

> embodied in the indigenous Arabs of Palestine and, supporting them, Egyptians, Syrians, Lebanese, and Jordanians who were descendants of the various Semitic tribes, including the Arab Midianites, whom the Israelites had first encountered south of Palestine and with whom they had a rich exchange. (41)

With the establishment of the state of Israel,

> what had once been a diverse multiracial population of many different peoples—European and non-European, as happened to be the case—there occurred a new re-schematization of races and peoples, which . . . seemed like a parodistic re-enactment of the divisions that had been so murderous before. (41)

With regard to Freud, Said's reading of this passage—which is, aside from the other passage he misread above, the sole specific textual basis of his claim that Freud wants to Europeanize the Jews (against Freud's better judgment and against his "knowledge" of the Egyptian origins of Moses)—is questionable. The macho, castration-anxious language of "limp" with reference to Freud's argument here is embarrassingly symptomatic of Said's discomfiture and no substitute for more detailed and precise interpretive argumentation. For example, when Freud says that the Jews descend from "remnants of Mediterranean peoples and inherit their culture," he is not arguing that they are European but that their cultural site is neither inside nor outside of Europe, since parts of the Mediterranean world are European, parts are African, parts are perhaps something in between. By "Asiatic race"—as unclear as his invocation of race was in this context (although initially a mention or quotation of the anti-Semites' usage)—Freud might well mean something more like South Asian to East Asian.[40] Indeed, in the continuation of the passage, which Said conveniently omits to quote as a whole, Freud writes: "Yet they [the Jews] are different—although sometimes it is hard to define in what respects—especially from the Nordic peoples, and racial intolerance [or rather: intolerance of the masses] finds stronger expression, strange to say, in regard to small differences than to fundamental ones" (*Aber sie sind doch anders, oft in undefinierbarer Art anders als zumal die nordischen Völker, und die Intoleranz der Massen äußert sich merkürdigerweise gegen kleine Unterschiede stärker als gegen fundamentale Differenzen*) (116, 538). Thus Freud explicitly posits here a difference between the Jews and the Europeans, but a difference of small degree and indeterminate kind, not one of being on different foundations—not a difference of essence. Whether Freud is thinking there is a sliding scale—that is, differences in degree but not in kind—from Europe to East Asia in this regard is not proven definitively by this passage, but it certainly seems probable. But what is quite clear is that Freud is not trying to place the Jews squarely inside Europe as opposed to non-Europeans.

Given that Said had to both ignore the sentences immediately after the ones he quoted and skip over a crucial phrase in order to make the passage seem like proof that Freud was trying to sneak the Jews back inside of Europe, it is appropriate to wonder about the structure Said is unwittingly attempting to impose on the textual and historical matters at hand. He is evidently not entirely comfortable with Freud's placement of the Jew on the border between the inside and the outside of Europe, even though he praises Freud for this placement. Nor is he entirely comfortable with either regarding the Jews as nonforeigners in the Middle East (because this might legitimate Zionism in one form or another) or entertaining the idea that he would be in a position analogous to that of the anti-Semitism that rejects Jews unfairly as foreigners. Therefore, he has to make them truly foreigners *in* the Middle East, and responsible for their own exclusion *from* the Middle East. Thus his argument suggests that even the most advanced of Jews, like Freud—he will later call them "non-Jewish Jews" (and I'll return to this briefly)—sooner or later lay claim to European identity.[41] And this is exactly what Said needs them to do. Jews who are European evidently do not belong in the resolutely non-European Middle East, the Middle East that identifies as non-European.[42] Moreover, as will appear surprising, Said ultimately supports his unhappiness about Israeli politics in the lecture on Freud by means of a rhetoric that appeals, in not so subtle ways, to Christian patterns of anti-Jewish thought (viz., the figural logic that Erich Auerbach tried to explain).

The starting point of this development is Said's appreciation of Freud's activities as "archaeological," his method as one of "excavation" (27). Against the background of Freud as one whose archaeological work he admires, because this work opens Judaism at its origins to the non-Jewish and the non-European (despite the Freudian backsliding Said also claims to observe), Said then rightly develops a critique of some of the literal archaeology currently practiced in Israel, an archaeology he sees as marginalizing remains of non-Israelite cultures and non-Jewish heritages in the service of "consolidating" Jewish "identity in secular time" (45) as the foundation of Israel qua Jewish state.[43] Although this is an important argument, the way in which Said makes it is problematic:

> I wish I had the time to go into this here, and to discuss how the nationalist thesis of separate Israeli and Palestinian histories has begun to shape archaeological disputes in the West Bank, and how, for instance, Palestinian attention to the enormously rich sedimentations of village history and oral traditions potentially changes the status of objects from dead monuments and artifacts destined for the museum, and approved historical theme parks, to remainders of an ongoing native life and living Palestinian practices of a sustainable human ecology. (49)

The shift from Jewish to Palestinian archaeology (the study of origins— the *arche*) means here the passage from "dead monuments and artifacts destined for the museum" to "ongoing native life and living Palestinian practices," and this is then augmented by "sustainable human ecology" (49). The Pauline rhetoric of the Jews as "dead letter" and the Christians as "living spirit" returns here with a vengeance.[44] How can one disagree with this, when one "knows," as a (Western) Christian reader, or for that matter a (culturally) Christianized (secular) Jewish reader, that the Jews have always been the dead letter, as what comes between "us" and our "native" origins, our immediate experience qua spiritual-sensuous unity under the aegis of the spiritual?[45] The Jews have traditionally been characterized as the invasion of the one who does not belong, in the sense of the one who alienates "us" from "our own" proper space.[46] This is because the Jews—qua "dead letter" or (pre)figural anticipation and belated debasement of the fulfillment—are the ones who represent the split between universal and particular, one and many, identity and difference, that is characteristic of representation, that is, of life in culture or human life as such. The Jews represent representation, hence alienation. Of course, it is correct and important to indicate that the Israeli government's settlement policies in the occupied territories, the creation of "facts on the ground," the endless provocations, and so on, are undergirded by certain streams of Israeli archaeology. And it is equally important to indicate that this violent game is reprehensible. Both the perpetuation of the occupation as it has been maintained by right-wing Israeli government policies, and Hamas-style forms of rejectionism, are equally grotesque, unnecessary, and endlessly sad. But Said misrepresents the factual situation by portraying it in terms of traditional Christian anti-Jewish stereotypes.

In any case, the follow-up is telling: "For a Palestinian, archaeology must be challenged so that those 'facts' and the practices that gave them a scientific pedigree are opened to the existence of other histories and a multiplicity of voices" (50). Here, Said aligns his group identification with multiplicity (which implicitly stands for "the good"), as against the ("bad") unity of Israel: The brother speaks to the rest of the brother-horde against the phantasm of the primal father—Israel as primal father, taking all for himself, including (and perhaps above all) mother earth, the source of native life. By these invocations of anti-Jewish stereotypes, Said places Palestinian identity on a metaphysical ideological foundation in the precise moment when he is arguing for multiplicity, which also means nolens volens nonsovereignty. He attempts to ground Palestinian identity in the immediacy of a tie to the land, in real experience, in the present. In contrast, the Israelis, as Jews, "naturally" fall into the position of the ones who disrupt the immediate self-identity of the unified multiplicity. Here, they are colonists from Europe who represent bad identity (or unity) and dead abstraction, the material letter, whereas Palestinians represent good difference (or multiplicity) and living concretion (as *voices*, which here carry a phonocentric charge).

To be sure, Said does say in this context that "nationalist agendas . . . tend to resemble each other" (50), but in many of his gestures and statements he nonetheless remains squarely within a national identification, even as he praises Freud for disrupting the foundations of Jewish identity. It is in the service of an identity narrative that he structurally needs the Jews to be European, and within that context he needs Freud's turn to Moses as Egyptian to appear exceptional:

> Freud seems to have made a special effort never to discount or play down the fact that Moses was non-European—especially since, in the terms of his argument, modern Judaism and the Jews were mainly to be thought of as European, or at least as belonging to Europe rather than Asia or Africa. (50)

But the Europeanization of the Jews was not undertaken within "the terms of" Freud's argument, nor indeed the project of many other Jews at that time (Buber and others), including most Zionists, nor was it the project of their enemies in Europe. It is, however, a crucial aspect of Said's project: "Palestinians gradually came to see that the people who arrived from abroad [the Jews] to take and settle on their land seemed just like the French who came to Algeria: Europeans who had superior title to the land over the non-European natives" (51). This statement—performatively equating the Zionists with the French in Algeria, despite the word "seemed"—effaces everything that differentiates the two projects (the fact that many Sephardic Jews have gone to Israel from Arab countries, that they certainly belong in the Middle East if anyone does; the fact that France existed prior to French colonialism and elsewhere; the fact of continuing Jewish presence in Palestine for centuries, and so on), turning an overlap into an identity. The Jews, according to Said's rhetoric, seem to be evil European colonialists, representatives of the deadly principle of identity.

Except that there is for Said definitely such a thing as a good Jew: It is the "non-Jewish Jew" (52). Of course, Said is referring to the modern, secular universalist, broadly liberal tradition when he speaks of the "non-Jewish Jew," and he is drawing the phrase from Isaac Deutscher's essay of that title. But not only is that essay strongly indebted to Marx's "On the Jewish Question," whose anti-Semitic dimension is nontrivial, but all of the Jews Deutscher admires there either converted, were excommunicated, or wrote deeply anti-Semitic tracts.[47] In this respect, it is striking that Said allows himself to say, as a very publicly nationally invested and identified Palestinian, as well as a prominent cultural studies scholar, that the only

Jew he finds acceptable—the only one who should be allowed into the group identity of the cosmopolites—is the one who repudiates Judaism. Moreover, one of the problems here is that the "non-Jewish Jews" in Israel have tended to be white-identified leftists of European origin who brought racism with them, including a sense of their own superiority to Jews from the Levant.

A certain inconsistency concerning the vexed question of sovereign identity beyond all disfigurative representation sadly threatens the discussion at every turn. For example, Said praises Freud for "refusing to resolve identity into some of the nationalist or religious herds in which so many people want so desperately to run" (53), and he ends up speaking in favor of a binational state in Israel/Palestine. Referring to the thought of identity as pervaded by difference, he asks:

> Can it ever become the not-so-precarious foundation in the land of Jews and Palestinians of a bi-national state in which Israel and Palestine are parts, rather than antagonists of each other's history and underlying reality? I myself believe so—as much because Freud's unresolved sense of identity is so fruitful an example, as because the condition he takes such pains to elucidate is actually more general in the non-European world than he suspected. (55)

But a binational state is, at this point in history, at best an unwitting synonym for the demographic marginalization of Jews in Israel/Palestine, the progressive silencing of Jewish Israeli "voices." Even more fundamentally, as it were, despite the admirably idealistic, reconciliatory pathos of this statement, the ultimate problem here remains the reference to a foundation and underlying reality for a self-determining binationality.

In sum, Said's apparently cosmopolitan reading of Freud is a curiously mixed and somewhat incoherent disfiguration of Freud's discourse on disfiguration, in which, moreover, the myth of the primal father's murder—surely symptomatically—is never even mentioned. To the degree that Said invokes the Christian rhetoric of typology against the Jews (of Israel), he demonstrates that he cannot quite do justice to his aspirations as a critic of identity—as indeed Jacqueline Rose suggests in her response to his lecture, though much more discreetly than I am doing here. Further, he thereby shows that he does not sufficiently grasp the sense in which Orientalism is structured by the typological thinking that defined the Jewish-Christian relationship since the times of Paul. Consequently, Said is not able to see the specific ways in which Freud's text undermines just this typological thinking. Nor does Said do justice to the Freudian emphasis on representation as distortion and loss of immediate reality, the sense in which the origin that the archaeologist Freud reveals is the loss of the origin, of the Real itself. Said's idealist and historicist hostility to the linguistic focus of structuralist and poststructuralist thought—a hostility that asserts itself strongly, for example, in the section on the textualism of *Orientalism* (perhaps the weakest part of that book), and despite his attempt to assimilate poststructuralism in his book *Beginnings*—blinds him to the deepest level of Freud's critique of identity. For the latter is also a critique of difference: The instance of difference (the brother-horde) repeats the violence of identity (the primal father), in that "the different" is always unified under some identity or other, the identity of those supposedly opposed to identity.

Indeed, that Said does not quite manage to confront this most difficult of aporias—the fact that not only is identity undone by difference but difference is totalized by identity—is indicated by Said's closing phrase, the suggestion that "the condition [Freud] takes such pains to elucidate is actually more general in the non-European world than he suspected" (55). This statement recapitulates the quintessentially Pauline gesture in universalizing the Jewish condition. But the universalization is limited, perhaps because total universalization of a group-determining trait is impossible. The unstated implication of this closing line is that the European world is not a place in which the diasporal condition or radical differentiation can be experienced as such, except by non-Europeans in Europe. "Europe" thus becomes the name for identity, "non-European" the name for difference, as "Jewish" is the name for identity (epitomized by Israeli archaeology) and "Palestinian" the name for difference (as the lively multiplicity of voices). The good European (or American), then, if he or she knows what is good about (and for) him or her, will identify with the non-European, as the place of difference that exceeds identity, whereas the bad European will identify with Europe as the place of identity.[48] Europe's Jewish prefiguration is now realized by the non-European, cosmopolitan universality of pure difference as symbolically concretized by Palestine, the site of difference as such, or the "son" as representative of the brother-horde, somewhere between Nazareth and Jerusalem. In contrast, when Said asks the questions, in his concluding remarks, whether this state of identity as undone by difference "has a real history—history being always that which comes after and, all too often, that which hides the flaw . . . [and] can so utterly indecisive and so deeply undetermined a history ever be written? In what language and with what sort of vocabulary?" (55), he begins to push beyond his idealist-realist, historicist predilections, toward a level of rigor that cannot be attained by the identitarian invocations of traditional Western, Christian metaphysics that I have been tracing. Here Said is in fact "refusing to resolve identity into some of the nationalist or religious herds into which so many people want so desperately to run" (53). But when he pushes the Jews into a white European identity that they—including many Israelis—by no means uniformly embrace or recognize, I'm not so sure.

Conclusion:
For an Abstract Historiography of the Nonexistent Present

What's the end result of this anamnestic journey through conceptual figurations of the Orient in major German texts—philosophical, literary, philological, political-ideological, and psychoanalytic—from the late eighteenth through the mid-twentieth century? I summarize this result briefly first in historical terms, then in psychoanalytic and especially philosophical ones, before drawing some methodological (or philosophico-historical) consequences. Finally, I say a word about Orientalism in postwar and contemporary Germany, and thereby illustrate the approach to the temporality of cultural history that this book implies.

In religiohistorical and cultural-political terms I have reviewed important determinations of Orient and Occident, and within the figure of the Orient, its various bifurcations into a "good" (appropriable) Orient and a "bad" (nonappropriable) one. We've seen that the nineteenth-century historicist thinkers invariably used the Christian construction of the Jewish-Christian relation, that is, supersessionist figuralism, as a model for their constructions of the Oriental-Occidental relation. In Enlightenment thinkers such as Lessing and Kant, whom I left in the background for reasons of space (although I treat them in detail elsewhere), the ahistorical ethical demand of tolerance interrupted supersessionist narratives to some extent, but at the cost of an abstraction that the historicists wanted to overcome. At the far end of the historicist vogue, critical modernists such as Kafka, Freud, and Mann made supersessionist Orientalist narratives the object of their irony, but likewise took their distance from the ahistorical formalism and moralism of the Enlightenment.

We've seen further how the various nineteenth-century bifurcations of the Oriental prefiguration culminate most destructively in the Semitic/Aryan split, and we've seen how this split tends to be doubled and shadowed in turn by a split between the "good Semite" and the "bad Semite" (a game we are still playing in the Middle East and in international public opinion today, with sad consequences for all). Thus, one of my main general points about the study of modern Orientalism, particularly—but I think not exclusively—in German thought (although I've restricted myself to readings of German texts here), has been that it cannot be pursued in isolation from the study of anti-Judaism and anti-Semitism and vice versa. Although the same might be said, with appropriate adjustments, for other European cultures, the particularly virulent development of the Aryan myth in and around the National Socialist movement in Germany makes this claim especially obvious and pressing with respect to German Orientalism.

In philosophical and psychoanalytic rather than religiohistorical or cultural-political terms, as we have seen, modern thinkers mobilize the determinations of the limits of East and West defensively in order to organize a whole series of binary oppositions. Through East-West border definition, Western thinkers attempt to situate these oppositions in geocultural space so that "we" (in what "we" imagine to be the West) always find "ourselves" associated with the desirable term in the given opposition.

The most important, or fundamental, opposition in the series, which is an ontological one, is evidently, from my perspective, that between foundations and their lack. This is the case, I believe, both because in modernity absolute foundations are pervasively in question and because, with particular explicitness in modernity since Leibniz, to be without foundations is to be thought not to exist. *Nihil est sine ratione. Omne ens habet rationem* (Nothing is without a reason. All that exists has a reason).[1] And who wants not to exist? What fun is that? I have argued that it tends to be precisely a panic, but in the psychoanalytic sense of an ego starting to dissolve in the absence of any ego ideal, and responding with an extreme hope and fear in urgent search of an elusive resolution. Fortunately, so to speak, Orientalism is there, in its various forms (including its colonialist and imperialist realizations), to disavow the absence of absolute foundations and so to reassure "us" of "our own" existence! Unfortunately, as we have seen, one can never reassure oneself of the stability of one's foundations by situating groundlessness elsewhere (e.g., in a pre-Orient or in the "bad" Orient), projecting it outward, because grounding and groundlessness interpenetrate. The use of ethnic or cultural identity categories for the sake of metaphysical assurances is both futile and destructive.

It is now necessary to reconsider the other key categories (beyond those of foundation and abyss) that Orientalism has been mobilized to organize and to organize "our" relationship to, for given such a reconsideration it will be possible to draw more positive methodological consequences from our negative insights concerning the Orientalist tradition. Specifically, it will be possible to sketch the outlines of a cultural historiography that would start out by trying to avoid the pitfalls of Orientalist metaphysics, that is, a cultural historiography that would try *not* to avoid the abyssal undecidabilities that Orientalism attempted to master and disavow. After considering this question, I close by considering a few respects in which the Orientalist problematic persists in postwar and contemporary Germany. Discussing this persistence briefly will enable me to illustrate what I mean by the "nonexistence" of the present, to which I think such a historiography should be peculiarly attentive.

What we've found in the various readings, as was not so surprising (especially after Derrida) yet still worth reviewing for its critical (or postcritical) implications, is that there is a relatively simple set of metaphysical homologies in operation. To begin with ontology, the two levels of material and spiritual are most generally associated with groundlessness (or insubstantiality) and (self-)grounding (or substantiality), respectively. The East must end up being material, while the West is spiritual. This remains the general Orientalist program even though the typological tradition completes this scheme in a dialectical manner. That is, the anticipatorily and externally combined but still split excessive spirituality and excessive materiality of the East condemn it (like the simultaneity of Jewish abstraction and Jewish ceremonial-legalistic fetishism from a Christian point of view) to an ultimate materiality, whereas the synthesis and overcoming of these two excesses gives rise in the West to "concrete" spirituality, as spirituality "properly" so called, the "realization" of spirituality. And so, in modal categories, matter is associated in historicist Orientalisms with potential, or unfulfilled possibility, whereas spiritual form is reserved for realization, or the ultimate reality itself.

In the language of fundamental logical terms or principles, the equivalent of these oppositions is the binary of difference and identity, which rhetorical philosophy translates as figural and literal. (These oppositions became particularly prominent in the Schlegel reading above and then remained important throughout the ensuing readings.) Figuration (the "dead letter") is the realm of difference (between the intended and the expressed, for example), whereas the literal represents the sphere of identity. And the Pauline and medieval doctrine of *figura* organizes the Jewish-Christian relationship (and later the East-West relationship) by combining the figural-literal opposition with the possibility-reality binary.

Further, in terms of what Kant called the forms of sense, space and time are bound up within this set of conceptual homologies as well. The *here* functions as the place of grounded existence, while the *there* is the place of groundless nonexistence (or the reverse, or the dialectical synthesis of the two in a higher or deeper *here*). In other words, unappropriated or unbridged spatial distance is associated with a lack of grounding (mediation), and absolute proximity or spatial self-coincidence characterizes the state of groundedness. In Goethe, for example, the reciprocal gift had to unite subject and object (bridging their mutual distance), and in Buber, *Entzweiung* had to be overcome by emphatic decision qua *teshuvah*. In temporal terms, the split duplicity of memory and anticipation (or pastness and futurity) constitutes the site of temporal nonidentity, while the unitary monologism of the pure present, or (as so prominently in Goethe) *Augenblick*, functions as temporal identity, self-assured existence, and so on.

But the system of homologies extends also to the realm of ethics, including a certain hermeneutic or semiological morality. In terms of ethical categories, freedom is obviously associated with spirit, and necessity is associated with matter—hence, the anxiety solicited by Spinozism that runs through all of nineteenth-century German Orientalism. On the level of the general and, as we saw, the pervasive worry about *Zusammenhang*—coherence or incoherence (or contextuality or noncontextuality), which ultimately concerns a morality of meaningfulness and of appropriate semiological types—the pole of coherence (or metaphor) coincides with grounded existence, and so on, and the pole of incoherence (or metonymy qua senselessly arbitrary juxtaposition) signifies abyssal exposure.

Finally, the often implicit system of homologies extends to overarching epochal determinations of method as well. In the tension between the Enlightenment's abstract formalist moralisms, on the one hand, and historicism's dogmatic teleologies, on the other hand, we can glimpse two mutually opposed ways of situating the matter-spirit opposition in relation to time. The former ultimately operates synchronically, the latter diachronically. Thus, Enlightenment ahistoricism tends to reduce material becoming to spiritual being, existence to the essence (or formal law) it ought to be or realize. And in contrast, historicism reduces material being (static structure) to the spiritual dynamism of its becoming, refers essence to the existence it is. Each movement involves a supersession, though not always one conceived principally as a historical development.

In following the trajectory of modern German Orientalism, however, we have seen that none of the extreme terms in these binary oppositions can be plausibly made to correspond to given cultural phenomena, or to the givings and misgivings of human manifestation. This is because the oppositions themselves remain structurally undecidable. We simply cannot have spirit (and the series of terms associated with it) in isolation from matter (and all the notions it traditionally implies). So how can we begin to reconfigure cultural historiography such that it would do what Hegel says no one ever does, namely, learn from (the mistakes of) history? The point would certainly not be to renounce historiography entirely (despite, for example, Paul de Man's misleading hyperboles), for to embrace an ahistoricism would be to repeat the illusory ambitions of an exclusively synchronic analysis (whether in its eighteenth-century versions or in its twentieth-century, structuralist avatars). Rather, it's still a matter of learning from the limitations of both Enlightenment formalist normativity and nineteenth-century historicism, and continuing to unfold the implications of advanced modernism for history. If the graphing of the existence (and nonexistence) of cultural artifacts were to attempt to do justice to the intractable undecidabilities that have been foregrounded by the readings above, then what would be some of its regulative principles and guiding questions?

We begin with panic, or radical anxiety (i.e., "hope and fear," as Spinoza put it): the acknowledgment that there is no absolute escape from the leaderless, foundationless position. That is, we find ourselves faced with the necessity of accepting a situation in which there are no absolute leaders or foundations, but a radical multiplicity of relative ones instead. We are subject to an absolute of relativization. This situation implies a radical responsibility for the distortional (or fictional, or performative) dimensions of historical representation, as Freud brought them out: One operates in the absence of any guarantees, including methodological alibis of diverse sorts.

Further, not only are cultural essentialisms—trying to situate, for example, materiality (or the body) in x cultural place and spirituality (or the mind) in y cultural place—patently false and uninteresting, but also methodological or discursive distinctions like that between a material—for example, political and social—history and a history of ideas (or cultural forms) are henceforth in principle untenable. This opens up new possibilities for the recombination of materialist accounts with idealist ones, and for their reconceptualization. Obviously, much interesting work in deconstruction and cultural studies has already productively explored such possibilities. But we're finished with this exploration neither in theory nor in practice. If the history of ideas is already a history of material forms, and if material history is already a history of ideas, and the disjunction between matter and spirit is not thereby simply overcome, then new representational economies and recombinations become both possible and necessary.

Indeed, the very narrative structures of history become open to reconsideration when one reflects on the inadequacy of the ontological-modal schemas of possibility and realization, anticipation and fulfillment. For example, what if, on the one hand, no potentials are ever realized, except completely within themselves (as incomplete), because what comes later is also in one sense radically new? And what if, on the other hand, no reality or situation ever ceases to be shot through with potentialities (both for the future and from the past) that render it essentially other than it is? How would reflection on these specifically modal aporias—which introduce unsettling discontinuities and continuities into history that are more resistant to monological description than the discontinuities Foucault pursued—alter our representations of individual works, epochs, and developments in history?[2]

To move on to the logical and rhetorical dimensions: If identity of cultures, languages, works, and authors is always shot through with difference (and vice versa), what becomes of the description and analysis of discrete cultural entities on these various levels? What legitimate and even necessary dispersions of object, theme, text, author, genre, and discourse must, or at least can, result? Likewise, when figural and literal language are inscribed onto a continuum, perhaps even "identical," as seems to be ineluctably the case (however much traditional historians may panic over the implications of "postmodernism"), what new ways of negotiating the relationships between history and fiction, science and art, emerge within the general space of a cultural historiography?

In addition, we have to reconsider cultural space and cultural time. If, for example, self-separation or unbridged internal distance is no longer degraded by contrast with, nor in principle excluded from, absolute self-proximity, what are the consequences for the negotiation of distances between cultural entities of various sorts, and for the analysis of given entities, oeuvres, movements, and so on? As Freud reminded us, displacement and disfiguration (*Entstellung*) render uncanny where we are, even when we try to counter this universal tendency by designating the "there" as the "here" in a simple spatial reversal of the cultural polarities of same and other (e.g., in exoticism or primitivism). Moreover, when one takes seriously the notion that there is (*pace* Goethe) no "present moment" or *Augenblick* (and thus no gaze) that is not dispersed into an endless multiplicity of pasts and futures, even while it remains radically separated from them, how will the adequate representation of a given moment in its originary diaspora proceed or take shape? If history has always attempted to describe a presumed (past) present or (present) past that, in fact, has never existed as such, then how will we write the history of a nonexistent present? To be sure, the inscription of the present in a temporal process has been the concern of historiography since the beginnings of historicism at the very least (perhaps all the way back to Herodotus, Thucydides, the Old Testament narratives, the Ramayana, etc.), not to mention oral traditions. Yet the passage beyond the model of a sequence of presents linked by various linear figures of potentiality and realization introduces (not entirely unprecedented but nonetheless) difficult and important forms of narrative (dis)continuity.

Further, concerning ethics, the limits of freedom and necessity being impossible to determine historically (as we saw in Herder and Hegel), the emergences and disappearances of freedom will henceforth coincide, it seems, with no end in sight. The limits of coherence (*Zusammenhang*) and incoherence on various levels are no longer in principle so easy to determine, as Kafka was so acutely aware, even if we are perhaps inclined to avoid this problem today by responding to the disarticulation of meaning with calls for relevance.

Finally, there is the question of how we choose to relate to the overarching epochal determinations of method given by the Enlightenment and historicist traditions. A cultural historiography of the nonexistent present necessarily participates in the abstraction—"cold" or "deadly" or "static" as it may seem—often characterized as the opposite of the concretion and dynamism that history is supposed to grasp in its living warmth. There is no separating separation from togetherness, at least where language is involved (and for the rest, who can say?). Context separates from itself in voids of many different kinds.

These, then, would be the most minimal indications and questions for a cultural historiography—of necessity abstract to the point where one might wish to call it a material theory—of the (nonexistent) present. The desirability of such a cultural historiography (or material theory) is implied by the foregoing analyses of German Orientalism, although these analyses themselves in fact proceed in a much more traditional manner.

Although I cannot adequately even begin to broach here a consideration of German Orientalism through World War II, the Cold War, the unification, and since, let me nonetheless close with a few illustrative and allusive remarks on German Orientalism in the (nonexistent) present of what we call present-day Germany.

After the high modernist episode, the first thing that happens with historicist German Orientalism is that it explodes into World War II and the Shoah as the National Socialist assertion of the Aryan myth in its most extreme form. Under the Nazis this myth becomes the principle of the limitless colonization of a world they view as subject to an ever-growing threat of Semiticization. The National Socialist ideology identifies the Aryan racial principle with immediate positive presence, while it reduces the Semitic (and specifically the Jewish Semitic) principle to mediation, negativity, and absence caused by representational excess, or (dis)figuration. The Nazis' rejection of high modernism and the modernist avant-gardes—as in the Degenerate Art exhibit—belongs to the more general denial of the impossibility of self-identical and self-grounded presence that also drives their anti-Semitism, an impossibility on which advanced modernists such as Kafka, Freud, Mann, and some others insisted.

Subsequent to the war, as neither metaphysics nor Eurocentrism nor racism simply disappeared with the collapse of the Nazi regime, many of the tendencies that we have been tracing since the eighteenth century of course persisted. Like other disavowals of traumatic loss, they repeated themselves (and still repeat themselves) in displaced forms.[3] The desire for foundations, for example, was initially absorbed, as if literally concretized, in the rebuilding of Germany from out of the ruins left by Allied bombing and the violence of the war in general. Ideologically and culturally, new foundations for the divided Germany were partly adopted from within and partly imposed from without (a free necessity, as it were) in the forms of Soviet communism and Western (and especially U.S. American) capitalism. Further, the Orient-Occident split continued to haunt German culture in various forms, such as its own division by the occupying powers into East and West, which bore the connotations of a punishment, a period of penance, and a delay of the phantasmatic return to the origins of self-constituting sovereignty, among others.[4] During this time, the East appeared to the West as a still precapitalist despotism destined to realize itself one day in capitalism, while the West appeared to the East as precommunist, in a reversal of East-West teleologies that retained the supersessionist (Hegelian-Marxist) narrative of a dialectically attained freedom. Thus, in the Cold War years, the supplementation of lacking absolute foundations persisted and even still or again revolved around an East-West decision and one or another teleological East-West narrative.

With the fall of the Berlin Wall on November 9, 1989 (unsettlingly, the same date as the Night of Broken Glass in 1938, and as the Hitler Beer-Hall Putsch in 1923, and as the proclamation of the Weimar Republic in 1918), both Germanies experienced, to a certain extent euphorically, but also with substantial anxiety, the mythical return to a phantasmatic and self-grounding national unity. With unification, however, came minirepetitions of the Nazi past in neo-Nazi skinhead violence, the repetition of de-Nazification memories in connection with investigations of the Stasi, and other signs of both the inscription of the present in the past and what Heiner Müller had called the *Zeitmauer* (the "wall of time"), division of the same nation into two different historical temporalities.[5] Although Europe provided the new politically grounding framework, questions about the grounding of Europe, its eastern borders, and its relations with its eastern neighbors and Middle Eastern politics persist.

Internally, given the relative cultural heterogeneity of contemporary Germany, the Orientalism problematic still plays an important role, although a changed one, most obviously and prominently in two dimensions: The complex Turkish-German intercultural relationship that arose, at least in appearance, out of the guest-worker policies beginning in 1961 (not by chance, the same year the East-West wall went up), and the German-Jewish relationship. The rich complexity of these relationships in the Germany of today, in cultural, political, social, religious, sociological, and psychological terms, makes it impossible even remotely to do them justice here. And, of course, there is an extensive and significant literature on these relationships.[6] Nonetheless, a couple of remarks are in order, with a view to suggesting the temporal and cultural-spatial dispersion of present cultural entities.[7]

With globalization in general, as well as the maturation of one or even two generations of Turkish foreigners (*Ausländer*) living in Germany (and going back and forth between Germany and Turkey), in addition to the alteration of the citizenship laws in 2000, the opposition between Germans as Westerners and Turks as a non-Western, non-European people has begun to erode. There are now a host of culturally articulate Turkish Germans or German Turks—cineastes, literary authors, journalists, essayists, musicians, and so on—who are pervaded by, identified with, and thoroughly versed in both cultures.[8] The mutual exclusiveness of these cultures hence appears as disproven by the fact of their cohabitation in the minds of the individuals who live their intermingling.[9] And the same goes for a number of other East-West, North-South, and European–non-European polarities in today's world of "hyphenated" German identities and cultural production.[10]

Nonetheless, Orientalist schemas and stereotypes from yesteryear persist in many respects, including the pressure to determine a "good," assimilable, Oriental origin and a "bad," nonassimilable, one. With respect to Turkish-German relations, this pressure takes innumerable concrete forms that I cannot specify here, sometimes, for example, by opposing a "good" Turkey to a "bad" one, sometimes by opposing a "good" Turkish Orient to another Orient designated in some sense as "bad" or the reverse.[11]

The "bad" Orient always represents, here as elsewhere, the site of the projection of "bad" traits potentially characteristic of the West in general and of Germany in particular. One sees here the same structure as the projection of Western sexism onto the Oriental despot in Mozart's *Abduction from the Seraglio*, where the choice of an apparently appropriate object masks the self-exculpating projection. For example—as is too rarely discussed—one of the overdeterminations of the image of Turkey as "bad," when it is regarded as such, is the implicit and even unconscious identification of Turkey with precisely the German (Nazi and more generally predemocratic) past qua land of despotism and genocidal brutality, and a land that, moreover, the old German Empire supported in World War I against the West. When this projective identification is active, the appearance of Turkish culture as a land of (Oriental) despotism becomes all the more powerfully reinforced, while German culture represses its own past, including its nineteenth- and twentieth-century involvements in Ottoman Turkish affairs.[12]

This is just one illustration of the reason for which, and one sense in which, the present can realistically be called "nonexistent": It always represses its relationship to (and at the same time its displaced repetition of) certain moments in the past with which it wishes to have nothing to do. The past reasserts itself partially in the present; the present remains partially inscribed in its past.[13] (And although we know this, we don't necessarily reflect it in our historiographical practices or in our still largely metaphysical conceptions of history.)[14] This is not to say that serious political discussions cannot be conducted, nor that values cannot be negotiated between different cultures who articulate values differently, but simply that such discussions and negotiations are always overdetermined by historical hauntings (and their emotional echoes) that tend to play a disavowed role in ostensibly rational proceedings.

Another complex illustration is the contemporary Jewish-Christian or Jewish-German relation, which in turn (by comparison, contrast, and competition) to some degree overdetermines and is overdetermined by the Turkish-German one on conceptual, historical, and phantasmatic levels.[15] Even apart from that overdetermination, the old question of "good" versus "bad" Orient repeats itself here in connection with the search for foundations, in various ways, which are all complicated by the continuous haunting of the Shoah. In the context of the "Special Relationship" between Israel and the Federal Republic, for example, the question of Israeli-Palestinian politics is necessarily complicated for any contemporary German-identified subject by at least two factors. First, as indicated, it is overdetermined by the haunting presence of an Orientalist structural imperative to distinguish the "good" Semite, that is, the one who is most easily reconcilable with the way in which the West wants to imagine itself, from the "bad."[16] And second, it is marked by a more specifically German (and potentially Austrian) complication, for the Shoah bears in fact a significant part of the responsibility for the felt necessity and actual origination of the modern State of Israel. And the conscience of any reasonably serious German subject remains (althoughly increasingly distantly) somewhat vexed in relation to the figure of the Jew, even if at this point in history more in terms of residual shame (and also resentment) than in terms of guilt.[17] The foundation here understandably sought, then, is that of a clear conscience, as the possibility of an unashamed and un-self-conscious national-cultural self-assertion.[18] And the "good" Semite would be precisely the mirror in which that clear conscience could catch a glimpse of itself. In this situation, a certain desire to moralistically devalue and blame the Israelis in a sweeping manner as "bad" Semites, while exculpating the Palestinians as "good" Semites and victims of the Jews, is thus both supported (because, in a word, "bad" Jews make Germans look better) and undermined (because condemning Israeli Jews may appear unbecoming to those who are implicated in the Shoah by familial and/or national societal association and whose ancestors likely contributed to the situation in which the Israeli Jews find themselves now violently at odds with many violently hostile neighbors). To choose the more subtle and rational middle position, in favor of the maximally equitable reconciliation of a tragic conflict, leaves one exposed to the anxiety of both positions at once. For on each side of the equation, one makes oneself both guilty and innocent in different senses. Yet despite the fact that one cannot quite find the "good" or the "bad" Semite, one is compelled by both the lingering Orientalist tradition and the conflict itself to continue looking for him (or her).

Can one find the "good" Semite in Jewish cultural formations outside of the ongoing Israeli-Palestinian disaster? The situation is hardly alleviated by the complexity of the associations of Judaism with the main political-economic options (i.e., foundations) available in postwar Germany. Since Jews were associated by the Nazis both with capitalism and with bolshevism, one has two possible ways of trying to satisfy with respect to diasporal Judaism any conscious or half-conscious interest one may retain in compensatory identification with the murdered Jews. On the one hand, one can pursue the Western, and more specifically U.S. American cultural identification by way of New York and L.A. (as prominent sites of Jewish cultural production). This is one familiar tendency since the war and in our own times. On the other hand, one can (or at least for a time one could) move in the direction of Marxist, Eastern European cultures, which are (or were) associated with a different sort of Jewish universalism and assimilation. (A certain Frankfurt School culture, for example, arguably participates in this phantasm.) Either way, however, one finds oneself potentially opposed to oneself through one's very choice. There's no real relief of the tension, no noncontradictory identification, because capitalism and socialism/communism remain at odds, and even overdetermined by an East-West divide. There ends up being no reliably easy phantasm of safety for a postwar German (or Austrian) conscience with respect to the ghostly soul of Jewish culture.[19] This is among the reasons why so frequently people choose simply to turn away, to forget the whole thing, that is, to seek phantasms of self-grounding elsewhere, for example in other Orientalist figures (not that these figures will easily satisfy the desire to deny groundlessness either), or in other modes of imagined groundedness, intellectual or not. Even turning away, however, as understandable and, given the passing of time, legitimate as it may be in certain regards, does not prevent the ostensible present from interpenetrating with the ostensible past such that a pure present never escapes its radical historicity to come into being as such. Working through and acting out are endless in principle and in practice—and multiple in theme—even if they may asymptotically approach forgetting over time.

But the present is connected not just to the past but also to the future: It is coming toward us from up ahead. And the world's cultures and nations are becoming reconfigured from out of that future (or rather those futures), as well as out of our past(s). Like Hegel in the *Lectures on the Philoso-*

phy of History, we cannot know the histories of the future, or the futures of history (see chapter 5 in this book). Unlike Hegel, however, we can know the historical (dis)continuity ensuring that history both is already over and has not yet started at every moment, even as that moment also participates (still) in multiple pasts and (already) in multiple futures. And we can know, in contrast to Hegel and the historicist tradition, that our historical interest does not concern the eternal teleological will or spirit. Yet our historical representations of complicatedly temporal processual events are compelled to configure them in fragments characterized by a certain abstraction, just as our theoretical claims must materialize in forms marked by a degree of opacity that we will never overcome.

NOTES

INTRODUCTION: ORIENTALISM AS TYPOLOGY,
OR HOW TO DISAVOW THE MODERN ABYSS

1. See Immanuel Wallerstein, *The Modern World-System*, 2 vols. (New York: Academic Press, 1974–80). For important work on the history of anxiety and fear in early modernity, see Jean Delumeau, *La peur en occident (XIVe–XVIIIe siècles): Une cité assiégée* (Paris: Fayard, 1978).

2. In addition to Delumeau, see, e.g., Djelal Kadir, *Columbus and the Ends of the Earth: Europe's Prophetic Rhetoric as Conquering Ideology* (Berkeley: University of California Press, 1992); Nabil Matar, *Turks, Moors, and Englishmen in the Age of Discovery* (New York: Columbia University Press, 1999); Bartolomé Bennassar and Lucile Bennassar, *1492: Un monde nouveau?* (Paris: Perrin, 1991); Marvin Lunenfeld, ed., *1492: Discovery, Invasion, Encounter—Sources and Interpretations* (Lexington, Mass.: D. C. Heath, 1991); John Docker, *1492: The Poetics of Diaspora* (London: Continuum, 2001); Joseph Perez, *The Spanish Inquisition*, trans. Janet Lloyd (New Haven: Yale University Press, 2005); and Margarita Zamora, *Reading Columbus* (Berkeley: University of California Press, 1993).

3. The processes of the "long sixteenth century" to which I refer include the expansion of printing (which had already been invented by Gutenberg in 1440), the first developments of the Atlantic slave trade, the Reformation, the Copernican revolution, the English revolution, the Thirty Years' War, and the rise of modern rationalism and empiricism, just to name the most obviously all-encompassing.

4. Reinhard Koselleck, *Kritik und Krise: Eine Studie zur Pathogenese der bürgerlichen Welt* (Frankfurt am Main: Suhrkamp Verlag, 1959), 13.

5. The phrase is Koselleck's, under the partial influence of Carl Schmitt.

6. This is the somewhat hyperbolic phrase Heinz Kittsteiner uses repeatedly in his very useful *Die Stabilisierungsmoderne: Deutschland und Europa 1618–1715* (Munich: Hanser Verlag, 2010). Citations given henceforth parenthetically in text.

7. Heinz Kittsteiner characterizes this period as precisely the "Stabilisierungsmoderne" in his title.

8. Heinz Kittsteiner, *Die Stabilisierungsmoderne: Deutschland und Europa 1618–1715* (Munich: Carl Hanser Verlag, 2010). The epigraph for the current chapter quoting Droysen is found in this book by Kittsteiner, 30. Cf. Heinz Kittsteiner, "Die Angst in der Geschichte und die Re-Personalisierung des Feindes," *Jahrbuch für psychohistorische Forschung* 3 (2002): 113–31.

9. In this calculation Kittsteiner is roughly in line with his teacher Koselleck's account. But Kittsteiner also qualifies the notion of a "stabilization" in this period by recounting the continuous wars that immediately ensue, including France's wars against her neighbors from 1667 to 1697, the wars of the Spanish succession from 1701 to 1712, and so on.

10. See Paul Hazard's still useful discussion of the turn toward a more dynamic modernity in the years between 1680 and 1715, *La crise de la conscience Européenne* (Paris: Boivin, 1935).

11. This passage in Hobbes is apposite: "*Feare* of power invisible, feigned by the mind, or imagined from tales publiquely allowed, RELIGION; not allowed, SUPERSTITION. And when the power imagined, is truly such as we imagine, TRUE RELIGION. *Feare*, without the apprehension of why, or what, PANIQUE TERROR; called so from the Fables, that make *Pan* the author of them; whereas in truth, there is always in him that feareth, first, some apprehension of the cause, though the rest run away by Example; every one supposing his fellow to know why. And therefore this Passion happens to none but in a throng, or multitude of people" (*Leviathan* [London: Penguin, 1981], 124).

12. See, e.g., Frederick Beiser's summary of Wizenmann's debate with Moses Mendelssohn in *The Fate of Reason: German Philosophy from Kant to Fichte* (Cambridge, Mass.: Harvard University Press, 1987), 109–26.

13. Each of these manifestations of foundation is "metaphysical" in the sense of the "ontotheological constitution of Western metaphysics" that Martin Heidegger usefully circumscribes in the late essay of that title (in *Identität und Differenz* [Pfullingen: Günther Neske Verlag, 1957]). If God is being as highest being, then Monarch, Father, Truth, Goodness, and Beauty all concern essential transformations of this highest being or of his attributes. See also Martin Heidegger, *Der Satz vom Grund* (Pfullingen: Günther Neske Verlag, 1957). Needless to say, my interests here are—dividedly—as historical as they are theoretical, as ontic as ontological, as political as aesthetic. If the problematic of grounding is significant—and, of course, it is—this is because it ramifies not just across conceptualities but also across institutional arrangements, affective structures and experiences, and imaginal networks.

14. See Heidi Rosenbaum, *Formen der Familie: Untersuchungen zum Zusammenhang von Familienverhältnissen, Sozialstruktur und sozialen Wandel in*

der deutschen Gesellschaft des 19. Jahrhunderts (Frankfurt am Main: Suhrkamp Taschenbuch Verlag, 1982); and Neithard Bulst, Joseph Goy, and Jochen Hoock, eds., *Familie zwischen Tradition und Moderne: Studien zur Geschichte der Familie in Deutschland und Frankreich vom 16. bis zum 20. Jahrhundert* (Göttingen: Vandenhoeck und Ruprecht, 1981).

15. The prize question in the Berlin Academy of Sciences from 1763, which Moses Mendelssohn and Immanuel Kant answered, winning first and second prize respectively, illustrates the moment, in that the Academy (following the proposal of Sulzer) questioned the limits of rationalist metaphysics.

16. The erosion of the ground in these different discursive areas constitutes also the disruption of any possible general equivalent, and hence of any restricted economy that may have governed them. God, king, father, and so on are in such disarray in the period we are considering that measurelessness begins to take over—hence, perhaps, the high profile gained by the concept of the sublime in this epoch—yet in such a way as to lose its own contours in turn.

17. The problem of missing foundations in modernity is obviously still with us, in its crudest form through the disavowals on which all "fundamentalisms" currently rest, including that of Al Qaeda, "the foundation." See Tariq Ali, *The Clash of Fundamentalisms: Crusades, Jihads, and Modernity* (London: Verso, 2002); Mark Juergensmeyer, *Terror in the Mind of God: The Global Rise of Religious Violence* (Berkeley: University of California Press, 2000); Sudhir Kakar, *The Colors of Violence: Cultural Identities, Religion, and Conflict* (Chicago: University of Chicago Press, 1996); Ian Buruma and Avishai Margalit, *Occidentalism: The West in the Eyes of Its Enemies* (New York: Penguin, 2004); Raymond Ibrahim, ed., *The Al Qaeda Reader* (New York: Doubleday, 2007); Reza Aslan, *Beyond Fundamentalism: Confronting Religious Extremism in the Age of Globalization* (New York: Random House, 2010).

18. Sigmund Freud, "Massenpsychologie und Ichanalyse," in *Studienausgabe*, ed. Alexander Mitscherlich et al. (Frankfurt am Main: Fischer Taschenbuch Verlag, 1982), 9:61–134. Translated into English by James Strachey as *Group Psychology and the Analysis of the Ego* (New York: W. W. Norton and Company, 1959). I have modified translations for accuracy and given pages parenthetically in text, first for the German edition, then for the English translation. I translate "Massenpsychologie" as "Mass psychology," rather than the standard "Group psychology," because the connotations of materiality are, I believe, crucial to Freud's conception.

19. One of the standard accusations against the Jews during the Third Reich was that they were "zersetzend" or "disintegrative." Note also that, as soon as a mass becomes aware of itself (in any of its members) as a mass, that

is, as a composition of material figures against an absent ideal ground, then it begins to decompose.

20. Cf. Philippe Lacoue-Labarthe and Jean-Luc Nancy, "La panique politique," in English in their *Retreating the Political*, ed. Simon Sparks (London: Routledge, 1997), 1–31; for cultural studies analyses, see Jackie Orr, *Panic Diaries: A Genealogy of Panic Disorder* (Durham, N.C.: Duke University Press, 2006), and Devon Hinton and Byron J. Good, eds., *Culture and Panic Disorder* (Stanford: Stanford University Press, 2009). See also Jean-Pierre Dupuy, *La panique*, new ed. (Paris: Les empêcheurs de penser en rond, 2003).

21. See the first epigraph for chapter 6, where Schopenhauer speaks of how we all have, at certain moments, "misgivings about" (*irrewerden an*) the *principium individuationis*, misgivings that reveal a certain groundlessness, to which the subject reacts with "dread" (*Grausen*) and "fearful terror" (*ungeheures Entsetzen*) ("Die Welt als Wille und Vorstellung," in Arthur Schopenhauer, *Werke in zwei Bänden*, ed. Werner Brede, vol. 1 [Munich: Carl Hanser Verlag, 1977], 451; *The World as Will and Representation*, trans. E. F. J. Payne, vol. 1 [New York: Dover, 1969], 353.).

22. In *Civilization and Its Discontents* (*Das Unbehagen in der Kultur*), Freud indicates that the modern situation, especially as embodied by "Amerika," is one in which leaderlessness obtains, forcing social bonds to take place on a more strictly imaginary level of "identification" (*Studienausgabe*, 9:244).

23. In another context, Freud makes the point in the form of a series of questions: "We should consider whether groups with leaders may not be the more primitive and complete, whether in the others an idea, an abstraction may not take the place of the leader (a state of things to which religious groups, with their invisible head, form a transitional stage), and whether a common tendency, a wish in which a number of people can share, may not in the same way serve as a substitute. . . . The leader or the leading idea might also, so to speak, be negative; hatred against a particular person or institution might operate in just the same unifying way" (94; 40–41). For important elaborations of Freud's approach to group psychology, including his notion of panic, see W. R. Bion's *Experiences in Groups and Other Papers* (London: Routledge, 2010). On the potentially abstract and even narrative character of the leader figure: The "leader need not . . . be a person at all but may be identified with an idea or an inanimate object. In the dependent group the place of leader may be filled by the *history* of the group. A group, complaining of an inability to remember what took place on a previous occasion, sets about making a record of its meetings. This record then becomes a 'bible' to which appeal is made, if, for example, the individual whom the group has invested with leadership proves to be refractory material for moulding into the likeness proper to the dependent leader" (155). As we will see below,

in historicist Orientalism, this narrativization of the abstract foundation is exactly what happens.

24. See Sigmund Freud, "Fetischismus" and "Die Ichspaltung im Abwehrvorgang," in *Studienausgabe*, 3:379–96. Octave Mannoni, "I Know Very Well, But All the Same," in *Perversion and the Social Relation*, ed. Molly Anne Rothenberg, Dennis A. Foster, Slavoj Žižek (Durham, N.C.: Duke University Press, 2003), 68–91, enrichingly expands the psychoanalytic paradigm of fetishistic disavowal by applying the notion of disavowal to the problem of belief in general and specifically to any attempt either to deny the existence of whatever places a belief in question or to deny that one continues to embrace a belief that one thinks of oneself as having renounced, as in superstitions or the upholding of illusions in children (or, we might add, as in the continuing of religion in the form of comparative philology, etc.). I have found inspiration in David Levin, *Richard Wagner, Fritz Lang, and the Nibelungen: The Dramaturgy of Disavowal* (Princeton: Princeton University Press, 1998), who shows how in Wagner and Lang the Jewish figures function to enable these artists to disavow a certain lack of control over representation, and an excess of representation over presence, by situating the cause of this lack or excess in the Jewish figures who can then be destroyed. I am also sympathetic to Homi Bhabha's use of the notion of "fetishism" in connection with colonialism in "The Other Question: Stereotype, Discrimination, and the Discourse of Colonialism," in *The Location of Culture* (London: Routledge, 1994), 66–84. Although it does seem true that, as his critics allege, he tends to dehistoricize, to universalize, to minimize the difference between colonizer and colonized, and to do scant justice to the question of gender, all of which are weaknesses, these weaknesses do not render his attempt to mobilize "fetishism" in a critical reflection on colonialism useless or uninteresting, just flawed. For critiques of Bhabha in the terms mentioned, see Bart Moore-Gilbert, *Postcolonial Theory: Contexts, Practices, Politics* (London: Verso, 1997); and notes in Nigel Gibson, "Losing Sight of the Real: Recasting Merleau-Ponty in Fanon's Critique of Mannoni," and Kelly Oliver, "Alienation and Its Double; or, The Secretion of Race," both in, *Race and Racism in Continental Philosophy*, ed. Robert Bernasconi and Sybol Cook (Bloomington: Indiana University Press, 2003), 129–50 and 176–95, respectively. See Dorothy M. Figueira, *The Exotic: A Decadent Quest* (Albany: State University of New York Press, 1994), 5–6. I am largely in accord with the reading of Jews and Orientals as both fetishes and fetishists in Jay Geller's *The Other Jewish Question: Identifying the Jew and Making Sense of Modernity* (New York: Fordham University Press, 2011), 11–27. His emphasis on the resentment and fear of the Jews that comes along with their continuing survival beyond the point of their obsolescence from a Christian point of view (10) suggests strikingly that the failure of Christian

supersessionist figuralism is among the causes of an anxiety about otherness to which the fetishistic renewal of supersessionism in East-West terms is a desperate response. On fetishism in the U.S. engagement in Iraq after 9/11, as an extension of the Orientalist tradition, see Jeffrey S. Librett, "Perversion and Freedom at Abu Ghraib," in *Les enjeux de perversion aujourd'hui/The Stakes of Perversion Today*, ed. Willy Apollon et al. (Quebec: GIFRIC, 2005), 63–78.

25. The position of China as prominent interlocutor of the West, in the Confucianist enthusisasm of the Jesuits and the early Enlighteners such as Leibniz, was not that of a historical origin but of an equal partner from afar. See Julia Ching and Willard G. Oxtoby, *Discovering China: European Interpretations in the Enlightenment* (Rochester, N.Y.: University of Rochester Press, 1992). On the frequently drawn analogies between Jews and Chinese centering around the fetishistic image of the *Zopf* (braid) and its double, the circumcised penis, see the very rich analyses in Geller, *Other Jewish Question*, 50–87.

26. Erich Auerbach, "Figura," in *Gesammelte Aufsätze zur romantischen Philologie* (Bern: Francke Verlag, 1967), 55–92, for *littera-figura-veritas*, see 73; *Scenes from the Drama of European Literature* (Minneapolis: University of Minnesota Press, 1984), 11–78, and on *littera-figura-veritas* see 47; Northrop Frye, *The Great Code: The Bible and Literature* (New York: Harcourt Brace Jovanovich, 1982); Frank Talmage, "Apples of God: The Inner Meaning of Sacred Texts in Medieval Judaism," in *Jewish Spirituality from the Bible through the Middle Ages*, ed. Arthur Green (New York: Crossroad, 1996), 313–55.

27. For a penetrating reading of letter-spirit in Paul, Moses Mendelssohn, and Jacques Derrida, a reading that explores both the classical backgrounds and in particular the media-theoretical consequences of the Pauline distinction, see David Martyn, "Der Geist, der Buchstabe, und der Löwe: Zur Medialität des Lesens bei Paulus und Mendelssohn," in *Transkribieren: Medien-Lektüre*, ed. Ludwig Jäger and Georg Stanitzek (Munich: Wilhelm Fink Verlag, 2002).

28. For essays on Jewish Orientalists, Jews as Orientals, and Orientalism in various aspects of modern Jewish life, see, e.g., John Efron, "From Mitteleuropa to the Middle East: Orientalism through a Jewish Lens, *Jewish Quarterly Review* 94, no. 3 (2004): 490–520; and Ivan Davidson Kalmar and Derek J. Penslar, *Orientalism and the Jews* (Hanover, N.H.: University Press of New England, 2005). The latter collection is a partial proceedings volume for the conference from 2001 on Orientalism and the Jews at which I presented a reading of Orientalism in Lessing that was subsequently published as two essays, "Destabilizing Typologies: Jewish Works, Christian Faith, and the Passage from Orient to Occident in G. E. Lessing's *Ernst und Falk: Gespräche*

für Freimäurer," Germanic Review 78, no. 4 (2003): 301–18; and "How Does One Orient Oneself in Giving? Cultural-Political and Theological Implications of Problematic Generosity in G. E. Lessing's *Nathan the Wise*," *Lessing Yearbook* 35 (2003): 35–59. For an insightful more recent analysis of Christian views of Oriental despotism in early modernity that overlaps in various respects my own approach to the question of Orientalism, see Ivan Kalmar's later book, *Early Orientalism: Imagined Islam and the Notion of Sublime Power* (London: Routledge, 2012). In particular, I find support in Kalmar's rich work—which builds also on Alain Grosrichard's psychoanalytic approach to "despotism"—for my concern with modern groundlessness, for my interest in the connections between anxiety and Orientalism, and for my emphasis on the importance of figural interpretation for the Orientalist problematic. See also Susannah Heschel, *Abraham Geiger and the Jewish Jesus* (Chicago: University of Chicago Press, 1998); Jonathan M. Hess, *Germans, Jews, and the Claims of Modernity* (New Haven: Yale University Press, 2002).

29. On the Aryan-Semite distinction, see Léon Poliakov, *The Aryan Myth: A History of Racist and Nationalist Ideas in Europe*, trans. Edmund Howard (London: Sussex University Press and Heinemann Educational Books, 1974); Maurice Olender, *The Languages of Paradise: Race, Religion, and Philology in the Nineteenth Century*, trans. Arthur Goldhammer (Cambridge, Mass.: Harvard University Press, 1992); Gil Anidjar, *Semites: Race, Religion, Literature* (Stanford: Stanford University Press, 2008), and *The Jew, the Arab: A History of the Enemy* (Stanford: Stanford University Press, 2003), as well as Ammiel Alcalay, *After Jews and Arabs: Remaking Levantine Culture* (Minneapolis: University of Minnesota Press, 1993). See Tuska Benes, *In Babel's Shadow: Language, Philology, and the Nation in Nineteenth-Century Germany* (Detroit: Wayne State University Press, 2008), especially 66–112 on leading theories of the Indo-Germanic in early nineteenth century philology, and then 197–240 for the transformation of the Indo-Germanic into the Aryan after 1830.

30. On the way in which figural interpretation is an always unstable proposed solution to the intractable problem of the *border* within the "context" of a spiritualizing (i.e., antimaterialist) philosophical anthropology, see the opening pages of chapter 5.

31. Jeffrey S. Librett, *The Rhetoric of Cultural Dialogue: Jews and Germans from Moses Mendelssohn to Richard Wagner and Beyond* (Stanford: Stanford University Press, 2000).

32. We might say that with the Spinoza controversy Jews become the "exemplary" Orientals.

33. On the Spinoza debates in Germany, see, e.g., Sylvain Zac, *Spinoza en Allemagne: Mendelssohn, Lessing et Jacobi* (Paris: Méridiens Klincksieck, 1989); David Bell, *Spinoza in Germany from 1670 to the Age of Goethe* (London:

University of London, 1984); Yirmiyahu Yovel, *Spinoza and Other Heretics: The Adventures of Immanence* (Princeton: Princeton University Press, 1989); and Beiser, *Fate of Reason*. Jan Assmann, *Moses der Ägypter: Entzifferung einer Gedächtnisspur* (Frankfurt am Main: Fischer Taschenbuch Verlag, 2000), 118–30., 205–12, shows that the "all-in-one" philosophy (and slogan) of the Spinoza enthusiasm that runs from Lessing through Goethe and the early romantics and beyond goes back to Ralph Cudworth's *True Intellectual System of the Universe* (1678), which is itself responding to Spinoza and "finding" his thought in ancient Egyptian religion. Assmann's enthusiasm for Spinoza as signaling the return of the "cosmotheism" of late antiquity is somewhat problematic, however, for two reasons. First, this enthusiasm participates in the very conventional Orientalization of Spinozism. Even more important, insofar as Spinoza's philosophy proposes itself as the "true" philosophy, and one with strong monotheistic aspects (one "substance," for instance), it runs counter to Assmann's idea of "cosmotheistic" (and supposedly natural) religions. On Spinoza in the context of Jewish seventeenth-century Amsterdam, see Adam Sutcliffe, *Judaism and Enlightenment* (Cambridge: Cambridge University Press, 2003). For the final avatar of Jacobi's critique of Spinoza, see his Jewish reincarnation as Leo Strauss, whose *Die Religionskritik Spinozas als Grundlage seiner Bibelwissenschaft* (Berlin: Akademieverlag, 1930) represents Jacobi's position in a twentieth-century form and—oddly—from a Jewish perspective.

34. Benedict de Spinoza, *A Spinoza Reader: The Ethics and Other Works*, ed. and trans. Edwin Curley (Princeton: Princeton University Press, 1994). In the *Ethics*, see especially the Appendix to part 1 (109–15). I return to that text in chapter 1 in some detail. In the *Theologico–Political Treatise*, see chapter 3, "Of the Vocation of the Hebrews," and especially the discussion of "God's guidance" as "the fixed and immutable order of nature" (24–25).

35. Cf. the analysis of fear and hope as intertwined in the *Ethics*, for example in part 3, "Definition of the Affects," definitions 12 and 13. Hope is "an inconstant joy, born of the idea of a future or past thing whose outcome we to some extent doubt," whereas fear is "an inconstant sadness, born of the idea of a future or past thing whose outcome we to some extent doubt," and "there is neither hope without fear, nor fear without hope" (190). In panic, one hopes for an escape from danger that at the same time one doubts and fears will fail, and while fleeing in fear one continues to hope that the flight will amount to an effort at self-salvation.

36. See, for example, in *Ethics*, part 1, proposition 32: "The will cannot be called a free cause, but only a necessary one. . . . Corollary 1: . . . God does not produce any effect by freedom of the will" (105–6); and in *Ethics*, part 2, proposition 48: "In the mind there is no absolute or free will, but the

mind is determined to will this or that by a cause which is also determined by another; and this again by another, and so to infinity" (146); and proposition 49: "In the mind there is no volition, or affirmation and negation, except that which the idea involves insofar as it is an idea" and its corollary: "The will and the intellect are one and the same" (147).

37. On the noon hour of Pan, see Roger Caillois, "The Noon Complex," in his *The Edge of Surrealism: A Roger Caillois Reader*, ed. Claudine Frank (Durham, N.C.: Duke University Press, 2003), 124–29. For a Jungian-mythological approach to panic and nightmare through the figure of Pan, see James Hillman and Wilhelm Heinrich Roscher, *Pan and the Nightmare: Two Essays* (New York: Spring Publications, 1972).

38. Jeffrey S. Librett, "How Does One Orient Oneself in Giving? Cultural-Political and Theological Implications of Problematic Generosity in Lessing's *Nathan der Weise*"; "Destabilizing Typologies: Jewish Works, Christian Faith, and the Passage from Orient to Occident in G. E. Lessing's *Ernst und Falk: Gespräche für Freimaurer*": "Preventing Historicism: G. E. Lessing's 'Grounding' of the Spirit of Religion and Family (*Nathan the Wise* and *The Education of the Human Race*)," in circulation; and "What Does It Mean: To Orient Oneself in the Want of Reason? Kant's Critique of Herder (from Regulative Teleology to Racism," in circulation.

39. The attempt to provide a "dynamic" rather than a "static" view of the world, an attempt that as Karl Mannheim notes (in "Historicism," in his *Essays on the Sociology of Knowledge* [New York: Oxford University Press, 1952], 84–133, especially 129–33) is characteristic of historicism, is no doubt conditioned by the "acceleration of time" that, according to Kittsteiner, as we saw, modernity imposes, particularly from the late eighteenth century onward. The dynamism of narrative always competes, however, with the requirement of meaning that unavoidably appeals to a static structure. And around we go.

40. Georg Iggers, *The German Conception of History: The National Tradition of Historical Thought from Herder to the Present* (Middletown, Conn.: Wesleyan University Press, 1983). On historicism see also Herbert Schnädelbach, *Philosophy in Germany, 1831–1933*, trans. Eric Matthews (Cambridge: Cambridge University Press, 1984), 33–65. Schnädelbach rightly and usefully argues that nineteenth-century consciousness liberated itself from idealism in the name of "science" and "history," and that while in general "science" was pursued instead of a philosophical system, "historical science" was pursued instead of a philosophy of history. Yet Schnädelbach also traces how such history shared basic assumptions with the idealist philosophy of history (41). "For Hegel as for the Historical School, history is spirit . . . not nature, but depends on freedom, on action which is capable of becoming conscious and creative individuality, and hence is intelligible" (45). Schnädelbach also points

out that Hegel and the historicists in the narrower sense shared a notion of history as "objective spirit" (45–46), a certain contemplative attitude, and a tendency toward conservatism, even though the historicists also considered Hegel to be a kind of "repetition of rationalist metaphysics" (45) that they had to resist, "in a way analogous to that in which Hamann, Herder, and Novalis had once resisted Enlightenment theories of history" (45). It is the shared assumptions of the idealists and the historicists that justify my broad use of the term historicism for nineteenth-century Orientalist texts.

41. Because historicism in a narrower sense, as a defense of historical knowledge per se in the nineteenth century, has to defend itself against the natural sciences, on the one hand, and against philosophy, on the other hand, its rejection of concepts in favor of the individual is necessary to its taking-of-distance from philosophy, but its insistence on meaning as opposed to mere data, spirit rather than mere matter (or letter), is necessary to its taking-of-distance from the natural sciences. The ambivalent oscillation of historicism, as an ideology and discourse more generally, between affinities with Hegelian philosophy of history and affiinities with Goethean antitheoreticism, is written into this disciplinary situation. See Schnädelbach, *Philosophy in Germany*, 33–65.

42. As one example of a formulation in which historicism itself is subject to the typo-logic of the fulfillment of essence (or potential), but a formulation that also shows how historicism as narrative returns to the structure that contradicts its desire to be movement itself: "Historicist theory fulfills its own essence only by managing to derive an ordering principle from this seeming anarchy of change, only by managing to penetrate the innermost structure of this all-pervading change" (Mannheim, "Historicism," 86).

43. See Karl Mannheim, "Historicism," who argues explicitly at various points (87, 127) that the proper place of historicism is that of the "metaphysics" of earlier times. The groundlessness it overcomes is that of "relativism," he argues also in this essay. The way in which historicism overcomes relativism, for Mannheim, is through engagement, that is, the alignment of the will of the subject with the forces (teleology) of history: "The historical philosophically relevant subject is just that kernel of the human personality whose being and dynamism is consubstantial with the dominant active forces of history" (102).

44. On the "crisis" of historicism, see Iggers, *The German Conception of History*, 124–229; Schnädelbach, *Philosophy in Germany*, 50–65. A detailed reading of Nietzsche—of his later hostility to "Buddhism," his critique of Judaism and of anti-Semitism, his critique of historicism, his Zoroastrian allusion throughout "Thus Spake Zarathustra"—would belong properly to this study, and is lacking here only for reasons of space and time. What makes his

absence perhaps somewhat less of a problem is the fact that Schopenhauer, whom I treat here in detail, establishes to such a great extent the terms in which the Orient must or can appear for Nietzsche. On the manifestations of the crisis of historicism within the fields of philology and linguistics, see Benes, *In Babel's Shadow*, 241–82.

45. The opposition between Enlightenment models and their historicist opponents replays in displaced ways the earlier one between rationalism and empiricism. As I argue in "The Finitude of Method: Mourning Theory from the New Criticism to the New Vitalism," *Comparative Literature Journal* 64, no. 2 (2012): 121–49, the early modern methods of rationalism and empiricism can be usefully seen as responses of incompleted mourning to the (partially impending) loss of the absolute, or objective universality, which they accelerate. In psychoanalytic terms, rationalism can be shown to follow a course akin to melancholy, whereas empiricism follows a path akin to mania. The same would be true, mutatis mutandis, of Enlightenment and historicism, respectively.

46. For an intellectual history that contests Said's perspective aggressively but not injudiciously, see Michael Curtis, *Orientalism and Islam: European Thinkers on Oriental Despotism in the Middle East and India* (Cambridge: Cambridge University Press, 2009); for a Lacanian reading of the logic of the fantasy of despotism with regard to the Ottoman Empire, see Alain Grosrichard, *The Sultan's Court: European Fantasies of the East*, trans. Liz Heron (London: Verso, 1998), originally published in French in 1979, and for the role of fetishism in the fantasy of the despot, see xv in Mladen Dolar's useful introduction; for an informative sweeping history of Europe's contacts with the Mediterranean worlds of Islam, see the work by the Italian medieval historian Franco Cardini, *Europe and Islam* (Oxford: Blackwell, 1999). On the position of Muslim women in Western representations, which Said only minimally discusses, see, for example, Mohja Kahf, *Western Representations of the Muslim Woman: From Termagant to Odalisque* (Austin: University of Texas Press, 1999); and Lynne Thornton, *Women as Portrayed in Orientalist Painting* (Paris: ACR Édition international, 1994). The range of work on Orientalism in relation to South Asia is illustrated by the Subaltern Studies group; Sara Suleri's literary-historically focused questioning of the binarisms of Western and "other" Oriental in Said's and related work, in *The Rhetoric of English India* (Chicago: University of Chicago Press, 1992); Richard King's introduction of postcolonial studies into religious studies, *Orientalism and Religion: Postcolonial Theory, India, and the "Mystic East"* (London: Routledge, 1999); Partha Chatterjee's critical analysis of Indian nationalism, *Nationalist Thought and the Colonial World: A Derivative Discourse* (Minneapolis: University of Minnesota Press, 1993); and the poststructuralist psychoanalytic reading of

Indian philosophy in Catherine Clément, *Syncope: The Philosophy of Rapture*, trans. Sally O'Driscoll and Deirdre M. Mahoney (Minneapolis: University of Minnesota Press, 1994). For an exemplary study of Orientalism in French literature, see Madeleine Dobie, *Foreign Bodies: Gender, Language, and Culture in French Orientalism* (Stanford: Stanford University Press, 2001), and for her interesting engagement of the notion of fetishism, 167.

47. From among the unsurveyable onslaught of books and essays since the 1990s that provide sustained critical responses to Said's work and/or case studies that test and modify his theories, one might consider, for example, Timothy Mitchell, *Colonising Egypt* (Berkeley: University of California Press, 1991); Bryan S. Turner, *Orientalism, Postmodernism, and Globalism* (London: Routledge, 1994), who illuminates Orientalism through sociology, especially Max Weber's rationalization theory; Bart Moore-Gilbert, *Postcolonial Theory: Contexts, Practices, Politics* (London: Verso, 1997), a book that weighs theoreticism against historicism in the work of Said, Spivak, and Bhabha; Alexander Lyon Macfie, ed., *Orientalism: A Reader* (New York: New York University Press, 2000), which provides a useful sampling and overview of responses to Said, and further explorations, as well as nineteenth-century and earlier twentieth-century sources; Chandreyee Niyogi, ed., *Reorienting Orientalism* (New Delhi: Sage, 2006), a collection of essays that recognizes Said's work while performing the capacity of Oriental cultures to represent themselves; Diane Long Hoeveler and Jeffrey Cass, eds., *Interrogating Orientalism: Contextual Approaches and Pedagogical Practices* (Columbus: Ohio State University Press, 2006), which elaborates on Said's legacy in British letters; Daniel Martin Varisco, *Reading Orientalism: Said and the Unsaid* (Seattle: University of Washington Press, 2007), a summary of all criticism of Said to date; Ibn Warraq, *Defending the West: A Critique of Edward Said's Orientalism* (Amherst, N.Y.: Prometheus, 2007), which stresses the extent to which the Occident has been characterized by the "defining values" of "rationalism, universalism, and self-criticism" (12); and Robert Irwin, *Dangerous Knowledge: Orientalism and Its Discontents* (Woodstock, N.Y.: Overlook, 2006), which tries to retell the story of scholarly Orientalism, with respect mostly to the Arab and Muslim traditions, in a manner less damning to the Orientalists' intentions and attitudes.

48. Edward W. Said, *Orientalism* (New York: Vintage Books, 1978).

49. Said does point out in this context (28)—but how small is a context? how close is close?—the resemblance between anti-Arab Orientalism and Western anti-Semitism, but he does not expand much on this very important insight, for understandable but perhaps not ultimately good enough reasons. He also discusses in this context the idea that the East cannot represent itself, quoting Marx (21), but strikingly he never makes the connection to the tradi-

tion of Christian typology, in terms of which the Jews ultimately need to be represented by the Christians, despite the fact that one of his most admired predecessors is Erich Auerbach, the author of the essay "Figura."

50. Mannheim, for example, argues for engagement in his essay "Historicism" and traces its use also by Troeltsch.

51. In "The Finitude of Method: Mourning Theory from the New Criticism to the New Vitalism" I show how realism and symbolism both share this ontology. The main tradition of German historicism also adopts these symbolist assumptions.

52. Said fails to reflect adequately on the ways in which the methodological (and ontological) dilemmas he faces not only faced the Orientalists but constituted the situation in which it first occurred to them to be interested in the Orient, and formed the character, direction, parameters of their interest in an Orient in the first place. That is, he inadequately reflects on the connections between his object and his method. In still other words: He fails to reflect adequately on the history of his methodological dilemmas, despite the beginning he made in *Beginnings: Intention and Method* (Baltimore: Johns Hopkins University Press, 1975).

53. I would distinguish blame from critique of domination. The former appears intermittently, mixed up with the latter. For example, when Said writes, "In brief, because of Orientalism the Orient was not (and is not) a free subject of thought and action" (*Orientalism*, 3), such a statement removes all responsibility for themselves from the "Oriental" subjects. Of course, elsewhere Said is very critical of contemporary leaders in the Arab Middle East, so he is not one-sided in this matter, but statements like the one just quoted also appear intermittently throughout his writings, statements whose lack of rigor and whose ethical and intellectual inadequacy is striking, and culpably misleading to Said's more credulous readers.

54. Said speaks in *Orientalism*, for example, of Schlegel's "abstractions" (98), of the "general category" that is imposed on the particular (102), of H. A. R. Gibb's way of accusing the Orient of being caught in the "separateness and the individuality of the concrete events" (105), etc.

55. Earlier works that were produced in a relatively apolitical style of history of ideas and "images," such as Raymond Schwab's *La renaissance orientale* (Paris: Payot, 1950), René Gérard's *L'Orient et la pensée romantique allemande* (Paris: Didier, 1963), A. Leslie Wilson's *A Mythical Image: The Ideal of India in German Romanticism* (Durham, N.C.: Duke University Press, 1964), and Wilhelm Halbfass's *India and Europe: An Essay in Understanding* (Albany: State University of New York Press, 1988), nonetheless remain important and useful. Kamakshi P. Murti's innovative work, *Die Reinkarnation des Lesers als Autor: Ein rezeptionsgeschichtlicher Versuch über den Einfluß der altindischen*

Literatur auf deutsche Schriftsteller um 1900 (Berlin: Walter de Gruyter, 1990), applied reception aesthetics insightfully to three German modernists—Wedekind, Feuchtwanger, and Hesse—in their productive reception of classical Indian literature.

56. Dorothy M. Figueira was among the first to explore German Orientalism after Said and to insist (perhaps somewhat too stridently) that the imperialism and colonialism paradigm is not without further ado applicable to the German tradition. See *Translating the Orient: The Reception of Sakuntala in Nineteenth-Century Europe* (Albany: State University of New York Press, 1991), *The Exotic: A Decadent Quest*, and *Aryans, Jews, Brahmins: Theorizing Authority* (Albany: State University of New York Press, 2002). Figueira has usefully reconstructed debates from the late eighteenth century to the present, including Indian reception of Western ideas about the Aryan. In particular the understanding of Orientalism as responding to a crisis of "authority," as she discusses this in the most recent of these books, is closely related to what I theorize as the loss of foundations in its connection with Orientalism.

57. Todd Kontje's *German Orientalisms* (Ann Arbor: University of Michigan Press, 2004) provides an informative and insightful overview of the specifically literary history of German involvements with the Orient from the Middle Ages to the present. Kontje usefully stresses the liminal position of Germany (as "Middle Europe") between East and West, and then understands modern German Orientalism as a function of the German project to construct a national identity as Western, but yet as distinct from Western Europe in the sense of France, England, etc. Like Figueira, and in appealing to the work of Russell Berman and Susanne Zantop, Kontje emphasizes, against Said's sometime one-sidedness, that the German tradition is not uniformly xenophobic but also at times welcomes the stranger and affirms otherness.

58. See Nina Berman, *German Literature on the Middle East: Discourses and Practices, 1000–1989* (Ann Arbor: University of Michigan Press, 2011). Berman argues for the combination of a history of "practices" with a history of literary and cultural "discourses." That is, she polemicizes against the excesses and lingering deleterious effects of the "linguistic turn" and text-centered approaches in principle. She then provides an impressively encyclopedic and informative overview of a very broad range of phenomena—political, economic, cultural—concerning the interactions and exchanges between German and Middle Eastern nations, states, individuals, and so on. Needless to say, I have more sympathy with the "linguistic turn" than she, but I think also that the acute attention to language, and to philosophical questions, need not blind us to important aspects of human history, even if it means that certain details necessarily get magnified to the detriment of many others. My

own focus on the close reading of philosophical, literary, philological, and psychoanalytic texts is at the opposite end of the methodological spectrum from such a work. But it seems to me that—if pluralistic tolerance can still be tolerated—each end of the spectrum has perspectives to offer that are worthy of consideration.

59. In *Der andere Orientalismus: Regeln deutsch–morgenländischer Imagination im 19. Jahrhundert* (Berlin: Walter de Gruyter, 2005), Andrea Polaschegg has produced an intriguing, theoretically sophisticated, and stylistically powerful reading of nineteenth-century German literary Orientalism. She organizes this reading largely around the distinction between two axes, an axis of difference between self and other, and an axis of distance between the familiar and the foreign, which she claims then to historicize. Her polemical point here is that recent studies of Orientalism collapse this distinction and fail to glimpse its historical variability. This distinction, however, which rests on that between the constitution of identity and hermeneutic processes of understanding, strikes me as more fluid than she allows, and this in principle, not just in our own day. Like all versions of the distinction between being and having, the distinction is a difference that tends to undermine itself. Jacques Derrida's analyses of the endless improprieties of the "propre," as concerning the "own," the "clean," "property," and original, literal "meaning," which build on Martin Heidegger's problematically performative and historically unsettling but significant examinations of the play of the "eigen" in *Eigentlichkeit, Ereignis*, and so on, would seem to have made this point irrefutably. To understand is (sooner or later) to identify with, and vice versa. All claims to the contrary can always be assimilated to this structure with a modicum of critically suspicious reflection. What the distinction *does* accomplish, however, despite its illusoriness, is to allow Polaschegg to determine intermediate territories where foreignness and familiarity, or sameness and otherness, overlap or paradoxically coincide. She simply regards these as instances where the foreign is same, or the familiar is other. These intermediate zones are those, in my typologically centered analysis, that function as "figura" between the "littera" or "foreign other" and the "veritas" or "familiar same."

60. Suzanne L. Marchand's *German Orientalism in the Age of Empire: Religion, Race, and Scholarship* (Cambridge: Cambridge University Press, 2009) focuses on scholarly Orientalism. It provides a compendious, insightful, and well-balanced "critical history of the practice of oriental scholarship" (xx) in German-speaking lands. Like all the other authors mentioned, Marchand consciously avoids Said's political reduction of Oriental scholarship to imperialist and colonialist projects and goals without disavowing the great degree to which such scholarship has quite often been implicated in imperialism and colonialism. Resisting presentist modernism, she further rightly emphasizes

the sense in which post-1780 Orientalism remains connected to Reformation and Renaissance concerns, notably biblical criticism and classical antiquity. Although I am more concerned than she with the undermining of foundations that modernity entails and although I stress the specific role of typology in (German) Orientalism more broadly, my emphasis on the continuity of the concern with absolute foundations both before and after the Enlightenment is in accord with Marchand's insistence on certain continuities between early modern and post-Enlightenment Orientalism.

61. See Russell A. Berman's seminal *Enlightenment or Empire: Colonial Discourse in German Culture* (Lincoln: University of Nebraska Press, 1998), and Sara Friedrichsmeyer, Sara Lennox, and Susanne Zantop, eds., *The Imperialist Imagination: German Colonialism and Its Legacy* (Ann Arbor: University of Michigan Press, 1998). On Wilhelmine involvements in Ottoman Turkey, see Sean McMeekin, *The Berlin-Baghdad Express: The Ottoman Empire and Germany's Bid for World Power* (Cambridge, Mass.: Harvard University Press, 2010). See also the catalogue from an exhibition in 2005 at Sanssouci, *Der Traum vom Orient: Kaiser Wilhelm II. im Osmanischen Reich* (Potsdam: Stiftung Preussische Schlösser und Gärten Berlin–Brandenburg, 2005); and the interesting study of German views of Eastern Europe, Vejas Gabriel Liulevicius, *The German Myth of the East: 1800 to the Present* (Oxford: Oxford University Press, 2009).

62. Although Halbfass's *India and Europe* is useful, it is surprising the degree to which the question of anti-Semitism disappears from view, except in the most egregious cases where it cannot possibly be ignored (such as Gobineau or Rosenberg). In the Festschrift that was recently dedicated to his legacy, *Sanskrit and "Orientalism": Indology and Comparative Linguistics in Germany, 1750–1958*, ed. Douglas T. McGetchin, Peter K. J. Park, and D. R. SarDesai (New Delhi: Manohar, 2004), in which the question of the applicability of Said's perspective is a vital one, Halbfass does argue against making German Indology an exception to the rule of Orientalism as imperialism, which is a good start. On the role of German Indology in colonization and domination, see Sheldon Pollock, "Deep Orientalism? Notes on Sanskrit and Power beyond the Raj," in *Orientalism and the Postcolonial Predicament: Perspectives on South Asia*, ed. Carol A. Breckenridge and Peter van der Veer (Philadelphia: University of Pennsylvania Press, 1993), 76–133.

1. ORDERING CHAOS: THE ORIENT IN J. G. HERDER'S TELEOLOGICAL HISTORICISM

1. Jeffrey S. Librett, "How Does One Orient Oneself in Giving? Cultural-Political and Theological Implications of Problematic Generosity in Lessing's *Nathan der Weise*," *Lessing Yearbook* 35 (2003): 35–60; Jeffrey S. Librett,

"Destabilizing Typologies: Jewish Works, Christian Faith, and the Passage from Orient to Occident in G. E. Lessing's *Ernst und Falk: Gespräche für Freimaurer*," *Germanic Review* 78, no. 4 (2003): 301–18; Jeffrey S. Librett, "Preventing Historicism: G. E. Lessing's 'Grounding' of the Spirit of Religion and Family (*Nathan the Wise* and *The Education of the Human Race*)," in circulation. On Herder's contestation of Lessing's notion of transmigration in the text "Palingenesie: Vom Wiederkommen menschlicher Seelen," see René Gérard, *L'orient et la pensée romantique allemande* (Paris: Marcel Didier, 1963), 49–51.

2. Jeffrey S. Librett, "What Does It Mean: To Orient Oneself in the Want of Reason? Kant's Critique of Herder (from Regulative Teleology to Racism)," in circulation.

3. Unless otherwise indicated, references to Herder in German concern *Werke in zehn Bänden*, ed. Martin Bollacher et al. (Frankfurt am Main: Deutscher Klassiker Verlag, 1989). "Ideen zur Philosophie der Geschichte der Menschheit" in volume 6 is cited by pages parenthetically in the text, first the German, then the English edition, the latter in Johann Gottfried Herder, *On World History: An Anthology*, ed. Hans Adler and Ernest A. Menze, trans. Ernest A. Menze with Michael Palma (Armonk, N.Y.: M. E. Sharpe, 1997). I provide my own translations of all Herder passages, and I give the page numbers of the corresponding passages in the Menze and Palma translation for reference and comparison.

4. Raymond Schwab, *The Oriental Renaissance: Europe's Rediscovery of India and the East, 1680–1880*, trans. Gene Patterson-Black and Victor Reinking (New York: Columbia University Press, 1984).

5. On Herder's writings as constitution of the romantic myth of India, see A. Leslie Wilson, *A Mythical Image: The Ideal of India in German Romanticism* (Durham, N.C.: Duke University Press, 1964), 49–72.

6. This fact can become obscured by Herder's defense of Spinoza in *God: Some Conversations* (1787), but one must not forget that the defense is accompanied by a refusal of Spinoza's rejection of teleology.

7. Kant's response to the Spinoza debates (a response in which he is critical of Jacobi's irrationalism as well as of Spinoza's determinism) is intimately bound up with his response to Herder's philosophy of history, in which Kant likewise criticizes Herder's irrationalism while saving teleology in a "regulative" mode. Both of these responses belong to Kant's attempt to question rationalism as well as antirationalism, dogmatic metaphysics as well as empiricism (and traditionalist irrationalism, which often accompanies German empiricism in this period), and to point out the ways in which metaphysics and empiricism ultimately and unwittingly serve each other's interests, although they remain in principle mutually opposed. For a useful summary of the

debate, see Manfred Riedel, "Historismus und Kritizismus: Kants Streit mit G. Forster und J. G. Herder," *Kant-Studien* 72, no. 1 (1981): 41–57.

8. Benedict de Spinoza, *A Spinoza Reader: The Ethics and Other Works*, ed. and trans. Edwin Curley (Princeton: Princeton University Press, 1994), 110. Hereafter page references are given parenthetically in text.

9. In other words, "incomplete nihilism" will consist for Nietzsche in the stubborn maintenance of the teleological impulse in the face of its failure.

10. Kant tries to sidestep this problem by proposing not only a regulative but a non-eudaemonistic teleology, for which latter emphasis Herder and many subsequent critics (from Schiller on) will take him to task.

11. More precisely, Jacobi uses the word "nihilism" with reference to Fichte's philosophy, which he considers an inverted Spinozism, as is well known.

12. Herder's position contrasts starkly with Kant's ultimate transcendental inscription of teleology—splitting the middle between dogmatic teleology and its dogmatic negation—as a regulative, rather than a constitutive, principle. Kant prepares this development in his essays of the mid to late 1780s on philosophy of history and on the pantheism panic. Then he treats it most fully in the section of the *Critique of Judgment* (1790) titled the "Critique of Teleological Judgment."

13. Kant complains in his reviews about these rhetorical means, both in general terms and with some examples, but he makes no specific reference to the preface per se. And his own attempt to escape figural rhetoric and sophistical argumentation remains itself problematic.

14. At the same time, it performs the "spontaneity" of his appeal to the reader, the "natural" lack of manipulativeness in his address.

15. The passage is striking because it seems to "anticipate" texts such as Kafka's fragments on the building of the tower of Babel (see chapter 8 below) or Walter Benjamin's figure of the stormwinds of history piling more and more ruins up in front of the angel of history, who is blown backward into the future.

16. See Herder, "Ideen zur Philosophie der Geschichte der Menschheit," book 15, chapter 1, titled "Humanity Is the Purpose of Human Nature and God Delivered, with This Purpose, His Own Fate into the Hands of This [Human] Race."

17. See Herder, "Ideen zur Philosophie der Geschichte der Menschheit," book 12, chapter 6, "Further Ideas about the Philosophy of Human History" (*Weitere Ideen zur Philosophie der Menschengeschichte*): "Alles, was sein kann, ist: alles, was werden kann, wird; wo nicht heut, so morgen" (510; 272).

18. Herder emphasizes that he has sought his philosophy of the history of humanity not through "metaphysical speculations" (16; 113) but by "reading

the fate of humanity out of the book of creation" (16; 113), that is, by "experience and analogies of nature" (16; 113–14). Empiricism and faith are here melded together, in that "everywhere the great analogy of nature has led me to the truths of religion" (17; 114). In this enterprise, Herder speaks of God's intentions through a strategy of "personification" of "nature" or "organic forces" (17; 114) meant ostensibly to avoid using God's name in vain. Instead of "Adonai," Herder says "Natur," and thus "realizes" the Jewish gesture as a panentheistic variant of Lutheran piety (17; 114).

19. He also—with an astonishing explicitness—reads Genesis here as a prefigurative "philosophy of history," which he claims to realize by stripping it of its ornamental language. "A glance at it [*or its glance at us: Ihr Anblick*] should tell us what these brief, simple leaves want to be and can be, in that we will see them not as history but as tradition or as an old *philosophy of human history*, which I therefore also immediately strip of its Oriental poetic jewelry" (*die ich deswegen auch sogleich von ihrem morgenländischen poetischen Schmuck entkleide*) (402–3; 212). The ornaments of Oriental language (*morgenländischen poetischen Schmuck*) are now marked as bad, in the sense of excessively material, whereas in the preface, Oriental ornamentation (*Morgenschmuck*) was marked as good, in the sense of early fullness. This ambivalence has to mark the historical "origin" (and the linguistic vehicle of meaning's origination) all along the line.

20. The artificiality of human culture—which Herder emphasizes in this context, repeatedly using the word "künstlich"—becomes precisely the reason why nature had to bring us forth in one place where a single language and tradition could be given to us as a revelatory education. That is, in granting artificiality, Herder disavows it in naturalizing and Christianizing terms.

21. Despite the fact that Herder in principle contests Kant's racial theory, we should not forget that Herder is equally racist in particulars, as Maurice Olender points out in *The Languages of Paradies: Race, Religion, and Philology in the Nineteenth Century* (Cambridge, Mass.: Harvard University Press, 1992), 45–46. Olender quotes Herder as writing that nature "placed the Black next to the ape" and polemicizing against Africans as sensuous but lacking "nobler gifts" and so on. René Gérard corroborates this view in *L'orient et la pensée romantique allemande* (Paris: Marcel Didier, 1963), 58–59.

22. The vocal metaphor rhymes with Herder's unsurprisingly phonocentric approach to the Orient in general: For example, he considers the myths of other parts of the world to be "strewn [or diasporic] sounds of lost echo as opposed to the voice of the Asiatic origin-world, which loses itself in fable" (*zerstreute Laute der verirreten Echo gegen die Stimme der Asiatischen Urwelt, die sich in die Fabel verliert*) (396–97; 208).

23. Concerning the mention of "the invention of language" here, let me note in passing that in this text Herder takes the opposite position on the origin of language from the one he took in his earlier treatise, *Origin of Language*. Whereas he had argued there for a human invention of language, now he argues that language and reason are a divine gift. See Frederick Beiser, *The Fate of Reason: German Philosophy from Kant to Fichte* (Cambridge, Mass.: Harvard University Press, 1987), chap. 5, "Herder's Philosophy of Mind," 127–64, esp. 130–40; and Jürgen Trabant, "Herder and Language," in *A Companion to the Works of Johann Gottfried Herder*, ed. Hans Adler and Wulf Koepke (Rochester, N.Y.: Camden House, 2009), 117–39. Trabant usefully underlines Herder's positive contribution to the modern recognition of the embeddedness of thought in language.

24. "The Mosaic tradition, however, cuts off this chaos and represents immediately the cliff; also those chaotic monsters and miraculous forms of the older tradition go thereby into the abyss" (*Die Mosaische Tradition schneidet aber auch dies Chaos ab und schildert sogleich den Felsen; auch jene chaotischen Ungeheuer und Wundergestalten der ältern Traditionen gehen damit in den Abgrund*) (403; 212).

25. The ambiguity of "pregnant with life"—suggesting death about to produce life, or efficient causality about to give rise to final causality—encapsulates the uncanny status of the "dead letter" that speaks.

26. Cf. Franz Rosenzweig, "The Hebrew Bible's Direct Influence on Goethe's Language," in Martin Buber and Franz Rosenzweig, *Scripture and Translation*, trans. Lawrence Rosenwald and Everett Fix (Bloomington: Indiana University Press, 1994), 70–72. Rosenzweig discusses Goethe's translation of the verb in the passage as "brooding," and Herder's earlier text on the "Oldest Document of Humankind" as using the translation "hovers," which suggests that there was some influence passing between Herder and Goethe in the 1780s concerning this passage, but which does not clarify which way (or ways) various aspects of the influence may have gone. Rosenzweig cites Rashi as one medieval Jewish authority who indeed supports the translation as "broods," but he nowhere entertains the vitalist-biological vocabulary Herder employs in *Ideas*. For Martin Buber's discussion of the translation of this passage ("Braus Gottes schwingend über dem Antlitz der Wasser"), see "People Today and the Jewish Bible: From a Lecture Series," in *Scripture and Tradition*, 5–21, especially 14–18. Buber, too, attempts to see *ruach* as "neither natural nor spiritual but both in one; it is the creative breathing that brings both nature and spirit into being" (15).

27. For example: "They lack motivation [*Triebfedern*]: for ancient habit [*uralte Gewohnheit*] works against every new motivation. How slowly even Europe learned its best arts!" (462; 248).

28. Note that the term "hieroglyphics" takes on much more positive connotations in early romanticism and is often employed there as a metaphor for interesting poetical texts.

29. Herder seems to be objecting to Leibniz's attempt to renew such hieroglyphic character-languages when he writes: "All hieroglyph-wisdom of more modern times is thus a stubborn block against all freer Enlightenment, because in the older times themselves hieroglyphics was always only the most imperfect writing" (505–6; 268). See Julia Ching and Willard G. Oxtoby, eds., *Discovering China: European Interpretations in the Enlightenment* (Rochester, N.Y.: University of Rochester Press, 1992), especially 82–117.

30. But the Chinese are nonetheless one step further than the Egyptians, as Herder writes in the chapter on Egypt: "The Chinese themselves advance further than the Egyptians, developing from similar hieroglyphs real thought-characters, to which the latter, as it appears, never attained" (504; 267). Herder is responding here to the debate between Joseph de Guignes, who argued that Chinese culture was an offshoot of Egyptian culture, and Cornelius de Pauw, who opposed him.

31. The Native Americans, in contrast, are relegated to an inferior status in connection with their "hieroglyphic" languages. "Hieroglyphs represent the earliest untaught attempt of the human mind in its infancy seeking symbols to express its thoughts; the most primitive savages of America had hieroglyphs sufficient for their needs" (504; 267).

32. Dorothy Figueira, *The Exotic: A Decadent Quest* (Albany: State University of New York Press, 1994), 21–24, 51–52.

33. See Christoph Bultmann, "Herder's Biblical Studies," in *A Companion to the Works of J. G. Herder*, ed. Hans Adler and Wulf Koepke (Rochester, N.Y.: Camden House, 2009), 233–46. On Herder's idealization of the ancient Hebrew constitution in *Vom Geist der hebräischen Poesy* (1782–83), the flip side of the disparagement of medieval and modern Jewry, see "The Political Theory of J. G. Herder," in Frederick Beiser, *Enlightenment, Revolution, and Romanticism: The Genesis of Modern German Political Thought, 1790–1800* (Cambridge, Mass.: Harvard University Press, 1992), 189–221, esp. 213–14. For a defense of Herder against Paul Lawrence Rose, see Ernest A. Menze, "Herder's 'German Kind of "Humanity"' and the Jewish Question: Historical Context and Contemporary Criticism," in *Johann Gottfried Herder: Geschichte und Kultur*, ed. Martin Bollacher (Würzburg: Königshausen und Neumann, 1994), 213–28. Menze errs in the opposite direction, however, by downplaying Herder's participation in anti-Jewish discourse.

34. Herder asserts that "outside Palestine there ought not to be any Jews" (*so dürfte es außer Palestina keinen Juden mehr geben*) (512; 273) and that the Jews have been "nearly since their origin a parasitic plant on the stems

of other nations" (*eine parasitäre Pflanze auf den Stämmen andrer Nationen*) (492; 263). The development, which manifestly feels itself parasitic upon the origin, here calls the origin parasitic, in order to externalize its own parasitic dimension (a universal one). And the appropriated origin becomes parasitic here through its very appropriation.

35. For example, Herder writes that it does not come from the sun but is

> a light that breaks out of the interior of this organic mass. . . . It is not the rays of the sun that give and nourish the life of creatures; with inner warmth all is impregnated . . . the first elementary flame . . . the separating force, the warming balsam of nature . . . which gradually sets everything in motion [*ein Licht, das aus dem innern dieser organischen Masse hervorbricht. . . . Nicht die Strahlen der Sonne sinds, die allen Geschöpfen das Leben geben und nähren; mit innerer Wärme ist alles geschwängert . . . die erste elementarische Flamme . . . die scheidende Kraft, der wärmende Balsam der Natur . . . der alles allmählich in Bewegung setzte*].
> (404; 213)

36. "The fire developed and then bound again, the living forces are limited by organizations and then freed again" (*das Feuer entwickelt und wieder gebunden, die legendigen Kräfte mit Organisationen beschränkt und wieder befreiet werden*) (410; 217).

37. After the end of the first creation—that is, after God has begun to rest, when evolution ceases, so to speak—"the whole creation lives off of each other/itself" (*die ganze Schöpfung lebt jetzt von einander*) (410; 217), and "the wheel of the creatures runs around, without adding anything to itself" (*das Rad der Geschöpfe läuft umher, ohne daß es hinzutue*) (410; 217). In the form of this closed circuit, the "artwork" of creation is the field in which the chaotic forces of nature pass from containment to freedom and back again.

38. Cf. the useful discussion of Herder by Todd Kontje in *German Orientalisms* (Ann Arbor: University of Michigan Press, 2004), 64–82, which traces, like Olender (see the following note), the tensions between Herder's linear narrative of history and his emphasis on organic individuality of cultures.

39. See Maurice Olender, *The Languages of Paradise: Race, Religion, and Philology in the Nineteenth Century*, trans. Arthur Goldhammer (Cambridge, Mass.: Harvard University Press, 1992), 31–50: "When Herder's cultural pluralism ran up against his Christianity, it metamorphosed into a history of religion with undisguised priorities" (44, 49).

40. See John Boeing's "Herder and the White Man's Burden: The *Ideen zur Philosophe der Geschichte der Menschheit* and the Shaping of British Colonial Policy," in *Johann Gottfried Herder: Language, History, and the Enlighten-

ment, ed. Wulf Koepke (Columbia, S.C.: Camden House, 1990), 236–45. On Herder's anticolonialism in its uncomfortable combination with his racism, see Gérard, *L'orient et la pensée romantique allemande*, 62.

2. FIGURALIZING THE ORIENTAL, LITERALIZING THE JEW: FROM LETTER TO SPIRIT IN FRIEDRICH SCHLEGEL'S ON THE LANGUAGE AND WISDOM OF THE INDIANS

1. Friedrich Schlegel, *Über die Sprache und Weisheit der Indier*, in *Studien zur Philosophie und Theologie*, ed. Ernst Behler and Ursula Struc-Oppenberg (Munich: Ferdinand Schöningh, 1975) 105–433, vol. 8 of *Kritische Friedrich-Schlegel-Ausgabe* (hereafter referred to as *KA*), ed. Ernst Behler, Jean-Jacques Anstett, and Hans Eichner. Translations of this and other texts are my own. For a useful overview of literary German romantic Orientalism, specifically concerning India, see *A Mythical Image: The Ideal of India in German Romanticism* (Durham, N.C.: Duke University Press, 1964), and on Schlegel, 199–220. For an overview of German philosophical approaches to India, see Helmuth von Glasenapp, *Das Indienbild deutscher Denker* (Stuttgart: K. F. Koehler Verlag, 1960).

2. The concept of "supplement" has been developed by Jacques Derrida at some length, especially in *De la grammatologie* (Paris: Éditions de Minuit, 1967).

3. See my *The Rhetoric of Cultural Dialogue: Jews and Germans from Moses Mendelssohn to Richard Wagner and Beyond* (Stanford: Stanford University Press, 2000).

4. For an excellent discussion of the place of *Über die Sprache und Weisheit der Indier* within the development of Schlegel's career, see René Gérard, *L'Orient et la pensée romantique allemande* (Paris: Didier, 1963). Gérard characterizes the text on India as the moment when Schlegel begins to discover that the Orient will not satisfy his desire for a historically given purity that would exceed the purity of the Judaeo-Christian tradition. Gérard does not, however, explore in detail the language-theoretical or rhetorical dimensions of Schlegel's text. For a useful review article on this book, along with other contributions to the topic in the 1960s, see Ernst Behler, "Das Indienbild der deutschen Romantik," *Germanisch-Romanische Monatsschrift* 18 (January 1968): 21–37. On Schlegel's Orientalism within the context of modern philology, see Suzanne L. Marchand, *German Orientalism in the Age of Empire: Religion, Race, and Scholarship* (Cambridge: Cambridge University Press, 2009), 58–65.

5. On political and theological dimensions of Schlegel's concern with ancient India, see Raymond Schwab's important work originally published in French in 1950, *The Oriental Renaissance: Europe's Rediscovery of India and*

the East, 1680–1880, trans. Gene Patterson-Black and Victor Reinking (New York: Columbia University Press, 1984), 67–78, here 76. On Orientalism in German romantic literature in general, see especially 203–21.

6. See, for example, Schlegel's early essays "Georg Forster" and "Über Lessing, in *Charakteristiken und Kritiken I* (1796–1801), ed. Hans Eichner (Munich: Ferdinand Schöningh, 1967), 78–99 and 100–126, vol. 2 of *KA*. Especially in "Über Lessing," Schlegel's sense of the work as fragment is derived in large part from the problematization of works in Lessing's writings. On the complex relationship between Schlegel and the Enlightenment in these essays, see Hans Eichner, *Friedrich Schlegel* (New York: Twayne, 1970), 32–34.

7. See Gérard, *L'Orient et la pensée romantique allemande,* especially the section "Les idées politiques de 1805 et l'Orient," 107–9.

8. See Alfred von Martin, "Romantische Konversionen," *Logos* 8 (1928): 141–64.

9. Cf. Philippe Lacoue-Labarthe and Jean-Luc Nancy, with the collaboration of Anne-Martin Lang, *L'absolu littéraire: Théorie de la literature du romantisme allemande* (Paris: Éditions du Seuil, 1978), 181–205. In English: *The Literary Absolute: The Theory of Literature in German Romanticism,* trans. and ed. Philip Barnard and Cheryl Lester (New York: State University of New York Press, 1988) 59–78.

10. For Schlegel's views on the relations between church and state in this period, see *Vorlesungen über Universalgeschichte (1805–6),* ed. Jean-Jacques Anstett (Munich: Ferdinand Schöningh, 1960), especially 151–57, 165–74, 211–17, 253–56, vol. 14 of *KA*.

11. Moses Mendelssohn, *Schriften zum Judentum,* ed. Alexander Altmann (Stuttgart-Bad Cannstatt: Friedrich Frommann Verlag, 1983), vol. 8 of *Gesammelte Schriften, Jubiläumsausgabe,* ed. Fr. Bamberger et al. (Stuttgart-Bad Cannstatt: Friedrich Frommann Verlag, 1971–).

12. This structural possibility has indeed given rise on occasion (for example, in Benno von Wiese and Jean-Jacques Anstett) to the argument that Dorothea was one of the main impulses behind Friedrich's conversion. But, in fact, at least some time prior to her Catholic conversion, during her Protestant phase, Dorothea saw Catholicism as close—indeed, too close—to Judaism, as a religion focused on ritual law and works. She wrote in a letter to Schleiermacher in 1802 (quoted in Ernst Behler's "Einleitung" to *KA* 8: cxviii, and discussed also in von Martin, "Romantische Konversionen," 146) that Catholicism had "too much similarity with the old Judaism," while Protestantism seemed to her "entirely the religion of Jesus . . . and the religion of culture [*Bildung*]," and that thus, "In my heart, I am entirely Protestant,"

which is not surprising, since the Protestantism by which she was surrounded defined itself as the religion of the heart as such.

13. Just as, according to the Schlegel's *Vorlesungen über Universalgeschichte*, Dominicans and Franciscans had already played out the distinction between Jewish letter and Protestant/Christian spirit within Catholicism itself (156–57).

14. "Since in general all science is genetic, it follows that history is the most universal, most general, and highest of all sciences. . . . History in this sense has merely the human being himself as its object. . . . Therefore moral development, to which above all religion and politics belong, is the actual object of universal history [*der eigentliche Gegenstand der Universalhistorie*]" (*Vorlesungen über Universalgeschichte*, 3).

15. See Immanuel Kant, *Kritik der reinen Vernunft*, vol. 4 of *Werkausgabe*, ed. Wilhelm Weischedel (Frankfurt: Suhrkamp, 1974), 695–99.

16. It is quite striking to remark the sharp contrast between Schlegel's suspicion of "mixing" in this later text and his affirmation, indeed his exaltation, of "mixing" in the earlier work of the *Athenäum* phase, e.g., the famous *Athenäum* fragment 116 on romantic poetry as progressive universal poetry, as well as fragments 239 and 448 (*KA* 2:182, 205, 254).

17. Schlegel is extending, but also displacing, suspending, or destroying here his earlier notion of "reflexion": From "Reflexion" we have moved to "Flexion" as the guiding concept. But what is missing from this doctrine of "Flexion" is the chemical mediation between identity (or the organic) and difference (or the mechanical). It is as if the "Re" of "Reflexion" had been lopped off, its heart finally circumcised, the difference and doubling that characterize "Re-flexion" effaced in favor of a self-identical unfolding of pure continuity. It is no longer the case that "understanding is mechanical spirit, wit is chemical spirit, genius is organic spirit [*Verstand ist mechanischer, Witz ist chemischer, Genie ist organischer Geist*]" (*Athenäum* fragment 366 [*KA* 2:232]). Chemical spirit has been absorbed into mechanical spirit, and the break between mechanical and organic must now be dogmatically posited as absolute.

18. In the wake of Kant, the organic is generally opposed to the mechanical, as the living to the dead, in terms of the opposition between reason and understanding as developed in Kant's three *Critiques*. On the tension between organic and mechanical in the background of Schlegel's thought, see Frederick Beiser, *The Fate of Reason: German Philosophy from Kant to Fichte* (Cambridge, Mass.: Harvard University Press, 1987).

19. The general ideological force and cultural-political implications of Schlegel's distinction between organic and mechanical languages have been

briefly discussed by Said and Bernal. However, neither of these scholars has closely examined the workings of Schlegel's text, never mind explored its local philosophical, psychoanalytic, and theopolitical "contextual" elements or determinants, or attempted to elucidate—by way of an "internal" reading—the ontorhetorical "foundations" of the culturally political level of ideology in Schlegel's discourse. For Said's correct characterization of the general arbitrariness of Schlegel's distinction between organic and mechanical languages, see *Orientalism* (New York: Vintage, 1978), 98–99, 115. For Bernal's generally convincing inscription of Schlegel's position on ancient Indian culture within a striking (not to say horrifying) narrative of a (racially motivated) displacement, throughout the nineteenth century, of Egypt by India as image of the origin of the Greco-Roman West, see *The Fabrication of Ancient Greece, 1785–1985* (New Brunswick, N.J.: Rutgers University Press, 1987), 230–33, vol. 1 of *Black Athena: The Afroasiatic Roots of Classical Civilization*, 2 vols.

20. Schlegel is thus distancing himself from Herder's theory to the extent that Schlegel posits two different origins of language, one for the mechanical, and another for the organic language(s), the former being an origin in the imitative cry of the animals, the latter in the pure knowledge of *Besonnenheit*, the prosaic light of an original revelation.

21. Dorothy Figueira, in *The Exotic: A Decadent Quest* (Albany: State University of New York Press, 1994), 55–62, has attempted to contest the ways in which Said and Bernal have developed a critical political perspective on Schlegel. While rightly pointing out that, in their haste, they do not always do justice to the particulars of a given author, text, or context, Figueira in turn exaggerates and oversimplifies when she says, for example, that in Said's work, "all Orientalists become indistinguishable" (56) and that "they are static, fixed, and artificial objects of Said's own discourse" (56). Her admirable concern with particularity does make it possible, however, for her to remind us of certain useful facts about the context of Schlegel's interest in India: For example, as Schlegel indeed indicates at the end of the Preface, his third oldest brother, Karl August Schlegel, had died there in 1789. This is no doubt one more good reason for Schlegel to have been both interested in India and ambivalent, such that it was difficult for him to decide whether it was a culture of life or death.

22. Although Schlegel acknowledges that this ought by rights to include some treatment of Indian "mythology," he excuses himself from undertaking such a treatment both because of the lack of available scholarly philological materials and because "mythology is the most entangled artifact of the human spirit [*das verflochtenste Gebilde des menschlichen Geistes*]; infinitely rich, but also highly changeable in its meaning, whereas meaning is alone the essential thing.... The sense, the meaning is alone the essential thing, and how this

forms itself nearly always and everywhere differently! [*der Sinn, die Bedeutung ist doch eigentlich allein wesentlich, und wie gestaltet sich diese fast immer und überall anders?*]" (*Über die Sprache und Weisheit der Indier*, 195). By putting the problem in this way, Schlegel manifests quite clearly once again that his concern at this phase of his career is with spirit and meaning, with respect to which the letter has become merely "inessential," secondary, fallen.

23. Moses Mendelssohn, *Schriften zur Philosophie und Ästhetik*, ed. Leo Strauss (Stuttgart-Bad Cannstatt: Friedrich Frommann Verlag, 1974), 1–176, here 114–24, vol. 3, part 2 of *Gesammelte Schriften, Jubiläumsausgabe*, ed. F. Bamberger et al. (Stuttgart-Bad Cannstatt: Friedrich Frommann Verlag, 1971–74).

24. I assume that the historical reliability of Schlegel's argument is so problematic as hardly to merit serious discussion. Cf. Gérard's discussion (*L'Orient et la pensée romantique allemande*, 121–27) of Schlegel's gradual disillusionment when he realized that his schema of the history of Indian thought was not historically substantiated.

25. Cf. Schlegel's discussions of Jacobi in "Jacobis Woldemar" (*KA* 2:57–77), and in "Über F. H. Jacobi: Von den göttlichen Dingen und ihrer Offenbarung. 1812" (*KA* 8:441–58).

26. Schlegel characterizes (*Über die Sprache und Weisheit der Indier*, 229–31) the symmetrical dilemmas of emanationism (as a version of idealism) and pantheism as follows: On the one hand, in positing a difference between identity and difference, emanationism sanctions the reality, self-identity, and quasi substantiality of difference, and thus destroys the unity of the world. It denies differences in the sense of the crossing-from-the-same-to-the-other, leaving only the same of the good and the same (difference) of the evil, separated by an abyss with no possibility of mediation. On the other hand, the problem with pantheism is that, in denying the difference between identity and difference, it gives rise to a total dominion of difference, so that there is nothing but crossing left, but no terms between which to cross. The difference between idealism and pantheism, then, is that idealism posits difference and thereby destroys difference, while pantheism posits identity and thereby destroys it. The doctrine of the two principles is supposed to mediate between these two extremes, but it in effect repeats the position of emanationism. The position midway between idealism and materialism is never actually formulated by Schlegel within this treatise.

27. For example: "When pantheism ... appears as a system, it is never as anything other than such a mere combinative play of positive and negative [*nie etwas anders als ein solches nach einem bloßen Kombinationsspiel aus einem Positiven und Negativen*]" (*Über die Sprache und Weisheit der Indier*, 247). Pantheism is the mechanical game of positive and negative, not unlike Schlegel's

own rather mechanical opposition between the "positive" infinity of emanationism and the "negative" infinity of pantheism (217).

28. For example: "Meanwhile, one would completely misunderstand me if one believed that I wanted to exalt the one main language type exclusively, and denigrate the other in an unconditional fashion. . . . Who can deny the high art, the dignity and sublime power of the Arabic and Hebrew languages? They stand incontrovertibly on the highest pinnacle of formation and perfection *in their type*, to which they furthermore do not belong so exclusively that they should not in various respects approach the other type. But that this art was propped onto the old raw stem, in part violently, is something that those experts most familiar with these languages have often expressed" (163, emphasis added, and see also 185–87). Propping or grafting of the artful organicity of the inflected languages onto the mechanical ones reflects here nolens volens the propping or grafting of Schlegel as German onto the Hebraic family stem of the Mendelssohn-Veits through Friedrich's union with Dorothea.

29. It is here that Schelling will intervene when he argues, with repeated reference to Schlegel's text on ancient Indian culture and other texts by Schlegel from the same period, that evil is not merely nothing but has indeed a positive presence in the world, for which Schlegel fails in his text on ancient India to account. Friedrich Wilhelm Joseph Schelling, *Philosophische Untersuchungen über das Wesen der menschlichen Freiheit und die damit zusammenhängenden Gegenstände*, in *Schriften von 1806–1813* (Darmstadt: Wissenschaftliche Buchgesellschaft, 1968), 275–360, vol. 9 of *Ausgewählte Werke*. See especially 282, 293, 296, 353.

3. GOETHE'S ORIENTALIZING MOMENT (I): "NOTES AND TREATISES FOR THE BETTER UNDERSTANDING OF THE WEST-EAST DIVAN"

1 See Dorothy Figueira, *The Exotic: A Decadent Quest* (Albany: State University of New York Press, 1994), 63–89.

2. All references to the *West-Östlicher Divan* are from Erich Trunz, ed., *Goethes Werke*, Hamburger Ausgabe in 14 Bänden (Munich: C. H. Beck Verlag, 1982), II: *Gedichte und Epen II*. Page numbers are given parenthetically in text. Translations from the "Notes and Treatises" are mine. Translations of the poems are from J. W. von Goethe, *Poems of the West and East (West-Eastern Divan—West-Östlicher Divan): Bilingual Edition of the Complete Poems*, trans. John Whaley (Bern: Peter Lang, 1998).

3. In "Goethe und die geschichtliche Welt" (in Ernst Cassirer, *Goethe und die geschichtliche Welt*, ed. Rainer A. Bast [Hamburg: Felix Meiner Verlag, 1995], 1–26), Cassirer demonstrates this skepticism (6–8). On Goethe's historical skepticism treated within an insightful analysis of the Goethean "mo-

ment" in *Faust*, see Nicholas Rennie, *Speculating on the Moment: The Poetics of Time and Recurrence in Goethe, Leopardi, and Nietzsche* (Göttingen: Wallstein Verlag, 2005), 64–91. See also E. Menke-Glückert, *Goethes Geschichtsphilosophie* (Leipzig: R. Voigtländer Verlag, 1907).

4. See Hugh Barr Nisbet, "Naturgeschichte und Humangeschichte bei Goethe, Herder und Kant," in *Goethe und die Verzeitlichung der Natur*, ed. Peter Matussek (Munich: Beck, 1998), 15–43.

5. Ibid., 38–41.

6. Ibid., 38, 40.

7. Ibid., 19–21, 27–30.

8. Ibid., 29.

9. "Jede Epoche ist unmittelbar zu Gott, und ihr Wert beruht gar nicht auf dem, was aus ihr hervorgeht, sondern in ihrer Existenz selbst." In Leopold von Ranke, *Weltgeschichte: Neunter Theil, zweite Abtheilung: Über die Epochen der neueren Geschichte: Vorträge dem Könige Maximilian von Bayern gehalten*, ed. Alfred Dove (Leipzig: Duncker and Humblot, 1888), 5.

10. Cassirer characteristically misquotes Goethe here as saying that he had the gift "die 'Vergangenheit und Gegenwart in eins zu sehen'" (12), which turns a feeling into a seeing, rendering it under the masterful control of the gaze of knowledge.

11. For an overview of recent criticism on Orientalism in the *West-East Divan*, see Volker C. Dörr, "Orient und Okzident: Der *West-Östliche Divan* als postkoloniales Paradigma," *Goethe Yearbook* 16 (2009): 219–33. Dörr argues ultimately, and not entirely without plausibility, that the "Notes and Treatises" contain more Orientalism than the poetry, but he idealizes the poetry in the process. Karl J. Fink, "Goethe's West-Östlicher Divan: Orientalism Restructured," *International Journal of Middle East Studies* 14, no. 3 (1982): 315–28, reads Goethe, too apologetically, as anticipating Said's skepticism about "authority"; Andrea Fuchs-Sumiyoshi, in *Orientalismus in der deutschen Literatur: Untersuchungen zu Werken des 19. und 20. Jahrhunderts, von Goethes West-Östlichem Divan bis Thomas Manns Joseph-Tetralogie* (Hildesheim: Georg Olms Verlag, 1984), stresses the literary-intellectual nature of Goethe's interest in the Orient; Mirjam Weber, in *Der, wahre Poesie-Orient': Eine Untersuchung zur Orientalismus-Theorie Edward Saids am Beispiel von Goethes, West-Östlichem Divan' und der Lyrik Heines* (Wiesbaden: Harrassowitz Verlag, 2001), suggests Said's position is one-sided, and that the West is changed through its encounter with the East. None of these positions engage with groundlessness or with typology. On the *Divan* as critique of anti-Napoleonic *Freiheitslyrik*, see Monika Lemmel, *Poetologie in Goethe's West-Östlichem Divan* (Heidelberg: Carl Winter Universitätsverlag, 1987). Walter Veit, "Goethe's Fantasies about the Orient," *Eighteenth-Century Life* 26, no. 3 (2002):

164–80, sees Goethe's turn to the Orient as motivated by his desire to flee the "turmoil" (165) of his day. For a media-theoretical approach to the *Divan*, see Gerhart von Graevenitz, *Das Ornament des Blicks: Über die Grundlagen des neuzeitlichen Sehens, die Poetik der Arabeske und Goethes "West-Östlichen Divan"* (Stuttgart: Verlag J. B. Metzler, 1994).

12. The fact that he begins by quoting the Old Testament already indicates the predicament and project: How will he appropriate his voice (as presence) from the (Hebraic/Judaic) otherness in which the voice begins?

13. The great aestheticizing modernist readings like those of Friedrich Gundolf (*Goethe* [Berlin: Georg Bondi, 1922], 638–70) or Max Kommerell (*Gedanken über Gedichte* [Frankfurt am Main: V. Klostermann, 1943], 249–318) recognize the metaphysical dimension, but they credulously overemphasize the success with which Goethe attains his metaphysical goals and an auratic work in Walter Benjamin's sense.

14. Moreover, the summary does not only present the cycle as it now stands (in the 1819 edition), but also anticipates its future completion. It thus eradicates in advance (as intention) the current incompleteness of the cycle.

15. The letter from the wife of the Emperor of Persia to the Emperor Mother of Russia engages two themes to which we will return below: the exchange of gifts as constitutive of unity insofar as it bridges the distance between activity and passivity (or spontaneity and receptivity of subject and object) and the "Eastern" rhetoric of hyperbole and yoked comparisons.

16. Indeed, in the "Revision," which proceeds upon the "Conclusion" and repeats it, Goethe's explicit concern is with how the letters of the Western alphabets should spell correctly the sounds of the names from different, Eastern alphabets: The continuity of letter and (phonic) spirit is the concern with which the *Divan* closes. On Goethe's imitation of the Arabic script, see Andrea Polaschegg, *Der andere Orientalismus*, 316–26, 331–35.

17. Of course, if things last beyond their time, then it is hard to see how they actually have their own time. But the way in which Goethe tries to avoid the contradiction here (between enduring presence and punctual occurrence) is by insisting on the developmental continuity of a linear narrative.

18. See Emmanuel Levinas, *Totalité et infini: Essai sur l'extériorité* (Paris: Livre de poche, 1992).

19. According to the motif of the *Zug*, Moses traces—and so writes or inscribes—the history of the nation as a wandering. Hence, if he governs the history intentionally, he nonetheless only anticipates (or belatedly recalls) the true leadership of spirit, since the entirety of the journey is inscribed as an inscription, rather than as the spirituality of voice, and writing is always both too early and too late for pure meaning. By underscoring Moses' inability to speak (211), moreover, Goethe makes this viewpoint still more plausible.

20. In this sense, the Moses of the Bible is reminiscent of the Goethe of the "Noten und Abhandlungen"—a man of action who has decided to undertake the passive work of self-explanation. Hence, Goethe's anxiety about the wanderings of the Israelites wanders into the space of his anxiety about the connection between his own activity and his own passivity, an anxiety that the poems explicitly play out and incessantly attempt to resolve. Freud will expand on the question of the "right place" in the motif of "Entstellung" in his text *Moses and Monotheism*, which, as is well known, follows up on Goethe's suggestion that Moses was Egyptian. See my chapter 8 on Freud's *Moses* below.

21. Moses was, for example, "driven by his nature to the greatest of deeds [*durch seine Natur zum größten getrieben*]" (224).

22. Elsewhere Goethe situates the "highest character" of Oriental poetic arts in "what we Germans call 'spirit' [*Geist*], the predomination of that which leads from above [*das Vorwaltende des oberen Leitenden*]" (165). And this "spirit" of top-down leadership is what the Oriental poets presumably share with the Germans, not only because "we" have named it but also because "Spirit belongs chiefly [*vorzüglich*] to age or to an aging world epoch" (165), and both the East and the West can be seen as old (more on this below), depending on whether one sees the West as the aging of the (ever youthful) East (Occident as sundown, Orient as sunrise) or the East as aged, while the West is newly arisen out of it.

23. In the realm of poetry (once we have been linked to the East by the historical narrative Goethe provides), in order both to overcome the barrier to the East and to let the East be the East, we have to leave the East to its place in the narrative, to have faith also in the narrative (which is a narrative of the faith in narrative, or history), to have faith that the East actually comes down to us. But in order to leave things in their places we must refrain from comparisons between East and West, as Goethe at one point insists. The fact that Goethe nonetheless undertakes comparisons (183–86) between Eastern and Western poetry indicates the impossibility of completely absorbing structure into developmental narrative.

24. On the debate between Benjamin and Scholem concerning the notion of a revealed tradition that retains "force without significance" because it is a revelation with a lost key, see Giorgio Agamben, *Homo Sacer: Sovereign Power and Bare Life*, trans. Daniel Heller-Roazen (Stanford: Stanford University Press, 1998), 49–62.

25. See all the poems about the tension between clergy, or religious authority, and the poet, which are scattered in "Buch des Sängers" (e.g., "Dreistigkeit" and "Derb und Tüchtig"), "Buch Hafis" (from "Anklage" to the second "Fetwa" poem, "Offenbar Geheimnis"), and "Buch des Unmuts"

(throughout) especially, and which group Goethe together with Hafis as the poets who constitute necessary exceptions to the rule of religious (and overlapping with this, moral) law. What guarantees that the Oriental poets do not fall away from the source they represent is that the figures that provide the foundation of their poetry are natural figures, what Goethe calls "Urtropen," as tropes that do not ever really turn away from the proper and natural referents with which they begin (179–82).

26. Although the pure and eternal presence of the rising sun, as of spirit and matter fused, constitutes for Goethe the center of the old Parsee religion, this "noble, pure, nature religion" (135) already breaks down, he writes, in Zoroastrian culture, where eternal presence splits into the fleeting moment of transient temporality, on the one hand, and the "long time" of boredom, on the other hand, in which time stretches out infinitely. On boredom, see Walter Benjamin, *Gesammelte Schriften*, I, 2, ed. R. Tiedemann and H. Schweppenhäuser (Frankfurt: Suhrkamp Taschenbuch Verlag, 1974), 682, and Martin Heidegger, *Grundbegriffe der Metaphysik: Welt, Endlichkeit, Einsamkeit* (Frankfurt am Main: V. Klostermann, 1992).

27. Hendrik Birus, "Goethe's 'Orientalism,'" in Margaret Higonnet and Sumie Jones, *Visions of the Other*, ed. Margaret Higonnet and Sumie Jones, Proceedings of the XIIIth Congress of the International Comparative Literature Association (Tokyo: University of Tokyo Press, 1995), 572–81, attempts, in terms of this symmetry, to rescue Goethe from the charge of Orientalism. Ehrhard Bahr also defends against the charge of Orientalism, but he oversimplifies the question of mixing traditions in a manner similar to Birus (Bahr, "East Is West, and West Is East: The Synthesis of Near-Eastern and Western Rhetoric and Imagination in Goethe's West-Östlicher Divan," in *Aufnahme— Weitergabe: Literarische Impulse um Lessing und Goethe*, ed. John A. McCarthy and Albert A. Kipa, Festschrift für Heinz Moenkemeyer zum 68. Geburtstag [Hamburg: Helmut Buske Verlag, 1982], 144–52).

28. As worshippers of the sun and fire, the Persians are already Western insofar as they are situated in the West with respect to the Eastern sunrise of the Orient: "Praying to the creator, they turned toward the rising sun, as toward the most strikingly glorious appearance. Therein they believed themselves to glimpse the throne of God, surrounded by shining angels" (135). They therefore represent both the Oriental sunrise and the objectification of that sunrise from an Occidental position, the self-reflexion of Orientality. And so Goethe explicitly characterizes them—like Hegel, in his wake—as the West of the East, the part of the East that is always already Western: "The possibility of a higher culture lay in it, which spread itself into the Western part of the Eastern world" (138). In this sense they anticipate the West and differentiate themselves from the East (qua Indian,

for example): "But to me what is most worthy of admiration is that the fatal proximity of the Indian idolatry could have no effect on them" (138). But they are also more advanced than the West in that they are still immediately connected with nature—"The old Parsees' divine worship was grounded in the observation of nature" (135)—and their religion combines monotheistic abstraction with pantheistic concreteness in perfect balance, as it has been "grounded upon the all-presence of God in his works in the sensuous world" (136).

29. Although Goethe plays for the most part, in the poetic cycle, with medieval Persian poetry, he sees this poetry as expressing the essential and eternal "character" of the Persians (134).

4. GOETHE'S ORIENTALIZING MOMENT (II): THE POETRY OF THE WEST-EAST DIVAN

1. Cf. the later poems, "Des Paria Gebet" and "Legende," in which Goethe's understanding of Indian culture attains a more nuanced level (1:361–66).

2. Thus, for example, he repeatedly defines "Islam" as "devotion [*Ergebenheit*]," in an interesting trope on Lessing's motif of "devotion to God [*Ergebenheit in Gott*]" as it functions in *Nathan der Weise*. (See, for example, this poem: "If *Islam* means 'devoted to God,' Then we all live and die in Islam [*Wenn* Islam *Gott ergeben heißt, / Im Islam leben und sterben wir alle*]" [56]). This approach to Islam enables us to see how much Katharina Mommsen exaggerates when she asserts Goethe's extreme proximity to Islam in *Goethe und der Islam* [Frankfurt am Main: Insel, 2001]—although her work also makes an informative and useful contribution.) On Spinozism and pantheism in Goethe's *Divan*, see, for example, Konrad Burdach, "Die Kunst und der dichterisch-religiöse Gehalt des West-östlichen Divans," and Ursula Wertheim, "Herr und Meister Benedikt Spinoza," both of which are reprinted in *Studien zum West-östlichen Divan Goethes*, ed. Edgar Lohnert (Darmstadt: Wissenschaftliche Buchgesellschaft, 1971), 48–91 and 375–90, respectively. Although Goethe eroticizes and demoralizes Lessing's construction of the gift, proposing a less skeptical and more egocentric version of the gift as supplement of presence, he continues to make gestures that link him to Lessing's work and to the latter's magnanimous humanity, gestures that would include, for example, the implicit allusion to "Al-Hafi" in the very name of "Hafis."

3. Goethe also takes his distance from the patriotic poetry being written at the time in connection with the wars of liberation. See Eberhard Lämmert, "Die vaterländische Lyrik und Goethes *Westöstlicher Divan*," in *Literaturwissenschaft und Geschichtsphilosophie*, Festschrift für Wilhelm Emrich, ed. Helmut Arntzen et al. (Berlin: Walter de Gruyter, 1975), 341–56.

4. The three nominalized infinitive verbs, "Lieben, Trinken, Singen" ("loving, drinking, singing"), summarize the three dimensions that I analyze below: "Loving" is realized between Hatem and Suleika; "drinking" is the topic of the relationship between Hatem and Saki, the *Schenke*; and "singing" is the theme of Goethe's relationship with Hafis.

5. On the *Augenblick* in Goethe's lyric, see David Wellbery, *The Specular Moment: Goethe's Early Lyric and the Beginnings of Romanticism* (Stanford: Stanford University Press, 1996). This extraordinarily rigorous book, equally learned in Goethe scholarship and in contemporary theory, manages more or less single-handedly to retrieve Goethe studies from the nineteenth century (where they have been languishing for about a hundred and fifty years) to the early twenty-first century. Although my reading of the theme of the present in Goethe's *Divan* preceded my discovery of Wellbery's book, his analyses of Goethe's early lyric in terms of this theme provided essential inspiration for my completion of this reading.

6. See, for example, the three essays by H. E. Hass ("Über die strukturelle Einheit des West-östlichen Divans"), Carl Becker ("Das Buch Suleika als Zyklus"), and Ingeborg Hillmann ("Das Ganze im Kleinsten") in Lohnert, *Studien zum West-östlichen Divan Goethes*, 431–43, 391–430, and 444–68, respectively; and Hans-J. Weitz's commentary in J. W. Goethe, *West-östlicher Divan*, ed. Hans-J. Weitz (Frankfurt am Main: Insel, 1974), 297–98.

7. See the suggestive article by Jonathan Culler, "Apostrophe" in *The Pursuit of Signs: Semiotics, Literature, Deconstruction* (Ithaca, N.Y.: Cornell University Press, 2002).

8. Hafis's middle or his present—which as *offenbar* ("openly" or, as it were, "revealedly") suggests a revelation (*Offenbarung*)—is the same as his end and his beginning, insofar as, being without beginning or end properly speaking, he is all middle, pure present and pure presence.

9. Goethe develops the motif of the gift as an interplay between activity and passivity that guarantees presence (hence, the present as presence) further in some poems that appear in the "Book of Reflexions." In these poems, we can see him struggling ambivalently between the affirmation of activity as presence, on the one hand, and the (more penetrating) acknowledgment that only a balance between activity and passivity could ever guarantee full presence. See, for example, "Fünf Andere," "Lieblich ist des Mädchens Blick, der winket," and "Und was im Pend-Nameh steht." On temporality more generally, in the "Book of Reflexions," see especially "Den Gruß des Unbekannten ehre ja!," "Woher ich kam? Es ist noch eine Frage," "Es geht eins nach dem andern hin," and "Das Leben ist ein Gänsespiel," as well as "Dschelâl-eddîn Rumi spricht," and "Suleika spricht."

10. On fetishistic disavowal elsewhere in Goethe, see Hartmut Böhme, "Fetisch und Idol: Die Temporalität von Erinnerungsformen in Goethes *Wilhelm Meister, Faust,* und *Der Sammler und die Seinigen,*" in *Goethe und die Verzeitlichung der Natur,* ed. Peter Matussek (Munich: n.p., 1998), 178–202.

11. Further, the mouth and song, throat and heart listed in sequence throughout the second strophe remain placed metonymically next to each other; their identification in and with the poet, Hafis, as source is nowhere explicitly achieved.

12. See the poem "Zwiespalt" in "Buch des Sängers." This poem registers the ineluctable and literally maddening tension between what Freud will call eros and thanatos, as the tension between the flutes of Cupid and the trumpets of Mars. The necessary intermingling of appropriative desire and destructive aggression appears here strikingly as an internal division the poet is not able to overcome.

13. "Das Leben ist kurz, der Tag ist lang," is evidently a trope on the utterance, "life is short, art is long."

14. In the famous line, "Stirb und werde" or "die and become" (in "Selige Sehnsucht" [18–19]), Goethe attempts to make the condition of presence—here named, for example, "das Lebendige" or "the living" (18)—precisely the splitting into pastness (*Stirb*) and futurity (*werde*) of the moment, as if the affirmation of the splitting could overcome it.

15. I am alluding in the "shifts, subverts, and anagrammatizes one's name" to a line in Hart Crane's poem, "O Carib Isle."

16. This command echoes (for example) the grateful outstretched hand and gaze of the poor receiver of the charitable gift in "Lieblich ist des Mädchens Blick, der winket."

17. For biographical treatments of this relationship, see Dagmar von Gersdorff, *Marianne von Willemer und Goethe: Geschichte einer Liebe* (Frankfurt am Main: Insel, 2003); Richard Friedenthal, *Goethe: Sein Leben und seine Zeit* (Munich: Piper, 1963), 591–615; and, from among the older, "classical" essays, Herman Grimm, "Goethe und Suleika" (1869); Konrad Burdach, "Goethes West-östlicher Divan in biographischer und zeitgeschichtlicher Beleuchtung" (1896); and Hans Pyritz, "Goethe und Marianne von Willemer" (1943), all three of which are in Lohnert, *Studien zum West-Östlichen Divan Goethes,* 285–309, 310–51, and 352–74, respectively. See also Sulpiz Boisserée, *Briefwechsel/Tagebücher* (Göttingen: Vandenhoeck and Ruprecht, 1970).

18. On the history of the relationship between Johann Jakob von Willemer and Marianne von Willemer, see Dagmar von Gersdorff, *Marianne von Willemer und Goethe: Geschichte einer Liebe* (Frankfurt: Insel Verlag, 2003), and on the scandalous character of the relationship at the time, 21–23. See also

the account in Richard Friedenthal, *Goethe: Sein Leben und seine Zeit* (Munich: R. Piper & Co Verlag, 1963), 591–614.

19. The images of the *Blick* ("glance" or "look") and the *Augenblick* ("moment") pervade the poetry of eros in this cycle in a way that constantly connects desire with presence as its goal, and with such frequency in these poems that we have had to content ourselves with discussion of several selected instances.

20. Cf. Jacques Lacan, *The Four Fundamental Concepts of Psychoanalysis*, trans. Alan Sheridan (New York: Norton, 1977), "Of the Gaze as objet petit a," 67–122. If the gaze can be its own object, this is because the gaze is split off from itself as its subjective and its objective component. The objet a is, in this sense, not an externally existing object pure and simple, even if it is also not an object that can ever be internalized. Goethe's eternal presence/present or *Augenblick* would be like the realization of the synthesis of the subjectivity and objectivity of the gaze, the synthesis of the objet a as gaze with itself. But rather than pursue the psychoanalytic translation of Goethe, I have tried to understand him as closely as possible in his "own" terms.

21. I have altered Whaley's translation of the fourteenth and twenty-fourth lines translated here so as to accord better with my understanding of the German.

22. Similarly, in "Full Moon Night [*Vollmondnacht*]," a poem that celebrates the unification of the lovers in the phrase "Dieses ist der Augenblick," the unification remains radically incomplete and in need of supplementation. In fact, the moment of fulfillment turns out to be here only the moment of the fulfillment of the lovers' promise to state their *desire* in the phrase, "I want to kiss! Kiss! I say" (*Ich will küssen! Küssen! sag' ich*) (85) when the full moon appears to each during their separation. The fulfillment of the promissory prefiguration is here the restatement of a desire that remains prefigural, in that it still only anticipates the lovers' actual unification (and in that this desire, moreover, remains questionably abstract—a desire to kiss, but whom or what?). Indeed, desire becomes in this collection one of the fundamental names for the disavowal of distance, so long as the desire is mutually given and received. The individual erotic-aesthetic relationship replaces the history of religion as the site of the realization of an anticipated absolute, in accordance with the privatization of the absolute and consequent absolutization of the private (feeling) carried out by European sentimentalism and romanticism in general (to which Goethe has been a major contributor ever since *Die Leiden des jungen Werther* and the other *Sturm und Drang* works). As a result of these various elements in its construction, the poem embodies in an exemplary manner the interdependence of desire and renunciation that characterizes so much of the cycle as a whole.

23. See also "Sie haben wegen der Trunkenheit" (92). This poem connects "love-drunkenness" (Liebestrunkenheit), which it also calls "love-, song-, and wine-drunkenness" (*Lieb-, Lied- und Weines Trunkenheit*) to an indifference to time that suggests the overcoming of time (within time), using phrases such as "from day to night, from night to day" (*Von Tag zu Nacht, von Nacht zu Tag*) and "whether it's night or day" (*ob's nachtet oder tagt*) to indicate this indifference.

24. Note that the language of "Sorgen" here links this poem precisely to the "geheime Sorgen" of "Lieb' um Liebe, Stund' um Stunde," where Goethe/Hatem expressed the worry about losing Suleika to the young Jussuph, and about being unfair to her in not being able to give her what the young man could have given.

25. The triadic structure of Hafis, Suleika, and Saki is indicated in the line "Lieb-, Lied- und Weines Trunkenheit" in "Sie haben wegen der Trunkenheit" (92), as also in the very first stanza of the first poem of the cycle, discussed at the outset of the current chapter: "Unter Lieben, Trinken, Singen/Soll dich Chisers Quell verjüngen" (There in loving, drinking, singing/Youth from Chiser's well is springing).

26. On the homoerotic dimension of the "Cupbearer's Book," in connection with Winckelmann's aesthetics, see Joachim Heimerl, "'In aller Reinheit behandelt': Das 'Buch des Schenken' aus *Goethes West-Östlichem Divan* und die Polarität der Liebe," in *Zeitschrift für Deutsche Philologie* 122, no. 2 (2003): 200–217.

27. See Spinoza's preface to his *Theological-Political Tractate*, and the section in the *Ethics* on "fear" and "hope," part 3, proposition 18, scholium 2, et passim. Fear and hope, as intertwined, in their extreme forms have the structure of panic, as I suggested above.

28. I believe the only other similar passage would be this one from the summary of Pietro Della Valle's voyages, which would itself merit analysis: "Presents are brought, great magnificence is on display, and yet they are haughtily disdained, and soon therefore Jewishly marketed, and thus the majesty oscillates always between the highest and the lowest" (*Geschenke werden gebracht, großer Prunk damit getrieben, und doch werden sie bald hochfahrend verschmäht, bald darum jüdisch gemarktet, und so schwankt die Majestät immer zwischen dem Höchsten und dem Tiefsten*) (235).

5. THRESHOLDS OF HISTORY: INDIA AND THE LIMITS OF EUROPE IN HEGEL'S LECTURES ON THE PHILOSOPHY OF HISTORY

1. See, for example, Jacques Derrida, "Le parergon," in *La vérité en peinture* (Paris: Flammarion, 1978), 21–168. I will not engage here with Derrida's extended reading of Hegel (with Jean Genet) in *Glas: Que reste-t-il du savoir*

absolu (Paris: Denoël/Gonthier, 1981), but for his discussion of Hegel on the Jews, see 54–84. Derrida's approach to the question of Christian supersessionism in Hegel is indicated here: "Mais de même que le christianisme se représente et s'anticipe seulement dans le judaïsme qui en est la *Vorstellung*, de même la religion absolue qu'est le christianisme reste la *Vorstellung* du *Sa* [*Savoir absolu/Ça*] comme philosophie. La structure de la *Vorstellung* ouvre la scène de la sainte famille sur la *Sa*" ("But just as Christianity represents itself and anticipates itself solely in Judaism, which is its *representation*, so the absolute religion that is Christianity remains the *representation* of the SA [Absolute Knowledge, or Id, according to Derrida's pun]," my translation) (43).

2. The ancient Jewish, that is, "Old Testament," discourse struggles similarly, of course, against "idolatry," but in a different, two-step structure of transcendence and repeated relapse (and at the same time perhaps without such a radically antimaterial gesture), as Christian discourses have often made into an argument against Judaism.

3. G. W. F. Hegel, *Vorlesungen über die Philosophie der Geschichte*, in *Werke in zwanzig Bänden: Theorie Werkausgabe* (Frankfurt am Main: Suhrkamp Verlag, 1970), 12:120–29; 91–99. The English translation to which I make reference is G. W. F. Hegel, *The Philosophy of History*, trans. J. Sibree (Amherst, N.Y.: Prometheus Books, 1991). I indicate pagination in parentheses in my text, first from the German, then (after semicolon) from the English edition. For quotations from this edition, translations have been modified according to my sense of the text and my interpretive argument. The Suhrkamp edition of the lectures that I have used is based on the Karl Hegel edition of 1840, and thus constitutes a problematic, retroactively created palimpsest edition in various respects. Although I am certain that it can be extremely productive to work between the various editions and versions of the lecture course to try to differentiate between Hegel's diverse positions at different times in his development (as, e.g., Robert Bernasconi has done magnificently in the essays I cite), neither the status of the authorial referent, "Hegel," nor the status of his "philosophy of history" would be thereby entirely simplified, of course, nor is it, I think, without validity and significance to work closely with the composite text I have used in order to construct a reading of it as an important document on what we would call Hegel's philosophy of history. As I have ignored editorial and philological considerations in developing this reading, so have I set aside for the sake of space the complex job of comparing and contrasting Hegel's treatments of the various so-called Oriental cultures in the several philosophical subdisciplines on which he lectured, especially the *Aesthetics* and the *Philosophy of Religion*.

4. Martin Bernal argues in *Black Athena: The Afro-Asiatic Roots of Classical Civilization* (New Brunswick, N.J.: Rutgers University Press, 1987–2006) that

India replaces Egypt (as "too African") in nineteenth-century narratives of the origins of Greek, hence Western, civilization. Hegel sees India has insufficiently distancing "us" precisely from Africa (as well as the New World), while he brings Egypt closer to Europe by characterizing it as Oriental and non-African. Hegel's narrative includes both India and Egypt, yet confirms Bernal's claims that racism is key to such narratives. But one fails to comprehend the logic at stake if one does not take modern groundlessness prominently into account as I do here.

5. On Hegel's response to the romantic Orient, see Rodolphe Gasché, "Hegel's Orient or the End of Romanticism," in *History and Mimesis*, ed. Irving J. Massey and Sung-Won Lee (Buffalo: State University of New York, 1983), 17–29. Gasché criticizes Said's residual vitalism and empiricism, which he likens intriguingly to what Hegel characterizes in his *Aesthetics* as the return, at the end of romantic art, to Oriental beginnings of art, in a desired intimacy with the object (27).

6. Figueira, *The Exotic: A Decadent Quest* (Albany: State University of New York Press, 1994), 63–90.

7. On the struggles within early nineteenth-century philology to determine whether there are any essential affinities between Indo-Germanic and Semitic languages, and on the theological and religio-historical stakes of these struggles in the context of the emancipation of Jewry, see Tuska Benes, *In Babel's Shadow: Language, Philology, and the Nation in Nineteenth-Century Germany* (Detroit: Wayne State University Press, 2008), 95–112. Sanskrit and Indo-Germanic come to supplant the Hebraic position. This is why the theologians tend to try to show an affinity between the Indo-Germanic and the Semitic languages groups: so that Hebrew is not displaced and replaced by Sanskrit (or Indo-Germanic) as the originary (and so anticipatory) language.

8. The "Unbändigkeit" [unruliness, inner disconnectedness] that Hegel posits as the character of blacks is striking as the image of what might be threatening from within the European consciousness. Hegel illustrates this "unruliness" by describing how, when the King of Dahomey dies, "the bonds of society are immediately torn" (128; 98, trans. modified), giving way to a pervasive panic and uncontrolled violence and looting. For a precise and informative reading of Hegel's account of Africa in the context of Hegel's potential and real sources, see Robert Bernasconi, "Hegel at the Court of the Ashanti," in *Hegel after Derrida*, ed. Stuart Barnett (London: Routledge, 1998), 41–63, and on Hegel's critique of African "fetishism," 52–55. Although one might object to my own invocation of psychoanalytic thought on "fetishism" that it continues the tradition of colonialist and Eurocentric thinking, my hope is that this tradition is significantly and even radically

displaced when the concept of fetishism is applied to discourses that have constructed it in Eurocentric ways. In fact, the denial of lacking absolute foundations is understandable as an attempt to maintain the illusion of control and safety. And for Hegel the fetishism of African magical (non)religion consists in the refusal/incapacity to acknowledge that one is not in control of otherness (i.e., the denial that the subject does not control substance), and in the arbitrary choice of a representation of human power over nature, a representation that remains changeable. But whether the (Hegelian) philosophy of spirit in the end entirely escapes such a description one is entitled to doubt. So not only is the notion of disavowal that I invoke here applicable to Hegel, but it further helps us see and underline his nontrivial resemblance to what he wants to posit as the other of (European) history pure and simple.

9. "For the Christian world is the world of completion [*Vollendung*]; the principle is fulfilled [*das Prinzip ist erfüllt*], and therewith the end of days has become full" (*Vorlesungen über die Philosophie der Geschichte*, 414; 342, trans. modified). And the three subperiods of the Christian world recapitulate the three periods of Orient (here, named for its culmination in Persia), Greece, and Rome. The three phases in question are: (1) the time from the origin of Christianity to the time of Charlemagne; (2) the middle ages from Charlemagne to the early sixteenth century; and (3) modernity, "die neue Zeit," from the Reformation until Hegel's own times. Hegel characterizes the first explicitly as the realm of the father, the second as the realm of the son, and the third as the realm of the Holy Spirit. Hegel in turn likens these three phases to Persia (which here functions symptomatically as the culmination of the Oriental world), Greece, and Rome, respectively (417–18; 345–46).

10. Hegel explicitly makes the connection between the notion of the Orient as sole prefiguration and the notion that the Orient, Greece, and Rome taken together function as prefiguration when he writes: "China is quite properly [*ganz eigentümlich*] Oriental, India could be paralleled with Greece, and Persia paralleled with Rome" (145; 113, trans. modified). The unification of the structure of the *Lectures* proceeds largely, perhaps entirely, by means of homologies between different formulations or levels of their typological narrative.

11. "The Orientals have not attained the knowledge that Spirit—Man *as such*—is free; and because they do not know this, they are not free. They only know that *one is free* [*daß einer frei ist*]. . . . The consciousness of Freedom first arose among the Greeks, and therefore they were free; but they, and the Romans likewise, knew only that *some* are free—not man as such. . . . The Greeks, therefore, had slaves. . . . The German nations, under the influence of Christianity, were the first to attain the consciousness that man, as man,

is free: that it is the *freedom* of Spirit which constitutes its essence.... [This] supplies us with the natural division of Universal History, and suggests the mode of its discussion" (31–32; 18–19).

12. Through the "cunning of reason" or "List der Vernunft," the particular serves the universal; reason "lets the passions work for itself" (*sie die Leidenschaften für sich wirken läßt*) (49; 33).

13. Cf. Moses Mendelssohn in *Jerusalem, oder über religiöse Macht und Judentum*, where Catholicism stands for the unification of church and state, whereas Protestantism stands for their division. The importance of Hegel's struggle with *Jerusalem* in his early writings is well known.

14. "It is also to be noted that these incitements of the spirit are at first external, natural impulses [*Regsamkeiten*], then, however, equally internal alterations that occur within the human being himself, such as dreams or the insanity of the Delphic Priestess, which are first meaningfully interpreted by the *mantis*.... But the incitements that operated on the spirit of the Greeks are not to be limited to these objective and subjective ones, but rather the traditional materials [*das Traditionelle*] from foreign cultures [*aus der Fremde*], the already given culture, gods, and religious services [*die schon gegebene Bildung, Götter und Gottesdienste*] are to be considered here.... It is just as historical that the Greeks have received representations from India, Syria, and Egypt, as that the Greek representations are characteristic [*eigentümlich*] and the others foreign [*und jene anderen fremd*]" (291–92; 236–37, trans. modified).

15. For a brief, philologically focused overview of Hegel on the Orient, see Hans-Joachim Schoeps, "Die außerchristlichen Religionen bei Hegel," in his *Studien zur unbekannten Religions- und Geistesgeschichte* (Göttingen: Musterschmidt Verlag, 1963), 255–84. On Hegel and the Orient in historicism, see Ernst Schulin, *Die weltgeschichtliche Erfassung des Orients bei Hegel und Ranke* (Göttingen: Vandenhoeck and Ruprecht, 1958). Schulin argues that although the Orient was important to the origins of historicism, the Eurocentrism of universal history increased over the course of the nineteenth century. For a comprehensive overview of Hegel on the Orient, see Michel Hulin, *Hegel et l'Orient, suivi de la traduction annotée d'un essai de Hegel sur la Bhagavad-Gita* (Paris: Vrin, 1979).

16. On Spinozan "substance" in Hegel, see Klaus Düsing, *Hegel und die Geschichte der Philosophie: Ontologie und Dialektik in Antike und Neuzeit* (Darmstadt: Wissenschaftliche Buchgesellschaft, 1983), 160–95.

17. "In China the patriarchal principle dominates the immature ones [*Unmündigen*], for whose moral decision the ruling law and the moral oversight of the Emperor stands in" (174–75; 139, trans. modified).

18. In terms of political categories, the progress is from patriarchal kingship (in China) to aristocracy (in India), to monarchy (in Persia), where

monarchy is understood as a synthesis of the rule by the one and the rule by the many (144–45; 113–14).

19. For a scrupulously attentive and sophisticated reading of Hegel's construction of China in the *Philosophy of History*, see Haun Saussy, *The Problem of a Chinese Aesthetic* (Stanford: Stanford University Press, 1993), 151–84.

20. See Robert Bernasconi's illuminating expansion of this point in his analysis of Hegel's racism, "'With What Must the Philosophy of World History Begin?' On the Racial Basis of Hegel's Eurocentrism," *Nineteenth-Century Contexts* 22, no. 2 (2000): 171–201.

21. The former passage is this one: "The third great form [*Gestalt*], which now enters the stage against the static One of China [*das bewegungslose Eine Chinas*] and the roaming, unbound Indian unquiet [*die schweifende ungebundene indische Unruhe auftritt*], is the Persian Empire" (145; 113, trans. modified).

22. See Arvind Mandair, "The Repetition of Past Imperialisms: Hegel, Historical Difference, and the Theorization of Indic Religions," *History of Religions* 44, no. 4 (2005): 277–99, who interestingly questions whether "historicism in itself can provide the proper element for thinking about postcolonial agency" (281); Balachandra Rajan, *Under Western Eyes: India from Milton to Macaulay* (Durham, N.C.: Duke University Press, 1999), 100–117, on Hegel's appropriation of the ancient Hebrew (but also Calvinist) rhetoric of the "chosen" and "elect," 114–15; Wilhelm Halbfass, *India and Europe: An Essay in Understanding* (Albany: State University of New York Press, 1988), 84–99; Figueira, *Exotic*, 63–91.

23. By "specter" I mean here that Hegel is haunted by this idea in his own work and also that India represents a beginning of life that falls back into death, like a stillborn baby or a death at birth.

24. For a different approach to Hegel's relationship to India, but an approach likewise marked by Derridean deconstruction, see Gayatri Chakravorty Spivak, *A Critique of Postcolonial Reason: Toward a History of the Vanishing Present* (Cambridge, Mass.: Harvard University Press, 1999), 37–67. Spivak undertakes "to deconstruct the opposition between Hegel and the *Gītā*," as an example of the "structural complicity of dominant texts from two different cultural inscriptions" (39). What the texts share in common is that "Time graphed as Law manipulates history seen as timing in the interest of cultural political explanations" (43). Both Hegel and the Bhagavad Gita, in other words, if I understand this correctly, efface the abyss of the "vanishing present"—"history seen as timing"—by asserting a teleology that accomplishes an apology for a given political state of affairs. The commonalities to which Spivak points are additional reasons why, for Hegel, the ancient Indian culture comes "too close" for (his) comfort. Spivak's powerful and sympa-

thetic gesture is perhaps best condensed in the assumption that "an ethnicity untroubled by the vicissitudes of history and neatly accessible as an object of investigation" (60) is not given.

25. Accordingly, Hegel figures—or dreams—India through the allegorical concretion of a "peculiar beauty" seen in women, he claims, in the days after they give birth (175–76; 140). In turn, Hegel associates this beauty with a painting of the dying Mary, mother of Jesus, and with somnambulism, the oneiric connection with another world. These figures of the maternal origin as simultaneous place of birth and death, waking and sleeping, are appropriate to the status of Hegel's India as the sunrise of sunrise, the "not yet" but "already" of the "not yet" but "already" that is Persia. Because India is the origin, it will not progress, but must remain eternally what it is as origin: It must remain an origin linked to its own death. The feminization of the Orient is widespread in modern Orientalism, but does not exclude its double, the figure of the Orient as patriarchal despot (which in Hegel's Orient is embodied initially in China).

26. Hegel finds it self-evident that women and children should be excluded from the political process: "Equality in civil life is something absolutely impossible; for individual distinctions of sex and age will always assert themselves; and even if an equal share in the government is accorded to all citizens, women and children are immediately passed by, and remain excluded [*so übergeht man sofort die Weiber und Kinder, welche ausgeschloßen bleiben*]" (182; 145).

27. For an illuminating attempt at "rescuing the idea of universal human history from the uses to which white domination has put it," see Susan Buck-Morss, "Hegel and Haiti," *Critical Inquiry* 26, no. 4 (2000): 821–65. Buck-Morss traces the influence of the Haitian revolution on Hegel's treatment of the "master-slave" dialectic.

28. An illustration of this polemical language: "Annihilation—the abandonment of all reason, morality and subjectivity—can only come to a positive feeling and consciousness of itself by extravagating in a boundlessly wild imagination; in which, like a desolate spirit, it finds no . . . settled composure, . . . as a man who is quite reduced in body and spirit finds his existence altogether stupid and intolerable, and is driven to the creation of a dream-world and a delirious bliss in Opium" (208; 167)

29. The abstract establishment of Brahma as the substantial spiritual unity that is to absorb by negation all particularity is, of course, threateningly similar to the abstractness of which Hegel himself is often accused. India thus comes "too close" to Hegel in one of two ways. Its resemblance to his thought means either that he has not achieved the concreteness that he thinks

he has, or that Indian thinking perhaps already achieved all the concreteness necessary. Either history has not yet started, or it started so long ago that Hegel's achievement of history, and that of his age, is superfluous.

30. Hegel's interest in and perhaps anxiety around the question of the status of Sanskrit is reflected further in his denial in 1822 that, as Schlegel maintained, Sanskrit was the ultimate source of Greek, Latin, and German, for example, and his defense of Sir William Jones's position that there must have been a prior source. On this point see Robert Bernasconi, "With What Must the History of Philosophy Begin? Hegel's Role in the Debate on the Place of India within the History of Philosophy," in *Hegel's History of Philosophy: New Interpretations*, ed. David A. Duquette (Albany: State University of New York Press, 2003), 35–50. Bernasconi explores here Hegel's ambivalence—his increasing willingness to grant Indian thought something like the status of philosophy, but his continuing unwillingness to include it within philosophy properly so-called qua European philosophy. Concerning the question of the beginning of the history of (European) philosophy, Indian thought remains just at the limit of the limit: anticipatory, but not a realization of philosophy as such. On the contemporaneous debates about Sanskrit versus Indo-Germanic as "original" language, see Benes, *In Babel's Shadow*, 65–112.

31. Hegel allows himself this move despite the fact that a major part of his reading of world history includes the spiritual characteristics of geographical and geological formations. See the part of the introduction dedicated to "Geographische Grundlage der Weltgeschichte" (105–32; 79–102).

32. Hegel not only calls India "the land of desire" (or the desired land: *das Land der Sehnsucht*) (174; 139), but also calls America "a land of desire" (or a desired land: *ein Land der Sehnsucht*) (114; 86), a comparison that is connected to the status of America as world of the new, of originality and futurity, to which we return below.

33. The cultural-historical trajectory Hegel traces out will be quite precisely reversed by Schopenhauer. For Hegel, the Persian Empire and the Zoroastrian religion of Ormuzd and Ahriman mean the beginning of the rise of Judaeo-Christianity out of Indian debasement. For Schopenhauer, Ormuzd and Ahriman mean the beginning of the fall from Indian pessimism (for which all the world is darkness) into Judaeo-Christian optimism (of which the optimistic element is the Jewish one), since in the Persian religion darkness is only one aspect of the world.

34. For recent work on Hegel and the Jews, see Yirmiyahu Yovel, *Dark Riddle: Hegel, Nietzsche, and the Jews* (University Park: Pennsylvania State University Press, 1998); Wolf-Daniel Hartwich, *Romantischer Antisemitismus: Von Klopstock bis Richard Wagner* (Göttingen: Vandenhoeck and Ruprecht, 2005), 89–103; for Hegel's account of the Jews from his early writings on, see

Hans Liebeschütz, *Das Judentum im deutschen Geschichtsbild von Hegel bis Max Weber* (Tübingen: J. C. B. Mohr [Paul Siebeck], 1967), 1–42; and for the U.S. American Hegelianist discussion see Lawrence S. Stepelevich, "Hegel and Judaism," *Judaism: A Quarterly Journal of Jewish Life and Thought* 24, no. 2 (1975): 215–24, which stresses Hegel's anti-Semitism, and the subsequent friendly criticism of this article by Eric von der Luft, "Hegel and Judaism: A Reassessment," *Clio: A Journal of Literature, History, and the Philosophy of History* 18, no. 4 (1989): 361–78; on Hegel's treatment of the Jews in his early writings on Christianity, Bruce Rosenstock, *Philosophy and the Jewish Question: Mendelssohn, Rosenzweig, and Beyond* (New York: Fordham University Press, 2010), 205–30; and Werner Hamacher, "Pleroma—zu Genesis und Struktur einer dialektischen Hermeneutik bei Hegel," in G. W. F. Hegel, *Der Geist des Christentums: Schriften 1796–1800: Mit bislang unveröffentlichten Texten*, ed. and introd. Werner Hamacher (Frankfurt: Ullstein Verlag, 1978), 11–333. On Jews and Muslims in Hegel, see Gil Anidjar, *The Jew, the Arab: A History of the Enemy* (Stanford: Stanford University Press, 2003), 128–33.

35. Hegel sees in the Adonis cult the divinization of the figure of the dead son. In this cult, pain as such is honored, and therefore subjectivity is given its due, as life also its value. When the god dies, moreover, there is a synthesis of the light and dark principles that merely struggle with one another in Zoroastrianism. Negativity becomes part of God, along with affirmation, in death combined with resurrection, and in this combination consists the concreteness that for Hegel is required for Spirit in the proper sense of the term (239–40; 193–94).

36. The topic of Egypt's role in Hegel's thought is more complex than I can explore here, of course, especially given Egypt's importance in the discussions of symbolic art, and of architecture in the *Aesthetics*. For some contemporary perspectives, see Stuart Harten, "Archaeology and the Unconscious: Hegel, Egyptomania, and the Legitimations of Orientalism," in *Egypt and the Fabrication of European Identity*, ed. Irene A. Bierman (Los Angeles: UCLA Center for Near Eastern Studies, 1995), 3–33.

37. Hegel stresses the similarity between the Jewish and Indian principles, as well as their specific difference, by explicit reference to the shared "sublimity" of each religion: "Compared with this sublimity, the Indian sublimity is merely that of the measureless. Through spirituality as such, the sensuous and unethical is now no longer privileged, but rather diminished as the nondivine" (*Gegen diese Erhabenheit gehalten ist die indische nur die des Maßlosen. Durch die Geistigkeit überhaupt wird nun das Sinnliche und Unsittliche nicht mehr privilegiert, sondern als das Ungöttliche herabgesetzt*) (242; 196, trans. modified).

38. The proximity of the Jewish God to the Indian Brahma is also implied by the fact that, in the section on China, Hegel explicitly contrasts the

materialized substance of Chinese with the spiritualized substance of Jewish culture in order to clarify initially the meaning of Chinese culture. Yet the explicit opposite of China is India. Further, in the following passage, the characterization of the Jewish God as the negation of the individual recalls the Indian tendency toward self-negation in the attempt to approach the universal substance. Speaking of the patriarchal Chinese emperors, Hegel writes: "The universal will enacts itself immediately through the individual: the latter has no knowledge of himself in opposition to substance, which it does not yet posit as a power standing over against it, as, e.g., in Judaism the jealous God is known as the negation of the individual. In China, the universal will immediately commands what the individual is to do, and the latter complies and obeys with proportionate renunciation of reflexion and personal independence [*ebenso reflexions- und selbstlos*]" (152; 120, trans. modified).

39. Hence, here (as—problematically—also in Greece), "the possibility of a historical view is present; for it is here the prosaic understanding that puts the limited and circumscribed into its place and grasps it as a peculiar form of finitude: humans are taken to be individuals" (243; 196, trans. modified).

40. India's religious service involves a "chaos of ceremonies, which propose prescriptions for even the most extreme meaningless activity" (*Wust von Gebräuchen, welche auch für das äußerlichste unbedeutendste Tun Vorschriften erteilen*) (188; 150, trans. modified).

41. For recent discussions of the "end of history" in Hegel, especially in relation to the posthistoire-debate and the theories of postmodernity, see Hans von Fabeck, *Jenseits der Geschichte: Zur Dialektik des Posthistoire* (Munich: Wilhelm Fink Verlag, 2007); Jere O'Neill Surber, "On Giving Hegel His Due: The 'End of History' and the Hegelian Roots of Postmodern Thought," *Philosophy Today* 51, no. 3 (2007): 330–42; Barry Cooper, *The End of History: An Essay on Modern Hegelianism* (Toronto: University of Toronto Press, 1984); Joseph L. Esposito, "Hegel, Absolute Knowledge, and the End of History," *Clio: A Journal of Literature, History, and the Philosophy of History* 12, no. 4 (1983): 355–65.

42. Cf. Hegel's remark in his review of Humboldt's essay on the Bhagavad Gita: "As old a world as India is, in terms of the general familiarity of Europeans with this land, it is an only recently discovered new world [*neue Welt*] for us in terms of its literature, its sciences, and its arts" (131).

43. In fact, however futural America may be, it is actually older than Europe, a belated echo—or *Widerhall*—of the European world. Its future lies beyond the end, presence, and realization of history, which is Christian Europe as a Germanic Europe and as the place of the new.

44. In the introduction to the *Lectures*, Hegel states emphatically the embeddedness of history in a metaphysics of presence: "While we are thus

concerned exclusively with the Idea of Spirit, and in the History of the World regard everything as only its manifestation, in traversing the past—however extensive its periods—we have only to do with what is *present*; for philosophy, as occupying itself with the True, has to do with the *eternally present*" (105; 79,).

45. This appropriation takes a number of stages, at each of which the language of sunrise is restated. In the case of Persia, which is the ending of the Orient and in this sense the beginning of the Occident (as interplay between identity and difference), the sun appears as the divine principle of light. In the case of Greece, the sunrise appears in the imagery with which Hegel opens the part on "the Greek World," in a sentence that tellingly once again recalls and then pushes aside the fact that the Western languages descend from Sanskrit: "Among the Greeks we feel ourselves immediately at home [*heimatlich*], for we are on the ground of Spirit [*wir sind auf dem Boden des Geistes*], and although the origin of nations, as well as differences of language, can be traced further back to India, the authentic rise [*eigentliche Aufsteigen*—like the rising of a sun] and the true rebirth of the Spirit is first to be found in Greece" (275; 223, trans. modified). This Spirit of youth, that is Greece, goes on to realize itself in conquering its own origins, the Oriental spirit as represented by Persia, and in Alexander's movement all the way to India, displacing the site of sunrise thus Westward, through Greece to Rome, and so on.

46. If Greece does not become the object of hostile polemic—despite the fact that in some respects it functions as prefigurative—this is because India and Judaea and the Orient in general become the focus of this polemic, while Greece must be spared, since it is conventionally understood as the origin of the philosophical Western logos. Hegel consciously rejects Hölderlin's association of Greece with the *Morgenland* here, and the latter's focus on Dionysos as god arriving from the Indian Orient.

47. On Hegel's characterization of medieval philosophy, see Joël Biard, "The Middle Ages in Hegel's History of Philosophy," *Philosophical Forum* 31, no. 3–4 (2000): 248–60.

48. These two tendencies reflect those of church and state respectively, as spirit and matter, which develop in this period, as Hegel had said, independently of one another before entering into contradiction in the second period of the Germanic world.

49. Edward W. Said, *Orientalism* (New York: Pantheon, 1978), 60–73.

50. Cf. Hegel's famous analysis of the French Revolutionary "terreur," "Absolute Freedom and Terror," in *Phänomenologie des Geistes, Theorie Werkausgabe* (Frankfurt am Main: Suhrkamp Verlag, 1970), 3:431–40.

51. Through the "intuition [*Anschauung*] of the infinite nobility of heart of Oriental bravery," the hearts of the Knights are "fired" to purification

(475; 396, trans. modified). "For Christianity too has the moment of infinite abstraction and freedom in itself, and the Oriental Knightly spirit found an echo therefore in Occidental hearts, which formed them to a more noble virtue" (475–76; 396, trans. modified).

52. On Hegel's ongoing positive investment in the French Revolution, see Joachim Ritter's crucial essay on "Hegel und die französische Revolution," in his *Metaphysik und Politik: Studien zu Aristoteles und Hegel* (Frankfurt am Main: Suhrkamp, 1969).

53. See, e.g., Léon Poliakov, *The Aryan Myth: A History of Racist and Nationalist Ideas in Europe*, trans. Edmund Howard (London: Sussex University Press and Heinemann Educational Books, 1971); Dorothy Figueira, *Aryans, Jews, Brahmins: Theorizing Authority through Myths of Identity* (Albany: State University of New York Press, 2002).

6. TAKING UP GROUNDLESSNESS, FULFILLING FULFILLMENT: SCHOPENHAUER'S ORIENTALIST METAPHYSICS BETWEEN INDIANS AND JEWS

1. Yet Friedrich Schelling ultimately places Indian culture in a preliminary, mythological domain, as Wilhelm Halbfass explains in *India and Europe: An Essay in Understanding* (Albany: State University of New York Press, 1988), 100–105.

2. For example: "All willing springs from lack, from deficiency, and thus from suffering. Fulfillment [*Erfüllung*] brings this to an end; yet for one wish that is fulfilled there remain at least ten that are denied. . . . But even the final satisfaction itself is only apparent; the wish fulfilled at once makes way for a new one." Arthur Schopenhauer, *Werke in zwei Bänden*, ed. Werner Brede (Munich: Carl Hanser Verlag, n.d.), vol. 1, *Die Welt als Wille und Vorstellung*, 262. In English, from *The World as Will and Representation*, trans. E. F. J. Payne, 2 vols. (New York: Dover, 1969), 1:196. References to these editions are given below parenthetically in the text, first to the German and then to the English edition. Translations here as elsewhere occasionally modified to represent more accurately the German original.

3. See Chetan Batt, "Primordial Being: Enlightenment, Schopenhauer, and the Indian Subject of Postcolonial Theory," *Radical Philosophy* 100 (March/April 2000): 28–41. This essay argues that deconstructive postcolonial theory often repeats a problematic, traditional Western claim that the Indian Orient exceeds all proper Western articulation.

4. On Schopenhauer's philosophy and Indian thought, see René Gérard, *L'orient et la pensée romantique allemande* (Paris: Marcel Didier, 1963), 215–51; Moira Nicholls, "The Influences of Eastern Thought on Schopenhauer's Doctrine of the Thing-in-Itself" (which contains a useful appendix listing

Schopenhauer's references to Oriental sources), in *The Cambridge Companion to Schopenhauer*, ed. Christopher Janaway (Cambridge: Cambridge University Press, 1999), 171–213; Lakshmi Kapani, "Schopenhauer et son interprétation du 'Tu es cela,'" in *L'inde inspiratrice: Réception de l'Inde en France et en Allemagne (XIXe et Xxe siècles)*, ed. Michel Hulin and Christine Maillard (Strasbourg: Presses universitaires de Strasbourg, 1996), 45–70; Ram Adhar Mall, "Wie indisch ist das Indienbild Schopenhauers?" *Schopenhauer-Jahrbuch* 76 (1995): 151–72; and Douglas L. Berger, *"The Veil of Maya": Schopenhauer's System and Early Indian Thought* (Binghamton, N.Y.: Global Academic Publishing, 2004). On Indian thought in modern Germany since Schopenhauer, see Heinz Bechert, "Flucht in den Orient?" *Schopenhauer-Jahrbuch* 62 (1981): 55–66. On Schopenhauer's version of the Aryan-Semitic opposition, see Gregory Moore, "From Buddhism to Bolshevism: Some Orientalist Themes in German Thought," *German Life and Letters* 56, no. 1 (2003): 20–42. On Schopenhauer and Buddhism, see Roger-Pol Droit, *Le culte du néant: Les philosophes et le Bouddha* (Paris: Éditions due Seuil, 1997), 135–53, and Peter Abelsen, "Schopenhauer and Buddhism," *Philosophy East and West* 43, no. 1 (1993): 255–78.

5. In *India and Europe*, Halbfass notes this tension between Schopenhauer's self-subordination to ancient Indian wisdom and his claims to constitute its "standard and fulfillment" (114).

6. Like the "state of willed exception" under German fascism, this sustained sovereign decision on the state of metaphysical exception is marked by the structure of disavowal. See Giorgio Agamben, *Homo Sacer: Sovereign Power and Bare Life*, trans. Daniel Heller-Roazen (Stanford: Stanford University Press, 1998), 168.

7. The debasement of the Muslim "Semitic" dimension goes along with this. See Douglas L. Berger, "'The Poorest Form of Theism': Schopenhauer, Islam, and the Perils of Comparative Hermeneutics," *Islam and Christian-Muslim Relations* 15, no. 1 (2004): 135–46.

8. Arthur Schopenhauer, *Parerga und Paralipomena: Kleine philosophische Schriften*, in *Schopenhauers Sämmtliche Werke in fünf Bänden, Großherzog Wilhelm Ernst Ausgabe* (Leipzig: Insel Verlag), 5:412. In English, *Parerga and Paralipomena: Short Philosophical Essays*, 2 vols., trans. E. F. J. Payne (Oxford: Oxford University Press, 1974), 2:378. Further references are given parenthetically in the text, first to the German, then to the English edition. We should note in passing the fact that "fundamental characteristic" or "Grundcharakter" is itself a problematic concept in the "context" of a will—a world—that is groundless.

9. See my *The Rhetoric of Cultural Dialogue: Jews and Germans from Moses Mendelssohn to Richard Wagner and Beyond*, 220–24.

10. Schopenhauer favors its Catholic manifestations. In this respect, he is still sympathetic to a romantic perspective like the later Schlegel's. But he is not so sympathetic as to recapitulate Schlegel's—or more generally the German neo-Catholic romantic—take on the history of religions.

11. Spinoza too is an opponent of hope in its collusion with doubt, but in a very different sense from Schopenhauer.

12. On the "Doctrine of Immortality" or "Unsterblichkeitslehre," see *Parerga and Paralipomena*, vol. 2, chap. 12, "Additional Remarks on the Doctrine of the Suffering of the World" ("Vom Leiden der Welt"), §156 (327; 30); and on metempsychosis, see the same text, §177 (368; 365–66). And in turn, Schopenhauer's preference for the doctrine of reincarnation over the doctrine of creation out of nothing and his hostility to the idea of miracles—at least if one follows on this point the reasoning of Carl Schmitt—seem to contradict rather than support the possibility of the transcendent and redemptive exception that is represented by the self-negation of the will.

13. Against established religions, see 427–28; 392; and against the medieval founding of state on religion, see 374; 345.

14. See the insightful essay by Hent de Vries, "Zum Begriff der Allegorie in Schopenhauers Religionsphilosophie," in *Schopenhauer, Nietzsche, und die Kunst*, ed. Wolfgang Schirmacher (Vienna: Passagen Verlag, 1991), 187–97.

15. The use of "paralysis" here contrasts strikingly with Franz Rosenzweig's use of the term with reference to Parmenidean metaphysics.

16. See further the section "On Language and Words," in *Parerga and Paralipomena*, vol. 2.

17. If one takes the term "Vor-stellung" (as it were) literally, it looks very much like pre-figuration, even if *Vorstellungen* in Schopenhauer are pre-prefigured (nonfigurally) in the will.

18. The Jews are represented by Schopenhauer as figures of theft (387; 357), stealing from the Egyptians their gold and silver, hence that which stands for the medium of exchange, the medium of the determination of value, their "language" of money. The Jews represent here the stealing away of money and language at once.

19. If one encourages intermarriage, he says, one can get rid of the "tragic-comic nonessence [*Unwesen*]" in the quietest way possible, and so within about one hundred years "the ghost" (*das Gespenst*) could be "entirely exorcized, Ahasuerus buried and the chosen people will not know where it has gone" (286; 264).

20. Note the contrast between the *foetor Judaicus* in Schopenhauer, on the one hand, and his sense of India's spirit as possessing "the fragrance of a bloom" quoted above, on the other hand.

21. Even if in the mouth of the character Philalethes, the utterance fits with those to which Schopenhauer signs his own name elsewhere, concerning the eventual, potential replacement of religion by philosophy.

22. For a politically ambiguous perspective on pessimism from the 1940s, see Gottfried Benn, "Pessimismus" (1943), in *Gesammelte Werke in der Fassung der Erstdrucke*. 4 vols., ed. Bruno Hillebrand (Frankfurt am Main: Fischer Taschenbuch Verlag, 1989), 3:393–8.

23. References to the "Epiphilosophie," given parenthetically in text, concern the Werner Brede German edition and the Payne translation indicated above, in both cases the second volume.

24. Wilhelm Humboldt is an important exception to the general rule here, in that he sees Indian thought as genuinely theistic, and not merely as pantheistic. For an introductory discussion, see Dorothy Figueira, *The Exotic: A Decadent Quest* (Albany: State University of New York Press, 1994), 63–90.

25. Cf. "A few words on pantheism" in *Parerga and Paralipomena*, 2:116–19; 99–102.

26. The Kantian language here rings a little bit hollow, since to grasp "the essence of the world" ("das Wesen der Welt") as Schopenhauer claims to—to describe the "thing-in-itself" as will, and so on—would have been, for Kant, to go rather far beyond the limits of possible experience, if only by virtue of the "impoverished" concept of experience that Walter Benjamin has shown Kant to possess.

27. Rüdiger Safranski, *Schopenhauer und die wilden Jahre der Philosophie: Eine Biographie* (Munich: Carl Hanser Verlag, 1987), 320–23.

7. DIALECTICAL DEVELOPMENT OR PARTIAL CONSTRUCTION? MARTIN BUBER AND FRANZ KAFKA

1. The epigraph is from Arthur Schopenhauer, *The World as Will and Representation*, trans. E. F. J. Payne, vol. 2 (New York: Dover, 1958), chap. 38, "On History," 441–43.

2. In his essay on "Historicism" first published in 1924 (republished in *Essays on the Sociology of Knowledge*, ed. Paul Kecskemeti (New York: Oxford University Press, 1952), 84–133, Karl Mannheim tries to answer the relativism accusation in a series of reflections that bear witness to the aporias affecting any attempt to save historicism. Mannheim claims, for example, that historicism "fulfills its own essence only by managing to derive an ordering principle from this seeming anarchy of change, only by managing to penetrate the innermost structure of this all-pervading change" (86), but such a "fulfillment" of historicism would involve a return to an Enlightenment style "structure." This (re)turn makes Mannheim's protestations ring hollow, when

he claims that those who object to historicism's relativism are hung up on an Enlightenment model of supratemporal reason (90–91). Further on in his argument, he is still trying to reconcile the formalist and life-philosophical frameworks (or *Geist* and *Seele*), which he says descend from Hegel and the German historical school respectively. But these are displaced versions of the Enlightenment and historicist paradigms (107), the overcoming of whose mutual incompatibility he then envisions only by directing each to different objects, the former to philosophy, sciences, economy, and so on, and the latter to the arts, religion, and so on.

3. On this development, see Herbert Schnädelbach, *Philosophy in Germany, 1831–1933*, trans. Eric Matthews (Cambridge: Cambridge University Press, 1984), 33–66, chap. 2, "History," esp. 38–40.

4. See Schnädelbach, *Philosophy in Germany*, on historicism as involving the turning of Enlightenment arguments against the "ahistorical dogmatism" of Enlightenment (36), and on the development of historicist methodology, between the scylla of ahistorical universal principles and the charybdis of the historical self-relativization of one's own principles, in Droysen, Dilthey, Windelband, and Rickert, from the 1850s to the early 1900s (50–59). Schnädelbach spells out each of these positions in detail in his earlier book *Geschichtsphilosophie nach Hegel: Die Probleme des Historismus* (Freiburg: Verlag Karl Alber, 1974). On these same developments, see Georg Iggers, *The German Conception of History: The National Tradition of Historical Thought from Herder to the Present*, rev. ed. (Middletown: Wesleyan University Press, 1968), 124–229.

5. Later in his career, that is, in the long essay, "Two Types of Belief" (*Zwei Glaubensweisen*), from 1950 (written after both the Holocaust and Buber's extensive collaboration with Franz Rosenzweig, the great critic of Hegelian thought), Buber registers a more critical awareness of Hegelian Paulinism: "In our age a philosopher, Hegel, tore the Pauline conception out of its rootedness in the soil of its reality of faith [*dem Wurzelgrund ihrer Glaubenswirklichkeit entrissen*] and transplanted it into the system" (Martin Buber, *Werke, 1. Band, Schriften zur Philosophie* [Munich: Kösel Verlag and Heidelberg: Verlag Lambert Schneider, 1962], 651–782, here 718, trans. mine). Buber goes on to argue that Jesus' faith is compatible with *emunah*, whereas Paul's more Greek conception of *pistis* is not, and Buber contests Paul's reduction of Jewish *torah* to law *qua* dead letter (especially 686–726).

6. Martin Buber, "Der Geist des Orients und das Judentum," in Martin Buber, *Der Jude und sein Judentum: Gesammelte Aufsätze und Reden*, ed. Robert Weltsch (Cologne: Joseph Melzer Verlag, 1963), 46–65. My translations, pages given parenthetically in text. For an English translation, which I also consulted in considering translations, see "The Spirit of the Orient and

Judaism," in Martin Buber, *On Judaism*, ed. Nahum N. Glatzer (New York: Schocken, 1967), 56–78.

7. Rabid political, racial anti-Semitism takes off in Europe in the late 1870s with Wilhelm Marr, Adolph Stoeker, the Orientalist Paul de Lagarde, Heinrich von Treitschke, Edouard Drumont, and so on.

8. When Max Weber determines Judaism as a "pariah"-religion (e.g., in *Das antike Judentum*, vol. 3 of *Gesammelte Aufsätze zur Religions-soziologie* [Tübingen: J. C. B. Mohr/Paul Siebeck, 1966]), and Hannah Arendt follows him in speaking of Jews as "pariahs" ("The Jew as Pariah: A Hidden Tradition" in *The Jew as Pariah: Jewish Identity and Politics in the Modern Age*, ed. Ron Feldman [New York: Grove Press, 1978], 67–90), the Jews are being theorized as outcastes within a world conceived in terms of the ancient Indian—or Aryan—caste system. This strange structure inscribes Judaism as an internal exterior within Aryan culture.

9. On Aryan Christianity during the Third Reich, see Susannah Heschel, *The Aryan Jesus: Christian Theologians and the Bible in Nazi Germany* (Princeton: Princeton University Press, 2008). On the Aryan myth in Herder, F. Schlegel and the romantic mythographers, and through Renan, Max Müller, Gobineau, Houston Steward Chamberlain, and Alfred Rosenberg, see Dorothy M. Figueira, *Aryans, Jews, Brahmins* (Albany: State University of New York Press, 2002). On Renan's racist distinction between Semitic and Aryan, as organized around the opposition between a static origin and a dynamic development, see Maurice Olender, *The Languages of Paradise: Race, Religion, and Philology in the Nineteenth Century*, trans. Arthur Goldhammer (Cambridge, Mass.: Harvard University Press, 1992), 51–81, esp. 54–57). For an overview, see Léon Poliakov, *The Aryan Myth: A History of Racist and Nationalist Ideas in Europe*, trans. Edmund Howard (London: Sussex University Press and Heinemann Educational Books, 1974).

10. See Paul Mendes-Flohr, *Divided Passions: Jewish Intellectuals and the Experience of Modernity* (Detroit: Wayne State University Press, 1991). Although Mendes-Flohr usefully underlines the importance of Schopenhauer, he misses the importance of Hegelian patterns of thought for Buber's early essay.

11. See the useful discussion of the "Jew as Oriental" in Nina Berman, *Orientalismus, Kolonialismus und Moderne: Zum Bild des Orients in der deutschsprachigen Kultur um 1900* (Stuttgart: J. B. Metzler Verlag, 1997), 264–91.

12. Buber will depict the Jewish Oriental (in continuity with the Indian, Chinese, and Persian Orientals) as the one who identifies with the world will qua longing for unity. He thus contests Schopenhauer's view of the Jew as superficial optimist: "He [the Jew] has not just experienced the anxiety of the world, he has suffered it; in his will to becoming-one beats the longing of

the world, and what he completes with himself . . . he also does in a primally secret connection [*in urgeheimem Zusammenhang*] to the heart of the world" ("Der Geist des Orients und das Judentum," 55).

13. "The Jews are a straggler of the Orient" (*Die Juden sind ein Spätling des Orients*) (52).

14. "Everything I've said of the Oriental counts with particular clarity for the Jew" (53).

15. On Buber's approach to Bergsonian intuition, see "Zu Bergsons Begriff der Intuition," *Werke*, I, 1071–78.

16. Buber writes, for example, that the "inwardness" in which the Oriental's movement is grounded (*gegründet*) is itself not movement, but rather "he feels it within him untouchably and unchangeably restful, elevated above all multiplicity and opposition like a primal ground [*urgrundhaft*], the maternal womb [*Mutterschoß*], that bears and swallows up all multiplicity and opposition, the nameless core and meaning" (49).

17. The Orient recognizes, according to Buber, that the "originally intended unity is split and disfigured" (*die urgemeinte Einheit gespalten und entstellt ist*) (51). Below, we will see this motif of *Entstellung*—disfiguration—reappear in Freud.

18. Similarly, in decision "the unity of Being is fulfilled" (*es erfüllt sich die Einheit des Seins*) (54).

19. See Buber, "Die Lehre vom Tao," *Werke* I, 1021–52.

20. Although Christianity takes up much from Hellenism, "the enduringly fruitful in Christianity was originally Jewish substance" (*das dauernd Zeugende im Christentum war jüdisches Urgut*) (58).

21. See my discussion of Zionism and metaphysical anti-Judaism in "Schizotechnotheology in Some Zionist Texts: Melanie Klein and Martin Heidegger in the Promised Land," *American Journal of Semiotics* 10, no. 3–4 (1993): 27–80.

22. In addition, in the first published version of the text—cut from subsequent editions—Buber designates Germany as the one European nation on whom one can rely to use the mediating Jewish people to renew Oriental-Occidental relations. (I refer to the 1916 edition of Martin Buber, *Vom Geist des Judentums: Reden und Geleitworte* [Leipzig: Kurt Wolff Verlag, 1916], translations in what follows are my own.) Buber argues this because he sees in Germany both the country "whose life in spirit and whose metaphysical creation alone in modern Europe are related to those of the great Oriental peoples" (46) and the country that has been most influential on "the wandering Jew" in "his language and his life-forms" (47) as well as conversely the one that has "received the strongest impressions from Judaism" (47). Here, Buber mentions the examples of Luther's Bible translation, Spinoza as hav-

ing been "alone in Germany a deep and fruitful possession of the decisive minds," and the socialism of Marx and Lassalle as having been "completely assimilated" (*völlig assimiliert*) (47) only in Germany. Finally, he argues that this is "no chance but meaningful context [*sinnvoller Zusammenhang*]. The moment appears to me near in which it will be able to test itself in a context of activity [*Zusammenhang der Aktivität*]" (47–48). Buber's strikingly naïve overvaluation of Germany's interests in East-West reconciliation, of its intimacy with Oriental cultures, and of its friendliness toward Jewish culture was in some degree typical of the age, as the example of Hermann Cohen also demonstrates, on which topic see Jacques Derrida, "Interpretations at War: Kant, the Jew, the German," *New Literary History* 22, no. 1 (1991): 39–95. Thanks are due to my colleague and friend John McCole for pointing out to me this earlier edition of Buber's essay and the references to Germany cut from the later editions.

23. For the later Buber's approach to Kafka, see §16 of "Two Types of Faith" (*Werke*, 773–79). Here, Buber mobilizes Kafka as an illustration of the sensibility of a moment in history where Paulinism without any prospect of redemption has penetrated deeply into Jewry, but also as an answer on behalf of, or in terms of, *emunah*. "The way of the world appears here [in Kafka] more darkly than ever before, and yet with an even deeper 'despite all of that,' *emunah* is proclaimed anew, quite softly and hesitantly, but unambiguously" (779). Buber's late reading of Kafka as a figure of faith builds on certain of Kafka's own late theological aphorisms, and usefully underlines Kafka's distance from Pauline patterns of thought, but risks exaggerating Kafka's adherence to the traditional framework of *emunah*. On Buber's "Two Types of Faith," see the brief but useful general summary in Paul Mendes-Flohr, *Divided Passions*, 230–31, 257.

24. For an analysis of this phrase, which Kafka wrote on a postcard to Felice Bauer in 1916, see Weiyan Meng, "China and Chinese in Kafka's Works," in *Kafka and China*, ed. Adrian Hsia (Bern: Peter Lang, 1996), 75–96.

25. Franz Kafka, *Gesammelte Werke in zwölf Bänden, nach der kritischen Ausgabe*, ed. Hans-Gerd Koch, vol. 6, *Beim Bau der chinesischen Mauer und andere Schriften aus dem Nachlaß* (Frankfurt am Main: Fischer Taschenbuch Verlag, 2002), 146. Translations are my own unless otherwise indicated, page numbers are given parenthetically in text.

26. Franz Kafka, "The Great Wall of China," ibid.

27. For important recent contextual readings of Kafka that include his Jewish and Orientalist contexts, see Noah Isenberg, *Between Redemption and Doom: The Strains of German-Jewish Modernism* (Lincoln: University of Nebraska Press, 1999), 19–50; Rolf Goebel, *Constructing China: Kafka's*

Orientalist Discourse (Columbia, S.C.: Camden House, 1997); and Sander Gilman, *Franz Kafka, The Jewish Patient* (New York: Routledge, 1995); as well as the biographies by Hartmut Binder, Max Brod, Ronald Hayman, Anthony Horthey, Ernst Pawel, and Christoph Stölzl. These works attempt to ground their readings by grounding the texts they read in contexts of origination. External context—*Zusammenhang*—serves as unifying ground. Such readings, however, are always haunted by the danger that they will fail to do justice to the internal complexity and coherence of Kafka's texts, to their relentlessly self-qualifying character. However, mere formalism—reading for internal coherence, another mode of *Zusammenhang*—cannot suffice. No texts simply escape (infinite) contextual inscription, and Kafka's texts in particular emphasize, among other things, a certain passivity or impotence of the characters with respect to their (indeterminable) surroundings. Hence, we have to read Kafka in terms of neither internal nor external *Zusammenhang*, and both.

28. Kafka, *Beim Bau der chinesischen Mauer*, 80–83.

29. For example: "Unity! Unity! Breast beside breast, a round dance of the people, blood, no longer locked into the pitiful circulation of the body but rolling sweetly and yet returning through infinite China" (68).

30. For a reading of architectural metaphors in Kafka, which, however, considers neither architectonics in the philosophical sense nor Orientalism, see Gerhard Neumann, "Chinesische Mauer und Schacht von Babel: Franz Kafkas Architekturen," *Deutsche Vierteljahrschrift für Literaturwissenschaft und Geistesgeschichte* 3 (2009): 452–71.

31. The allusion to the sublime, as a nontotalizable excess and a confrontation of the finite mental capacities with an infinite thing, appears not only in the narrator's general description of the wall, but also in the tension between "narrow enough" limits on his "capacity to think" and the "endless" region his mind has to traverse to comprehend the "leadership" (71); in the tension between "Auffassung" and "Zusammenfassung" through which Kafka explicitly invokes Kant's language (70, 78–80); and in the explicit claim that "the leadership wanted something nonpurposive" (70), that is, that there is a counterpurposive purposiveness at work in the "system of partial construction" (for the sublime is a counterpurposive purposiveness). Kafka confronts us with a hermeneutic sublime, placing in question any possible delimitation of the subject of understanding.

32. For Kant's articulation of the opposition between an architectonics and a rhapsody, which as we saw above Friedrich Schlegel used as the basis for his distinction between organic and mechanical languages, see the section of the *Critique of Pure Reason* titled "The Architectonic of Pure Reason."

33. See Jay Geller, *The Other Jewish Question: Identifying the Jew and Making Sense of Modernity* (New York: Fordham University Press, 2011), 50–87,

for the dense and perverse tradition of analogies drawn between the Chinese and the Jewish gathered around the figure of the pigtail and the circumcised penis, which Kafka is prolonging here. Geller rightly stresses the complex overdeterminations of these "fetishized images of the Other" (87), and prudently leaves the question "undecided: are European identifications of Jew and Chinese parallel effects of the West's fetishizing logic, or is the *Zopf* a displacement from Sinai to Sinology" (87). My own analysis emphasizes and argues for the great importance, although not the exclusive importance, of the latter dimension.

34. For this characterization of the oral law as a fence around the written law, which stems from Rabbi Akiba ben Joseph, see *The Ethics of the Talmud* (*Pirkei Avot*), ed. R. Travers Herford (New York: Schocken, 1945), III, 17, p. 85. As in Kafka's Prague one of the most prominent organizations for Jewish renewal was the Bar Kochba Verein, and as Akiba was the main supporter of Bar Kochba among the rabbis, himself put to death by the Romans in 135 C.E., the resonance of any allusion to Akiba in this story published in *Selbstwehr* would have significance. Clement Greenberg had the perspicacity to see in this Kafka story an allusion to the fence around the law ("At the Building of the Great Wall of China," in *Franz Kafka Today*, ed. Angel Flores and Homer Swander (Madison: University of Wisconsin Press, 1958), 77–82, but he misread Kafka's interest in Judaism by overemphasizing Kafka's chagrin over the condition of diaspora Jewry, as if Kafka's writings (rather than, say, his biographical persona) were much closer to the Zionist rejection of diaspora culture than my reading would suggest. Using the Chinese discourse to signify the Jewish discourse constitutes here a parody of the Orientalist gesture. Further, concerning the figure of the oral law as Great Wall, Kafka can be seen to be asserting both the uselessness and the superfluity of the oral law here, while affirming it in a sense. It is useless because people pillage and interpretively abuse the Old Testament anyway, superfluous because we cannot know what it finally means. This would be one place to intervene in the Scholem/Benjamin debate summarized well by Robert Alter in *Necessary Angels: Tradition and Modernity in Kafka, Benjamin, and Scholem* (Cambridge, Mass.: Harvard University Press, 1991) and pursued further by Giorgio Agamben in *Homo Sacer: Sovereign Power and Bare Life*, trans. Daniel Heller-Roazen (Stanford: Stanford University Press, 1998), 49–58. The point of departure would be as follows: Insofar as China, within its wall, figures Torah itself, Kafka would be implying here that there is indeed a revealed text, but that we (nomadic reader-barbarians) both cannot access it *and* can access it all too easily, despite and because of the fact that this oral law—the Wall—discontinuously intervenes.

35. Given the prominence of Buber and his writings on the Far East, and on Eastern Judaism, as well as the facts that Kafka is communicating

with Buber at this time (e.g., he sends Buber a package of stories in April 1917) and that he gives his sister a volume of *Chinesische Volksmärchen* in the same month, one wonders whether Kafka may even have had Buber in mind when he wrote in the same notebook as the one in which "The Great Wall of China" was written down, just a few pages later," "This (perhaps all too Europeanizing) translation of some old, Chinese manuscript pages has been placed at our disposal by a friend of action" (83). It is almost as if he were saying that Buber, a "friend of action" by comparison with Kafka, has placed this topos of China as Jewish-Oriental origin onto his agenda, prompting him to write the text. But like Kafka's text, this speculation "is a fragment. There is no hope that its extension could be found." The fragment then concludes: "Here follow some more pages, which, however, are too damaged for anything definite to be gleaned from them" (83).

36. The narrator suggests that the emperor is deluded if he thinks he has ordained the building of the wall.

37. The people in turn function as the emperor's center insofar as we are told that they constitute his foundations, or "Stützen" (73). In this sense, too, they are decentered (and doubled) with respect to themselves.

38. This panicky anxiety of hope combined with fear, or despair (hopelessness), is reminiscent of that condition Spinoza encouraged us to leave behind in the diminution of the passions, and of the condition that was induced in Herder by the possible absence of any teleology, that is, by the possibility of the impossibility of a historicism.

39. The motif of indecision is, of course, prominent in all of Kafka's texts, from the early story "Resolutions" to the great novels, *The Trial* and *The Castle*, as in such wonderful refrains as "Official decisions are shy like young girls" (*Amtsentscheidungen sind scheu wie junge Mädchen*), to somewhat more private texts such as the "Letter to the Father" (regarding the choice of a profession), and so on.

40. So the ground of the unity of the people is their incapacity to represent their leader to themselves. This makes them like the Jews and like the "community without community" of which Jean-Luc Nancy writes (*La communautée désoeuvrée* [Paris: Christian Bourgois, 1986]), since what they share is no grasp of their common essence. But perhaps above all, in terms of Freud's *Group Psychology and the Analysis of the Ego*, it makes them a community or mass on the edge of panic, on the verge of disintegration, because their grounding leaders are only tenuously present.

41. In Walter Benjamin's radio-essay, "Franz Kafka: Beim Bau der chinesischen Mauer" (*Gesammelte Schriften*, vol. II.2 [Frankfurt am Main: Suhrkamp Verlag, 1980], 676–83, trans. mine), an essay worth its own essay, Benjamin argues that Kafka's creatures are on all levels "in solidarity only

in the one sole feeling of anxiety [*Angst*]. An anxiety that is not a reaction but an organ" (681). In this sense, Kafka speaks directly of the anxiety that has underlain Orientalist historicism all along. Benjamin also writes of the "panic horror" (*panisches Entsetzen*) (678) mixed into the "astonishment" with which the reader must react to the "nearly incomprehensible disfigurations of existence" (*fast unverständlichen Entstellungen des Daseins*) (678) that ironically "(ful)fill" (*erfüllt*) (678) Kafka, disfigurations that make up "his one and only object" (*seine einen und einzigen Gegenstand*) (678). With these *Entstellungen* and the "signs, indications, and symptoms of displacements" (*Zeichen, Anzeichen, und Symptome von Verschiebungen*) Benjamin grasps Kafka by means of a Freudian vocabulary we will treat in detail in the following chapter.

42. In another small fragment on Babel from the *Nachlaß*, Kafka writes that at the beginning of the project the order "was perhaps too great," which led to further delays in the construction of the "foundations" (Kafka, *Gesammelte Werke*, vol. 7, *Zur Frage der Gesetze und andere Schriften aus dem Nachlaß*, 143). Here order creates disorder, and the coming together of people is disrupted by their struggles for prestige.

43. In *Ernst und Falk: Dialogues for Freemasons*—a text that belongs to the allusive background or context of Kafka's "Wall of China" text owing to the common thematic figure of "masonry"—G. E. Lessing similarly explores the notion that the inevitable accompaniment of social unification is social division.

44. Cf. the very thorough Lacanian-oriented commentary on Kafka's Chinese Wall and Tower of Babel texts by Wolf Kittler, *Der Turmbau zu Babel und das Schweigen der Sirenen: Über das Reden, das Schweigen, die Stimme und die Schrift in vier Texten von Franz Kafka* (Erlangen: Verlag Palm und Enke, 1985), 11–110. Although Kittler's reading, which I discovered only after nearly completing my own, does not concern itself with Orientalism, historicism, or typology, it does thematize questions of grounding, language, subjectivity, and borderlines in a manner with which I am in substantial agreement, as our shared poststructuralist point of departure assures.

45. Franz Kafka, *Historisch-Kritische Ausgabe sämtlicher Handschriften, Drucke und Typoskripte, Oxforder Oktavhefte 3 und 4*, ed. Roland Reuß and Peter Staengle (Frankfurt am Main: Stroemfeld Verlag, 2008).

46. Franz Kafka, *The Complete Stories* (New York: Schocken, 1971).

47. On the question of whether or not a message always arrives at its destination, see Jacques Derrida's critical reading of Jacques Lacan's reading of Edgar Allan Poe's "The Purloined Letter," in *La carte postale: De Socrate à Freud et au-delà* (Paris: Flammarion, 1980), 439–524. For a more measured adjudication of the debate, see Barbara Johnson's "The Frame of Reference: Poe, Lacan, Derrida," in *The Critical Difference: Essays in the Contemporary*

Rhetoric of Reading (Baltimore: Johns Hopkins University Press, 1980), 110–46. Walter Benjamin notes, in "Franz Kafka: Beim Bau der chinesischen Mauer" (which begins with a long quotation of "An Imperial Message"), as against Max Brod's religiophilosophical reading of Kafka, that the only (ironic) mercy (*Gnade*) in Kafka is the fact that the law never appears there, that the stories remain "pregnant with a moral they do not deliver" (679), and thus radically anticipatory even in their repetition of the lack of full presence. Kafka's writing is "(ful)filled" with "configurations of forgetting" (*Konfigurationen des Vergessens*) (82). This is one important way in which it displaces Pauline "fulfillment."

8. THE DREAMWORK OF HISTORY: ORIENTALISM AND ORIGINARY DISFIGURATION IN FREUD'S *MOSES AND MONOTHEISM*

1. The epigraph from Franz Kafka is from "Ein altes Blatt," in *Beim Bau der chinesischen Mauer und andere Schriften aus dem Nachlaß, Gesammelte Werke in zwölf Bänden, Nach der Kritischen Ausgabe*, ed. Hans-Gerd Koch, v. 6 (Frankfurt am Main: Fischer Taschenbuch Verlag, 1994), 81–83. Translation my own.

2. Sigmund Freud, *Der Mann Moses und die monotheistische Religion: Drei Abhandlungen*, in Studienausgabe, vol. 9, ed. Alexander Mitscherlich et al. (Frankfurt am Main: Fischer Taschenbuch Verlag, 1982), 455–584, here 504. The epigraphs taken from this text are from pages 503, 493, and 554, in the order in which they appear. Translations are my own. Pages hereafter are given parenthetically in the text.

3. This is why trying to decide the question of whether Freud is "Jewish"—addressed with subtlety by Yerushalmi, Gay, and others—is something of a false path: Of course Freud is Jewish, and of course that's complicated, and he understands himself also to be other and more (or less) than that. See Peter Gay, *A Godless Jew: Freud, Atheism, and the Making of Psychoanalysis* (New Haven: Yale University Press, 1987); Yosef Hayim Yerushalmi, *Freud's Moses: Judaism Terminable and Interminable* (New Haven: Yale University Press, 1991); Jacques Derrida, *Archive Fever: A Freudian Impression*, trans. Eric Prenowitz (Chicago: University of Chicago Press, 1996); and Barbara Johnson's recent attempt to argue for a multicultural, rather than a Jewish nationalist, Moses (or Freud) in *Moses and Multiculturalism* (Berkeley: University of California Press, 2011). For a constantly informative, insightful, and witty examination of the way in which Freud's Jewishness pervades his body/corpus, see Jay Geller, *On Freud's Jewish Body: Mitigating Circumcisions* (New York: Fordham University Press, 2007). Geller's explorations of circumcision, castration, feminization, homosexualization, and racial othering surrounding the figure of the Jew in Freud's Vienna (and thus in his experience and

works) are strikingly illuminating, including the final chapter devoted to *Moses and Monotheism*. If the Jew is figured as—made responsible for— disfiguration (i.e., made responsible for figural representation as disfiguration, or for language as death) in the Christian culture at large, then this aligns in terms of gender with the feminine, since in Christian supersessionist ideology the literal (spirit) supersedes the figural (material letter) as the masculine supersedes the feminine (as the latter's "noncastrated" norm, etc.). Being ungrounded tends to get constructed in gendered terms as feminine whereas being grounded gets figured as masculine, even as the ground of the masculine is often posited as the feminine, which nonetheless anticipates "him." In these terms, Geller's more body- and gender-focused analysis and my more theotypological and semiological analysis are concentrating on closely related structures at different levels. The circumcised penis functions like a figural signifier, a sign that has become unwhole. In Christian and (then) Occidental discourse, first the Jews and then the Orientals more generally function to fill (i.e., to disavow) the hole in language and the body (i.e., whatever makes them unwhole) with and as the cause of that very hole, an unwholeness (and unholiness) that nonetheless stands as the (fetishistic) beginning of a possible (Christian/Western) wholeness.

4. James Henry Breasted offered Freud the analysis of Moses' name as Egyptian and also, alongside A. Weigall, the story of Ikhnaton as inventor of monotheism; Ernst Sellin extended the tradition (to which Goethe also contributed) of the assumption that Moses was murdered in the desert; Eduard Meyer provided Freud with the hypothesis that Moses was Pharaoh's daughter, with the derivation of circumcision from Egypt, and with an account of the Israelites' assumption of the Jahve religion in Maribat-Qades.

5. Jan Assmann looks like he is attempting to turn hostility back on the Jews—despite his protestations to the contrary, and perhaps not quite consciously—by calling "monotheism" the "Mosaic distinction" even though he grants that it is an Egyptian invention, for example in *Moses der Ägypter: Entzifferung einer Gedächtnisspur* (Frankfurt am Main: Fischer Taschenbuch Verlag, 2007) and its English version, *Moses the Egyptian: The Memory of Egypt in Western Monotheism* (Cambridge, Mass.: Harvard University Press, 1997). It is hard, moreover, for Assmann persuasively to argue that he is not determining as a kind of false religion precisely the counterreligion that he problematizes for having introduced intolerance and the loss of nature into the human world by distinguishing between true and false religion. At the end of *The Price of Monotheism* (Stanford: Stanford University Press, 2009), Assmann says that he wants to retain the distinction between truth and falsity (120), including in religion, but that he wants to "work through" or "sublimate" (120) the trauma of the distinction itself. He also writes that Freud "refuses to

acknowledge the Christian radicalization of religious spirituality as evidence of progress in intellectuality" (102) and asserts the (Pauline and Lutheran) arguments that monotheism—the "Mosaic distinction"—involves a turn from speech to writing. Assmann envisages progress beyond the Mosaic distinction, then, as some sort of mediation between transcendent and immanent religions—as in father and son—that would resynthesize artifice and nature. Assmann's argument certainly favors a Christian-style solution, even though he does not admit this, as offering a compromise between monotheism and paganism, and despite the fact that he says that Christianity in no way enables a return to paganism (since, indeed, a mediation, an *Aufhebung*, but not a complete return is what he desires). Although one can learn an enormous amount from Assmann, nonetheless, he problematically makes monotheism responsible for what language universally introduces: a certain loss of being.

6. See Martin Bernal, *Black Athena: The Afro-Asiatic Roots of Classical Civilization*, vol. 1, *The Fabrication of Ancient Greece, 1785–1985* (New Brunswick, N.J.: Rutgers University Press, 1987), most narrowly chapter 5, 224–80. For critical reviews of Bernal's project, see Mary R. Lefkowitz and Guy MacLean Rogers, eds., *Black Athena Revisited* (Chapel Hill: University of North Carolina Press, 1996). For Bernal's counterresponse, see *Black Athena Writes Back: Martin Bernal Responds to His Critics*, ed. David Chioni Moore (Durham, N.C.: Duke University Press, 2001). For a measured analysis, see Jacques Berlinerblau, *Heresy in the University: The Black Athena Controversy and the Responsibilities of American Intellectuals* (New Brunswick, N.J.: Rutgers University Press, 1999). Concerning the constitutive role of ancient Egyptian culture with respect to ancient Greece, Bernal clarifies in *Black Athena Writes Back* that his "Revised Ancient Model" (now) merely proposes a combination of influences from "north" and "south" on ancient Greece. His examination of eighteenth- and nineteenth-century attitudes toward race within the context of Orientalist and classicist discussions of Egypt, Phoenicia, and so on, remains informative.

7. I summarize Freud, *Der Mann Moses und die monotheistische Religion*, 528–31, in the following paragraphs.

8. Thomas Mann's story, "The Transposed Heads" ("Die vertauschten Köpfe"), in Thomas Mann, *Die Erzählungen*, vol. 2 (Frankfurt am Main: Fischer Taschenbuch Verlag, 1978), draws on Heinrich Zimmer's "The Indian World-Mother," in Heinrich Zimmer, *Die indische Weltmutter: Aufsätze*, ed. Friedrich Wilhelm (Frankfurt am Main: Insel Verlag, 1980), 17–56, which in turn follows Johann Jakob Bachofen, to sketch out the fantasy of a matriarchal period preceding the Aryan. In this way, Mann honors in 1940 an ancient Indian tradition, but a specifically non-Aryan and nonmasculinist tradition, with playful seriousness. By making the story further turn in a tragicomic

mode around the nonsynthesizable binary opposition of body and spirit, as represented by the two friends Nanda and Schridaman, respectively, Mann invokes Schillerian aesthetics of grace as synthesis of inclination and duty, a neoclassicizing gesture, while ironizing the possibility of any totalization of these principles. Finally, as the two friends, like the principles they represent, long for each other, Mann includes as often a homoerotic element, which takes this Indian story even further from the contemporaneous Aryan-Nazi ideology with its virulent homophobia.

9. The attempt to put to rest a matriarchal dimension would be one aspect of Fritz Lang's Orientalist films, *The Tiger of Eshnapur* and *The Indian Tomb*, that would be worthy of complex discussion in this context of analytic and modernist perspectives on Orientalism. Lang's two postwar remakes of the earlier versions of this material based on Thea von Harbou's novel present a host of Orientalist stereotypes in the form of kitsch, but to such an extent that one is almost tempted to read the films as exposing the absurdity of the clichés they manipulate, from the repair of the architectural foundations of the palace to the abduction of the Western woman from the "seraglio" (to recall Mozart's operatic precedent). The return of the lepers from the underground resonates interestingly, moreover, with the discussion of leprosy in Freud's text (discussed later in this chapter), especially since when they emerge from below they have the appearance of "muslims" in the Nazi death camps. But to do justice to these films in their historical, biographical, and formal contexts exceeds the scope of this book. For an entry into the discussion, see Barbara Mennel, "Returning Home: The Orientalist Spectacle of Fritz Lang's 'Der Tiger von Eschnapur" and 'Das indische Grabmal,'" in *Take Two: Fifties Cinema in Divided Germany*, ed. John E. Davidson and Sabine Hake (New York: Berghahn, 2007), 28–43; and Michael Tratner, "Lovers, Filmmakers, and Nazis: Fritz Lang's Last Two Movies as Autobiography," *Biography* 29, no. 1 (2006): 86–100. The many other important Orientalist or Orientalism-related German films, from *The Golem*, *Gypsy Blood*, and *The Adventures of Prince Achmed* to the films of Fatih Akin and other contemporaries, constitute a topic for a book of their own.

10. The ascetic, idealizing aspect of religion, which Freud underscores, is a trait that Schopenhauer wants to appropriate and monopolize for his own philosophical refoundation of ancient Hinduism, while denying it has any place, for example, in Judaism.

11. What complicates this picture from the beginning, however, is what Lacan characterized as the imaginary dimension, with all its aggression. Freud, of course, also appreciates this aggressivity and duplicity of the imaginary.

12. Freud cites in a footnote here (537) Goethe's "Israel in der Wüste," which I discussed in chapter 3.

13. Roman Jakobson, "Two Aspects of Language and Two Types of Aphasic Disturbances" (in *Selected Writings*, vol. 2, *Word and Language* [The Hague: Mouton, 1971], 239–60: "A competition between both devices, metonymic and metaphoric, is manifest in any symbolic process, be it intrapersonal or social. Thus in an inquiry into the structure of dreams, the decisive question is whether the symbols and the temporal sequences used are based on contiguity (Freud's metonymic 'displacement' and synecdochic 'condensation') or on similarity (Freud's 'identification and symbolism')" (258).

14. See, for example, Jacques Lacan, *Écrits* (Paris: Éditions du Seuil, 1966), especially "L'instance de la lettre dans l'inconscient ou la raison depuis Freud," 493–530, in particular 505–23. For a commentary of Lacan's on Freud's *Moses and Monotheism*, see Jacques-Alain Miller, ed., *Le Séminaire de Jacques Lacan, Livre XVII, L'envers de la psychanalyse (1969–70)* (Paris: Éditions du Seuil, 1991), 117–63, 241–46. For a compelling Lacanian reading of the ten commandments, see Kenneth Reinhard and Julia Reinhard Lupton, "The Subject of Religion: Lacan and the Ten Commandments," *Diacritics* 33, no. 2 (2003): 71–97.

15. One wonders also whether the primal scene—or the sexual difference as incomprehensible—is not more closely connected to the beginnings of language and culture than Freud accounts for in *Moses* (or even *Totem and Taboo*), where the primal father and his annihilation by the brothers, rather than, for example, father and mother in their tension, become the Ur-trauma, despite the fact that, for example, in the passage just cited (527) the not yet linguistically inscribed subject observes parental sexuality. Freud's masculinist obsession with paternity no doubt plays a disfiguring role here of its own.

16. In terms of the Kafka fragments we considered, religion is the development of a Babelian project.

17. Sigmund Freud, *Die Traumdeutung*, in *Studienausgabe*, vol. 2 (Frankfurt am Main: Fischer Taschenbuch Verlag, 1982).

18. On *Entstellung* in *The Interpretation of Dreams*, see Samuel Weber, *The Legend of Freud* (Minneapolis: University of Minnesota Press, 1982), 66–68.

19. As Freud puts it in *Moses and Monotheism*: "The passageways of thought and what may be analogous to them in the It, are in themselves unconscious [*an sich unbewußt*] and attain access to the consciousness only through linkage with memory-remainders of perceptions of sight and hearing by way of the linguistic function" (544–45).

20. Strikingly, Freud defines *Entstellung* in *Moses* in both metaphorical and metonymical terms: "One would like to lend 'Entstellung' the double sense to which it has a claim, although it makes no use of that double sense today. It should not only mean: to alter in its appearance, but also: to bring to a different place, to displace to somewhere else [*anderswohin verschieben*].

Thus, in many cases of textual disfiguration [*Textentstellung*] we can count on finding the suppressed and denied somewhere hidden, even if altered and torn from its context [*abgeändert und aus dem Zusammenhang gerissen*]. Only it won't always be easy to recognize it" (493). Since "to alter in its appearance" is tantamount to "to substitute" along an axis of "similarity"-"dissimilarity," whereas "to bring to a different place" is tantamount to "to combine" anew along an axis of "contiguity," Freud's definition of *Entstellung* in *Moses* supports my evocation of Jakobson and Lacan to characterize the term.

21. The verbal motif of *Entstellung* appears on pages 477, 483, 488, 491, 493, 495–96, 514–15, 517, 518, 530, 533, 535, 542, 548, 569, 572, 574, 580. To trace its conceptuality thoroughly, however, one would have to connect it with other uses of "stellen" and "Stelle," including "Vorstellung," and so on, as well as the related motif of "Setzung" and all of its variants (including "Besetzung"), which proliferate across the text unsettlingly, in a zone where it is quite difficult to discern where intention ends and the dynamics of the language itself begin.

22. For a discussion of "distortion" in *Moses and Monotheism* and Freud's relation to Moses more broadly, see Bluma Goldstein, *Reinscribing Moses: Heine, Kafka, Freud, and Schoenberg in a European Wilderness* (Cambridge, Mass.: Harvard University Press, 1992), 97–102.

23. See Michel de Certeau on this subject, "The Fiction of History: The Writing of *Moses and Monotheism*," in his *The Writing of History*, trans. Tom Conley (New York: Columbia University Press, 1988), 308–54.

24. The two prefaces to part 3, the first written in Vienna, the second in London, and which "contradict each other, indeed suspend each other [*ja einander aufheben*]" (506), explain in the first instance why Freud will not publish part 3, and then in the second case why he will. Although on one level the prefaces certainly provide a historical record of Freud's intentions, one could also say that the two prefaces, precisely in their simultaneity and incompatibility, perform the double nature/culture of the human—as cut off from the world and as part of the world—that accounts for, or restates, the possibility and necessity of *Entstellung*.

25. Freud comes back to this figure later, in the second preface to part 3, when he writes that to his own "critique . . . this work that takes off from the man, Moses, appears like a dancer balancing on the point of one toe" (507). The reason is that the foundations of humanity—the origination of human culture out of the Real of nature—appear simultaneously with their erasure, if these foundations occur as the primal father and his murder and cannibalization by the sons, that is, as representation beginning with identity and difference.

26. Thomas Mann, in "The Tablets of the Law" ["Das Gesetz"] (in Thomas Mann, *Die Erzählungen*, Bd. 2 (Frankfurt am Main: Fischer Taschen-

buch Verlag, 1978), rewrites the "exposure" myth in the wake of Freud and Rank, restoring the tale to a more classical version, such that Moses is the Pharaoh's daughter's baby, but then humanizing and humorizing this version, by making the father a young Hebrew to whom the Pharaoh's daughter had taken a fancy. Mann's playfully sympathetic reimagining of the exodus story, written in 1943 under commission by Armin L. Robinson as a contribution to the war against fascism, draws on Goethe and Freud in various further respects. It has to be read together with Mann's tetralogy of novels, *Joseph and His Brothers*, written during the fascist period, which incorporates the Akhenaten story (on the authority of Weigall and other sources Freud also consulted) and fuses it with the biblical narrative in a complex manner that resists the Nazi terminus of Orientalism.

27. One can see a similar attempt to rehabilitate teleology through a doctrine of the individual will, in some cases that of the historian himself, in the historicist tradition. In his essay "Historicism" Karl Mannheim summarizes Ernst Troeltsch's "central thesis" as stating that "historical knowledge . . . presupposes a subject harboring definite aspirations regarding the future and actively striving to achieve them" (102), and Mannheim similarly suggests that "the historico-philosophically relevant subject is just that kernel of the human personality whose being and dynamism is consubstantial with the dominant active forces of history" (102).

28. Freud discusses the tradition that Moses was "of heavy tongue" (*schwer von Sprache*) (482) and comments that this might have been literally true, or that it might indicate "in a light disfiguration" (*in leichter Entstellung*) that Moses was "one who spoke differently" (*ein Anderssprachiger*) (483), that is, that he was an Egyptian.

29. Nor can "faith" change the situation. That is, it cannot re-embed the human in a natural context of either inner intention or external reality. Freud makes this clear when he at once invests in, and parodies, the language of faith in one of the drily humorous passages of the text, his "confession of faith": "We confess therefore the faith that the idea of a single God as well as the rejection of magically effective ceremonial and the emphasis on the ethical demand in his name were in fact Mosaic doctrines, which . . . after a long intermediary time came to effect and . . . asserted themselves in an enduring fashion" (515).

30. For a fascinating historical explanation of the ancient Egyptian Manetho's narrative of the uprising of the lepers, see Jan Assmann, *Price of Monotheism*, 57–66, which elaborates on his earlier account in *Moses the Egyptian*, 29–44. My own approach underlines that the trauma separating the human from nature is not first monotheism, but language, whereas Assmann attributes this separation to monotheism. See, for example, his discussion of

the sense in which monotheism implies separation and loss of "meaning" in chapter 4 of *The Price of Monotheism* (42)—a discussion which is problematic insofar as one doesn't simply have a meaninglessness of existence in monotheisms—and his opposition of "primary" to "secondary" religions in terms of the binary opposition between writing and speech in chapter 5, and so on. In this nostalgic tendency, Assmann illustrates the model of Orientalism I am outlining in this book: Oriental cosmotheism functions for him as the natural origin (or foundation) that gets lost when (first Egyptian or cognitive, then the much worse Jewish or political) monotheism supervenes (35–43), and Christianity at least makes some progress toward returning to the synthesis of repressed nature with repressing law, even if more still needs to be done in this regard by modern Egyptologists.

31. One could align Hegel's China with Freud's primal father as initial imposition of the principle of identity, and Hegel's India with Freud's brother-horde, as the introduction of the principle of difference, but in Freud there is no Persia, still less a Greece, but just repetition of China in Egypt, and subsequent repetitions of China and India.

32. Assmann argues in *The Price of Monotheism* that he first (in *Moses the Egyptian*) saw Freud as suspending the monotheistic negation of polytheism, but now has decided that Freud is defending that negation (86). This alternative—does Freud vote yes or no for "progress in spirituality" (and thus, for Judaism)—strikes me as much too simple to do justice to Freud or to the matter at hand, for if, as Assmann sees it, polytheism embeds humans in nature whereas monotheism separates humans from nature, then with a little reflection on modern intellectual history we can see that there is no choice between polytheism and monotheism. We have to choose both simultaneously. Modern intellectual history tells us this because romanticism tries the path of what Assmann calls polytheism here—naturalism—but when this fails (or reveals its one-sidedness), decadence (1890s) tries the opposite path of artifice—culturalism—and when this fails, modernists—such as Freud—intelligently (and rightly) attempt to combine these two perspectives and to work through their mutual incompatibility. Freud affirms in their mutual contradictoriness not just rationality and ego but also irrationality and id, being in language and living in a world that exceeds language, so he both affirms "progress in spirituality" and the recognition that this progress comes at the constantly paid price of an irrevocable loss, a loss of a "nature" that, inevitably but never entirely, also returns.

33. Cf. Kafka's untitled manuscript fragment on Babel (Franz Kafka, *Zur Frage der Gesetze und andere Schriften aus dem Nachlaß, Gesammelte Werke in zwölf Bänden, nach der Kritischen Ausgabe*, vol. 7, 143–44, in which it is precisely "order" that leads to "disorder," thus dispersing the peoples who wish

to build the tower and turning them against each other before they even start building: "In the beginning at the building of the Tower of Babylon everything was in decent order, indeed the order was perhaps too great" (143). By arguing that monotheism makes impossible the "translation" between the gods of others and the gods of one's own culture (*Price of Monotheism*, 18), Assmann argues essentially that monotheism—and this means essentially Judaic, revolutionary monotheism—is the building of the tower of Babel, that is, responsible for the limits of communication among humans, a deeply problematic claim.

34. Edward Said, *Freud and the Non-European*, intro. Christopher Bollas, response by Jacqueline Rose (London: Verso, 2003).

35. This mutual entanglement occurs on three levels: in the use of typology within Orientalism generally, in the frequent traditional designation of Jews as (exemplary) Orientals, and in the necessity of splitting the Orient into good and evil, which for the German right wing of the early twentieth century took the form of the Aryan-Semitic split, and now frequently takes the form of the Jewish-Arab, Israeli-Palestinian split. At times Said falls into implying in an oversimplifying manner that the Palestinians are the "good" Semites while the Israelis are the "bad" ones, as I will show here. Such a counterproductive competition remains bound up with the notion of sovereign self-determination, which always entails the infinite (and therefore both violent and nonattainable) domination or mastery of the "other."

36. "Orientalism Reconsidered," in Edward Said, *Reflections on Exile and Other Essays* (Cambridge, Mass.: Harvard University Press, 2000), 198–215. On this subject, in "Orientalism Reconsidered," Said points us back to the passages in *Orientalism* on Proust and Renan where this comes up (e.g., 293). See James Pasto, "Islam's 'Strange Secret Sharer': Orientalism, Judaism, and the Jewish Question," *Comparative Studies in Society and History* 40, no. 3 (1998): 437–74, for key points of reference in German biblical scholarship and in the political-ideological history of the "Jewish Question" since the emancipatory epoch; for a judicious evaluation and expansion of Said's remarks on the similarities between Orientalism and anti-Semitism; and finally for an insightful analysis of the limitations of Said's exploration of this topic.

37. "One of the legacies of Orientalism, and indeed one of its epistemological foundations, is historicism. . . . What has never taken place is an epistemological critique of the connection between the development of . . . historicism . . . and . . . the actual practice of imperialism" ("Orientalism Reconsidered," 210). I work toward such a critique in this book.

38. Edward Said, *Humanism and Democratic Criticism* (New York: Columbia University Press, 2004), 103.

39. Said's summary of Nazi anti-Semitism here—"Jews were foreign, and therefore expendable" (40)—displays little comprehension of the structure of Nazi anti-Semitism, for which the Jews were not just "foreign" and not just "expendable" but the antirace par excellence, the undermining of nature, and the source of all the world's (or at least of Germany's) ills. They represented death and matter as antispirit, difference, and so on. The same structure, generally in less rabidly racist and exterminationist terms, is tendentially applied to the Orient (more specifically to the nonassimilable aspect of the Orient) across all of historicist modern Orientalism. Nazism is indeed, in part, one "outgrowth" of this Orientalism, which is not limited in its object to the Arab and Muslim Orient but very much includes it. While Said says in "Orientalism Reconsidered" that no one has yet offered him a good reason as to why he "should have" included Germany more substantially in his book, the foregoing would perhaps supply the reason.

40. Freud was, of course, subject to the influence of the racist thought of his times. See Celia Brickman, *Aboriginal Populations in the Mind: Race and Primitivity in Psychoanalysis* (New York: Columbia University Press, 2003), and on *Moses and Monotheism*, 150–53. Nonetheless, not only in *Moses and Monotheism* but even in *Totem and Taboo*, Freud attributes repression to the most "primitive" of cultures, and in this way undercuts the progressive historicist narrative he still upholds in some other respects.

41. Israel is "adopted by the Atlantic West" and functions "as, in effect, a quasi-European state" (Said, *Freud and the Non-European*, 41). This is not entirely untrue, but its history is a complex one for which many different actors—whether "European," "non-European," or something in between—must be given, and assume, their portion of responsibility.

42. In "Orientalism Reconsidered," when Said speaks of "the white European democracy that is Israel" (208), the same sometime tendency makes itself felt. Namely, one sees here the tendency to push Israeli Jews away from any right to be in the Middle East by trying to force on them a European and white identity, while blaming them for assuming this identity. This is the type of discursive gesture to which Said rightly objects when he complains that Orientalists speak "as if Islam were one simple thing" (205). Here the cycle of violence repeats itself on the level of discourse, as Jacqueline Rose says she fears it will, in her all-too-measured response to Said's lecture on Freud, where she stresses the difficulty of escaping from both identity and traumatic repetition ("Response to Edward Said," in *Freud and the Non-European*, 74–78). See her subtle and articulate subsequent texts, *The Question of Zion* (Princeton: Princeton University Press, 2005), and *The Last Resistance* (London: Verso, 2007). This latter includes a eulogistic text "Continuing the

Dialogue: On Edward Said" (193–99), in which Rose reads Said with a gracious generosity that, although ethically admirable, risks effacing problems in Said's writings that should be discussed.

43. For current presentations of German archaeology in the ideological and museological context of the new Berlin, see Dietrich Wildung, *Preussen am Nil* (Berlin: G+H Verlag, 2002); Christina Hans, Verena Lepper Friederike Seyfried, and Olivia Zorn, *Wegbereiter der Ägyptologie: Carl Richard Lepsius 1810–1884* (Berlin: Staatliche Museen zu Berin—Stiftung Preussischer Kulturbesitz, 2010); and for the ambiguous cultural-political program for the renovated Berlin museums, in which "in der Mitte Berlins kehren die außereuropäischen Sammlungen in ein Ensemble zurück, in dem sie das abwertende Stigma des Exotischen verlieren" ("the extra-European collections are returning as a group to the center of Berlin, where they will lose the derogatory stigma of the exotic") (26), see Hermann Parzinger, *Das Humboldt-Forum. "Soviel Welt mit sich verbinden als möglich,".Aufgabe und Bedeutung des wichtigsten Kulturprojekts in Deutschland zu Beginn des 21. Jahrhunderts* (Berlin: Stiftung Berliner Schloss–Humboldtforum, 2011).

44. When Said writes earlier: "The whole idea of cultural difference itself—especially today—is far from the *inert thing* taken for granted by Freud" (22, emphasis added), this implies that "cultural difference" (the site of "living spirit" today) is a dead letter for Freud. This is, however, a historically shortsighted claim. Why would cultural difference have been "inert" for Freud, writing in the late 1930s, as a Jewish citizen in the remains of the ethnically complex Austro-Hungarian Empire, whose multicultural conflicts were constant and rich in tensions and productivity, and had been for centuries?

45. One of the things that make Said broadly appealing, as well as deeply problematic, is his embrace of vitalistic motifs. An example is his criticism of Hayden White, in whose work "the lived experience, and the geography or setting of that experience, is alchemically transmuted into an unrecognizably slender form, and a totally European one at that" (*Reflexions on Exile and Other Essays*, xix). Said's allergy to the "textualism" of Orientalism is a much larger example. On the backgrounds of "vitalism," see the chapter titled "Life" in Herbert Schädelbach, *Philosophy in Germany, 1831–1933* (Cambridge: Cambridge University Press, 1984), 139–60.

46. It may be that the Israeli policy of creating "facts on the ground" unwittingly or unconsciously realizes this stereotypical anti-Jewish slander. In this case, the Israeli government would be self-destructively defying the world and victimizing Palestinians by acting out internalized negative views of "the Jew"—a tragic and disastrous state of affairs.

47. See the chapter on Karl Marx's "On the Jewish Question," in Jeffrey S. Librett, *The Rhetoric of Cultural Dialogue: Jews and Germans from Moses Mendelssohn to Richard Wagner and Beyond* (Stanford: Stanford University Press, 2000), 219–40.

48. Said runs into a similar snag—the problem is the aporia of (not) constituting an identity for the group of those who question identity—in "Orientalism Reconsidered," where he enumerates an intentionally heterogeneous series of examples of criticism that he sees as loosely aligned with "anti-Orientalist critique" (212) in their embrace of multiplicity and difference. But in saying what they have in common, he is reduced to stating that "instead of seeking common unity by appeals to a center of sovereign authority, methodological consistency, canonicity, and science, they offer the possibility of common grounds of assembly between them" (214). Trying to say that difference is not involved with identity—that the brother-horde does not repeat the violence of the primal father—Said is reduced to claiming that these critics have nothing in common but what they have in common: "common grounds." He then proceeds to enumerate the traits they effectively share in common—praxis, secularity, etc.—a series of traits that ineluctably constitutes the unity of their identity as a group. In other words, Jacqueline Rose is wise, in her understated "Response" to Said's lecture on *Moses and Monotheism*, to counsel us not to think that we can get rid of identity all too quickly.

CONCLUSION: FOR AN ABSTRACT HISTORIOGRAPHY
OF THE NONEXISTENT PRESENT

1. Martin Heidegger, *Der Satz vom Grund* (Pfullingen: Verlag Günther Neske, 1978), 16, 26, 31. The quoted phrases constitute the constant theme of this Heideggerian text.

2. See Giorgio Agamben, "On Potentiality," in *Potentialities: Collected Essays in Philosophy*, trans. Daniel Heller-Roazen (Stanford: Stanford University Press, 1999), 177–84.

3. On the radically different ways in which East and West Germany processed (or did not) the Shoah, see Jeffrey Herf, *Divided Memory: The Nazi Past in the Two Germanys* (Cambridge, Mass.: Harvard University Press, 1997), and on the obstacles to the work of mourning in postwar Germany, Alexander Mitscherlich and Margarete Mitscherlich, *Die Unfähigkeit zu trauern: Grundlagen kollektiven Verhaltens* (Munich: Piper Verlag, 1967).

4. Seyla Benhabib, "Citizens, Residents, and Aliens in a Changing World: Political Membership in the Global Era," in *The Postnational Self: Belonging and Identity*, ed. Ulf Hedetoft and Mett Hjort (Minneapolis: University of Minnesota Press, 2002), 85–119: "During the time of the cold war, the terms

east and west came to designate a geopolitical division of regimes. Whereas once the term *east*, or the *Orient*, would have been reserved for that border which separated Europe from the Ottoman Empire, after 1945 and the division of Germany, the line separating "east" from "west" ran through the heart of Europe, that is, the city of Berlin. The communist regimes of Europe became, oddly enough, part of the Orient; "Eastern Europe" designated differences in types of political regime by making communism appear as part of 'them,' the East, as opposed to 'us,' 'the free West'" (89).

5. Heiner Müller, "Deutschland ortlos: Anmerkung zu Kleist: Rede anläßlich der Entgegennahme des Kleist-Preises," in *Schriften*, ed. Frank Hörnigk (Frankfurt am Main: Suhrkamp Verlag, 2005), 382. The expression was used earlier by Ernst Jünger, *An der Zeitmauer (Along the Wall of Time)* (Stuttgart: Klett, 1959).

6. For a few key cultural, literary, and social perspectives, see, for example, Ruth Mandel, *Cosmopolitan Anxieties: Turkish Challenges to Citizenship and Belonging in Germany* (Durham, N.C.: Duke University Press, 2008); Azade Seyhan, *Writing Outside the Nation* (Princeton: Princeton University Press, 2001); David Horrocks and Eva Kolinsky, eds., *Turkish Culture in German Society Today* (Providence, R.I.: Berghahn, 1996); and Claus Leggewie and Zafer Senocak, eds., *Deutsche Türken: Das Ende der Geduld* (Hamburg: Rowohlt, 1993).

7. Cf. the remarks on "the jumble of the non-synchronous, the recognition of temporal difference" (9) in our contemporary age, in Andreas Huyssen, *Twilight Memories: Marking Time in a Culture of Amnesia* (New York: Routledge, 1995).

8. These cultural producers include Zafer Senocak, Emine Sevgi Özdamar, Feridun Zaimoglu, Seyran Ates, Fatih Akin, and Kemal Kurt, just to name a few of the most prominent.

9. Turkish cultural identity is itself also altered in part by these interactions, as can be seen in novels by Orhan Pamuk like *Snow*. See Ülker Gökberk, "Beyond Secularism: Orhan Pamuk's *Snow* and the Contestation of 'Turkish Identity' in the Borderland," in *Konturen* 1 (2008), http://konturen.uoregon.edu/vol1_Gokberk.html.

10. The example of the extraordinary Japanese German literary writer Yoko Tawada is one of the most striking. For useful readings that press beyond identity categories, see John Namjun Kim, "Ethnic Irony: The Poetic Parabasis of the Promiscuous Personal Pronoun in Yoko Tawada's 'Eine leere Flasche,'" *German Quarterly* 83, no. 3 (2010): 333–52; and David Martyn, "'Schiffe der Wüste,' 'Schiffe des Meeres': Topographien der Metapher bei Emine Sevgi Özdamar, Salim Alafenisch und Yoko Tawada," in *Topographien*

der Literatur, DFG Symposion 2004, ed. Hartmut Böhme (Stuttgart: Metzler, 2005), 724–44.

11. For example, one sees Fatih Akin both struggling with and analyzing this question in his films such as *Gegen die Wand*, in terms of distinctions between both "good" and "bad" versions of the Orient and "good" and "bad" versions of the Occident.

12. See, for example, Sean McMeekin, *The Berlin-Baghdad Express: The Ottoman Empire and Germany's Bid for World Power* (Cambridge, Mass.: Belknap Press of Harvard University Press, 2010).

13. See Dominic LaCapra, "Acting Out and Working Through," in *Representing the Holocaust: History, Theory, Trauma* (Ithaca, N.Y.: Cornell University Press, 1994), 205–23.

14. The problem does appear, however, albeit somewhat obliquely, in recent discussions of nostalgia, especially *Ostalgie*, in contemporary Germany. See, for example, Dominic Boyer, "*Ostalgie* and the Politics of the Future in Eastern Germany," *Public Culture* 18, no. 2 (2006): 361–81. See also Julia Hell and Johannes von Moltke, "Unification Effects: Imaginary Landscapes of the Berlin Republic," *Germanic Review* 80, no. 1 (2005): 74–95. Hell and von Moltke illuminatingly argue that a post-1989 logic of return manifests itself in an obsessive concern with imaginary spaces that function as potential sites of a lost object. While the hauntings the authors trace deal not only with temporality but register the search for stable grounding in spatial images, these hauntings nonetheless of course bear witness to an inscription of the past in the present and present in the past that unsettles the integrity of each temporal dimension.

15. See Leslie Adelson, *The Turkish Turn in Contemporary German Literature: Toward a New Critical Grammar of Migration* (New York: Palgrave Macmillan, 2005), and "Touching Tales of Turks, Germans, and Jews: Cultural Alterity, Historical Narrative, and Literary Riddles for the 1990s," *New German Critique* 80 (Spring–Summer 2000): 93–124. See also Zafer Senocak's novel, *Gefährliche Verwandschaft* (Munich: Babel Verlag, 1998).

16. Jeffrey Herf, in *Nazi Propaganda for the Arab World* (New Haven: Yale University Press, 2009), illuminatingly traces the links the Nazis made through radio propaganda and by other means with what they took to be the "good" Arab Semitic world as against the "bad" Jewish one.

17. The effects of the Shoah propagate themselves in Israel-Palestine in many different ways, while Europe to some extent washes its hands of the problem and blames Israel (whose right-wing policies and endless occupation at the same time, in part, culpably and destructively act out the fruitless denial of past helplessness).

18. Dominic Boyer argues insightfully in "*Ostalgie* and the Politics of the Future in Eastern Germany" that *Ostalgie* is in significant degree generated by a Western desire to make the East responsible for the fascist German past by positioning the East as nostalgic for the authoritarian past. This is another ruse of conscience-purification.

19. See Rafael Seligmann's exhaustive satirical investigation of the complexities of both German philo-Semitism and the new German-Jewish cultural position in *Der Musterjude* (Hildesheim: Claassen Verlag, 1997); and Frederick Alfred Lubich, "Der Musterjude: A Master Parody of German-Jewish Führer Phantasies," *German Studies Review* 27, no. 2 (May 2004): 229–48; and his "Jews in Germany Today—Contradictions in Progress," in *Wendewelten—Paradigmenwechsel in der deutschen Literatur- und Kulturgeschichte nach 1945* (Würzburg: Königshausen & Nemann, 2002), 111–20.

INDEX

Adelson, Leslie, 351n15
Agamben, Giorgio, 309n24, 327n6, 335n34, 349n2
Alcalay, Ammiel, 285n29
Alter, Robert, 227, 335n34
Anidjar, Gil, 285n29, 323n34
Anquetil-Duperron, Abraham Hyacinthe, 30
anxiety, xi, 1, 3, 8, 18; in Buber, 331n12; and Delumeau, Jean, 279n1; in Freud, 248; after German (re)unification, 273, 275; in Goethe, 74, 80, 94, 101, 119–20, 124, 126, 309n20; about groundlessness, 268–69, 285n28; in Hegel, 131, 138–41 passim, 161, 169, 322n30; in Kafka, for Benjamin, 337n41; of otherness, 284n24. See also panic
Arnim, Achim von, 52
Assmann, Jan, 286n33, 339–40n5, 344n30, 345n32, 346n33
Auerbach, Erich, 9, 177, 254, 259, 284n26, 291n49. See also figural interpretation; Testaments, Old and New; typology

Beckett, Samuel, 1
Behler, Ernst, 301nn1,4, 302n12
Beiser, Frederick, 280n12, 286n33, 298n23, 299n33, 303n18
Benes, Tuska, 285n29, 289n44, 317n7, 322n30
Benhabib, Seyla, 349n4
Benjamin, Walter, 222, 296n15, 308n13, 309n24, 310n26, 329n26, 335n34, 336n41, 338n47
Benn, Gottfried, 329n22
Berman, Nina, 26, 292n58, 331n11
Berman, Russell, 292n57, 294n61

Bernal, Martin, 237, 304n19, 304n21, 316n4, 340n6
Bernasconi, Robert, 228n24, 316n4, 317n8, 320n20, 322n30
Bhabha, Homi, 9, 283n24, 290n47
Bion, W. R., 282n23
Böhme, Hartmut, 313n10, 351n10
Brickman, Celia, 347n40
Buber, Martin, 17, 18, 209–19, 228–29, 298n26, 329–38 passim

Caillois, Roger, 287n37
Cassirer, Ernst, 75–76, 306n3, 307n10
China, 284n25; in Hegel, 134, 142–57 passim, 165, 172, 211–12, 215, 318n10, 319nn17–18, 320nn19,21, 321n25, 323n38, 345n31; in Herder, 46–47, 299n29; in Kafka, 218–34 passim, 333n24, 334n29; in Schlegel, 71
context. See Zusammenhang
Culler, Jonathan, 312n7

Delumeau, Jean, 279nn1–2
Derrida, Jacques, 11, 130–31, 267, 284n27, 293n59, 301n2, 315n1, 333n22, 337n47, 338n3
De Vries, Hent, 328n14
disavowal, xi, xii, 7–9; and Agamben, 327n6; in Cassirer, 76; Freud and Mannoni on, 283n24; and fundamentalisms, 281n17; in Goethe, 99, 103, 313n10, 314n22; in Hegel, 153, 163, 318n8; in Herder, 35–36, 43–44, 49, 51; in postwar Germany, 272; in Schopenhauer, 180, 182, 187, 194, 197, 199, 205. See also fetishism
Dobie, Madeleine, 290n46
Droysen, Johann Gustav, 1, 280n8, 330n4

353

Egypt, 41, 286*n*33, 304*n*19, 340*n*6; in Freud, 236–37, 241, 246, 248, 249, 252, 255, 257, 258, 261, 339*nn*4–5, 344*nn*28,30–32; in Goethe, 82, 86, 124, 309*n*20; in Hegel, 153, 157, 160, 317*n*4, 319*n*14, 323*n*36; in Herder, 45–47, 299*n*30; in Schopenhauer, 184, 328*n*18. *See also* hieroglyphs
Eisenberg, Noah, 333*n*27
Enlightenment, 3–7, 10–11, 16–25 passim, 29–30, 35, 37, 49, 55, 65, 66, 74, 90, 155, 164, 167, 171, 187, 203, 204, 210, 225–27, 265–71 passim, 284*n*25, 288*n*40, 289*n*45, 294*n*60, 299*n*29, 302*n*6, 326*n*3, 329*n*2, 330*nn*2,4

fear. *See* anxiety; panic
fetishism, xi, xiv, 9, 24, 39, 134, 267, 283*n*24, 284*n*25, 289*n*46, 290*n*46, 304*n*21, 313*n*10, 317–18*n*8, 335*n*33, 339*n*3. *See also* disavowal
Figueira, Dorothy, 26, 133, 283*n*24, 292*nn*56–57, 299*n*32, 304*n*21, 306*n*1, 317*n*6, 320*n*22, 326*n*53, 329*n*24, 331*n*9
figural interpretation, 9–10; 130–31; 285*n*30; in Goethe, 78, 88, 91, 124; in Herder, 42; in historicist Orientalism, 209; in Said, 254; in Schopenhauer, 182, 195. *See also* Testaments, Old and New; typology
Forster, Georg, 31, 296*n*7, 302*n*6
foundations. *See* groundlessness
Freud, Sigmund, xii, 7–9, 17, 18, 19, 37, 187, 197, 210, 222, 235–64, 266, 269, 271, 272, 281*n*18, 282*nn*22–23, 283*n*24, 309*n*20, 313*n*12, 332*n*17, 336*n*40, 337*n*41, 338–48
Friedrichsmeyer, Sara, 294*n*61

Gasché, Rodolphe, 317*n*5
Gay, Peter, 338*n*3
Geller, Jay, 9, 283*n*24, 284*n*25, 334*n*33, 338*n*3
Gérard, René, 55, 291*n*55, 295*n*1, 297*n*21, 301*n*40, 302*n*7, 305*n*24
gift, ethics of, 29, 311*n*2; in Freud, 242, 268; in Goethe, 75, 94, 96, 103–5, 110–15, 268, 307*n*10, 308*n*15, 311*n*2, 312*n*9, 313*n*16; in Hegel, 170; in Herder, 48, 297*n*21, 298*n*23; in Schopenhauer, 184; Spinoza on, 33

Gilman, Sander, 334*n*27
Goebel, Rolf, 333*n*27
Goethe, Johann Wolfgang von, 16, 17, 21, 33, 47, 69, 73–128, 163, 170, 174, 198, 214, 271, 306–15; anti-Semitism in, 123–27; and Biblical criticism, 80–89, 298*n*26, 341*n*12; and historicism, 74–76, 288*n*41; and Moses, 84–85, 241, 339*n*4, 344*n*26; and typology, 88–89
Gökberk, Ülker, 350*n*9
Greece, 134, 139–44 passim, 150, 157, 165, 169, 211, 215, 255, 304*n*19, 318*nn*9–10, 324*n*39, 325*n*45, 340*n*6, 345*n*31
Grosrichard, Alain, 289*n*46
groundlessness, 7, 12, 23; in contemporary German Orientalism, 276; in Goethe, 82; in Hegel, 139, 141; in Herder, 38; in modern Orientalism, 267; and relativism in historicism, 288*n*43; in Schopenhauer, 176–79, 183, 191, 194, 200, 282*n*21
Gundolf, Friedrich, 308*n*13

Hafis, 88, 93–100, 111–13, 115, 119, 122, 309–15 passim
Halbfass, Wilhelm, 291*n*55, 294*n*62, 320*n*22, 326*n*1, 327*n*5
Hebrews, 43, 48–49, 286*n*34
Hegel, Georg Wilhelm Friedrich, 7, 18, 21, 27, 36, 47, 57, 69, 74, 128, 129–75, 178–79, 198, 204, 209, 211–15, 217, 219, 240, 252, 269, 271, 276–77, 315–26, 346*n*31; Buber on, 330*n*5; and historicism, 287*n*40, 288*n*41; on India, 131–33,147–56; on Islam, 167–74; on Judaea, 156–60; Kafka and, 225–32 passim; on modernity, 160–75; on Persia, 145–46, 310*n*28; and typology, 133–34
Heidegger, Martin, 280*n*13, 293*n*59, 310*n*26, 349*n*1
Hell, Julia, 351*n*14
Herder, Johann Gottfried, 16–17, 29–51, 71, 73, 127, 135, 140, 155, 209, 214, 217, 240, 271, 287*n*38, 288*n*40, 294–301, 304*n*20, 331*n*9, 336*n*38
Herf, Jeffrey, 349*n*3, 351*n*16
Hess, Jonathan, 285*n*28
hieroglyphs, 44–47, 299*nn*28–31. *See also* Egypt

historicism, 16–18, 269, 271, 287nn39–40, 288nn41–43, 291n51, 319n15, 330n4, 344n27; crisis of, 210, 288n44; in Herder, 29–30, 35–39, 336n38; and relativism, 329n2; in Said,19–26, 254, 290n47, 346n37
Hobbes, Thomas, 188, 280n11
Hsia, Adrian, 333n24
Hulin, Michel, 319n15, 327n4
Humboldt, Wilhelm von, 73, 129, 133, 324n42, 329n24

Iggers, Georg, 17–18, 209, 287n40, 288n44, 330n4
India, 2, 23; in Aryan myth, 213, 237; Clément on, 290n46; in Goethe, 90; in Hegel, 129–75 passim, 211, 315–26 passim; in Herder, 31–2, 41, 43,47; in Lang, 210, 341n9; and Mann, 340n8; in Schlegel, 52–72, 301–6 passim; in Schopenhauer, 176–206 passim, 326–29 passim

Jacobi, Friedrich Heinrich, 12, 15, 17, 35, 65–6, 201, 202–3, 285n33, 295n7, 296n11, 305n25
Jakobson, Roman, 38, 59, 243, 342n13, 343
Jones, Sir William, 322n30
Judaea, 131, 132, 142, 156–61, 168, 174, 325n46
Jung-Willemer, Marianne, 94, 104–5, 107, 113

Kafka, Franz, 17, 18, 146, 181, 198, 209–11, 217–34, 235, 236, 239, 243, 266, 271, 272, 296n15, 329–38 passim, 342n16, 345n33,
Kant, Immanuel, 5, 6, 7, 17, 18, 30, 35, 253, 265, 268, 281n15; and Hegel, 143; and Herder, 39, 44, 49, 50, 58, 287n38, 296nn7,10,12–13, 297n21; and Kafka, 225, 226, 334nn31–32; and Schlegel, 58, 303n15; Schopenhauer and, 178, 197–99, 201, 329n26; and time, 98
Kim, John Namjun, 350n10
Kittler, Wolf, 337n44
Kittsteiner, Heinz, 2–3, 270n6, 280nn7–9, 287n30
Kommerell, Max, 308n13

Kontje, Todd, 26, 292n57, 300n38
Koselleck, Reinhard, 2–5

Lacan, Jacques, 182, 289n46, 337nn44,47, 342n14; ego in, 248, 341n11; the gaze in, 314n20; imaginary, symbolic, and real in, 246; *jouissance* in, 247; metaphor and metonymy in, 243; 343n20
LaCapra, Dominic, 351n13
Lacoue-Labarthe, Philippe, 282n20, 302n9
Lämmert, Eberhard, 311n3
Lang, Fritz, 210, 283n24, 341n9
Leibniz, Gottfried Wilhelm von, 135, 178, 231, 266, 284n25, 299n29
Lessing, Gotthold Ephraim, 3, 17, 29, 30, 33, 53, 65, 66, 133, 174, 209, 240, 265, 284n28, 286n33, 287n38, 302n6, 311n2, 337n43
Levin, David, 9, 283n24
Levinas, Emmanuel, 83, 86, 308n18
Luther, Martin, 5, 17, 53, 56, 83, 138–39, 209, 297n18, 332n22, 340n6

Mann, Thomas, 210, 340n8, 343n26,
Mannheim, Karl, 287n39, 288nn42–43, 329n2, 344n27
Mannoni, Octave, 9, 199, 283n24
Marchand, Suzanne L., 26, 294n60, 301n4,
Martyn, David, xv, 284n27, 350n10
Mendelssohn, Moses, 12, 15, 30, 55, 65, 84, 280n12, 281n15, 284n27, 302n11, 305n23, 319n13
Meng, Weiyan, 333n24
modernism (twentieth-century), 17–18, 184, 210, 269, 272
Moltke, Johannes von, 351n14
Murti, Kamakshi, 291n55

Nancy, Jean-Luc, 282n20, 302n9, 336n40
Novalis (Friedrich von Hardenberg), 52, 121, 187, 214, 288n40

Olender, Maurice, 285n29, 297n21, 300nn38–39, 331n9

panic, xi, xii, 3, 5, 7–8, 18, 266, 269, 270, 282n20, 287n37; in Goethe, 94; in Hegel, 131, 138–42, 161, 167–69, 317n8; in Herder, 36–37, 44, 296n12; in

panic (*continued*)
  Kafka, 337*n*41; and pantheism, 11–16, 197; in Spinoza, 286*n*35, 315*n*27, 336*n*38. *See also* anxiety
pantheism, 11–16, 64–66, 149; in Spinoza, 32–35. *See also* Spinoza, Baruch
Pasto, James, 346*n*36
Persia, 22; in Buber, 331*n*12; in Goethe, 73, 76, 79, 80, 86, 88–89, 94–95, 105, 115, 125, 308*n*15, 310*n*28, 311*n*29; in Hegel, 132–34, 140, 142, 144–50 passim, 156–60, 163, 165, 174, 211, 237, 318*nn*9–10, 319*n*18, 320*n*21, 321*n*25, 322*n*33, 325*n*45; in Schlegel, 58–59, 63; in Schopenhauer, 183–86
Polaschegg, Andrea, 26, 293*n*59, 308*n*16
Poliakov, Léon, 285*n*29, 326*n*53, 331*n*9

Rajan, Balachandra, 320*n*22
Ranke, Leopold von, 74, 307*n*9, 319*n*15
Rennie, Nicholas, 307*n*3
Rome, 134, 142, 157, 165, 255, 318*nn*9–10, 325*n*45

Said, Edward, 19–26, 167, 291*nn*52–54, 326*n*49, 347*n*42, 348*nn*44–45; on Freud, 253–64; on historicism, 346*n*37; on identity of the different, 263–64, 349*n*48; on Nazi anti-Semitism, 347*n*39; on Orientalism and anti-Semitism, 289*n*49, 346*n*36; reception of, 289*n*46, 290*n*47, 292*nn*56–57, 293*n*60, 294*n*62; on Schlegel, 304*n*19
Saussy, Haun, 320*n*19
Schelling, Friedrich Wilhelm Joseph, 177, 306*n*29, 326*n*1
Schlegel, August-Wilhelm, 73, 133
Schlegel, Dorothea Veit, 55–56, 302*n*12, 306*n*28
Schlegel, Friedrich, xiii, 16, 52–72, 73, 90, 132–33, 153, 301–6, 334*n*32
Schnädelbach, Herbert, 287*n*40, 288*n*41, 330*n*4
Schopenhauer, Arthur, 12, 16, 17, 69, 133, 174–75, 176–206, 209, 213, 215, 237, 282*n*21, 289*n*44, 322*n*33, 326–29, 331*n*12, 341*n*10
Schwab, Raymond, 30, 31, 291*n*55, 295*n*4, 301*n*5
Seligmann, Rafael, 352*n*19

Senocak, Zafer, 350*nn*6,8
Seyhan, Azade, 350*n*6
Shoah, 272, 275, 349*n*3, 351*n*17
Spinoza, Baruch, xii, 3, 5, 11–16, 29, 30, 32–35, 37, 38, 65, 90, 118, 143, 152, 180, 188, 197–205, 285*nn*32–33, 286*n*34, 295*nn*6–7, 315*n*27, 319*n*16, 328*n*11, 332*n*22, 336*n*38. *See also* pantheism
Spivak, Gayatri, 290*n*47, 320*n*24
Stepelevich, Lawrence S., 323*n*34
Strauss, Leo, 286*n*33, 305*n*23
Sutcliffe, Adam, 286*n*33

Tawada, Yoko, 350*n*10
teleology, xiii, 7; critique of, in Kant, 30, 287*n*38, 296*nn*10,12; dogmatic, in Herder, 35–9, 43–44, 336*n*38; in Hegel, 136, 140, 320*n*24; in historicism, 18, 74, 76, 288*n*43, 344*n*27; modernism and, 210, 249–50, 252; Spinoza's critique of, 32–35
Testaments, Old and New, 10, 316*n*2; in Goethe, 80–88 passim, 122–27 passim, 308*n*12; in Herder, 41–44; in Kafka, 335*n*34; in Schlegel, 69–71; in Schopenhauer, 182, 184–86, 194–96, 198, 201, 204. *See also* figural interpretation; typology
theodicy, 33, 35, 135–38
Thirty Years War, 2–7
typology, xi–xii, 9–12, 17, 24–25, 130–33; in Freud, 236–38, 252–53; in Goethe, 73, 76, 79, 89, 90; in Hegel, 130–34; in Herder, 45, 48, 50; in Kafka, 225–26, 229, 232; in Said, 259–62, 291*n*49; in Schlegel, 52–58, 68–72; in Schopenhauer, 177–87, 194–206; and the structure of the frame, 130–31. *See also* figural interpretation; Testaments, Old and New

Weber, Max, 331*n*8
Weber, Samuel, 342*n*18
Wellbery, David, 312*n*5
Wilkins, Sir Charles, 30
Wilson, A. Leslie, 291*n*55, 295*n*5

Yerushalmi, Yosef Hayim, 338*n*3
Yovel, Yirmiyahu, 286*n*34, 322*n*34

Zimmer, Heinrich, 340n8
Zusammenhang (i.e. "context"), 1, 21, 280n14, 306n29; in Buber, 217, 332n12, 333n22; in cultural historiography, 271; in Freud, 343n20; in Goethe, 79, 91–94; in Hegel, 146, 153–54, 211; in Herder, 41, 60; in Kafka, 222, 224, 225, 227–28, 334n27; in Orientalism, 268; in Schlegel, 60, 71; in Schopenhauer, 176, 178, 198–99, 202

www.ingramcontent.com/pod-product-compliance
Lightning Source LLC
Chambersburg PA
CBHW022026290426
44109CB00014B/767